THE COLMPLETE COLOUR COOKBOOK

Colour Cookbook

EDITED BY GILL EDDEN

octopus

Contents

First published 1977 by
Octopus Books Limited
59 Grosvenor Street
London W1

© 1977 Octopus Books Limited

ISBN 0 7064 0635 4

Printed in Czechoslovakia

APPETIZERS

Frosted tomato cocktail

Metric/Imperial
1 kg./2 lb. ripe tomatoes
4 tablespoons water
salt and pepper
good pinch of sugar
little lemon juice
Worcestershire sauce to taste
mint

American
2 lb. ripe tomatoes
5 tablespoons water
salt and pepper
good pinch of sugar
little lemon juice
Worcestershire sauce to taste
mint

Serves 4
Chop the tomatoes and put them in a pan with the water, seasoning and sugar. Heat for a few minutes only to extract the juice from the tomatoes. Rub the tomatoes through a sieve (strainer) and add lemon juice, Worcestershire sauce and any extra seasoning required (e.g. celery salt, cayenne pepper or chilli sauce). Put into a freezing tray and freeze lightly.

Chop the frozen mixture and spoon into chilled glasses. Garnish with mint.

Buckling and horseradish cream

Metric/Imperial
4 buckling
few lettuce leaves
2 tomatoes, sliced
parsley sprigs

Sauce
150 ml./¼ pint double cream
1 tablespoon redcurrant jelly
2 teaspoons grated horseradish
salt and pepper

American
4 buckling
few lettuce leaves
2 tomatoes, sliced
parsley sprigs

Sauce
⅔ cup heavy cream
1¼ tablespoons redcurrant jelly
2 teaspoons grated horseradish
salt and pepper

Serves 4
Slit the skin of the buckling along the backbone and gently pull it away from the flesh on both sides. Place the lettuce leaves on a serving dish and arrange the buckling on top. Garnish with the tomato slices and parsley sprigs.

Lightly whip the cream so that it just holds its shape. Melt the redcurrant jelly in a small saucepan over a low heat, then carefully fold into the cream with horseradish and seasoning. Serve the sauce separately.

Buckling are whole smoked herrings, which become cooked during smoking; they are similar in flavour to smoked trout which could be used instead.

Artichokes vinaigrette

Metric/Imperial
4 globe artichokes
salt
Vinaigrette or French dressing

American
4 globe artichokes
salt
Vinaigrette or French dressing

Serves 4
Wash the artichokes in cold salted water. Cut away any stalk and pull off any tough outer leaves. The leaves may be cut in a straight line with scissors, if wished.

Cook the artichokes in boiling, salted water until tender. Small, very young artichokes take about 25 minutes, very large ones take about 40 minutes. When a leaf can be pulled away easily, they are done. Allow to cool, then remove the centre choke.

Serve the dressing separately or spoon it into the centre of each artichoke. To eat artichokes, pull away each leaf, dip the base in the dressing and eat the tender part. The base of the artichoke, often called the heart, is eaten with a knife and fork.

Quick chicken liver pâté

Metric/Imperial
butter for frying
1 small onion, finely chopped
1 garlic clove, crushed with ½ teaspoon salt
225 g./8 oz. chicken livers, cleaned and chopped
1 teaspoon dried thyme
2 tablespoons brandy or sherry
salt and freshly ground black pepper
Melba toast

American
butter for frying
1 small onion, finely chopped
1 garlic clove, crushed with ½ teaspoon salt
8 oz. chicken livers, cleaned and chopped
1 teaspoon dried thyme
2½ tablespoons brandy or sherry
salt and freshly ground black pepper
Melba toast

Serves 4
Melt a knob of butter in a frying pan (skillet). Add the onion, garlic, livers and thyme and fry gently for about 5–10 minutes or until the juices of the liver are only faintly pink. Remove from the heat and leave to cool slightly. Mince (grind) the mixture finely or purée in a blender until smooth. Work in another knob of butter and the brandy or sherry with a wooden spoon, then season to taste. Press firmly into a serving dish and refrigerate. Serve with Melba toast.

APPETIZERS

Asparagus on artichoke hearts

Metric/Imperial	American
4 artichoke hearts	4 artichoke hearts
1 kg./2 lb. asparagus	2 lb. asparagus
4 eggs, hard boiled	4 eggs, hard cooked
hollandaise sauce	hollandaise sauce

Serves 4

Poach the artichoke hearts, then leave them to cool. Trim off the white and brown jagged ends of the asparagus and cut all the sticks to an average length. Scrape off the rough skin near the cut end with a sharp knife. Wash well in cold water. Tie into bundles and cook in boiling, unsalted water for 15–20 minutes.

Chop the eggs, mix with some of the asparagus tips and place on the artichoke hearts. Place the remaining asparagus tips on top and pour over the hollandaise sauce.

Taramasalata

Metric/Imperial	American
2 slices white bread, crusts removed	2 slices white bread, crusts removed
50 g./2 oz. smoked cod's roe, skinned	2 oz. smoked cod's roe, skinned
1 garlic clove, crushed	1 garlic clove, crushed
150 ml./¼ pint vegetable, olive or corn oil	⅔ cup vegetable, olive or corn oil
4 tablespoons lemon juice	5 tablespoons lemon juice
1 tablespoon hot water	1¼ tablespoons hot water
freshly ground black pepper	freshly ground black pepper
parsley	parsley

Serves 4

Put the bread in a small bowl, cover with cold water and leave to soak for 10 minutes. Squeeze dry.

Using an electric or rotary beater, beat the cod's roe until smooth. Beat in the soaked bread and garlic, then work in the oil drop by drop, beating well as for mayonnaise. As the taramasalata becomes thicker, the oil can be added faster. If the mixture separates, crumble in a little more white bread to absorb the oil. Beat constantly until all the oil is incorporated, then stir in the lemon juice and hot water.

Spoon the taramasalata into a serving dish and chill in the refrigerator for at least 2 hours before serving. Sprinkle with pepper. Garnish with parsley.

Simple terrine

Avocado with prawns (shrimp)

Metric/Imperial	American
½ kg./1 lb. mixed pork and veal, minced	1 lb. ground pork and veal
225 g./8 oz. sausage meat	8 oz. sausage meat
225 g./8 oz. pig's or lamb's liver, minced	8 oz. pig's or lamb's liver, ground
1 onion, finely chopped	1 onion, finely chopped
1 tablespoon chopped fresh herbs or 1 teaspoon dried herbs	1¼ tablespoons chopped fresh herbs or 1 teaspoon dried herbs
50 g./2 oz. fresh breadcrumbs	1 cup fresh breadcrumbs
1 egg	1 egg
salt and pepper	salt and pepper
225 g./8 oz. thin bacon rashers	8 oz. thin bacon slices
bay leaves	bay leaves

Serves 12

Oven setting: 170°C./325°F./Gas Mark 3

Mix the veal and pork and mince (grind) thoroughly with the sausage meat, liver, chopped onion, herbs, breadcrumbs, beaten egg and salt and pepper.

Line a terrine or straight-sided ovenproof casserole with overlapping rinded bacon rashers (slices). Fill the terrine with the meat mixture, pressing down firmly into the corners, and smooth the surface. Cover with more bacon rashers (slices) and place the bay leaves on top. Cover with foil and the lid of the casserole.

Stand in a pan with enough boiling water to come halfway up the side of the dish. Place in the centre of the preheated oven and cook for 1–1½ hours, or until firm to the touch.

Remove from the pan, remove the lid and foil, cover with a piece of clean foil and press with a heavy weight until cold. Serve in thick slices with brown bread or freshly-made crisp toast.

Metric/Imperial	American
2 ripe avocados	2 ripe avocados
juice of ½ lemon	juice of ½ lemon
350 g./12 oz. cooked and shelled prawns	1 cup cooked and peeled shrimp
Dressing	*Dressing*
150 ml./¼ pint double cream	⅔ cup heavy cream
2 tablespoons wine vinegar	2½ tablespoons wine vinegar
1 teaspoon Dijon-style mustard	1 teaspoon Dijon-style mustard
1 teaspoon sugar	1 teaspoon sugar
1 garlic clove, crushed with ½ teaspoon salt	1 garlic clove, crushed with ½ teaspoon salt
2 teaspoons chopped chives	2 teaspoons chopped chives
2 teaspoons chopped parsley	2 teaspoons chopped parsley

Serves 4

Halve the avocados and remove the stones (pits). Brush the cut surfaces of the flesh with the lemon juice.

To make the dressing, beat the cream and vinegar together in a bowl. Add the remaining ingredients and beat until thoroughly combined. Alternatively, put all the ingredients in a screw-top jar, cover and shake.

In a mixing bowl combine the prawns (shrimp) with the dressing, ensuring that they are thoroughly coated. Spoon into the avocado halves and serve immediately with brown bread and butter.

APPETIZERS

Stuffed peaches

Metric/Imperial
175 g./6 oz. cream cheese
2 tablespoons sultanas,
   plumped in hot water
2 tablespoons chopped walnuts
2 large ripe peaches, or 4
   canned peach halves
4 crisp lettuce leaves

American
¾ cup cream cheese
2½ tablespoons seedless
   raisins, plumped in hot
   water
2½ tablespoons chopped
   walnuts
2 large ripe peaches, or 4
   canned peach halves
4 crisp lettuce leaves

Serves 4

Mix the cheese, sultanas (raisins) and nuts, and form into
12 small balls. If the balls are very soft, chill the mixture for
a short time. Arrange each peach half on a lettuce leaf in a
small bowl and place three cheese balls on each. Serve
chilled.

Cheese and tomato meringues

Metric/Imperial
4 large tomatoes
25 g./1 oz. butter, softened
4 eggs, separated
salt and pepper
4 tablespoons grated Parmesan
   cheese
1 tablespoon chopped chives or
   parsley

American
4 large tomatoes
2 tablespoons butter, softened
4 eggs, separated
salt and pepper
5 tablespoons grated Parmesan
   cheese
1¼ tablespoons chopped chives
   or parsley

Serves 4

Oven setting: 200°C./400°F./Gas Mark 6

Make sure the tomatoes stand quite firmly, then cut a slice
from the top of each tomato. Scoop out the pulp with a
teaspoon, chop this finely and mix with the softened
butter, egg yolks and seasoning. Add half the cheese and
half the herbs. Pour the mixture back into the tomato
cases. Arrange the tomatoes in an ovenproof dish and
cook in the preheated oven for 10 minutes. Beat the egg
whites until stiff, fold in the seasoning and remaining
cheese and herbs. Bring the tomatoes out of the oven and
top with the meringue. Lower the heat to
180°C./350°F./Gas Mark 4, and cook for a further 5
minutes. Serve at once.

Walnut and avocado salad

Metric/Imperial
1–2 tablespoons lemon juice
2 ripe avocados
2 crisp, sweet apples
50 g./2 oz. walnuts
3–4 tablespoons French
    dressing
1 garlic clove (optional)
salt and pepper

Garnish
few lettuce leaves

American
1¼–2½ tablespoons lemon
    juice
2 ripe avocados
2 crisp, sweet apples
½ cup walnuts
4–5 tablespoons French
    dressing
1 garlic clove (optional)
salt and pepper

Garnish
few lettuce leaves

Serves 4
Put the lemon juice into a bowl. Halve the avocados and remove the stones (pits). Scrape the flesh gently into the bowl without damaging the skins. Mash with the lemon juice; this stops it turning brown. Peel and core the apples, chop them and the walnuts into small pieces and mix with the avocado pulp, the French dressing, crushed garlic, if using, and a little seasoning. Blend well and refill the avocado skins. Garnish with lettuce leaves.

Ham, tuna and fennel appetizer

Metric/Imperial
4 large slices lean ham
1 × 100 g./4 oz. can tuna
150 ml./¼ pint mayonnaise
3 tablespoons grated or finely
    chopped fennel
12 black olives
1 canned red pepper

Garnish
chopped parsley

American
4 large slices lean ham
1 × 4 oz. can tuna
⅔ cup mayonnaise
4 tablespoons grated or finely
    chopped fennel
12 black olives
1 canned red pepper

Garnish
chopped parsley

Serves 4
Halve the slices of ham, roll neatly and put on to a flat serving dish. Drain the tuna and break the flesh into smallish chunks. Stand in a line on top of the ham. Combine the mayonnaise and fennel together. Spoon over the tuna then stud with olives. Cut the pepper into thin strips and decorate the rolls with a criss-cross of pepper strips. Garnish with parsley.

APPETIZERS

Avocado dip (Guacamole)

Metric/Imperial	American
2 large avocados	2 large avocados
3 large tomatoes	3 large tomatoes
1 small onion	1 small onion
150 ml./¼ pint soured cream	⅔ cup sour cream
1 tablespoon lemon juice	1¼ tablespoons lemon juice
3 tablespoons mayonnaise	4 tablespoons mayonnaise
salt and pepper	salt and pepper
few drops Tabasco sauce	few drops Tabasco sauce

Serves 10–12
Halve the avocados, remove the stones (pits) and skin, and mash the flesh. Skin the tomatoes and onion and chop finely; add to the avocados. Add the remaining ingredients. Serve with crisps (potato chips), raw vegetables and biscuits (crackers).

Marinated herrings

Metric/Imperial	American
1 onion, sliced	1 onion, sliced
2 bay leaves	2 bay leaves
300 ml./½ pint dry white wine	1¼ cups dry white wine
100 ml./4 fl. oz. white wine vinegar	½ cup white wine vinegar
300 ml./½ pint water	1¼ cups water
1 teaspoon soft brown sugar	1 teaspoon light brown sugar
2 teaspoons salt	2 teaspoons salt
6 black peppercorns	6 black peppercorns
6 fresh herrings, cleaned, scaled, heads removed and boned	6 fresh herrings, cleaned, scaled, heads removed and boned

Serves 4–6
Place all the ingredients except the herrings in a shallow pan. Bring to the boil, then reduce the heat and simmer for 15 minutes. Add the herrings, cover the pan and simmer very gently for 10 minutes. Remove the pan from the heat and allow the fish to cool in the marinade. Chill and serve with brown bread and butter.

Mediterranean stuffed tomatoes

Mushrooms à la grecque

Metric/Imperial	American
4 large tomatoes	4 large tomatoes
50 g./2 oz. fresh white breadcrumbs	⅔ cup fresh white breadcrumbs
1 medium-sized onion, finely chopped	1 medium-sized onion, finely chopped
1 garlic clove, crushed	1 garlic clove, crushed
50 g./2 oz. mushrooms, finely chopped	½ cup finely chopped mushrooms
8 blanched almonds, finely chopped	8 blanched almonds, finely chopped
1 tablespoon chopped parsley	1¼ tablespoons chopped parsley
salt and pepper	salt and pepper
25 g./1 oz. butter	2 tablespoons butter
8 black olives to garnish	8 black olives to garnish

Serves 4
Oven setting 180°C./350°F./Gas Mark 4
Cut the tomatoes in half, scoop out the middle part and reserve. Turn the tomato shells upside down to drain. Strain the seeds from the reserved tomato and blend the pulp with the breadcrumbs, onion, garlic, mushrooms, almonds, parsley and seasoning. Pile the mixture into the tomato cases. Put a small knob of butter on top of each tomato and place in an ovenproof dish. Bake in the preheated oven for 15–20 minutes, or until golden brown. Garnish each tomato with an olive before serving.

Metric/Imperial	American
olive oil for frying	olive oil for frying
1 small onion, finely chopped	1 small onion, finely chopped
1 garlic clove, crushed with ½ teaspoon salt	1 garlic clove, crushed with ½ teaspoon salt
½ kg./1 lb. button mushrooms	4 cups button mushrooms
75 ml./3 fl. oz. dry white wine	⅓ cup dry white wine
freshly ground black pepper	freshly ground black pepper

Serves 4
Heat 2 tablespoons of oil in a frying pan (skillet). Add the onion and garlic and fry gently for 5 minutes or until golden. Add the mushrooms and cook for a further 5 minutes, stirring occasionally.

Add the wine to the pan. Bring just to boiling point, then remove immediately from the heat and add plenty of pepper. Stir well and leave to cool.

Chill for at least 2 hours before serving. Adjust seasoning and sprinkle with parsley, if desired.

APPETIZERS

Queensland cocktail

Metric/Imperial	American
1 large or 2 small avocados	1 large or 2 small avocados
mayonnaise	mayonnaise
1 × 85 g./2¾ oz. can crab meat	1 × 2¾ oz. can crab meat
1 green pepper, cored and diced	1 green pepper, cored and diced
lettuce	lettuce
1 lemon	1 lemon

Serves 4
Halve the avocados, remove the stones (pits) and skin, and dice the flesh. Blend with mayonnaise immediately so the flesh does not discolour. Mix with the crab meat and diced green pepper. Shred part of a lettuce finely, put at the bottom of 4 glasses. Top with the avocado mixture. Quarter the lemon and put a section on top of each glass. Serve with a teaspoon.
   To vary: Use fresh crab or other cooked shellfish.

Grapefruit cocktail

Metric/Imperial	American
½ kg./1 lb. canned grapefruit, drained	1 lb. canned grapefruit, drained
225 g./8 oz. canned mandarin oranges, drained	8 oz. canned mandarin oranges, drained
225 g./8 oz. canned cherries, drained and stoned	8 oz. canned cherries, drained and stoned
1 tablespoon caster sugar	1¼ tablespoons superfine sugar
Decoration	*Decoration*
1 egg white, beaten	1 egg white, beaten
caster sugar	superfine sugar

Serves 4
Mix the grapefruit, oranges and cherries together. Sprinkle with sugar. Frost the edges of the glasses by brushing with egg white and rolling the edges in sugar. Spoon the fruit into the glasses and chill before serving.

Peperonata

Metric/Imperial	American
4 red peppers	4 red peppers
3 tablespoons olive oil	4 tablespoons olive oil
1 tablespoon butter	1¼ tablespoons butter
1 small onion, very finely chopped	1 small onion, very finely chopped
½ garlic clove, crushed	½ garlic clove, crushed
salt and pepper	salt and pepper
4–5 ripe tomatoes, skinned, seeded and quartered	4–5 ripe tomatoes, skinned, seeded and quartered
chopped parsley	chopped parsley

Serves 4

Wash and dry the peppers, cut in half lengthways, remove seeds and pith and cut into strips. Heat the oil and butter in a pan, add the onion and garlic and cook until the onion is soft and transparent. Add the peppers and a little seasoning, cover, and sauté in the oil for about 15 minutes.

Add the tomatoes and cook over low heat for about 30 minutes, stirring occasionally, until the mixture is fairly thick and dry. Sprinkle with chopped parsley before serving.

Gnocchi

Metric/Imperial	American
600 ml./1 pint milk	2½ cups milk
pinch of grated nutmeg	pinch of grated nutmeg
salt and freshly ground black pepper	salt and freshly ground black pepper
100 g./4 oz. fine semolina	1 cup fine semolina flour
75 g./3 oz. grated Parmesan or Cheddar cheese	¾ cup grated Parmesan or Cheddar cheese
50 g./2 oz. butter	4 tablespoons butter
1 teaspoon made English mustard	1 teaspoon made hot mustard
1 egg, beaten	1 egg, beaten

Serves 4–6

Oven setting: 180°C./350°F./Gas Mark 4

Heat the milk in a pan, and add the nutmeg and seasoning to taste. Sprinkle in the semolina (semolina flour) and stir constantly until the mixture comes to the boil. Reduce the heat and cook gently for 1 minute, or until the mixture thickens. Remove the pan from the heat, and stir in 50 g./2 oz. (½ cup) of the cheese, half the butter, the mustard and beaten egg. Return the pan to the heat and cook, stirring constantly, for 1 minute. Turn the mixture into an oiled pan 20 × 30 cm./8 × 12 inches and spread the mixture out to ½ cm./¼ inch thick. Cover and leave in a cool place for at least 2 hours or until set. When firm, cut the mixture into 4 cm./1½ inch squares or circles and arrange the pieces overlapping in a buttered 600 ml./1 pint (2½ cup) ovenproof dish. Dot the surface with the remaining butter and cheese. Bake in the preheated oven for 35–40 minutes.

APPETIZERS

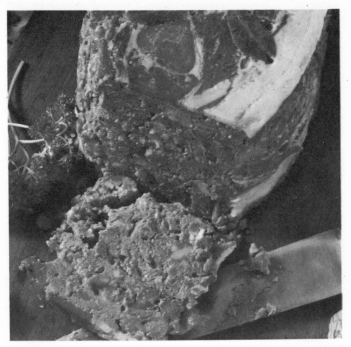

Tomato and herb ring

Metric/Imperial	American
1 × 400 g./14 oz. can and 1 × 225 g./8 oz. can tomatoes	1 × 14 oz. can and 1 × 8 oz. can tomatoes
4 tablespoons dry white wine	¼ cup dry white wine
finely grated rind and juice of ½ lemon	finely grated rind and juice of ½ lemon
4 peppercorns	4 peppercorns
1 garlic clove, crushed	1 garlic clove, crushed
1 teaspoon finely chopped fresh sage	1 teaspoon finely chopped fresh sage
2 teaspoons finely chopped fresh chives	2 teaspoons finely chopped fresh chives
1 teaspoon finely chopped fresh thyme	1 teaspoon finely chopped fresh thyme
salt	salt
pinch of sugar	pinch of sugar
4 tablespoons water	¼ cup water
1 tablespoon gelatine	1¼ tablespoons gelatin

Serves 4–6

Place the tomatoes in a pan with the wine, lemon rind and juice, peppercorns and garlic. Bring to the boil and simmer for 5 minutes. Remove the peppercorns and rub the mixture through a sieve (strainer). Stir in the fresh herbs, salt and the sugar.

Put the water in a small heatproof bowl or cup. Sprinkle over the gelatine (gelatin). Stir once and leave until spongy. Place the bowl or cup in a pan of hot water and stir over low heat until the gelatine (gelatin) has dissolved. Remove from the heat, strain the gelatine (gelatin) into the tomato pulp and stir well. Taste and adjust the seasoning.

Lightly oil a 600 ml./1 pint ring mould (2½ cup tube pan). Pour in the tomato mixture and leave until set. Turn out on to a flat serving plate. Fill the centre with watercress or cucumber tossed in French dressing.

Pâté de grillotin

Metric/Imperial	American
½ kg./1 lb. pig's liver	1 lb. pig's liver
225 g./8 oz. lean pork meat	8 oz. lean pork meat
225 g./8 oz. fat belly of pork	8 oz. pork arm steak
1–2 garlic cloves	1–2 garlic cloves
1 shallot or small onion	1 shallot or small onion
50 g./2 oz. lard or butter	4 tablespoons lard or butter
25 g./1 oz. flour	¼ cup flour
150 ml./¼ pint brown stock	⅔ cup brown stock
2 teaspoons chopped fresh herbs	2 teaspoons chopped fresh herbs
salt and pepper	salt and pepper
pinch of grated nutmeg	pinch of grated nutmeg
2–3 sage leaves	2–3 sage leaves
about ½ kg./1 lb. fairly streaky bacon	about 1 lb. fairly fatty bacon

Serves 8–10

Oven setting: 150–160°C./300–325°F./Gas Mark 2–3

Chop the liver, pork and belly of pork (pork arm steak) separately. If preferred, put through a coarse mincer (grinder). Crush the garlic, chop the shallot or onion. Toss for a few minutes in the lard or butter, stir in the flour and blend the stock gradually into the mixture. Bring to the boil and thicken. Add the herbs, seasoning and nutmeg. Put in all the meat. If you wish the meat in the pâté to be clearly defined, stir very little. Put a few sage leaves at the bottom of a baking pan or ovenproof dish, then line the bottom and sides with the bacon. Spoon in the pâté. Cover with greased foil or greaseproof (waxed) paper. Stand in a pan of hot water and bake in the preheated oven for about 1¼ hours. Allow to cool in the pan and place a small weight on top; this makes it easier to slice the pâté. Serve with hot toast and butter.

Salmon cream flan

Metric/Imperial
175 g./6 oz. plain flour
pinch of salt
75 g./3 oz. butter
water to mix

Filling
1 × 200 g./7 oz. can red
  salmon
2 eggs
¼ medium-sized cucumber,
  peeled and diced
300 ml./½ pint single cream
¼ teaspoon anchovy essence
3 spring onions, finely chopped
salt and pepper

Garnish
sliced cucumber
parsley

American
1½ cups all-purpose flour
pinch of salt
⅜ cup butter
water to mix

Filling
1 × 7 oz. can red salmon
2 eggs
¼ medium-sized cucumber,
  peeled and diced
1¼ cups light cream
¼ teaspoon anchovy extract
3 scallions, finely chopped
salt and pepper

Garnish
sliced cucumber
parsley

Serves 4–6
Oven setting: 220C./425°F./Gas Mark 7
Sieve the flour and salt. Rub in butter until the consistency
of fine breadcrumbs. Gradually add enough cold water to
make a rolling consistency. Roll out and line a 20 cm./8
inch flan tin (pan). Put a piece of greased greaseproof
paper into the pastry case (with the greased side touching
the pastry). Cover with beans and bake blind in the centre
of the oven for 10–15 minutes, until golden. Meanwhile
flake the salmon in a basin and beat in the eggs. Add the
cucumber, cream, anchovy essence (extract), onion
(scallion) and seasoning. Remove beans and paper from
flan case, and spoon in the fish mixture. Lower the oven to
160°C./325°F./Gas Mark 3 and bake for a further 30–35
minutes until the pastry is crisp and the filling firm.
Garnish with the thinly sliced cucumber and parsley.

Anchoïade

Metric/Imperial
4 slices brown bread, crusts
  removed
unsalted butter
1 × 50 g./2 oz. can anchovies
  in olive oil, drained and
  soaked in milk for 30 minutes
1 garlic clove, crushed
freshly ground black pepper

American
4 slices brown bread, crusts
  removed
unsalted butter
1 × 2 oz. can anchovies in olive
  oil, drained and soaked in
  milk for 30 minutes
1 garlic clove, crushed
freshly ground black pepper

Serves 4
Oven setting: 200°C./400°F./Gas Mark 6
Toast the bread on one side only and butter the untoasted
side. Cut into fingers. Drain the anchovies and pound to a
paste with the garlic in a mortar with a pestle. Season with
pepper to taste and spread over the buttered toast fingers.
Place on a baking sheet and cook in the preheated oven for
10 minutes, or until hot and crisp. Serve immediately.

APPETIZERS

Florida cocktail

Metric/Imperial	American
3 grapefruit	3 grapefruit
3 large oranges	3 large oranges
caster sugar	superfine sugar
2 tablespoons kirsch, (optional)	3 tablespoons kirsch, (optional)
6 glacé cherries	6 candied cherries

Serves 6

Peel the grapefruit and oranges with a sharp serrated knife, making sure all the white pith is removed. Cut the fruit into segments and place on a plate. Sprinkle with sugar to taste, and kirsch, if desired. Allow to stand at room temperature for 30 minutes.

Arrange the fruit in individual glasses, pour juice over, and decorate with a glacé (candied) cherry. Chill before serving.

Variation: Dry sherry may be used instead of kirsch.

Cheese aigrettes

Metric/Imperial	American
25 g./1 oz. butter or margarine	2 tablespoons butter or margarine
3 tablespoons water	4 tablespoons water
50 g./2 oz. flour, preferably plain	½ cup flour, preferably all-purpose
2 large eggs	2 large eggs
40 g./1½ oz. grated Parmesan cheese	6 tablespoons grated Parmesan cheese
salt and pepper	salt and pepper
oil for deep frying	oil for deep frying
Garnish (optional)	
grated Parmesan, or Parmesan and Cheddar cheese, or flaked almonds	Garnish (optional)
	grated Parmesan, or Parmesan and Cheddar cheese, or slivered almonds

Makes about 16–20

Put the butter or margarine with the water into a pan. Heat until the butter or margarine has melted, remove from the heat and stir in the flour. Return to the heat and cook gently for several minutes, until a firm ball. Again remove from the heat and gradually beat in the eggs until a smooth sticky mixture. Add the cheese (do not replace over the heat), season well. Heat the oil to 180°C./350°F. (until a tiny piece of the mixture turns golden within about a minute). Drop spoonfuls of the mixture into the hot oil, lower the heat and cook for about 7 minutes, turning during cooking. Drain well on absorbent paper. Sprinkle with the garnish if wished.

Note: These can be fried, put on a baking sheet in a low oven and kept hot for a very limited time only.

Salmon mousse

Metric/Imperial	American
2 ×215 g./7½ oz. cans red salmon	2 × 7½ oz. cans red salmon
2 tablespoons lemon juice	2½ tablespoons lemon juice
2 teaspoons tomato ketchup	2 teaspoons tomato ketchup
1 tablespoon finely chopped parsley	1¼ tablespoons finely chopped parsley
salt and freshly ground black pepper	salt and freshly ground black pepper
4 tablespoons cold water	5 tablespoons cold water
1 tablespoon gelatine	1 tablespoon gelatin
1 × 75 ml./3 fl. oz. can evaporated milk, chilled	1 × 3 fl. oz. can evaporated milk, chilled
2 egg whites	2 egg whites
sliced cucumber	sliced cucumber

Serves 8

Remove the skin and bones from the salmon and mash the fish to a smooth paste. Stir in the lemon juice, tomato ketchup, parsley and seasoning. Put the water in a small heatproof bowl or cup. Sprinkle over the gelatine (gelatin), stir once and leave until spongy. Place the bowl or cup in a pan of hot water and stir over a low heat until the gelatine (gelatin) has dissolved. Remove from the heat, strain the gelatine (gelatin) into the salmon mixture and mix well. Whisk the well-chilled evaporated milk until thick and nearly double in volume and fold into the salmon mixture.

Place the egg whites in a clean dry bowl, beat until standing up in peaks, then fold half of the whites into the salmon mixture with a metal spoon, lifting and folding throughout. Add the remaining whites and repeat the folding-in process which should result in a spongy froth. Turn the mixture into a lightly oiled 1¼ l./2 pint (5 cup) mould or individual moulds. Chill until set then turn out on to a flat serving plate. Garnish with sliced cucumber and parsley or shredded lettuce.

Tomato juice cocktail

Metric/Imperial	American
600 ml./1 pint tomato juice	2½ cups tomato juice
shake celery salt	shake celery salt
pinch cayenne pepper	pinch cayenne pepper
little Worcestershire sauce	little Worcestershire sauce
few bruised mint leaves	few bruised mint leaves
1 egg white	1 egg white
very finely chopped mint or parsley	very finely chopped mint or parsley

Serves 4–6

Blend the tomato juice with the celery salt, cayenne pepper, Worcestershire sauce and mint leaves. Chill. Frost 4–6 glasses by brushing the rims with egg white, turning upside down and dipping in very finely chopped mint or parsley. Serve the cocktail in the frosted glasses.

To vary: Add 1 tablespoon (1¼ tablespoons) chopped chives or parsley to the cocktail. Add about 3 tablespoons (4 tablespoons) very finely chopped celery in place of the celery salt. Garnish with small celery leaves.

APPETIZERS

Melon balls with lemon sauce

Metric/Imperial	American
1 melon	1 melon
2 lemons	2 lemons
little water	little water
2 tablespoons sugar	2½ tablespoons sugar
Garnish	Garnish
mint sprigs	mint sprigs
lemon twists	lemon twists

Serves 4–6

Halve the melon and remove the seeds. Make melon balls with a vegetable scoop and chill them. Keep fragments of melon left at the bottom of the fruit for the sauce.

Grate enough rind from the lemons to give 2 teaspoons. Squeeze the juice, measure and add enough water to give 150 ml./¼ pint (⅔ cup) of liquid. Simmer the rind in the liquid and sugar for about 5 minutes. Add the odd pieces of melon, then sieve or purée in a blender. Taste and add more sugar if wished. Spoon the sauce into 4 or 6 glasses and top with the melon balls. Garnish with mint and lemon.

Mixed hors d'oeuvres

Serves 6

Salami cornets

Twist 12 slices of salami into cones. Slice about 12 small raw button mushrooms, toss in oil and vinegar, season well. Spoon into the cones, top with halved stuffed olives. Alternatively, pipe in rosettes of thick mayonnaise and top with olives.

Red pepper and cucumber salad

Blend 3–4 tablespoons (4–5 tablespoons) diced cucumber with 3–4 tablespoons (4–5 tablespoons) diced canned red pepper. Toss in well seasoned oil and vinegar.

Carrot creamed coleslaw

Blend a little cream and lemon juice into about 3 tablespoons (4 tablespoons) mayonnaise. Toss 5–6 tablespoons (6–7½ tablespoons) shredded white cabbage and the same amount of coarsely grated carrot with the dressing.

Tomato and onion salad

Blend oil and vinegar with seasoning and a pinch of sugar. Cut 1 large onion and 4 tomatoes into rings. Toss in dressing.

Corn potato salad

Blend 2–3 tablespoons (2½–4 tablespoons) mayonnaise with a little oil and vinegar. Blend 3–4 tablespoons (4–5 tablespoons) cooked or canned sweetcorn, 2–3 tablespoons (2½–4 tablespoons) cooked or canned peas and 5–6 tablespoons (6–7½ tablespoons) diced cooked or canned potatoes. Toss in the dressing.

Stuffed egg mayonnaise

Hard boil (hard cook) 3–4 eggs, halve and remove the yolks. Mash these and blend with 4–5 chopped anchovy fillets. Press into the white cases. Put into a dish, top with mayonnaise flavoured with a little tomato ketchup and single (light) cream. Garnish with chopped parsley.

Herring or mackerel hors d'oeuvres

Metric/Imperial
4 medium-sized herrings or
   mackerel
salt and pepper
little oil
1 small onion, finely chopped
1 dessert apple, cored and
   chopped
little sherry
mayonnaise
curry powder
½–1 tablespoon tomato purée
2–3 tablespoons natural yogurt
1 raw carrot, peeled and grated
1 teaspoon grated raw onion
1 hard boiled egg
lettuce and watercress

Garnish
lemon twists

American
4 medium-sized herrings or
   mackerel
salt and pepper
little oil
1 small onion, finely chopped
1 dessert apple, cored and
   chopped
little sherry
mayonnaise
curry powder
¾–1¼ tablespoons tomato
   paste
2½–4 tablespoons plain yogurt
1 raw carrot, peeled and grated
1 teaspoon grated raw onion
1 hard cooked egg
lettuce and watercress

Garnish
lemon twists

Serves 4–6
Fillet the herrings or mackerel. Season, brush with a little oil and grill (broil) carefully so the flesh does not break — do not over-cook. Cool, then cut into neat pieces. Blend 1 fish with the finely chopped onion, finely chopped apple and a little sherry. Blend a second fish with mayonnaise flavoured with curry powder. Mix the tomato purée (paste) with the yogurt and toss the third fish in this mixture. Mix the last fish with the carrot, onion and chopped hard boiled (hard cooked) egg. Arrange the four mixtures on a bed of lettuce and watercress. Garnish with lemon twists.

Lemon and sardine pâté

Metric/Imperial
50 g./2 oz. butter
75 g./3 oz. fresh white or
   brown breadcrumbs
grated rind and juice of ½
   lemon
2 teaspoons finely chopped
   parsley
1 × 100 g./4 oz. can sardines,
   boned and mashed with can
   oil
salt and freshly ground black
   pepper
4–6 lemon slices

American
4 tablespoons butter
1½ cups fresh white or brown
   breadcrumbs
grated rind and juice of ½
   lemon
2 teaspoons finely chopped
   parsley
1 × 4 oz. can sardines, boned
   and mashed with can oil
salt and freshly ground black
   pepper
4–6 lemon slices

Serves 4–6
Melt the butter in a saucepan, then remove from the heat and stir in the breadcrumbs, lemon rind and juice, parsley, sardines and seasoning to taste. Beat together until smooth, taste and adjust the seasoning. Spoon the sardine mixture into 4 or 6 small dishes or 1 large dish.

    Place a slice of lemon on top and chill until firm. Serve chilled with hot toast and lemon wedges.

APPETIZERS

Melon and smoked ham

Metric/Imperial
1 small melon
100 g./4 oz. smoked ham
freshly ground black pepper
parsley sprigs

American
1 small melon
4 oz. smoked ham
freshly ground black pepper
parsley sprigs

Serves 6
Cut melon into 6 equal segments and remove the seeds. Chill the melon well. Slice the ham very thinly.

To serve, place melon on a plate. Lay rolled-up slices of smoked ham over each piece of melon and sprinkle with freshly ground black pepper. Serve immediately, garnished with sprigs of parsley.

Aubergines (eggplants) niçoise

Metric/Imperial
2 medium-sized aubergines
salt and pepper
1–2 cloves garlic
1 large onion
1 tablespoon oil
25 g./1 oz. butter
4–5 large tomatoes, skinned
*   and chopped*

Topping
chopped parsley

American
2 medium-sized eggplants
salt and pepper
1–2 cloves garlic
1 large onion
1 1/4 tablespoons oil
2 tablespoons butter
4–5 large tomatoes, skinned
*   and chopped*

Topping
chopped parsley

Serves 4
Wash and dry the aubergines (eggplants), slice thinly, but do not peel. Sprinkle lightly with salt and leave for about 15–20 minutes (to minimize the slightly bitter taste). Rinse under cold water. Crush the garlic, chop the onion. Heat the oil and butter in a pan. Fry the garlic and onion gently for a few minutes, then add the tomatoes. Simmer gently until the tomatoes become a purée. Add the aubergine (eggplant) slices and season well. Mix with the tomato purée, put a lid on the pan, and simmer steadily for 45–50 minutes. Serve hot, topped with chopped parsley.

French country-style liver pâté

Metric/Imperial	American
225 g./8 oz. pig's liver, ducts removed and minced	8 oz. pig's liver, ducts removed and ground
225 g./8 oz. belly of pork, boned and minced	8 oz. arm steak of pork, boned and ground
1 small garlic clove, crushed	1 small garlic clove, crushed
salt and freshly ground black pepper	salt and freshly ground black pepper
1 teaspoon dried mixed herbs	1 teaspoon dried mixed herbs
3 tablespoons dry white wine	4 tablespoons dry white wine
4 rashers streaky bacon	4 slices fatty bacon

Serves 6

Oven setting: 160°C./325°F./Gas Mark 3

Mix together the pig's liver and belly of pork (pork arm steak). Stir in the garlic, seasoning to taste, herbs and wine. Mix well and turn into a 600 ml./1 pint (2½ cup) ovenproof dish.

On a chopping board, flatten and stretch the bacon rashers (slices) with the blade of a knife. Cover the pâté with the bacon then cover tightly with foil. Stand the dish in a pan with enough boiling water to come halfway up the side of the dish. Bake in preheated oven for 1–1¼ hours, or until pâté has shrunk from the edges of the dish and a skewer inserted into it comes out clean. Pour off the excess fat. Allow to cool. Serve with hot toast or crusty French bread.

Watercress eggs

Metric/Imperial	American
4 eggs	4 eggs
salt and pepper	salt and pepper
squeeze lemon juice	squeeze lemon juice
2 tablespoons skimmed milk	2½ tablespoons skimmed milk
3–4 tablespoons chopped watercress leaves	4–5 tablespoons chopped watercress leaves
lettuce	lettuce

Serves 4

Hard boil (hard cook) the eggs and halve lengthways. Remove the yolks, mash with seasoning. Add the lemon juice, skimmed milk (to give a soft consistency) and the chopped watercress leaves. Press into the white cases and serve on a bed of lettuce.

To vary: Use chopped canned asparagus tips in place of watercress.

APPETIZERS

Haddock and mushroom scallops

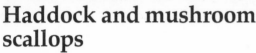

Metric/Imperial	American
25 g./1 oz. butter	2 tablespoons butter
100 g./4 oz. mushrooms, sliced	1 cup sliced mushrooms
300 ml./½ pint white coating sauce	1¼ cups white coating sauce
½ teaspoon made English mustard	½ teaspoon made hot mustard
225 g./8 oz. smoked haddock, cooked, skin and bones removed and flaked	8 oz. smoked haddock, cooked, skin and bones removed and flaked
freshly ground black pepper	freshly ground black pepper
25 g./1 oz. grated Cheddar cheese	¼ cup grated Cheddar cheese
15 g./½ oz. fresh white breadcrumbs	¼ cup fresh white breadcrumbs
½ kg./1 lb. potatoes, boiled	1 lb. potatoes, boiled
25 g./1 oz. butter	2 tablespoons butter
2 tablespoons milk	3 tablespoons milk
salt	salt

Serves 4
Oven setting: 200°C./400°F./Gas Mark 6
Melt the butter in a pan, add the mushrooms, and sauté for 3 minutes. Stir in the white sauce, mustard, fish and pepper to taste. Divide the mixture between 4 buttered scallop shells or small buttered ovenproof dishes and sprinkle with the grated cheese and breadcrumbs. Mash the potatoes with butter and milk until smooth, season to taste. Pipe a border of mashed potato round the edge of each shell or dish.

Dot with 15 g./½ oz. (1 tablespoon) butter and place on a baking sheet in the preheated oven for 15–20 minutes, or until topping is crisp and golden.

Chicken and pear vol-au-vents

Metric/Imperial	American
225 g./8 oz. puff pastry	2 cups puff pastry
1 egg, beaten	1 egg, beaten
225 g./8 oz. cold cooked chicken	2 cups cold cooked chicken
1 egg yolk	1 egg yolk
300 ml./½ pint béchamel sauce	1¼ cups béchamel sauce
juice of ½ lemon	juice of ½ lemon
½ kg./1 lb pears	1 lb pears
¼ teaspoon grated nutmeg	¼ teaspoon grated nutmeg
salt and pepper	salt and pepper

Serves 4
Oven setting: 240°C./475°F./Gas Mark 9
Roll out the dough on a lightly floured board to 1 cm./½ inch thick. Cut it into four 5 cm./2 inch rounds. Mark a circle in the centre of each round, using a smaller cutter, but cut only halfway through the pastry. Mark a criss-cross pattern in the centre circle with a knife. Leave the pastry in a cool place for 20 minutes before baking. Brush the tops with beaten egg, then bake for 10 minutes. Reduce the oven temperature to 190°C./375°F./Gas Mark 5 and cook for a further 10–15 minutes or until cooked.

Cut the chicken into bite-sized pieces. Add egg yolk to the béchamel sauce and reheat without boiling. Stir in the chicken and lemon juice. Peel, core and chop the pears and add to the sauce. Reheat and season with nutmeg, salt and pepper.

Remove the centre circle from each vol-au-vent case, taking care not to break it. Scoop out pastry in the middle and spoon in the sauce. Replace lid. Serve at once.

Bortsch

Metric/Imperial	American
butter for frying	butter for frying
1 large onion, sliced	1 large onion, sliced
1 large carrot, peeled and shredded	1 large carrot, peeled and shredded
2 large cooked beetroots, peeled and sliced	2 large cooked beets, peeled and sliced
½ small red cabbage, shredded	½ small red cabbage, shredded
1¼ l./2 pints beef stock, skimmed of fat	5 cups beef stock, skimmed of fat
1 tablespoon tomato purée	1¼ tablespoons tomato paste
1 tablespoon malt vinegar	1¼ tablespoons malt vinegar
1 tablespoon sugar	1¼ tablespoons sugar
salt and freshly ground black pepper	salt and freshly ground black pepper
300 ml./½ pint soured cream to finish	1¼ cups sour cream to finish

Serves 4

Melt a knob of butter in a large pan. Add the vegetables, cover and cook gently for 5 minutes. Stir in the remaining ingredients and bring to the boil. Lower the heat, cover and simmer gently for 20–30 minutes or until the vegetables are tender and the soup has a soft consistency. Adjust seasoning and serve with the soured cream (sour cream) handed round in a separate bowl.

Chilled summer soup

Metric/Imperial	American
1 medium-sized lettuce	1 medium-sized lettuce
40 g./1½ oz. butter	3 tablespoons butter
½ cucumber, peeled and chopped	½ cucumber, peeled and chopped
1 onion, chopped	1 onion, chopped
grated rind of 2 oranges	grated rind of 2 oranges
900 ml./1½ pints chicken stock	3¾ cups chicken stock
40 g./1½ oz. flour	6 tablespoons flour
salt and pepper	salt and pepper
300 ml./½ pint single cream	1¼ cups light cream
Garnish	Garnish
diced cucumber	diced cucumber
1 orange, sliced	1 orange, sliced

Serves 4–6

Wash and shred the lettuce, discarding any tough outer leaves. Heat the butter in a pan and add the lettuce, cucumber, onion and orange rind. Cook gently for 10 minutes, stirring. Add most of the stock, and simmer gently for 10 minutes, or until the vegetables are tender. Blend the flour with the remaining stock, add to the soup and cook until thickened. Season well. Work through a sieve (strainer) or blend the soup to give a very smooth purée. Allow to cool then whisk in the cream and chill. Garnish with diced cucumber and serve with orange slices.

SOUPS

Pot-au-feu

Metric/Imperial
1 kg./2 lb. clod or shin of beef
    with bones, excess fat
    removed
1 teaspoon salt
6 peppercorns, finely crushed
1 onion, peeled and stuck with a
    few cloves
1 bouquet garni
1 garlic clove, finely chopped
2 carrots, peeled and quartered
2 sticks celery, chopped
2 leeks, washed and sliced
½ kg./1 lb. potatoes, peeled
    and diced
chopped parsley

American
2 lb. lean beef chuck or plate of
    beef with bones, excess fat
    removed
1 teaspoon salt
6 peppercorns, finely crushed
1 onion, peeled and stuck with a
    few cloves
1 bouquet garni
1 garlic clove, finely chopped
2 carrots, peeled and quartered
2 sticks celery, chopped
2 leeks, washed and sliced
1 lb. potatoes, peeled and diced
chopped parsley

Serves 4–6
Put the meat and bones in a large pan. Cover with water, add the salt and bring slowly to the boil. Skim off the scum with a slotted spoon. Lower the heat, add the peppercorns, onion, bouquet garni and garlic, and half cover. Simmer very gently for 2½ hours or until the meat is just tender, skimming from time to time if necessary. Add more water if the liquid level in the pan becomes rather low.

Remove the bones, the bouquet garni and onion, then add the vegetables. Continue to simmer gently for a further 1 hour when both the meat and vegetables will be tender. Before serving, bring the soup quickly to the boil, skim well to remove any fat, adjust seasoning and sprinkle with plenty of chopped parsley.

Kidney and bacon soup

Metric/Imperial
225 g./8 oz. ox kidney
2 onions
2 rashers streaky bacon
25 g./1 oz. fat or beef dripping
750 ml./1¼ pints beef stock
salt and pepper
1 tablespoon flour
1 carrot (optional)

American
8 oz. ox kidney
2 onions
2 slices fatty bacon
2 tablespoons fat or beef
    dripping
3 cups beef stock
salt and pepper
1¼ tablespoons flour
1 carrot (optional)

Serves 4–6
Cut the kidney and peeled onions into very small pieces. Remove the bacon rinds and chop the rinds and bacon. Fry the bacon with the bacon rinds until the bacon is cooked. Lift out of the pan but continue frying the rinds until they are crisp. Remove these and put with the bacon. Heat the fat or dripping and toss the kidney and onions in this for 5 minutes. Add most of the stock with seasoning. Cover the pan and simmer gently for 1 hour. Blend the flour with the remaining stock, stir into the soup and cook until slightly thickened. Peel and grate the carrot, add to the soup and cook for 5 minutes (this could be omitted). Serve topped with the bacon and bacon rinds.

Green pepper soup

Metric/Imperial
2 tablespoons oil
50 g./2 oz. butter
225 g./8 oz. green peppers,
* cored, seeded and diced*
2 onions, chopped
40 g./1½ oz. flour
450 ml./¾ pint chicken stock
salt and pepper
450 ml./¾ pint milk
3 tablespoons single cream

American
2½ tablespoons oil
¼ cup butter
8 oz. green peppers, cored,
* seeded and diced*
2 onions, chopped
6 tablespoons flour
2 cups chicken stock
salt and pepper
2 cups milk
3¾ tablespoons light cream

Serves 4
Heat the oil in a saucepan, then add the butter. When it has melted, add the green peppers and onions and cook gently for 5 minutes. Blend in the flour and cook for 1 minute. Gradually stir in the stock and bring to the boil. Season and simmer, covered, for 30 minutes or until the vegetables are soft. Push the soup through a sieve or purée in a blender. Stir in the milk, and reheat gently. Add the cream just before serving.

Tomato and celery soup

Metric/Imperial
2 medium-sized onions
3–4 sticks celery
25 g./1 oz. butter
½ kg./1 lb. tomatoes, skinned
* and chopped*
300 ml./½ pint white stock
salt and pepper
1 tablespoon tomato purée

Garnish
celery leaves

American
2 medium-sized onions
3–4 sticks celery
2 tablespoons butter
1 lb. tomatoes, skinned and
* chopped*
1¼ cups white stock
salt and pepper
1¼ tablespoons tomato paste

Garnish
celery leaves

Serves 4
Chop the onions and celery. Toss in the melted butter for a few minutes. Add the chopped tomatoes and stock and simmer for 15 minutes. Work through a sieve (strainer) or purée in a blender. Return to the pan, heat for a few minutes, then add the seasoning and tomato purée (paste). Pour into soup bowls or a tureen. Garnish with chopped celery leaves. This soup is also excellent cold.

SOUPS

Chilled avocado soup

Metric/Imperial
2 large or 3 medium-sized ripe
*   avocados*
juice of 1 lemon
1 × 420 g./15 oz. can
*   consommé, or use 600 ml./1*
*   pint home-made beef or*
*   chicken stock*
150 ml./¼ pint natural yogurt
salt and pepper

Garnish
chopped chives or spring onions

American
2 large or 3 medium-sized ripe
*   avocados*
juice of 1 lemon
1 × 15 oz. can consommé, or
*   use 2½ cups home-made beef*
*   or chicken stock*
⅔ cup plain yogurt
salt and pepper

Garnish
chopped chives or scallions

Serves 4–6
Halve the avocados and remove the stones (pits). Scoop out the flesh and rub through a nylon sieve (strainer), using a wooden spoon. Blend in the remaining ingredients at once, except the chives or spring onions (scallions) and season well.

If preferred, place all the ingredients except the chives or spring onions (scallions) in a blender and set at high speed until the mixture is smooth. Serve chilled, topped with a few chopped chives or chopped spring onions (scallions).

Cock-a-leekie

Metric/Imperial
1 boiling fowl (about
*   1¼–1½ kg./2½–3 lb.),*
*   trussed, with the giblets*
*   (except liver and gall*
*   bladder)*
1 bouquet garni
salt and freshly ground black
*   pepper*
6 leeks, washed, halved and
*   sliced lengthways*
4–6 prunes, soaked overnight,
*   halved and stoned*

American
1 boiling fowl (about 2½–3 lb),
*   trussed, with the giblets*
*   (except liver and gall*
*   bladder)*
1 bouquet garni
salt and freshly ground black
*   pepper*
6 leeks, washed, halved and
*   sliced lengthways*
4–6 prunes, soaked overnight,
*   halved and pitted*

Serves 4–6
Put the fowl and bouquet garni in a large pan, season well and cover with water. Bring to the boil then lower the heat, half cover and simmer very gently for 2 hours, skimming with a slotted spoon from time to time if necessary to remove the scum. Add the leeks and more water to cover the fowl if required and continue to simmer, uncovered, for a further 1 hour or until both fowl and leeks are tender. The prunes should be added 30 minutes before the end of cooking time.

To serve, remove the fowl and discard the giblets and bouquet garni. Skim the broth and adjust seasoning. The fowl can be carved and some of the meat returned to the soup and reheated before serving, or it can be eaten separately as a main course.

Shrimp chowder

Metric/Imperial	American
1 large onion, sliced	1 large onion, sliced
15 g./½ oz. butter	1 tablespoon butter
150 ml./¼ pint boiling water	⅔ cup boiling water
3 medium-sized potatoes, peeled and diced	3 medium-sized potatoes, peeled and diced
salt and pepper	salt and pepper
½ kg./1 lb. shelled shrimps	1 lb. peeled shrimp
600 ml./1 pint milk	2½ cups milk
25–50 g./1–2 oz. grated cheese	¼–½ cup grated cheese
1 tablespoon chopped parsley	1¼ tablespoons chopped parsley

Serves 4

Fry the onion in the butter for 5 minutes, until soft but not coloured. Add the boiling water, potatoes and seasoning. Cover and simmer gently for 15–20 minutes, or until the potatoes are just cooked. Add the shrimps and the milk and reheat. Stir in the grated cheese and parsley. Serve hot with crusty bread or toast.

Minestrone

Metric/Imperial	American
100 g./4 oz. dried haricot beans	⅔ cup dried white (navy) beans
3 tablespoons oil	4 tablespoons oil
2 onions, sliced	2 onions, sliced
2 garlic cloves, crushed	2 garlic cloves, crushed
2–3 rashers bacon	2–3 slices bacon
4 tomatoes, skinned, seeded and chopped	4 tomatoes, skinned, seeded and chopped
125 ml./4 fl. oz. red wine	½ cup red wine
1 teaspoon chopped fresh marjoram	1 teaspoon chopped fresh marjoram
½ teaspoon chopped fresh thyme	½ teaspoon chopped fresh thyme
2 carrots, peeled and diced	2 carrots, peeled and diced
2 potatoes, peeled and diced	2 potatoes, peeled and diced
1 small turnip, peeled and diced	1 small turnip, peeled and diced
1–2 sticks celery, chopped	1–2 sticks celery, chopped
½ small cabbage, shredded	½ small cabbage, shredded
50 g./2 oz. small pasta	½ cup small pasta
1 tablespoon chopped parsley	1¼ tablespoons chopped parsley
salt and pepper	salt and pepper
grated Parmesan cheese	grated Parmesan cheese

Serves 4–6

Soak the beans overnight.

Heat the oil in a large pan. Add the onions, garlic and bacon and sauté for a few minutes. Add tomatoes, wine and drained beans. Add 1¾ l./3 pints (7½ cups) water, marjoram and thyme. Cover and simmer for about 2 hours.

Add carrots, cook about 10 minutes, then add potatoes and turnip. Cook a few minutes longer, then add celery, cabbage and pasta. Cook until pasta and all vegetables are tender, then add chopped parsley, salt and pepper to taste and stir in 2–3 tablespoons (2½–4 tablespoons) grated Parmesan. Serve with extra Parmesan.

SOUPS

Oxtail soup

Metric/Imperial
lard or beef dripping for frying
1 large onion, chopped
1 oxtail, chopped and excess fat
   removed
2–3 carrots, peeled and chopped
2–3 sticks celery, chopped
1 bay leaf
6 peppercorns
salt

American
lard or beef dripping for frying
1 large onion, chopped
1 oxtail, chopped and excess fat
   removed
2–3 carrots, peeled and chopped
2–3 sticks celery, chopped
1 bay leaf
6 peppercorns
salt

Serves 4–6
Melt a knob of fat in a large pan. Add the onion and oxtail and fry until brown. Add remaining ingredients and cover with water. Salt lightly. Bring to the boil, then lower the heat, cover and simmer gently for 3–4 hours, or until the oxtail is thoroughly tender and the meat is falling from the bone. Add more water during cooking if the liquid level becomes rather low.

   Take the pan from the heat. Remove the oxtail and take the meat off the bone with a sharp knife. Skim the stock well to remove any fat, using a spoon or absorbent paper towels. Return the meat to the soup, discarding the bone and bay leaf, and purée the soup in a blender. Thin with a little water if the soup is too thick and adjust seasoning. Return to the rinsed-out pan and reheat before serving.

Chicken bortsch

Metric/Imperial
1 × 290 g./10½ oz. can cream
   of chicken soup
little top of the milk or single
   cream
liquid from a 225 g./8 oz. can
   beetroot
chopped parsley

American
1 × 10½ oz. can cream of
   chicken soup
little light cream
liquid from an 8 oz. can beets
chopped parsley

Serves 4
Tip the soup into a pan and heat. Add a little top of the milk or cream and the beetroot (beet) liquid. Garnish with chopped parsley.

Watercress and potato soup

Crème chambertin

Metric/Imperial
butter for frying
1 small onion, finely chopped
2 bunches of watercress, finely chopped
225 g./8 oz. potatoes, peeled and diced
450 ml./¾ pint milk
450 ml./¾ pint chicken stock
salt and freshly ground black pepper
few reserved watercress leaves

American
butter for frying
1 small onion, finely chopped
2 bunches of watercress, finely chopped
2 cups peeled and diced potatoes
2 cups milk
2 cups chicken stock
salt and freshly ground black pepper
few reserved watercress leaves

Serves 4–6
Melt a knob of butter in a pan. Add the vegetables, cover and cook gently for 5 minutes. Stir in the milk and stock, bring to the boil and add seasoning. Lower the heat, half cover and simmer gently for 30 minutes, stirring occasionally. Purée the soup in a blender or work through a sieve (strainer). Return to the rinsed-out pan and reheat. Before serving adjust seasoning and float a few leaves of watercress on each soup bowl.

Metric/Imperial
2 medium-sized onions
2 medium-sized potatoes
50 g./2 oz. butter
600 ml./1 pint chicken stock
salt and pepper
25 g./1 oz. flour
300 ml./½ pint milk
1 large carrot, peeled and grated
2 tablespoons chopped fresh herbs, or 2 teaspoons dried herbs
300 ml./½ pint soured cream

American
2 medium-sized onions
2 medium-sized potatoes
4 tablespoons butter
2½ cups chicken stock
salt and pepper
¼ cup flour
1¼ cups milk
1 large carrot, peeled and grated
2½ tablespoons chopped fresh herbs, or 2 teaspoons dried herbs
1¼ cups sour cream

Serves 6–8
Chop the onions and potatoes. Toss in the hot butter for a few minutes; take care the vegetables do not brown. Add the stock and simmer gently for 30 minutes. Season lightly. Work through a sieve (strainer) or purée the soup in a blender and return to the pan. Blend the flour with the milk and stir into the vegetable purée. Continue stirring over a low heat until the mixture thickens. Add the carrot, herbs, half the soured cream (sour cream) and a little extra seasoning. Simmer for 5–10 minutes. Do not boil. Top with the remainder of the soured cream (sour cream).

SOUPS

Salmon chowder

Metric/Imperial
600 ml./1 pint milk
1 × 400 g./14 oz. can
    sweetcorn, drained
1 × 200 g./7 oz. can salmon,
    drained and flaked
25 g./1 oz. butter
salt and pepper
chopped parsley

American
2½ cups milk
1 × 14 oz. can sweetcorn,
    drained
1 × 7 oz. can salmon, drained
    and flaked
2 tablespoons butter
salt and pepper
chopped parsley

Serves 4
Put the milk and sweetcorn into a pan over high heat.
Bring to simmering point. Add the salmon, butter, salt,
pepper and parsley. Heat gently for a few minutes,
stirring, until hot. Remove pan from heat and serve.

Chicken broth

Metric/Imperial
1 chicken carcass and any
    leftover chicken, diced
½ teaspoon salt
6 peppercorns, finely crushed
1 bay leaf
1 bouquet garni
2 carrots, peeled and sliced
3 sticks celery, chopped
50 g./2 oz. long-grain rice

Garnish
chopped parsley
50 g./2 oz. chopped almonds

American
1 chicken carcass and any
    leftover chicken, diced
½ teaspoon salt
6 peppercorns, finely crushed
1 bay leaf
1 bouquet garni
2 carrots, peeled and sliced
3 sticks celery, chopped
⅓ cup long-grain rice

Garnish
chopped parsley
½ cup chopped almonds

Serves 4
Put the chicken carcass and any meat in a large pan, cover
with water and add the remaining ingredients. Bring to
the boil. Lower the heat, cover and simmer gently for 2
hours, skimming with a slotted spoon when necessary to
remove any scum. Add more water if the liquid in the pan
becomes low.

To serve, remove the carcass from the pan, making sure
that every scrap of meat is in the broth. Skim well to
remove any fat, using a spoon or absorbent paper towels.
Discard the bay leaf and bouquet garni, adjust seasoning
and serve the broth piping hot, topped with plenty of
parsley and the almonds.

Chilled tomato parsley soup

Metric/Imperial	American
½ kg./1 lb. canned tomatoes	1 lb. canned tomatoes
juice of ½ lemon	juice of ½ lemon
1 teaspoon salt	1 teaspoon salt
1 very small onion, chopped	1 very small onion, chopped
parsley sprig	parsley sprig
1 × 425 g./15 oz. can	1 × 15 oz. can condensed
condensed consommé	consommé

Garnish
2 tablespoons chopped parsley

Garnish
2½ tablespoons chopped
parsley

Serves 4–6
Place tomatoes, lemon juice, salt, onion and parsley sprig
in a blender and mix until smooth and well blended. Mix
tomato mixture with consommé. Chill well. Serve soup
chilled, garnished with chopped parsley.

Cauliflower soup

Metric/Imperial	American
50 g./2 oz. butter	4 tablespoons butter
1 large onion, sliced	1 large onion, sliced
1 garlic clove, crushed	1 garlic clove, crushed
1 medium-sized cauliflower, in	1 medium-sized cauliflower, in
sprigs	sprigs
1 l./1¾ pints chicken stock	4¼ cups chicken stock
salt and pepper	salt and pepper
4 tablespoons single cream	5 tablespoons light cream

Garnish
2 slices toast
chopped parsley

Garnish
2 slices toast
chopped parsley

Serves 6
Heat the butter in a large, heavy pan. Add the onion and
garlic and fry slowly until soft. Add the cauliflower and
stock, then cover and simmer for 1 hour.

Work the soup through a sieve (strainer) or purée in a
blender. Return it to the rinsed-out pan and check
seasoning. Stir in the cream and reheat the soup almost to
simmering point. Cut the toast into 1 cm./½ inch cubes
and scatter on top of the soup with the parsley just before
serving.

SOUPS

Celery soup

Metric/Imperial
1 head of celery, finely chopped,
   a few young leaves reserved
1 small onion, finely chopped
1 tablespoon flour
½ teaspoon celery salt
white pepper to taste
600 ml./1 pint milk

American
1 head of celery, finely chopped,
   a few young leaves reserved
1 small onion, finely chopped
1¼ tablespoons flour
½ teaspoon celery salt
white pepper to taste
2½ cups milk

Serves 4
Put all the ingredients, except the celery leaves, in a blender and purée until quite smooth. Pour into a pan and bring slowly to the boil, stirring constantly. Work through a sieve (strainer), return to the rinsed-out pan and reheat gently. Adjust seasoning. Garnish each bowl with a few celery leaves.

Creamed cauliflower soup

Metric/Imperial
1 small cauliflower
1 onion, chopped
600 ml./1 pint water
1 chicken stock cube
1 tablespoon dried milk
salt and pepper

American
1 small cauliflower
1 onion, chopped
2½ cups water
1 chicken bouillon cube
1¼ tablespoons dried milk
   solids
salt and pepper

Serves 2
Put the cauliflower into a saucepan with the onion, three quarters of the water and stock (bouillon) cube. Cover and simmer for about 1 hour. Remove the pan from the heat and whisk hard with an egg whisk or fork to break up the cauliflower. Mix the milk powder with the remaining water and stir into the soup. Season to taste with salt and pepper. Reheat gently and serve piping hot.

Mushroom vichyssoise

Metric/Imperial
2 large potatoes, peeled
3 large leeks, washed
600 ml./1 pint chicken stock
50 g./2 oz. button mushrooms,
  sliced
150 ml./¼ pint single cream
salt and pepper

Topping
little cream
chopped chives

American
2 large potatoes, peeled
3 large leeks, washed
2½ cups chicken stock
½ cup button mushrooms,
  sliced
⅔ cup light cream
salt and pepper

Topping
little cream
chopped chives

Serves 4–6
Chop the vegetables and simmer in the chicken stock for 35–40 minutes. Add the sliced mushrooms towards the end of the cooking time. Work through a sieve (strainer) or purée in a blender, then cool. Blend with the cream and season well. Top with cream and chopped chives.

French onion soup

Metric/Imperial
225 g./8 oz. onions, sliced
25 g./1 oz. butter
1 teaspoon caster sugar
1 tablespoon flour
900 ml./1½ pints beef stock
salt and pepper
slices French bread
50 g./2 oz. grated Gruyère
  cheese

American
1⅓ cups sliced onions
2 tablespoons butter
1 teaspoon superfine sugar
1¼ tablespoons flour
3¾ cups beef stock
salt and pepper
slices French or Italian bread
½ cup grated Swiss cheese

Serves 4
Brown the onions slowly in the butter. Add the sugar and cook for a few minutes. Add the flour and cook for 1 minute. Add the stock and bring to the boil, stirring. Simmer 20 minutes then add salt and pepper if necessary.

  Toast one side of the bread then sprinkle cheese on the untoasted side. Grill (broil) until the cheese has melted. Put slices of bread in each soup bowl and pour the soup on top.

SOUPS

Crab bisque

Metric/Imperial	American
1 medium-sized cooked crab or 1 × 225 g./8 oz. can crab meat	1 medium-sized cooked crab or 1 × 8 oz. can crab meat
450 ml./¾ pint fish stock* or water	2 cups fish stock* or water
1 lemon	1 lemon
salt and pepper	salt and pepper
bouquet garni	bouquet garni
1 onion	1 onion
50 g./2 oz. mushrooms	½ cup mushrooms
50 g./2 oz. butter	4 tablespoons butter
300 ml./½ pint single cream	1¼ cups light cream
2 egg yolks	2 egg yolks
2 tablespoons sherry	2½ tablespoons sherry

*made by boiling fish bones or a fish head

Serves 4–6

Remove all the meat from the fresh crab and put on one side. Put the stock or water, pared lemon rind, a little lemon juice, seasoning and the bouquet garni in a pan. Add the shell if using fresh crab. Cover the pan and simmer gently for 30 minutes. Chop the onion, slice the mushrooms and toss in the hot butter. Add the strained stock and the flaked crab meat and heat gently. Blend the cream with the egg yolks, add to the crab mixture and simmer gently just until thickened. Add the sherry.

Lentil and ham soup

Metric/Imperial	American
1 large onion, roughly chopped	1 large onion, roughly chopped
4 large sticks celery, roughly chopped	4 large sticks celery, roughly chopped
2 large carrots, peeled and chopped	2 large carrots, peeled and chopped
75 g./3 oz. split yellow lentils	½ cup split yellow lentils
1 large parsley sprig or ½ teaspoon dried parsley	1 large parsley sprig or ½ teaspoon dried parsley
few celery leaves	few celery leaves
salt and freshly ground black pepper	salt and freshly ground black pepper
2 cloves, crushed	2 cloves, crushed
900 ml./1½ pints home-made ham stock	3¾ cups home-made ham stock
cooked diced ham	cooked diced ham
chopped parsley to finish	chopped parsley to finish

Serves 4–6

Put all the ingredients, except the ham with 600 ml./1 pint (2½ cups) of the stock in a large pan. Bring to the boil, then lower the heat, cover and simmer very gently for 1–1½ hours, or until everything is soft and mushy. Purée in blender or work through a sieve (strainer). Return to the rinsed-out pan. Add the remaining stock and pieces of ham. Reheat gently. Adjust seasoning. Stir in plenty of chopped parsley and serve.

Chicken chowder

Metric/Imperial	American
2–3 rashers bacon, chopped	2–3 slices bacon, chopped
1 onion, chopped	1 onion, chopped
450 ml./¾ pint chicken stock	2 cups chicken stock
350 g./12 oz. diced raw root vegetables	2 cups diced raw root vegetables
300 ml./½ pint milk	1¼ cups milk
about 175 g./6 oz. diced cooked chicken	about 1 cup diced cooked chicken
3–4 tablespoons sweetcorn	4–5 tablespoons sweetcorn
salt and pepper	salt and pepper
Garnish	Garnish
chopped parsley	chopped parsley
paprika	paprika

Serves 4–6

Fry the bacon for a few minutes. Add the onion then cook together until the bacon is crisp. Add the stock. Bring to the boil, put in the vegetables and cook until just tender. Add the milk, chicken, sweetcorn and seasoning. Simmer for a few minutes then serve, topped with parsley and paprika.

Gazpacho

Metric/Imperial	American
½ kg./1 lb. ripe tomatoes, skinned, seeded and chopped	1 lb. ripe tomatoes, skinned, seeded and chopped
1 small onion, finely grated	1 small onion, finely grated
1 garlic clove, crushed with ½ teaspoon salt	1 garlic clove, crushed with ½ teaspoon salt
2 tablespoons lemon juice	2½ tablespoons lemon juice
1 tablespoon olive oil	1¼ tablespoons olive oil
1 × 425 ml./15 fl. oz. can tomato juice	1 × 15 fl. oz. can tomato juice
freshly ground black pepper	freshly ground black pepper

Serves 8

Purée the tomatoes in a blender, transfer to a bowl and add the onion and garlic. Stir in the lemon juice, olive oil, tomato juice and pepper to taste.

Beat well to produce a smooth consistency, taste and adjust the seasoning. Serve chilled with the classic accompaniments of diced cucumber, sliced green and red pepper, sieved hard boiled (hard cooked) egg yolk and ice-cubes.

FISH

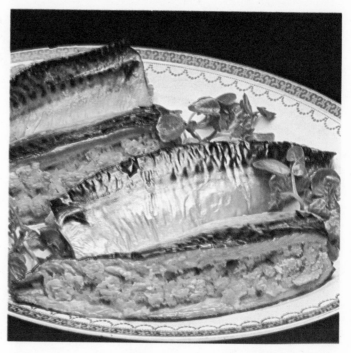

Soused fish

Metric/Imperial
6 herrings or mullets
1 onion, sliced
vinegar
water
4 bay leaves
2 cloves
12 allspice berries
2 mace blades
1 teaspoon salt

American
6 herrings or mullets
1 onion, sliced
vinegar
water
4 bay leaves
2 cloves
12 allspice berries
2 mace blades
1 teaspoon salt

Serves 6
Oven setting: 150°C./300°F./Gas Mark 2
Clean the herrings or mullets and remove the fins, tails
and backbones. Lay the fish, skin side down on a working
surface and place some sliced onion on the centre of each
fish. Roll the fish up from head to tail, secure with a
wooden cocktail stick (pick).

Place the fish in an ovenproof dish and add vinegar and
water to cover in the proportion of three parts vinegar to
one part water. Add the herbs, spices and salt. Cover and
cook in the preheated oven for 3 hours, or until the fish is
tender. The liquid must not boil.

Transfer the fish to a serving dish, strain over the liquor,
cool then chill in the refrigerator. The liquor sets into a soft
jelly.

Helpful hints
Herrings must be eaten very fresh. They should be stiff
and bright looking when you buy them; any which are
limp or slimy should be avoided.

Mackerel with lemon stuffing

Metric/Imperial
4 mackerel, about 175 g./6 oz.
   each, split and boned out
juice of ½ lemon
salt and freshly ground black
   pepper
1 bay leaf, crushed

Stuffing
butter for frying
1 small onion, finely chopped
75 g./3 oz. fresh white
   breadcrumbs
finely grated rind and juice of 1
   lemon
1 tablespoon chopped parsley
½ egg, beaten

American
4 mackerel, about 6 oz. each,
   split and boned out
juice of ½ lemon
salt and freshly ground black
   pepper
1 bay leaf, crushed

Stuffing
butter for frying
1 small onion, finely chopped
1½ cups fresh white
   breadcrumbs
finely grated rind and juice of 1
   lemon
1¼ tablespoons chopped
   parsley
½ egg, beaten

Serves 4
Oven setting: 160°C./325°F./Gas Mark 3
First prepare the stuffing. Heat a knob of butter in a pan.
Add the onion and fry gently for 5 minutes or until golden.
Transfer to a mixing bowl and combine with the remaining
stuffing ingredients.

Lay the mackerel flat on a board and sprinkle the flesh
with lemon juice and salt and pepper to taste. Spoon the
prepared stuffing into the fish and reshape. Place in an
ovenproof casserole, barely cover the bottom of the dish
with water and add the bay leaf and more salt and pepper
to taste. Cover with a lid, or greased greaseproof (waxed)
paper or foil and poach in the preheated oven for 15–20
minutes, or until the fish is tender. Drain and serve
immediately.

Prawns (shrimp) with vegetables

Metric/Imperial	American
½ kg./1 lb. prawns, shelled	1 lb. shrimp, peeled
1 red pepper, cored and seeded	1 red pepper, cored and seeded
2 sticks celery	2 sticks celery
2 Chinese dried mushrooms	2 Chinese dried mushrooms
2 spring onions	2 scallions
6 water chestnuts	6 water chestnuts
1 tablespoon cornflour	1¼ tablespoons cornstarch
1 tablespoon soy sauce	1¼ tablespoons soy sauce
pinch of sugar	pinch of sugar
1 tablespoon groundnut oil	1¼ tablespoons peanut oil
½ teaspoon very finely chopped fresh ginger	½ teaspoon very finely chopped fresh ginger
1 garlic clove, crushed	1 garlic clove, crushed
½ teaspoon salt	½ teaspoon salt
2 pineapple rings, chopped (optional)	2 pineapple rings, chopped (optional)
300 ml./½ pint chicken stock	1¼ cups chicken stock
25 g./1 oz. flaked toasted almonds	¼ cup flaked toasted almonds

Serves 4–6

If using large prawns (shrimp), de-vein them and cut in half. Cut the pepper into matchstick strips and slice the celery diagonally. Soak the mushrooms in warm water for 20 minutes, rinse and squeeze dry, discarding the stalks, and slice. Cut the spring onions (scallions) into 1 cm./½ inch lengths and slice the water chestnuts. Blend the cornflour (cornstarch) with soy sauce, sugar and 2 tablespoons of water.

Heat the oil and add the ginger, garlic and salt. Add the prepared vegetables, pineapple and stock. Bring to the boil and simmer, stirring, for 5 minutes. Add the cornflour (cornstarch) mixture and cook, stirring, for 2–3 minutes. Add the prawns (shrimp) and allow just to heat through.

Serve in a hot serving dish, scattered with flaked toasted almonds.

Stuffed plaice (flounder) with cream

Metric/Imperial	American
½ kg./1 lb. cooked mashed potatoes	2 cups cooked sieved potatoes
salt and pepper	salt and pepper
50 g./2 oz. butter	¼ cup butter
4 large, or 8 small plaice fillets	4 large, or 8 small flounder fillets
75 g./3 oz. mushrooms, sliced	¾ cup sliced mushrooms
4 rashers lean bacon, chopped	4 slices lean bacon, chopped
150 ml./¼ pint double cream	⅔ cup heavy cream

Garnish	Garnish
1 tomato, halved and cooked parsley	1 tomato, halved and cooked parsley

Serves 4

Oven setting: 180–190°C./350–375°F./Gas Mark 4–5

Beat the potatoes with seasoning and half the butter. Put into a cloth bag with a 1 cm./½ inch nozzle and pipe a border round the edge of a shallow oven-proof dish. Skin the fish, or ask the fishmonger to do this. Heat the remaining butter and fry the mushrooms and bacon in this for a few minutes. Spoon into the centre of the fish. Roll up the fillets from the tail to the head, securing with wooden cocktail sticks (toothpicks) and put into the dish. Season the cream. Pour over the fish. Cover the dish lightly with foil, do not press this down and spoil the potato piping. Bake in the centre of the oven for 15 minutes until the fish is tender; do not overcook.

Remove the foil and sticks (picks) from the fillets, and garnish with the tomato and parsley. Serve at once.

FISH

Grilled (broiled) sole

Metric/Imperial	American
4 medium-sized sole fillets	4 large or 8 small sole fillets
little milk	little milk
melted butter	melted butter
Garnish	Garnish
parsley	parsley
lemons	lemons

Serves 4

Soak the fish in a little milk for 30 minutes. Drain, brush with butter and grill (broil) until tender. Garnish with parsley and quartered lemons.

Helpful hints

Traditionally sole are cooked whole with the heads on. To save pan space, fillet the fish before cooking.

Fritto misto di mare

Metric/Imperial	American
fish (see method)	fish (see method)
oil for deep-frying	oil for deep-frying
100 g./4 oz. plain flour	1 cup all-purpose flour
good pinch of salt	good pinch of salt
3 tablespoons olive oil	4 tablespoons olive oil
225 ml./8 fl. oz. tepid water	1 cup tepid water
1 egg white	1 egg white
lemon wedges to garnish	lemon wedges to garnish

Serves 4

Sift the flour and salt into a mixing bowl. Add the oil and tepid water and beat well to a smooth creamy batter. Leave to stand in a cold place for 2 hours. When required for use, beat the egg white stiffly and fold it into the batter.

Choose a variety of fish, including prawns (shrimp). Prepare the fish according to type, cut into small pieces. Heat the oil until it is hot enough to turn a stale bread cube golden in 50 seconds (180°C./350°F. on a deep-fat thermometer). Dip in the batter and carefully lower into the hot oil. Fry for 3–5 minutes or until golden brown and crisp. Drain on absorbent paper and serve with lemon wedges and tartare sauce.

Fish cutlets with sauce

Prawn (shrimp) and turbot salad

Metric/Imperial	American
50 g./2 oz. butter	4 tablespoons butter
4 hake or cod cutlets	4 cod cutlets
1 onion, finely chopped	1 onion, finely chopped
2 tablespoons chopped capers	2½ tablespoons chopped capers
salt and pepper	salt and pepper
150 ml./¼ pint dry white wine	⅔ cup dry white wine
1 tablespoon flour	1¼ tablespoons flour
½ teaspoon made mustard	½ teaspoon made mustard
2 teaspoons chopped parsley	2 teaspoons chopped parsley
2 eggs, beaten	2 eggs, beaten
lemon slices	lemon slices

Serves 4
Oven setting: 180°C./350°F./Gas Mark 4
Heat half the butter in a flameproof serving dish, put in the fish and sprinkle with the onion, half the capers, salt and pepper. Add the wine, cover and cook in the preheated oven for about 20 minutes, or until the fish is tender. Heat the remaining butter in a pan, add the flour, cook for 1 minute. Gradually blend in the liquor remaining in the dish in which the fish was cooked and stir until boiling. Add mustard, parsley, remaining capers and beaten eggs. Reheat without boiling, correct the seasoning and pour the sauce over the fish. Garnish with lemon slices.

Metric/Imperial	American
175 g./6 oz. turbot	6 oz. turbot
salt and pepper	salt and pepper
100 g./4 oz. cooked and shelled prawns	⅔ cup cooked and peeled shrimp
50 ml./2 fl. oz. mayonnaise	¼ cup mayonnaise
1 teaspoon lemon juice	1 teaspoon lemon juice
1 small green pepper, cored, seeded and diced	1 small green pepper, cored, seeded and diced
1 small red pepper, cored, seeded and diced	1 small red pepper, cored, seeded and diced
lettuce or watercress	lettuce or watercress
Garnish	Garnish
black olives	black olives

Serves 4
Poach the fish in well seasoned water until just tender. Do not overcook as the fish continues to soften as it cools. Cut into small cubes and mix with prawns (shrimp).

Mix the mayonnaise with the lemon juice. Add the diced peppers and the fish.

Line 4 individual dishes with lettuce or watercress, (or use scallop shells, as shown in the picture). Spoon the fish mixture on top and garnish with olives.

Helpful hints
To vary, use any other white fish or well drained rollmop herrings in place of the cooked turbot. Omit the prawns (shrimp) and add diced gherkins and/or chopped celery and/or sliced tomatoes.

FISH

West country plaice (flounder)

Metric/Imperial
8 small plaice fillets, skinned
1 small onion, finely chopped
25 g./1 oz. butter
15 g./½ oz. cornflour
300 ml./½ pint dry cider
1 tablespoon French mustard
1 tablespoon finely chopped
  parsley
pinch of brown sugar
salt and freshly ground black
  pepper

American
8 small flounder fillets, skinned
1 small onion, finely chopped
2 tablespoons butter
2 tablespoons cornstarch
1¼ cups dry cider
1¼ tablespoons French
  mustard
1¼ tablespoons finely chopped
  parsley
pinch of brown sugar
salt and freshly ground black
  pepper

Serves 4
Oven setting: 190°C./375°F./Gas Mark 5
Roll up each fillet, arrange in a buttered shallow ovenproof dish and sprinkle over the onion.

Heat the butter in a pan, stir in the cornflour (cornstarch) and cook for 1 minute, stirring constantly. Gradually blend in the cider, mustard, parsley, brown sugar and seasoning to taste. Bring to the boil, stirring constantly, then remove from the heat and pour the sauce over the fish fillets. Bake the fish in the preheated oven for 10–15 minutes, or until tender.

Helpful hints
This sauce freezes well. To serve, unwrap and thaw at room temperature for 3 hours then cover and reheat in a fairly hot oven for 1 hour or until hot through.

Herrings with mushrooms

Metric/Imperial
4 herrings
1 large onion, very finely
  chopped
100 g./4 oz. mushrooms, finely
  chopped
3 tablespoons chopped parsley
1 tablespoon lemon juice
salt and pepper

Garnish
few parsley sprigs
½ lemon, sliced

American
4 herrings
1 large onion, very finely
  chopped
1 cup finely chopped
  mushrooms
4 tablespoons chopped
  parsley
1¼ tablespoons lemon juice
salt and pepper

Garnish
few parsley sprigs
½ lemon, sliced

Serves 4
Oven setting: 180°C./350°F./Gas Mark 4
Clean the herrings and remove the heads. Mix the onion, mushrooms, parsley, lemon juice and seasoning together and use to stuff the herrings. Lay the stuffed herrings in a shallow casserole or deep ovenproof plate. Cover and cook for 30 minutes. Garnish with parsley sprigs and lemon slices.

Salmon fish cakes

Metric/Imperial	American
1 × 350 g./12 oz. can salmon	1 × 12 oz. can salmon
350 g./12 oz. mashed potatoes	3 cups mashed potatoes
capers and anchovy essence	capers and anchovy extract
2 eggs, separated	2 eggs, separated
salt and pepper	salt and pepper
15 g./½ oz. flour	2 tablespoons flour
50 g./2 oz. dry breadcrumbs	⅔ cup dry breadcrumbs
50–75 g./2–3 oz. cooking fat	4–6 tablespoons cooking fat

Serves 4

Flake the salmon and mix with the potatoes; if using instant potato, make it a little stiffer than usual. Blend in 1–2 teaspoons capers and a little anchovy essence (extract). Blend with the yolks of the eggs and seasoning. Form into flat cakes, coat with flour, seasoned with salt and pepper. Brush the cakes with the egg whites and roll in breadcrumbs to ensure they are thoroughly covered. Fry in hot fat.

Helpful hints

If you find fried foods indigestible, bake fish cakes for 15 minutes on a well greased and heated baking tray (cookie sheet), at 200°C./400°F./Gas Mark 6.

Piquant fish casserole

Metric/Imperial	American
100–175 g./4–6 oz. mushrooms, sliced	1–1½ cups sliced mushrooms
25 g./1 oz. margarine or butter	2 tablespoons margarine or butter
1 tablespoon chopped spring onion or chives and/or 1 tablespoon chopped parsley	1¼ tablespoons chopped scallion or chives and/or 1¼ tablespoons chopped parsley
150 ml./¼ pint single cream	⅔ cup light cream
2 teaspoons Angostura bitters	2 teaspoons Angostura bitters
4 portions or 8 small fillets white fish	4 portions or 8 small fillets white fish
15 g./½ oz. butter	1 tablespoon butter
salt and pepper	salt and pepper

Serves 4

Oven setting: 180°C./350°F./Gas Mark 4

Toss the mushrooms in the hot margarine or butter. Add the spring onion (scallion) or chives and/or the parsley, cream and Angostura bitters. Put the fish into a buttered casserole, season and spoon over the mushroom mixture. Cover the dish and bake in the preheated oven for 40 minutes, or until the fish is tender.

Helpful hints

Angostura bitters, made from gentian and flavoured with spices, is a useful aromatic addition to sauces and all kinds of dishes. Use sparingly at first as the flavour can become overpowering.

FISH

Mackerel in cider sauce

Metric/Imperial
butter for frying
½ onion, very finely chopped
1 tablespoon flour
450 ml./¾ pint medium-dry or
 dry cider
salt and freshly ground black
 pepper
4 mackerel, about 175 g./6 oz.
 each, filleted
2 small dessert apples, peeled,
 cored and finely sliced
chopped parsley

American
butter for frying
½ onion, very finely chopped
1¼ tablespoons flour
2 cups medium-dry or dry cider
salt and freshly ground black
 pepper
4 mackerel, about 6 oz. each,
 filleted
2 small dessert apples, peeled,
 cored and finely sliced
chopped parsley

Serves 4

Heat a knob of butter in a large frying pan (skillet). Add the onion and fry gently for 5 minutes or until golden. Stir in the flour and cook for 1 minute, stirring constantly. Gradually blend in the cider. Season to taste and add the mackerel fillets. Cover the pan and simmer gently for 15 minutes, or until the mackerel is quite tender. Transfer the mackerel to a hot serving platter and keep warm.

Add the apples to the pan, increase the heat slightly and simmer for 5 minutes, or until the sauce is reduced to the consistency of double (heavy) cream and the apples are glazed. Adjust seasoning. Pour over the fish and sprinkle with parsley.

Prawns (shrimp) in cream sauce

Metric/Imperial
175 g./6 oz. prawns, cooked
 and shelled
freshly ground black pepper
pinch of grated nutmeg
40 g./1½ oz. butter
1 tablespoon brandy
150 ml./¼ pint double cream
1 teaspoon finely chopped
 parsley
boiled rice and lemon wedges for
 serving

American
6 oz. shrimp, cooked and peeled
freshly ground black pepper
pinch of grated nutmeg
3 tablespoons butter
1¼ tablespoons brandy
⅔ cup heavy cream
1 teaspoon finely chopped
 parsley
boiled rice and lemon wedges for
 serving

Serves 2

Rub the prawns (shrimp) with pepper and nutmeg. Heat the butter in a small frying pan (skillet) and sauté the prawns (shrimp) with brandy (warm brandy first in a large spoon or ladle, ignite and pour flaming into the pan). When the flames have died down, reduce heat to low and cook for a further 2 minutes. Increase the heat and add the cream. Cook until the cream thickens, shake the pan and stir the sauce. Stir in the parsley.

Serve hot on boiled rice, garnished with lemon wedges.

Helpful hints

An impressive recipe to try, ideal for cooking at the table in a chafing dish.

Trout with almonds

Seafood quiches

Metric/Imperial	American
4 trout, cleaned, with the heads on	4 trout, cleaned, with the heads on
flour	flour
salt and freshly ground black pepper	salt and freshly ground black pepper
butter for frying	butter for frying
50 g./2 oz. flaked blanched almonds	½ cup flaked blanched almonds
juice of 1 lemon	juice of 1 lemon
Garnish	Garnish
4 lemon wedges	4 lemon wedges
few parsley sprigs	few parsley sprigs

Serves 4

Coat the fish in flour, seasoned with salt and pepper. Heat a knob of butter in a large frying pan (skillet). Add the almonds and fry gently, stirring, for 2–3 minutes or until golden brown, being careful not to allow the butter to burn. Remove the almonds from the pan with a slotted spoon. Drain on absorbent paper and keep warm.

Wipe the pan clean and add another knob of butter. When it has melted, add the trout and cook gently for 5–8 minutes on each side, or until tender.

Transfer the fish to a hot serving platter, sprinkle with the almonds and lemon juice and serve immediately, garnished with lemon wedges and parsley sprigs.

Helpful hints

Almonds still in their skins keep best. Blanch a few at a time, as needed.

Metric/Imperial	American
Pastry	Pastry
350 g./12 oz. plain flour	3 cups all-purpose flour
pinch of salt	pinch of salt
225 g./8 oz. butter	1 cup butter
1 egg yolk	1 egg yolk
water to mix	water to mix
Filling	Filling
175 g./6 oz. smoked salmon	6 oz. smoked salmon
100 g./4 oz. shelled prawns	4 oz. peeled shrimp
1 tablespoon lemon juice	1¼ tablespoons lemon juice
4 large eggs	4 large eggs
150 ml./¼ pint single cream	⅔ cup light cream
450 ml./¾ pint milk	2 cups milk
salt and pepper	salt and pepper
chopped parsley	chopped parsley

Serves 6

Oven setting: 200°C./400°F./Gas Mark 6

Sift the flour and salt into a mixing bowl. Rub the butter into the flour until the mixture resembles fine breadcrumbs. Bind with the egg yolk and water. Knead the pastry lightly on a floured surface. Divide into six and roll out into circles large enough to line 7.5 cm./3 inch wide flan cases. Prick the base of each pastry case with a fork and flute the edges. Cut the smoked salmon into 2½ cm./1 inch pieces. Mix with the prawns (shrimp) and sprinkle with lemon juice. Beat the eggs, cream and milk together, season. Divide the salmon and prawn (shrimp) mixture between the pastry cases, cover with the egg mixture. Bake in the centre of the preheated oven for 15 minutes. Reduce the oven setting to 160°C./325°F./Gas Mark 3, and cook for about a further 20 minutes. Sprinkle with chopped parsley before serving.

FISH

Paella

Metric/Imperial	American
¼ teaspoon saffron powder or few strands saffron	¼ teaspoon saffron powder or few strands saffron
900 ml./1½ pints chicken stock	3¾ cups chicken stock
3–4 tablespoons olive oil	4–5 tablespoons olive oil
2 onions, chopped	2 onions, chopped
1–2 garlic cloves, crushed	1–2 garlic cloves, crushed
approx. 2 dozen mussels, scrubbed	approx. 2 dozen mussels, scrubbed
salt and pepper	salt and pepper
parsley	parsley
½ kg.–700 g./1–1½ lb. diced raw chicken meat	2⅔–4 cups diced raw chicken meat
175 g./6 oz. long-grain rice	1 cup long-grain rice
225 g./8 oz. shelled prawns	8 oz. peeled shrimp
few cooked peas	few cooked peas

Serves 6

Blend the saffron powder with the stock, or infuse the strands for 30 minutes, then strain. Heat the oil in a large pan and fry the onions and garlic until soft. Meanwhile, put the mussels into another pan with enough water to cover. Add seasoning and a bunch of parsley. Heat for about 10 minutes or until the mussels open (discard any that do not open). Allow to cool enough to handle, remove most of the mussels from *both* shells, but save a few on halved shells. Add the diced chicken and rice to the onions and garlic, toss in the oily mixture and pour in the saffron-flavoured stock. Simmer steadily in an uncovered pan, stirring occasionally, for 25–30 minutes, until the rice is almost tender. Add the prawns (shrimp), peas, mussels and seasoning and complete the cooking.

To vary: Fry 2 skinned, chopped tomatoes with the onions.

Cod bake

Metric/Imperial	American
275 g./10 oz. frozen chopped spinach	10 oz. frozen chopped spinach
salt and freshly ground black pepper	salt and freshly ground black pepper
¼ teaspoon grated nutmeg	¼ teaspoon grated nutmeg
50 g./2 oz. butter	4 tablespoons butter
4 cod steaks	4 cod steaks
Cheese sauce	Cheese sauce
25 g./1 oz. butter	2 tablespoons butter
25 g./1 oz. flour	¼ cup flour
450 ml./¾ pint hot milk	2 cups hot milk
100 g./4 oz. grated Cheddar cheese	1 cup grated Cheddar cheese

Serves 4

Oven setting: 190°C./375°F./Gas Mark 5
Cook frozen spinach according to packet directions. Season with salt, black pepper and the nutmeg and stir in half of the butter. Place in the bottom of a shallow ovenproof dish. Fry the cod steaks in the remaining butter for 2–3 minutes on each side, then place on top of the spinach in the dish.

To prepare the cheese sauce, heat the butter in a pan. Stir in the flour and cook for 1 minute, stirring constantly. Gradually add the milk, stirring vigorously. Bring slowly to the boil, stirring constantly. Lower the heat, add half the grated cheese and cook for 2–3 minutes, stirring constantly.

Cover the fish with the cheese sauce and sprinkle with the remaining grated cheese. Bake in the preheated oven for 20–30 minutes, or until the fish is tender and the top of the casserole is lightly browned and bubbling.

Scallops with peppers

Metric/Imperial	American
½ kg./1 lb. scallops	1 lb. scallops
1 tablespoon oil or melted lard	1¼ tablespoons oil or melted lard
2 spring onions, finely chopped	2 scallions, finely chopped
1 teaspoon salt	1 teaspoon salt
2 green or red peppers, cored, seeded and cut into small strips	2 green or red peppers, cored, seeded and cut into small strips
4 tablespoons water	5 tablespoons water

Serves 4
Trim the scallops and cut into slices. Heat the oil or lard and fry the scallops and spring onions (scallions) for about 3 minutes, stirring constantly. Add the salt and mix well. Add the peppers with the water and bring to the boil, stirring. Then lower the heat and simmer for about 2 minutes.

Helpful hints
Buy the scallops in their shells, save the shells, scrub them and use as individual starter dishes.

Fish and bacon whirls

Metric/Imperial	American
4 portions white fish	4 portions white fish
1 tablespoon flour	1¼ tablespoons flour
salt and pepper	salt and pepper
1 egg	1 egg
50 g./2 oz. dry breadcrumbs	⅔ cup dry breadcrumbs
oil or fat for frying	oil or fat for frying
4 rashers long streaky bacon	4 slices long fatty bacon
4 tomatoes, skinned and halved	4 tomatoes, skinned and halved

Serves 4
Coat the fish in the flour, seasoned with salt and pepper, then dip in the beaten egg and breadcrumbs, ensuring they are thoroughly covered. Fry in hot oil or fat until nearly cooked (approximately 4–5 minutes for plaice (flounder) fillets and 6–7 minutes for thicker pieces of cod or fresh haddock). Remove from the pan on to a plate.

Cut off any rinds from the bacon, cut each rasher (slice) in half lengthways and twist round the portions of fish. Secure with wooden cocktail sticks (picks), if necessary. Return the fish to the pan with seasoned tomatoes and cook for a further 2–3 minutes, turning once, so the bacon becomes crisp.

FISH

Kedgeree

Metric/Imperial	American
175 g./6 oz. long-grain rice	1 cup long-grain rice
salt and pepper	salt and pepper
1 onion, finely chopped	1 onion, finely chopped
100 g./4 oz. butter	½ cup butter
350 g./12 oz. cooked smoked haddock, skinned, boned and flaked	2 cups flaked cooked smoked haddock
4 hard boiled eggs, finely chopped	4 hard cooked eggs, finely chopped
1 tablespoon chopped parsley	1¼ tablespoons chopped parsley
3 tablespoons single cream	4 tablespoons light cream

Serves 4

Boil the rice in salted water until tender. Rinse well and drain.

Fry the onion in the butter until soft. Add the fish to the onion with the rice and eggs and mix well. Stir in the parsley, seasoning and cream.

Helpful hints

If freezing this dish do not add the cream until thawed. Thaw in a hot oven, lightly covered with foil, for about 50 minutes. Stir occasionally with a fork and stir in the cream just before serving.

Sole Véronique

Metric/Imperial	American
4 large sole fillets, skinned	4 large sole fillets, skinned
juice of ½ lemon	juice of ½ lemon
1 small onion, chopped	1 small onion, chopped
1 parsley sprig	1 parsley sprig
6 peppercorns	6 peppercorns
salt and freshly ground black pepper	salt and freshly ground black pepper
75 ml./3 fl. oz. dry white wine	⅜ cup dry white wine
25 g./1 oz. butter	2 tablespoons butter
25 g./1 oz. cornflour	¼ cup cornstarch
300 ml./½ pint milk	1¼ cups milk
175 g./6 oz. green grapes, skinned, halved and pips removed	6 oz. green grapes, skinned, halved and pips removed

Serves 4

Oven setting: 190°C./375°F./Gas Mark 5

Roll up each fillet and place in a buttered 600 ml./1 pint (2½ cup) ovenproof dish. Sprinkle over the lemon juice and add the onion, parsley, peppercorns and seasoning. Pour in the white wine and enough water barely to cover the fish. Cover with foil and bake in the preheated oven for 20 minutes. Lift out the fish and set aside. Tip the fish liquor into a saucepan and boil briskly to reduce it; strain and reserve 50 ml./2 fl. oz. (¼ cup). Return the fish to the washed, re-buttered ovenproof dish and keep it warm.

Heat the butter in a saucepan, add the cornflour (cornstarch) and cook gently for 1 minute, stirring constantly. Gradually blend in the milk and reduced fish liquor and bring to the boil, stirring constantly until the sauce thickens and is smooth. Season with salt and pepper, fold in the grapes and pour the sauce over the fish fillets.

Dressed crab

Normandy herrings

Metric/Imperial	American
1 medium-sized crab	1 medium-sized crab
salt and pepper	salt and pepper
¼ teaspoon mustard powder	¼ teaspoon mustard powder
1 hard boiled egg	1 hard cooked egg
crisp lettuce leaves	crisp lettuce leaves
lemon segments	lemon segments

Serves 1–2

If the crab is alive, put it in a large saucepan. Cover with salted water and bring slowly to the boil. Boil steadily for 10–15 minutes, then turn off the heat and leave to cool in the liquid. When quite cold, remove the crab from the cooking liquid and lay on its back on a board. Twist off the legs and claws and set aside. Pull the body and shell apart with the hands. Discard the stomach sac and any green matter in the outer shell part just below the head. Discard the 'dead men's fingers' — the pale-greyish coloured fronds — from the inner body part. With a teaspoon or skewer, scoop out all the soft dark meat from the shell and put in a bowl. Season well.

Knock away the shell around the dark rim and scrub and dry the shell.

Remove all the white meat from the reserved inner body part of the crab. With nutcrackers or a heavy weight, crack claws and legs. Take out the white meat with pincers or a skewer. Discard any cartilage. Flake the white meat carefully with a fork. Mix soft dark meat with mustard. Place dark meat across centre of the shell, with white meat on either side. Garnish with chopped egg white and sieved egg yolk. Serve crab on lettuce leaves with lemon.

Metric/Imperial	American
4 large herrings	4 large herrings
25 g./1 oz. flour	¼ cup flour
salt and pepper	salt and pepper
2–3 dessert apples, cored	2–3 dessert apples, cored
75 g./3 oz. butter or margarine	6 tablespoons butter or margarine
1 large onion, chopped	1 large onion, chopped
1 tablespoon lemon juice	1 tablespoon lemon juice
parsley	parsley

Serves 4

Clean the herrings and remove the heads, tails and fins. Remove the backbones. Coat the fish in the flour, seasoned with salt and pepper. Slice 1 apple for garnish, as in the picture, and chop the remainder. Heat about 50 g./2 oz. (4 tablespoons) of the butter or margarine in a large pan. Fry the apples and onion in the pan until they are soft. Add the lemon juice. Put the onion and apple mixture into a hot serving dish and keep warm; keep the apple slices separate. Heat the remaining butter or margarine in the pan and cook the fish until tender. Put on top of the mixture in the serving dish and garnish with the apple slices and parsley.

Helpful hints

To vary, use prawns (shrimp) in place of apples and onion. Fry the fish first, keep warm, then fry the prawns (shrimp) in a little extra butter. Add 1–2 tablespoons Calvados and spoon over the fish.

FISH

Halibut with egg and lemon sauce

Metric/Imperial	American
1 onion, sliced	1 onion, sliced
1 carrot, sliced	1 carrot, sliced
1 slice halibut, about ½ kg./1 lb.	1 slice halibut, about 1 lb.
150 ml./¼ pint water	⅔ cup water
salt and pepper	salt and pepper
juice and peeled rind of ¼ lemon	juice and peeled rind of ¼ lemon

Sauce	Sauce
2 teaspoons cornflour	2 teaspoons cornstarch
1 lemon	1 lemon
1 egg, beaten	1 egg, beaten

Garnish	Garnish
½ cucumber, sliced	½ cucumber, sliced
1 lemon, sliced	1 lemon, sliced
parsley sprig	parsley sprig

Serves 4

Put the onion and carrot in a shallow pan and place the fish on top. Add the water, seasoning and lemon juice and rind. Cover the pan, bring to the boil, then cook gently for about 15 minutes. When the fish is opaque, it is cooked. Carefully lift the fish and place it on a heated serving dish. Strain the liquid in the pan for use in the sauce.

To make the sauce, blend the cornflour (cornstarch) with the strained juice of the lemon. Bring the fish liquid to the boil and pour it over the cornflour (cornstarch) mixture. Return the mixture to the pan and cook for 1 minute. Allow the mixture to cool a little, then pour it into a bowl over the beaten egg. Mix and pour the sauce over the fish.

Arrange the cucumber and lemon slices round the fish and garnish with parsley.

Hungarian fish casserole

Metric/Imperial	American
1 kg./2 lb. cod fillets, skinned	2 lb. cod fillets, skinned
25 g./1 oz. butter	2 tablespoons butter
2 tablespoons corn oil	2½ tablespoons corn oil
1 medium-sized onion, sliced	1 medium-sized onion, sliced
1 garlic clove, crushed	1 garlic clove, crushed
15 g./½ oz. cornflour	2 tablespoons cornstarch
1 teaspoon paprika	1 teaspoon paprika
75 ml./3 fl. oz. dry white wine	⅜ cup dry white wine
1 tablespoon tomato purée	1¼ tablespoons tomato paste
3 large tomatoes, skinned, seeded and chopped	3 large tomatoes, skinned, seeded and chopped
salt and freshly ground black pepper	salt and freshly ground black pepper

Serves 4–6

Cut the fish into 5 cm./2 inch squares. Heat the butter and oil in a pan, add the onion and garlic and cook gently until soft. Add the cornflour (cornstarch) and paprika and cook gently, stirring constantly, for 1 minute. Gradually blend in the wine and bring to the boil, stirring constantly. Reduce the heat, stir in the remaining ingredients, cover and simmer for 5 minutes. Taste and adjust the seasoning.

Helpful hints

This freezes well. Thaw at room temperature for 4 hours then reheat, covered, in a fairly hot oven (190°C./375°F./Gas Mark 5) for about 25 minutes, stirring occasionally.

Skate with black butter

Metric/Imperial
1–2 wings skate, about
*   1 kg./2 lb.*
court bouillon
1 tablespoon chopped parsley

American
1–2 wings skate, about 2 lb.
court bouillon
1¼ tablespoons chopped
*   parsley*

Black butter
50 g./2 oz. butter
2 tablespoons wine vinegar
1 tablespoon capers
salt and freshly ground black
*   pepper*

Black butter
4 tablespoons butter
2½ tablespoons wine vinegar
1¼ tablespoons capers
salt and freshly ground black
*   pepper*

Serves 4

Poach the skate in the court bouillon for 15–20 minutes, or until just tender. Remove from the pan, drain and dry well on absorbent paper. Transfer to a hot serving dish and keep warm.

Heat the butter in a pan and cook until a rich brown. Stir in the vinegar and capers and boil to reduce slightly. Adjust seasoning. Pour over the skate on the serving dish and sprinkle with the parsley.

Helpful hints

To make a court bouillon simmer a carrot, an onion, a clove, a bouquet garni, 6 peppercorns and a little salt in 1 l./2 pints (5 cups) water plus 2 tablespoons vinegar for 15–20 minutes. Strain before using.

Tuna fish provençale

Metric/Imperial
2 × 200 g./7 oz. cans tuna
juice of ½ lemon
salt and pepper
4 anchovy fillets
1 tablespoon olive oil
1 onion, chopped
4 tomatoes, skinned, seeded and
*   chopped*
1 garlic clove, crushed
bouquet garni
150 ml./¼ pint white wine
chopped parsley

American
2 × 7 oz. cans tuna
juice of ½ lemon
salt and pepper
4 anchovy fillets
1¼ tablespoons olive oil
1 onion, chopped
4 tomatoes, skinned, seeded and
*   chopped*
1 garlic clove, crushed
bouquet garni
⅔ cup white wine
chopped parsley

Serves 4

Oven setting: 180°C./350°F./Gas Mark 4

Remove the tuna from the cans very carefully so that they stay in shape and place side by side on an ovenproof serving dish. Sprinkle them with lemon juice and season lightly with salt and pepper. Arrange the anchovy fillets on top.

Heat the olive oil in a small pan, add the onion and cook until softened. Add tomatoes, garlic, bouquet garni and wine. Bring to the boil and boil rapidly, uncovered, until reduced and thickened. Pour the sauce over the tuna fish, cover and bake in the oven for 10–15 minutes. Remove the bouquet garni and serve sprinkled with chopped parsley.

FISH

Sole with savoury butter

Curried seafood scallops

Allow one whole sole per person and have them skinned on both sides. Place them in the preheated grill (broiler) pan, heavily brushed with melted butter. Brush the soles with more butter, sprinkle with salt and pepper and grill (broil) for 5–6 minutes. Turn the fish over, brush with more butter and grill (broil) for 5–6 minutes more. Serve immediately with lemon slices and savoury butter pats. Garnish with parsley.

Helpful hints
Serve maître d'hôtel butter (flavoured with lemon and parsley) or anchovy butter (flavoured with crushed anchovy fillets and a little anchovy essence/extract). Unsalted butter is best.

Metric/Imperial	American
40 g./1½ oz. butter	3 tablespoons butter
40 g./1½ oz. flour	6 tablespoons flour
300 ml./½ pint milk	1¼ cups milk
2 teaspoons curry powder	2 teaspoons curry powder
salt and pepper	salt and pepper
3 tablespoons single cream	4 tablespoons light cream
½ kg./1 lb. mixed fish	1 lb. mixed fish

Garnish	Garnish
fine breadcrumbs	fine breadcrumbs
unpeeled prawns	unpeeled shrimp

Make a white sauce with the butter, flour and milk and stir in the curry powder. Add seasoning and the cream. Blend with the mixed fish. Put into scallop shells. Top with fine breadcrumbs and heat under the grill or in the oven. Garnish with prawns (shrimp).

Flaked cooked white fish, shellfish (either prawns (shrimp), scallops, or canned or fresh crab meat) and a little canned tuna would be a good mixture of fish to use.

Tasty tip
To make a more substantial dish, arrange a layer of cooked long-grain rice in a shallow heatproof dish. Top with the curry mixture and finish as above.

The sauce may be flavoured with cheese, anchovy essence (extract) or parsley instead of curry.

Bouillabaisse

Metric/Imperial
1½ kg./3 lb. fish, to include
white fish, oily fish and
shellfish
4 tablespoons olive oil
2 onions, chopped
1 leek, washed and sliced
4 tomatoes, skinned, seeded and
chopped
¼ teaspoon dried fennel
pinch of powdered saffron
1 bay leaf
3 parsley sprigs
salt and pepper
6–8 slices French bread

American
3 lb. fish, to include white fish,
oily fish and shellfish
5 tablespoons olive oil
2 onions, chopped
1 leek, washed and sliced
4 tomatoes, skinned, seeded and
chopped
¼ teaspoon dried fennel
pinch of powdered saffron
1 bay leaf
3 parsley sprigs
salt and pepper
6–8 slices French bread

Serves 6–8
Ask your fishmonger to fillet and skin the fish but keep the skin and bones for stock. Prepare the shellfish. Shell prawns (shrimp) but keep mussels in their shells. Put the skin, bones and shells from the fish and shellfish in a pan with 1½ l./2½ pints (6 cups) water. Bring to the boil and simmer for 20 minutes, then strain off the fish liquor. Reserve 1¼ l./2 pints (5 cups).

Heat the oil in a large pan, add the onions and leek and fry gently until soft. Add the oily fish, cut in chunks, to the pan and cook gently for 10 minutes, then add the remaining fish, in chunks, fish liquor and all other ingredients except the French bread. Simmer for about 10 minutes, until the fish is tender. Check the seasoning, discard the bay leaf and parsley. Put the bread in a tureen and pour over the fish mixture.

Moules marinière

Metric/Imperial
butter for frying
4 shallots or onions, finely
chopped
1 garlic clove, crushed with ½
teaspoon salt
300 ml./½ pint dry white wine
1 bouquet garni
freshly ground black pepper
4 dozen mussels, scrubbed
2 tablespoons chopped parsley

American
butter for frying
4 shallots or onions, finely
chopped
1 garlic clove, crushed with ½
teaspoon salt
1¼ cups dry white wine
1 bouquet garni
freshly ground black pepper
4 dozen mussels, scrubbed
2½ tablespoons chopped
parsley

Serves 4
Heat a knob of butter in a large pan. Add the shallots or onions and garlic and fry gently for 5 minutes or until golden. Stir in the wine, bouquet garni, pepper and mussels, cover the pan and cook the mussels for about 10 minutes, or until the shells open (discard any that do not open). Remove the top shells and place the mussels on individual serving plates. Taste the sauce for seasoning and pour over the mussels. If a thicker sauce is preferred, the cooking juice may be thickened with beurre manié. Cream together 2 tablespoons (2½ tablespoons) butter with 1 tablespoon (1¼ tablespoons) flour and stir into the juices in the pan after taking out the mussels. Bring slowly to the boil then simmer until sauce thickens. Sprinkle with the chopped parsley.

FISH

Fisherman's pie

Flaky fish and sweetcorn parcels

Metric/Imperial
Topping
1 kg./2 lb. potatoes, peeled
25 g./1 oz. butter
2 tablespoons cream or milk

Filling
600 ml./1 pint milk
½ kg./1 lb. haddock fillets
1 onion, sliced into rings
1 bay leaf
50 g./2 oz. butter
50 g./2 oz. flour
salt and freshly ground black
  pepper
100 g./4 oz. shelled shrimps
100 g./4 oz. grated Cheddar
  cheese

American
Topping
2 lb. potatoes, peeled
2 tablespoons butter
2½ tablespoons cream or milk

Filling
2½ cups milk
1 lb. haddock fillets
1 onion, sliced into rings
1 bay leaf
4 tablespoons butter
½ cup flour
salt and freshly ground black
  pepper
4 oz. peeled shrimp
1 cup grated Cheddar cheese

Serves 4
Cven setting: 200°C./400°F./Gas Mark 6
Cook the potatoes in boiling water, mash well while hot
and beat in the butter and cream or milk.

Place the milk in a pan, add the haddock, onion and bay
leaf, and poach for 15 minutes. Strain off and reserve the
liquor, discarding the flavourings. Flake the haddock,
removing the skin and bones.

Heat the butter in a pan and stir in the flour. Cook gently
for 1 minute, stirring constantly. Gradually blend in the
fish liquor and bring to the boil, stirring constantly until
the sauce thickens and is smooth. Remove from the heat
and stir in the flaked fish, seasoning to taste, shrimps and
cheese. Turn into a 1¼ l./2 pint (1½ quart) buttered pie
dish. Place the creamed potato in a piping bag fitted with a
large star nozzle (pastry bag fitted with a fluted nozzle)
and pipe over the entire surface of the fish. Put the dish in
the preheated oven and bake for 30 minutes, or until the
topping is browned and crisp.

Metric/Imperial
1 × 225 g./8 oz. packet frozen
  puff pastry, thawed
225 g./8 oz. smoked haddock,
  cooked, skin and bones
  removed and flaked
100 g./4 oz. sweetcorn
25 g./1 oz. butter, melted
1 teaspoon curry powder
salt and freshly ground black
  pepper
1 tablespoon double cream
2 tomatoes, skinned, seeded and
  sliced
1 egg, beaten

American
1 × 8 oz. packet frozen puff
  pastry, thawed
1⅓ cups flaked cooked smoked
  haddock
⅔ cup sweetcorn
2 tablespoons butter, melted
1 teaspoon curry powder
salt and freshly ground black
  pepper
1¼ tablespoons heavy cream
2 tomatoes, skinned, seeded and
  sliced
1 egg, beaten

Each parcel will serve 1
Oven setting: 230°C./450°F./Gas Mark 8
Roll out the pastry on a floured surface, then cut into large
squares.

Mix together the smoked haddock, sweetcorn, butter
and curry powder. Season to taste and stir in the cream.
Place equal amounts of the fish mixture on the centre of
each square and cover with the tomato slices. Brush the
edges with beaten egg and fold the squares across to form
triangles. Seal securely and glaze with remaining egg.
Bake in the preheated oven for 20 minutes; when puffed
reduce the oven setting to 200°C./400°F./Gas Mark 6 for a
further 10–15 minutes, or until the pastry is golden brown.

Salmon Walewska

Metric/Imperial	American
8 salmon cutlets	8 salmon steaks
225 g./8 oz. butter	1 cup butter
3 tablespoons lemon juice	4 tablespoons lemon juice
salt and pepper	salt and pepper
6 egg yolks	6 egg yolks
2 small or 1 large lobster, cut into small pieces	2 small or 1 large lobster, cut into small pieces
Garnish	Garnish
lemon	lemon
cucumber	cucumber
lobster claws	lobster claws

Serves 8
Oven setting: 180–190°C./350–375°F./Gas Mark 4–5
Brush the salmon with 50 g./2 oz. (¼ cup) melted butter, sprinkle with ½ tablespoon lemon juice and season lightly. Put into an ovenproof dish, cover with foil, and bake for 20–25 minutes in the centre of the preheated oven until just tender — do *not* over-cook.

Put the egg yolks, a little seasoning and remaining lemon juice into a bowl over a pan of hot, but not boiling, water and beat until thick. Gradually beat in the remaining butter, then add the lobster pieces. Keep warm but do not over-heat otherwise the sauce will curdle. Lift the salmon on to a serving platter, top with the sauce and garnish with the lemon, cucumber and the lobster claws.

Herrings in oatmeal

Metric/Imperial	American
4 herrings	4 herrings
100 g./4 oz. oatmeal	1 cup oatmeal
salt and freshly ground black pepper	salt and freshly ground black pepper
fat or oil for frying	fat or oil for frying

Serves 4
Clean the herrings and remove the heads, tails and fins. Slit the fish along the under side and remove the roe and blood vessels. Open out each fish, place cut side down on a board and press firmly down on the backbone to flatten the fish. Turn the fish over and remove the backbone. Rinse and dry with absorbent paper.

Mix the oatmeal, salt and pepper together and coat the fish in it. Fry in hot shallow fat until cooked through. Drain on absorbent paper before serving piping hot.

Helpful hints
Freeze the coated fish individually. To serve, fry from frozen for about 6 minutes on each side.

FISH

Seafood casserole

Metric/Imperial	American
½ kg./1 lb. cod, halibut or any firm white fish fillets, skinned	1 lb. cod, halibut or any firm white fish fillets, skinned
150 ml./¼ pint dry white wine	⅔ cup dry white wine
1 small onion, chopped	1 small onion, chopped
2 bay leaves	2 bay leaves
1 parsley sprig	1 parsley sprig
2 teaspoons cornflour	2 teaspoons cornstarch
1 × 400 g./14 oz. can lobster bisque	1 × 14 oz. can lobster bisque
juice of ½ lemon	juice of ½ lemon
salt and freshly ground black pepper	salt and freshly ground black pepper
225 g./8 oz. shelled prawns	8 oz. peeled shrimp
100 g./4 oz. crabmeat, frozen or canned	4 oz. crabmeat, frozen or canned
100 g./4 oz. jar of mussels (optional)	4 oz. jar of mussels (optional)
3 tablespoons fresh white breadcrumbs	4 tablespoons fresh white breadcrumbs
15 g./½ oz. butter	1 tablespoon butter

Serves 6

Oven setting: 220°C./425°F./Gas Mark 7

Cut the white fish into large chunks and place in a pan. Add the wine, onion, bay leaves and parsley, bring to the boil, then simmer gently for 5 minutes. Lift out the fish and reserve it. Strain the fish liquor, blend the cornflour (cornstarch) into it and return to the pan. Add the lobster bisque and bring to the boil, stirring constantly, then cook gently for 2 minutes. Add the lemon juice and season to taste.

Place the prawns (shrimp), crabmeat, mussels and reserved white fish in an ovenproof dish and pour over the sauce. Sprinkle the top with breadcrumbs and dot with butter. Put into the preheated oven for 20 minutes, or until the topping is brown.

Prawn (shrimp) cutlets

Metric/Imperial	American
8 large prawns	8 large shrimp
1 tablespoon sherry	1¼ tablespoons sherry
1 egg	1 egg
2 tablespoons cornflour	2½ tablespoons cornstarch
fat for deep-frying	fat for deep-frying

Serves 2

Hold the prawns (shrimp) firmly by the tail and remove the rest of the shell, leaving the tail piece intact. Split the prawns (shrimp) in half lengthways almost to the tail and remove the intestinal cord. Flatten the prawns (shrimp) to look like cutlets. Sprinkle with sherry.

Beat the egg and dip the cutlets in it, then in the cornflour (cornstarch). Do this twice. Fry the cutlets in deep fat for 2–3 minutes. Drain and serve plain or with a sweet and sour sauce.

Chablis halibut

Metric/Imperial
approx. 175 ml./6 fl. oz.
  Chablis or other dry white
  wine
4 halibut steaks (cutlets) or
  other white fish
salt and pepper
50 g./2 oz. butter

Garnish
canned sweetcorn, heated
red pepper, cored, seeded and
  sliced
parsley

American
approx. ¾ cup Chablis or other
  dry white wine
4 halibut steaks (cutlets) or
  other white fish
salt and pepper
4 tablespoons butter

Garnish
canned sweetcorn, heated
red pepper, cored, seeded and
  sliced
parsley

Serves 4
Put the wine in a shallow dish and leave the fish to soak in this marinade for 1 hour, turning once. Drain and discard the marinade, season the fish lightly. Melt the butter, brush the fish with this and cook under the preheated grill (broiler) for about 10 minutes, turning once.

Serve with the hot sweetcorn and top with red pepper and parsley. Heat any wine left in the dish and spoon over the fish before serving.

Helpful hints
If you have no wine opened, a glass of dry Vermouth gives an excellent flavour to white fish.

Scallops Breton-style

Metric/Imperial
½ kg./1 lb. scallops
100 g./4 oz. butter, melted
75 g./3 oz. fine browned
  breadcrumbs
½ garlic clove, well crushed
1 teaspoon finely chopped
  parsley
salt and freshly ground black
  pepper

Garnish
lemon slices
parsley sprigs

American
1 lb. scallops
½ cup butter, melted
¾ cup fine browned
  breadcrumbs
½ garlic clove, well crushed
1 teaspoon finely chopped
  parsley
salt and freshly ground black
  pepper

Garnish
lemon slices
parsley sprigs

Serves 4
Oven setting: 160°C./325°F./Gas Mark 3
Trim and wash the scallops. Drain them and cut them into thick pieces. Grease four scallop shells or small ovenproof dishes with a little of the melted butter. Sprinkle with half the breadcrumbs. Divide the sliced scallops equally between the four shells.

Mix the remaining breadcrumbs with the garlic and parsley, and season. Cover the scallops with the breadcrumb mixture and pour over the remaining melted butter. Bake, uncovered, for 15–20 minutes. Serve in the shells or dishes in which they are cooked. Garnish with lemon slices and parsley sprigs.

If the scallops are large, they may be cooked on skewers as shown in the picture.

FISH

Sole normande

Metric/Imperial	American
1 dozen mussels, scrubbed	1 dozen mussels, scrubbed
150 ml./¼ pint water	⅔ cup water
1 bouquet garni	1 bouquet garni
salt and pepper	salt and pepper
175 g./6 oz. prawns	6 oz. shrimp
few oysters	few oysters
1 onion or shallot, chopped	1 onion or shallot, chopped
150 ml./¼ pint white wine	⅔ cup white wine
8 sole fillets	8 sole fillets
75 g./3 oz. butter	6 tablespoons butter
50 g./2 oz. flour	½ cup flour
150 ml./¼ pint milk	⅔ cup milk
150 ml./¼ pint double cream	⅔ cup heavy cream
100 g./4 oz. button mushrooms, sliced	1 cup sliced button mushrooms

Serves 4–6

Put the mussels into a pan with the water, bouquet garni and seasoning. Heat until the mussels open (discard any that do not open). Lift the mussels out of the liquid. Shell the prawns (shrimp) and open the oysters. Add the prawn (shrimp) shells, the liquid from the oyster shells, the onion or shallot and wine to the mussel liquid. Simmer for 15 minutes. Strain carefully and return to the pan. Put the sole fillets into this; either fold or keep whole if the pan is sufficiently large. Simmer for 10–15 minutes until *just* tender. Lift the sole out of the liquid. Arrange on a flat dish or in individual dishes and keep warm.

Meanwhile heat 50 g./2 oz. (4 tablespoons) of the butter in a pan. Stir in the flour and cook for 1 minute, stirring constantly. Gradually blend in the milk, cream and reserved fish liquid and cook, stirring constantly until the sauce is thick and smooth. Fry the mushrooms in the remaining butter. Add with the shellfish to the sauce, warm for 1–2 minutes only (so the shellfish does not toughen). Spoon over the fish.

Cod mornay

Metric/Imperial	American
1 tablespoon instant potato	1¼ tablespoons instant potato
700 g./1½ lb. cod fillets, skinned	1½ lb. cod fillets, skinned
25 g./1 oz. butter	2 tablespoons butter
25 g./1 oz. cornflour	¼ cup cornstarch
300 ml./½ pint creamy milk	1¼ cups milk
50 g./2 oz. grated Cheddar cheese	½ cup grated Cheddar cheese
1 teaspoon made English mustard	1 teaspoon made English mustard
dash of Worcestershire sauce	dash of Worcestershire sauce
salt and freshly ground black pepper	salt and freshly ground black pepper
1 tablespoon grated Parmesan cheese	1¼ tablespoons grated Parmesan cheese
1 tablespoon dry white breadcrumbs	1¼ tablespoons dry white breadcrumbs
15 g./½ oz. butter, cut into pieces	1 tablespoon butter, cut into pieces

Serves 4

Oven setting: 180°C./350°F./Gas Mark 4

Lightly butter an ovenproof dish and sprinkle the base with the instant potato. Cut the cod into serving pieces and place in the ovenproof dish.

Heat the butter in a saucepan, stir in the cornflour (cornstarch) and cook, stirring constantly, for 1 minute. Gradually blend in the milk and bring to the boil, stirring constantly, until the mixture is smooth and thick. Remove from the heat and add the Cheddar cheese, mustard, Worcestershire sauce and seasoning to taste. Pour the sauce over the fish, sprinkle with the Parmesan cheese and breadcrumbs and dot with the butter. Cook in the preheated oven for 20 minutes, or until the fish is tender.

Rolled fillets of fish

Metric/Imperial
4 large fillets of white fish,
  skinned
2 tablespoons flour
salt and pepper
oil for deep-frying

Batter
100 g./4 oz. plain flour
pinch of salt
1 egg
approx. 12 tablespoons milk or
  milk and water

American
4 large fillets of white fish,
  skinned
2½ tablespoons flour
salt and pepper
oil for deep-frying

Batter
1 cup all-purpose flour
pinch of salt
1 egg
approx. 1 cup milk or milk and
  water

Serves 4
Roll up the fillets and secure with wooden cocktail sticks (picks). Coat in the flour, seasoned with salt and pepper, and set aside.

To make the batter, sift the flour and salt into a mixing bowl. Add the egg and milk or milk and water and beat well to a smooth batter.

Heat the oil until it is hot enough to turn a stale bread cube golden in 50 seconds (180°C./350°F. on a deep-fat thermometer). Dip the frying basket into the hot oil to heat it. Dip each piece of fish in the batter then arrange in the warmed basket. Fry for 5–6 minutes, until the batter is golden brown and crisp. Lift the basket from the oil and drain the fish on absorbent paper. Serve very hot, with tartare sauce.

Sautéed crab with almonds

Metric/Imperial
65 g./2½ oz. butter
½ kg./1 lb. fresh crabmeat
75 g./3 oz. almonds, halved
freshly ground black pepper
sea salt
150 ml./¼ pint soured cream
2 tablespoons chopped parsley

American
5 tablespoons butter
1 lb. fresh crabmeat
¾ cup almonds, halved
freshly ground black pepper
sea salt
⅔ cup sour cream
2½ tablespoons chopped
  parsley

Serves 4
Heat 40 g./1½ oz. (3 tablespoons) butter in a pan, add the crabmeat and toss lightly until delicately browned.

In a separate pan, heat remaining butter and sauté almonds until golden brown. Add pepper, salt and crabmeat. Add the cream and parsley and bring to the boil. Reduce heat and simmer for 2 minutes.
Serve hot with boiled brown rice.

SALADS

Mushrooms vinaigrette

Metric/Imperial
100 g./4 oz. mushrooms
3 tablespoons olive oil
1 tablespoon lemon juice
1 garlic clove, crushed
salt and freshly ground black
   pepper
1 teaspoon finely chopped
   parsley

American
1 cup mushrooms
4 tablespoons olive oil
1¼ tablespoons lemon juice
1 garlic clove, crushed
salt and freshly ground black
   pepper
1 teaspoon finely chopped
   parsley

Serves 2
Wipe the mushrooms with a clean, damp cloth and slice
thinly; do not remove the stalks.

   Combine the oil, lemon juice, garlic, salt, pepper and
parsley. Pour over the mushrooms and toss well. Chill,
covered, for several hours before serving. Raw
mushrooms are extremely absorbent so you may have to
add more dressing before serving. Serve chilled.

Helpful hints
Do not wash the mushrooms. Water will tend to soften
them and dilute the vinaigrette dressing.

Citrus green salad

Metric/Imperial
1 lettuce
1 bunch of watercress
2 grapefruit, peel, pith and pips
   removed and cut into
   segments
2 oranges, peel, pith and pips
   removed and cut into
   segments
100 ml./4 fl. oz. French
   dressing

American
1 lettuce
1 bunch of watercress
2 grapefruit, peel, pith and pips
   removed and cut into
   segments
2 oranges, peel, pith and pips
   removed and cut into
   segments
½ cup French dressing

Serves 6–8
Prepare the lettuce and watercress and crisp in the
refrigerator. Put the grapefruit and orange segments into a
chilled salad bowl. Add the lettuce, torn into bite-sized
pieces, and the watercress sprigs. Pour over the dressing
and toss well until each leaf is coated.

Helpful hints
Serve with a rich meat such as duck, pork, goose or game.

Potato salad

Metric/Imperial
700 g./1½ lb. new potatoes or
1 × 525 g./1 lb. 3 oz. can
new potatoes, drained
salt
1 bunch of spring onions, finely
chopped
150 ml./¼ pint thick
home-made mayonnaise
1 tablespoon lemon juice
freshly ground black pepper
2 tablespoons chopped fresh
mint or parsley to finish

American
1½ lb. new potatoes or 1 ×
1¼ lb. can new potatoes,
drained
salt
1 bunch of scallions, finely
chopped
⅔ cup thick home-made
mayonnaise
1¼ tablespoons lemon juice
freshly ground black pepper
2½ tablespoons chopped fresh
mint or parsley to finish

Serves 4
Boil the potatoes in their skins in salted water for 15
minutes or until just tender. Remove from the water and
allow to cool slightly. Peel off the skin. Cut the cooked or
canned potatoes into chunks and place in a mixing bowl
with the spring onions (scallions). Pour in the mayonnaise
and lemon juice and add black pepper to taste. Coat the
potato slices carefully in the mayonnaise, transfer to a
serving bowl and sprinkle with more black pepper and the
chopped mint or parsley.

Salami and potato salad

Metric/Imperial
½ kg./1 lb. cooked new
potatoes, diced
few cooked green beans
few radishes, sliced
5 cm./2 inch piece cucumber,
sliced
2–3 sticks celery, chopped
3–4 spring onions, chopped
little mayonnaise
lettuce
350 g.–½ kg./12 oz.–1 lb.
sliced salami or other sausage

American
4 cups diced cooked new
potatoes
few cooked green beans
few radishes, sliced
2 inch piece cucumber, sliced
2–3 sticks celery, chopped
3–4 scallions, chopped
little mayonnaise
lettuce
12 oz.–1 lb. sliced salami or
other sausage

Serves 4–6
Mix the potatoes with the beans, radishes, cucumber,
celery, spring onions (scallions) and mayonnaise to bind.
Pile in the centre of a bed of lettuce. Arrange the sliced
salami or other sausage round the edge of the dish.
   To vary: If preferred, the lettuce can be served
separately.

Helpful hints
Canned potatoes are excellent for this salad.

SALADS

Russian salad

Metric/Imperial
½ kg./1 lb. mixed root
   vegetables, prepared and
   diced
salt and pepper
150 ml./¼ pint mayonnaise
1–2 tablespoons chopped
   parsley

American
2⅔ cups diced mixed root
   vegetables
salt and pepper
⅔ cup mayonnaise
1¼–2½ tablespoons chopped
   parsley

Serves 4–6
Boil the vegetables in salted water until just tender; do not
over-cook as the vegetables soften slightly as they cool.
Drain well, blend with the mayonnaise and half the
parsley. Allow to cool and top with more parsley.

Helpful hints
Add diced cooked tongue or ham and chopped
hard boiled (hard cooked) eggs for a substantial first
course.

Coleslaw

Metric/Imperial
½ large white cabbage, about
   225 g./8 oz., finely shredded
2 large carrots, peeled and
   shredded
1 medium-sized onion, chopped
1 green pepper, cored, seeded
   and sliced (optional)
1 red apple, peeled, cored and
   chopped
150 ml./¼ pint thick
   home-made mayonnaise
juice of ½ lemon
salt and freshly ground black
   pepper

American
½ large white cabbage, about
   8 oz., finely shredded
2 large carrots, peeled and
   shredded
1 medium-sized onion, chopped
1 green pepper, cored, seeded
   and sliced (optional)
1 red apple, peeled, cored and
   chopped
⅔ cup thick home-made
   mayonnaise
juice of ½ lemon
salt and freshly ground black
   pepper

Serves 4–6
Put all the vegetables and apple in a large mixing bowl.
Bind with mayonnaise and stir in the lemon juice and
plenty of salt and pepper until all the vegetables are evenly
coated. Transfer to a serving dish. Cover and chill in the
refrigerator until required.

Helpful hints
When serving carrots in a salad, either use very young
ones or grate only the outer, red part, which has the most
flavour. Keep the yellow core for flavouring stock.

Scampi, apple and cheese salad

Metric/Imperial
225 g./8 oz. ricotta or cottage
  cheese
75 g./3 oz. chopped toasted
  nuts
escarole, Batavian endive or
  lettuce
1 dessert apple, cored, sliced
  and brushed with lemon
  juice
12–16 fresh or frozen scampi or
  prawns

Dressing
3 tablespoons oil
1 tablespoon lemon juice
salt and black pepper
½ avocado, peeled, stoned and
  mashed
1 tablespoon cream

American
1 cup ricotta or cottage cheese
⅔ cup chopped toasted nuts
escarole, chicory or lettuce
1 dessert apple, cored, sliced
  and brushed with lemon
  juice
12–16 fresh or frozen scampi or
  shrimp

Dressing
4 tablespoons oil
1¼ tablespoons lemon juice
salt and black pepper
½ avocado, peeled, pitted and
  mashed
1¼ tablespoons cream

Serves 4
Roll the cheese into balls about the size of a walnut, (if
cottage cheese is used, it should be sieved [strained]) then
roll in the chopped nuts. Chill while assembling the other
ingredients.

Put some shredded escarole or other salad plant into
four glasses or individual salad dishes and arrange the
cheese balls, apple slices and scampi on top.

Combine the oil and lemon juice for the dressing, add a
little salt and black pepper, the mashed avocado and
cream. Blend all the ingredients well and pour a little over
each salad just before serving.

Cucumber raita

Metric/Imperial
1 large cucumber, peeled,
  halved, seeded and sliced into
  small strips
½ teaspoon salt
1 teaspoon sugar
300 ml./½ pint natural yogurt
2 tablespoons chopped fresh
  mint
freshly ground black pepper
1 tablespoon olive oil

American
1 large cucumber, peeled,
  halved, seeded and sliced into
  small strips
½ teaspoon salt
1 teaspoon sugar
1¼ cups plain yogurt
2½ tablespoons chopped fresh
  mint
freshly ground black pepper
1¼ tablespoons olive oil

Serves 4
Put the cucumber strips in a bowl and sprinkle with the
salt and sugar. Stir to mix and leave to drain in a colander
for 30 minutes.

Mix the cucumber and yogurt together with half the
mint and plenty of pepper, then pile into a serving dish.
Pour the oil evenly over the surface of the raita, then
decorate with the remaining mint. Chill in the refrigerator
until required.

SALADS

Blue cheese and pear salad

Metric/Imperial
175–225 g./6–8 oz. blue cheese
little mayonnaise
8 canned pear halves
1 lettuce heart

Garnish
few grapes, seeded

American
6–8 oz. blue cheese
little mayonnaise
8 canned pear halves
1 lettuce heart

Garnish
few grapes, seeded

Serves 4
Crumble the cheese and blend with enough mayonnaise
to make a creamy consistency. Arrange the pear halves on
a bed of lettuce. Top with the cheese mixture and garnish
with the grapes.

Helpful hints
If you prefer to use fresh pears, sprinkle them with lemon
juice or French dressing to prevent them discolouring.

Tomato salad

Metric/Imperial
350 g./12 oz. tomatoes,
  skinned, seeded and sliced
1 tablespoon grated onion

Dressing
8 tablespoons olive oil
3 tablespoons lemon juice
1 garlic clove, halved
1 teaspoon chopped fresh basil
1 teaspoon caster sugar
1/2 teaspoon salt
freshly ground black pepper

American
12 oz. tomatoes, skinned,
  seeded and sliced
1 1/4 tablespoons grated onion

Dressing
2/3 cup olive oil
4 tablespoons lemon juice
1 garlic clove, halved
1 teaspoon chopped fresh basil
1 teaspoon superfine sugar
1/2 teaspoon salt
freshly ground black pepper

Serves 4
Arrange the tomatoes in a shallow serving dish and
sprinkle with the grated onion.

   To prepare the dressing, put all the ingredients, with
pepper to taste, in a screw-top jar. Shake vigorously until
thoroughly mixed. Leave for at least 30 minutes to allow
the garlic and basil to flavour the dressing. Remove the
garlic before using.

   Pour the dressing over the tomatoes. Chill in the
refrigerator until required, spooning over the dressing
from time to time.

Vegetables aïoli

Metric/Imperial	American
2–3 garlic cloves, crushed	2–3 garlic cloves, crushed
3 egg yolks	3 egg yolks
175 ml./6 fl. oz. vegetable or nut oil	¾ cup vegetable or nut oil
½ teaspoon salt	½ teaspoon salt
½ teaspoon pepper	½ teaspoon pepper
2 tablespoons lemon juice	2½ tablespoons lemon juice
½ small white cabbage, finely shredded	½ small white cabbage, finely shredded
100 g./4 oz. salami, cut into pieces	4 oz. salami, cut into pieces
50 g./2 oz. black olives	½ cup black olives
4 hard boiled eggs, quartered	4 hard cooked eggs, quartered

Serves 4

Blend the garlic and egg yolks in a bowl. Gradually beat in the oil as for mayonnaise. Stir in the seasoning and lemon juice.

Arrange the cabbage on a serving dish. Top with the salami, olives and egg quarters. Pour over the aïoli sauce just before serving.

Helpful hints

Both eggs and oil should be at room temperature for this dressing, to prevent it curdling. Add the oil drop by drop, whisking all the time.

Tomato and scampi salad

Metric/Imperial	American
4 large firm tomatoes	4 large firm tomatoes
3–4 tablespoons cooked rice	4–5 tablespoons cooked rice
2 tablespoons chopped capers	2½ tablespoons chopped capers
2–3 gherkins, chopped	2–3 gherkins, chopped
1 tablespoon chopped parsley	1¼ tablespoons chopped parsley
½ small red or green pepper, cored, seeded and chopped	½ small red or green pepper, cored, seeded and chopped
scampi, fresh, canned or frozen	scampi, fresh, canned or frozen
mayonnaise	mayonnaise
salt and pepper	salt and pepper
4 large black olives	4 large black olives
lettuce	lettuce

Serves 4

Cut a slice from the tops of the tomatoes and carefully remove the pulp. Discard the seeds and put the flesh into a bowl. Add the rice, capers, gherkins, parsley, pepper and scampi, reserving a few for garnish. Bind all the ingredients together with mayonnaise and correct the seasoning.

Fill the tomato cases, cover with a little more mayonnaise and garnish with a black olive and the remaining scampi. Serve on a bed of lettuce.

SALADS

American salad

Metric/Imperial
225 g./8 oz. cooked French
  beans
1 × 400 g./14 oz. can
  sweetcorn, drained
3 tablespoons finely diced red
  pimiento
100 g./4 oz. mushrooms, sliced
3 firm tomatoes, sliced
12 black olives
4 tablespoons French dressing
1 onion, sliced and pushed into
  rings

American
8 oz. cooked green beans
1 × 14 oz. can sweetcorn,
  drained
4 tablespoons finely diced red
  pimiento
1 cup sliced mushrooms
3 firm tomatoes, sliced
12 black olives
5 tablespoons French dressing
1 onion, sliced and pushed into
  rings

Serves 4
Mix the beans, sweetcorn, pimiento, mushrooms,
tomatoes and the olives together in a large bowl. Pour over
the French dressing and toss the salad well. Arrange the
salad in a large serving dish and top with onion rings.

Salad niçoise

Metric/Imperial
1 × 225 g./8 oz. can tuna
1 × 50 g./2 oz. can anchovy
  fillets
lettuce
3 tomatoes
2 hard boiled eggs
225 g./8 oz cooked new
  potatoes, sliced (optional)
225 g./8 oz. cooked beans
  (optional)
mayonnaise or oil and vinegar
salt and pepper
few black and green olives
  (optional)

American
1 × 8 oz. can tuna
1 × 2 oz. can anchovy fillets
lettuce
3 tomatoes
2 hard cooked eggs
2 cups sliced cooked new
  potatoes (optional)
1⅓ cups cooked beans
  (optional)
mayonnaise or oil and vinegar
salt and pepper
few black and green olives
  (optional)

Serves 4
Dice the tuna and separate the anchovy fillets. Make a
salad of lettuce, tomatoes and hard boiled (hard cooked)
eggs. Add cooked new potatoes and cooked beans when
available. Add the tuna and the anchovy fillets. Pour over
either mayonnaise or well seasoned oil and vinegar and
toss well. Garnish with black and green olives.

Helpful hints
This salad makes an excellent starter or a light lunch dish.
For a less strong flavour, soak the anchovy fillets in milk
for 30 minutes, drain and then use as in the recipe.

Savoury cheese log

Metric/Imperial
½ kg.–550 g./1–1¼ lb. grated
  Cheddar cheese
2–3 tablespoons each of diced
  cucumber, sliced stuffed
  olives, sliced radishes and
  chopped walnuts
mayonnaise

Garnish
olives
halved walnuts
radishes

American
4–5 cups grated Cheddar cheese
2½–4 tablespoons each of diced
  cucumber, sliced stuffed
  olives, sliced radishes and
  chopped walnuts
mayonnaise

Garnish
olives
halved walnuts
radishes

Serves 4–6
Blend the cheese, cucumber, olives, radishes and walnuts together. Bind with enough mayonnaise to make the consistency of very thick beaten cream. Form into a long roll. Garnish with olives, halved walnuts and radishes, chill well.

Serve on a bed of green salad with halved tomatoes, cooked peas (topped with chopped spring onions [scallions]) and sliced cucumber. Serve extra mayonnaise or oil and vinegar dressing separately.

To vary: Other hard cheeses, such as Gruyère, Edam and Jarlsberg can be used instead of Cheddar.

Chicory (endive) coleslaw

Metric/Imperial
1 small cabbage
1 carrot, peeled and grated
3–4 heads of chicory, chopped
4 tablespoons natural yogurt
1–2 teaspoons made mustard
squeeze of lemon juice
chopped parsley

American
1 small cabbage
1 carrot, peeled and grated
3–4 heads of endive, chopped
5 tablespoons plain yogurt
1–2 teaspoons made mustard
squeeze of lemon juice
chopped parsley

Serves 4
Shred the heart of the cabbage finely, mix with the carrot and the chopped chicory (endive) base. Blend the yogurt with the mustard and lemon juice. Pour over the vegetables and toss well. Put into a shallow dish, top with parsley and arrange the chicory (endive) tips round the dish.

Helpful hints
Add a few raisins and nuts to this recipe for extra interest.

SALADS

Seafood salad

Metric/Imperial
75 g./3 oz. long-grain rice
½ teaspoon salt
6 tablespoons mayonnaise
50 g./2 oz. cooked peas
50 g./2 oz. cooked sweetcorn
1 × 200 g./7 oz. can tuna or salmon
75 g./3 oz. prawns or canned or cooked crabmeat
5 cm./2 in. piece cucumber, diced

American
½ cup long-grain rice
½ teaspoon salt
7½ tablespoons mayonnaise
⅓ cup cooked peas
⅓ cup cooked sweetcorn
1 × 7 oz. can tuna or salmon
½ cup shrimp or canned or cooked crabmeat
2 in. piece cucumber, diced

Serves 4
Boil the rice in salted water until just tender. Drain, toss in the mayonnaise while the rice is still hot. Cool. Blend with the peas, sweetcorn, flaked tuna or salmon, chopped prawns (shrimp) or flaked crabmeat and cucumber.

Helpful hints
A first class starter salad. Sprinkle with lemon juice to sharpen the flavour.

Anchovy and egg salad

Metric/Imperial
1 large crisp lettuce
4 hard boiled eggs
4 tomatoes
1 × 50 g./2 oz. can anchovy fillets
few black olives
few capers
French dressing

American
1 large crisp lettuce
4 hard cooked eggs
4 tomatoes
1 × 2 oz. can anchovy fillets
few black olives
few capers
French dressing

Serves 4
Cut the lettuce into wedges, wash and drain well. Quarter the eggs and tomatoes and arrange on a plate with the lettuce sections. Arrange anchovy fillets on top and scatter with a few olives and capers. Pour over dressing to taste just before serving.

Helpful hints
As an alternative to French dressing, use mayonnaise; spoon the mayonnaise over before garnishing with anchovies, olives and capers.

Stuffed aubergines (eggplants)

Metric/Imperial
3 large even-sized aubergines,
  halved lengthways
salt
25 g./1 oz. fresh breadcrumbs
2 tablespoons chopped parsley
1 teaspoon chopped fresh
  oregano
6 anchovy fillets, finely
  chopped
12 large black olives, stoned and
  chopped
3 tomatoes, skinned, seeded and
  chopped
3–4 tablespoons olive oil

American
3 large even-sized eggplants,
  halved lengthways
salt
½ cup fresh breadcrumbs
2½ tablespoons chopped
  parsley
1 teaspoon chopped fresh
  oregano
6 anchovy fillets, finely
  chopped
12 large black olives, pitted and
  chopped
3 tomatoes, skinned, seeded and
  chopped
4–5 tablespoons olive oil

Serves 4
Oven setting: 180°C./350°F./Gas Mark 4
Sprinkle the aubergines (eggplants) with salt and leave for
30 minutes. Drain and dry.

Scoop out some of the aubergine (eggplant) flesh and
put it into a bowl. Mash well with a wooden spoon, then
add the breadcrumbs, parsley, oregano, anchovy fillets,
olives and tomatoes. Mix well.

Fill the aubergine (eggplant) halves with the mixture,
arrange in an ovenproof dish and pour over the oil. Cover
and cook in the preheated oven for about ¾–1 hour, or
until the aubergines (eggplants) are tender.

Cheese, potato and onion hotpot

Metric/Imperial
½ kg./1 lb. potatoes, peeled
  and sliced
½ kg./1 lb. onions, thinly
  sliced
225 g./8 oz. grated Cheddar
  cheese
salt and pepper
little melted margarine
150 ml./¼ pint milk

American
1 lb. potatoes, peeled and sliced
1 lb. onions, thinly sliced
2 cups grated Cheddar cheese
salt and pepper
little melted margarine
⅔ cup milk

Serves 4
Oven setting: 160–180°C./325–350°F./Gas Mark 3–4
Put layers of the potatoes, onions and cheese into a
casserole dish, seasoning each layer and brushing with a
little melted margarine, beginning and ending with
potatoes. Pour the milk over the mixture. Bake in the
centre of the preheated oven for 1¼ hours, or until the top
layer of potatoes is cooked through and brown on top.

Helpful hints
Serve with cold roast meat and pickles for a winter supper.

VEGETABLES

Courgettes (zucchini) and tomatoes au gratin

Metric/Imperial	American
½ kg./1 lb. courgettes, sliced	1 lb. zucchini, sliced
salt	salt
5 tablespoons butter	6 tablespoons butter
225 g./8 oz. tomatoes, skinned and chopped	8 oz. tomatoes, skinned and chopped
1 tablespoon chopped parsley	1¼ tablespoons chopped parsley
1 garlic clove, chopped	1 garlic clove, chopped
pepper	pepper
½ teaspoon sugar	½ teaspoon sugar
50 g./2 oz. cheese, grated	½ cup grated cheese
25 g./1 oz. fresh white breadcrumbs	½ cup fresh white breadcrumbs

Serves 4

Put the courgettes (zucchini) in a colander, sprinkle with salt and allow to drain for 1 hour. Rinse and pat dry. Melt 4 tablespoons (5 tablespoons) butter in a pan and cook courgettes (zucchini) gently until soft. Put in a shallow baking dish. Melt remaining butter and cook the tomatoes, parsley, garlic, pepper and sugar until a thickish purée forms. Pour over courgettes. Sprinkle with cheese and breadcrumbs. Grill (broil) under a hot grill (broiler) until cheese has melted and crumbs are golden brown.

Savoury vegetable strudel

Metric/Imperial	American
175 g./6 oz. flour	1½ cups flour
100 g./4 oz. hard cold butter	½ cup hard cold butter
150 ml./¼ pint water	⅔ cup water
1 teaspoon vinegar	1 teaspoon vinegar
Filling	*Filling*
2 tablespoons oil	2¼ tablespoons oil
2 onions, chopped	2 onions, chopped
100 g./4 oz. mushrooms, chopped	1 cup chopped mushrooms
2 tomatoes, skinned and chopped	2 tomatoes, skinned and chopped
350 g./12 oz. frozen spinach	12 oz. frozen spinach
1 tablespoon chopped nuts	1¼ tablespoons chopped nuts
½ teaspoon salt	½ teaspoon salt
pinch of pepper	pinch of pepper
pinch of dried mixed herbs	pinch of dried mixed herbs
1 tablespoon chopped parsley	1¼ tablespoons chopped parsley
Topping	*Topping*
1½ tablespoons melted butter	2 tablespoons melted butter
25 g./1 oz. dry breadcrumbs	¼ cup dry breadcrumbs
extra nuts or sesame seeds	extra nuts or sesame seeds

Serves 4–6

Oven setting: 220°C./425°F./Gas Mark 7

Sift the flour into a bowl and add the butter cut into large pieces. Mix with water and vinegar, adding enough to make a soft dough. Roll out the dough into an oblong and fold it in three, then seal the edges and turn to the left. Repeat this procedure twice, then refrigerate. Heat the oil in a pan and fry the onions until a pale brown. Add the mushrooms, tomatoes and spinach. Add the rest of the filling ingredients and cook for 10 minutes. Leave to cool. Cut the dough into two, roll out thinly into an oblong and brush with one-third of the melted butter and half the breadcrumbs. Spread half the filling to within 2.5 cm./1 inch of the edge. Wet edges, roll up, brush with melted butter and sprinkle with nuts or sesame seeds. Repeat with the rest of the dough and filling. Place on a greased baking sheet and cook for 20–30 minutes.

Rosti

Metric/Imperial
1 kg./2 lb. potatoes
salt and pepper
75 g./3 oz. grated Emmenthal
　or Gruyère cheese
100 g./4 oz. streaky bacon, cut
　into thin strips
75 g./3 oz. butter

American
2 lb. potatoes
salt and pepper
¾ cup grated Swiss cheese
4 oz. fatty bacon, cut into thin
　strips
6 tablespoons butter

Serves 4

Put the potatoes, unpeeled, into a pan of salted water and bring to the boil. Simmer for 20 minutes or until they are just cooked. Drain and when cool peel off the skins. Grate into a bowl and stir in the cheese.

Fry the bacon in one-third of the butter until golden brown and crisp. Drain, then stir into the potato mixture. Season well.

Melt the remaining butter in a frying pan (skillet). Add the potato mixture and cook gently for about 7 minutes.

Helpful hints

This is a Swiss dish — hence the Emmenthal or Gruyère cheese. To economize, use Cheddar or any hard English cheese.

Braised celery

Metric/Imperial
butter and oil for frying
1 medium-sized onion, chopped
4 tomatoes, skinned, seeded and
　chopped
2 heads of celery, stalks halved
　crossways
2 carrots, peeled and sliced
600 ml./1 pint chicken stock
1 bouquet garni
salt and freshly ground black
　pepper

American
butter and oil for frying
1 medium-sized onion, chopped
4 tomatoes, skinned, seeded and
　chopped
2 heads of celery, stalks halved
　crosswise
2 carrots, peeled and sliced
2½ cups chicken stock
1 bouquet garni
salt and freshly ground black
　pepper

Serves 4

Oven setting: 160°C./325°F./Gas Mark 3

Heat a knob of butter and a tablespoon of oil in a flameproof casserole, add the onion and fry until golden. Stir in the tomatoes, celery and carrots. Pour in just enough stock to cover the vegetables, and bring to the boil. Add the bouquet garni and seasoning to taste, and transfer to the preheated oven. Cook for 30–40 minutes, or until the celery is just tender. Adjust seasoning and discard the bouquet garni. Transfer to a hot serving dish with a little of the cooking liquid.

VEGETABLES

Green beans and tomatoes

Metric/Imperial
½ kg./1 lb. frozen, fresh or
  canned green beans
3–4 tomatoes, skinned and
  thickly sliced
salt and pepper

American
2⅔ cups frozen, fresh or
  canned green beans
3–4 tomatoes, skinned and
  thickly sliced
salt and pepper

Serves 4
Cook frozen or fresh green beans or heat canned beans.
Strain, then put into a pan with the tomatoes and
seasoning. Simmer for 10 minutes.
   To vary: Add a chopped onion to the pan and fry for 5
minutes in 25 g./1 oz. (2 tablespoons) butter or margarine,
then add the tomatoes and beans.
   Add chopped parsley, thyme or chives to the pan with
the tomatoes.

Helpful hints
Serve cold, with French dressing, as a starter.

Cauliflower surprise

Metric/Imperial
100 g./4 oz. margarine
2–3 medium-sized onions,
  sliced
2 tomatoes, skinned and sliced
6 mushrooms, sliced
1 × 175 g./6 oz. can sweetcorn,
  drained
few cooked or canned peas
few tablespoons diced cooked
  ham
1 cauliflower
50 g./2 oz. flour
450 ml./¾ pint milk
150 ml./¼ pint cauliflower
  stock
salt and pepper
100–175 g./4–6 oz. grated
  cheese

American
½ cup margarine
2–3 medium-sized onions,
  sliced
2 tomatoes, skinned and sliced
6 mushrooms, sliced
1 × 6 oz. can sweetcorn,
  drained
few cooked or canned peas
few tablespoons diced cooked
  ham
1 cauliflower
½ cup flour
2 cups milk
⅔ cup cauliflower stock
salt and pepper
1–1½ cups grated cheese

Serves 4–6
Heat half the margarine in a frying pan (skillet), add the
onions, tomatoes and mushrooms and fry until soft. Stir in
the sweetcorn, peas and ham. Simmer gently for 15
minutes.
   Meanwhile, boil the cauliflower in salted water for 10
minutes until just tender.
   Heat the remaining margarine in a saucepan and stir in
the flour. Cook, stirring, for 1 minute. Gradually add the
milk and stock and bring to the boil, stirring. Season to
taste and simmer for 3 minutes, stirring constantly, or
until the sauce has thickened. Stir about a quarter of the
sauce into the vegetable mixture and transfer the mixture
to a flameproof dish. Arrange the cauliflower on top. Stir
the cheese into the remaining sauce and spoon it over the
cauliflower. Put the dish under a hot grill (broiler) and grill
(broil) until the sauce has browned.

Stuffed artichokes

Metric/Imperial
4 globe artichokes
25 g./1 oz. butter
½ small onion, finely chopped
1 garlic clove, crushed
3–4 mushrooms, sliced
a few small florets cauliflower
2 tablespoons fresh
 breadcrumbs
1 tablespoon chopped parsley
salt and pepper
olive oil
6 tablespoons dry white wine

American
4 globe artichokes
2 tablespoons butter
½ small onion, finely chopped
1 garlic clove, crushed
3–4 mushrooms, sliced
a few small florets cauliflower
2½ tablespoons fresh
 breadcrumbs
1¼ tablespoons chopped
 parsley
salt and pepper
olive oil
½ cup dry white wine

Serves 4
Remove the stalks and any coarse outside leaves from the
artichokes and cut off about 2.5 cm./1 inch from the top of
the leaves. Pull the artichokes apart carefully and remove
the choke. Heat the butter in a pan, add the onion, garlic,
mushrooms and cauliflower and sauté for 5 minutes, then
stir in breadcrumbs and parsley. Season to taste and stuff
the artichokes. Heat a little oil in a pan large enough to take
the four artichokes. Put them in the pan and add the wine.
Cover, and simmer over very low heat for about 1 hour.

Helpful hints
In Italy vegetables are generally served as a separate
course, either before or after the meat, or as a first course.
This recipe makes an excellent but substantial starter.
Follow it with a light dish such as grilled (broiled) sole or
lamb cutlets.

Marrow (summer squash) provençale

Metric/Imperial
4 tablespoons olive oil
2 large onions, finely chopped
1 garlic clove, crushed
1 medium-sized marrow,
 peeled, seeded and cubed
6 large tomatoes, skinned and
 chopped
2 tablespoons tomato purée
2 teaspoons dried mixed herbs
salt and freshly ground black
 pepper

American
5 tablespoons olive oil
2 large onions, finely chopped
1 garlic clove, crushed
1 medium-sized summer
 squash, peeled, seeded and
 cubed
6 large tomatoes, skinned and
 chopped
2½ tablespoons tomato paste
2 teaspoons dried mixed herbs
salt and freshly ground black
 pepper

Serves 4–6
Heat the oil in a pan, add the onions and garlic and fry
until soft. Add the marrow (squash) and fry gently for 5
minutes. Stir in all the remaining ingredients and simmer,
stirring occasionally, for 30 minutes, or until the
vegetables are tender.

VEGETABLES

Ratatouille

Metric/Imperial	American
1 large aubergine	1 large eggplant
225 g./8 oz. courgettes	8 oz. zucchini
salt and pepper	salt and pepper
4 tablespoons olive oil	5 tablespoons olive oil
½ kg./1 lb. ripe tomatoes, skinned and chopped	1 lb. ripe tomatoes, skinned and chopped
4 medium-sized onions, chopped	4 medium-sized onions, chopped
2 garlic cloves, crushed	2 garlic cloves, crushed
1 green pepper, cored, seeded and diced	1 green pepper, cored, seeded and diced
1 red pepper, cored, seeded and diced	1 red pepper, cored, seeded and diced
Garnish	Garnish
parsley	parsley

Slice the aubergine (eggplant) and courgettes (zucchini). Put these vegetables into a bowl, sprinkle lightly with salt and leave for 30 minutes. Rinse under cold running water.

Heat the olive oil in a pan, add the tomatoes and onions and cook gently for a few minutes, to let the juice flow from the tomatoes. Add the rest of the vegetables, and stir well. Season and cover the pan with a tightly fitting lid. Simmer gently for about 30 minutes, or until tender.

Serve hot, garnished with parsley.

Helpful hints
The proportion of vegetables is entirely a matter of personal taste. Use mushrooms instead of red pepper, if wished.

Lyonnaise potatoes

Metric/Imperial	American
½ kg./1 lb. potatoes, peeled and thinly sliced	1 lb. potatoes, peeled and thinly sliced
1 large onion, thinly sliced	1 large onion, thinly sliced
50 g./2 oz. butter	4 tablespoons butter
salt and pepper	salt and pepper
chopped parsley	chopped parsley

Serves 4
Oven setting: 200°C./400°F./Gas Mark 6
Blanch the potatoes in boiling water for 1 minute, then drain. Fry the onion in the butter until soft. Layer the onion, potatoes and seasoning in a buttered 1 1./2 pint (5 cup) casserole, finishing with a layer of potatoes. Pour over any butter left in the pan, cover and bake in the preheated oven for 1½ hours. Remove the lid for the last 30 minutes to allow the potatoes to brown. Sprinkle with parsley before serving.

Helpful hints
A mandoline or rotary vegetable slicer will give perfect, thin potato slices for this dish, and quickly.

Leeks mornay

Metric/Imperial
8 large leeks, washed
salt and pepper
25 g./1 oz. butter
25 g./1 oz. flour
pinch of dry mustard
300 ml./½ pint milk or half
*   milk and half leek stock*
100 g./4 oz. grated cheese
paprika

American
8 large leeks, washed
salt and pepper
2 tablespoons butter
¼ cup flour
pinch of dry mustard
1¼ cups milk or half milk and
*   half leek stock*
1 cup grated cheese
paprika

Serves 4

Boil the leeks in salted water for 15–20 minutes, or until tender. Drain and transfer to a heated serving dish. Keep hot. (Save half the stock if necessary for the sauce.)

Heat the butter in a pan and stir in the flour and mustard. Cook, stirring, for 1 minute. Gradually add the milk or milk and stock and bring to the boil, stirring. Simmer for 3 minutes, stirring constantly, or until the sauce thickens. Stir in the cheese, and seasoning and simmer until the cheese melts.

Pour the sauce over the leeks and sprinkle with paprika.

Helpful hints

After cooking, drain the leeks thoroughly and dry over gentle heat for 1–2 minutes. Otherwise the cooking water will be retained between the leaves and will collect in the serving dish, spoiling the appearance of the sauce.

Red cabbage

Metric/Imperial
1 medium-sized red cabbage,
*   finely shredded*
½ kg./1 lb. cooking apples,
*   peeled, cored and sliced*
150 ml./¼ pint water
3 tablespoons sugar
1 teaspoon salt
4 cloves
5 tablespoons vinegar
50 g./2 oz. butter
1 tablespoon redcurrant jelly

American
1 medium-sized red cabbage,
*   finely shredded*
1 lb. cooking apples, peeled,
*   cored and sliced*
⅔ cup water
4 tablespoons sugar
1 teaspoon salt
4 cloves
6 tablespoons vinegar
4 tablespoons butter
1¼ tablespoons redcurrant
*   jelly*

Serves 4

Put the cabbage and apples into a saucepan and add the water, sugar, salt and cloves. Cover and simmer for about ¾–1 hour, or until the cabbage is tender. Remove the cloves and stir in the vinegar, butter and redcurrant jelly before serving.

Helpful hints

This freezes well, but use within 2 months. To serve, thaw at room temperature for 5–6 hours. Reheat gently in a saucepan, stirring frequently.

VEGETABLES

Stuffed cabbage leaves

Metric/Imperial	American
4 large cabbage leaves	4 large cabbage leaves
50 g./2 oz. butter	¼ cup butter
2 onions, chopped	2 onions, chopped
225 g./8 oz. lambs' liver, chopped	8 oz. lambs' liver, chopped
1 tablespoon tomato purée	1¼ tablespoons tomato paste
1 tablespoon water	1¼ tablespoons water
pinch of grated nutmeg	pinch of grated nutmeg
salt and pepper	salt and pepper

Serves 4
Oven setting: 180°C./350°F./Gas Mark 4
Cook cabbage leaves in a large pan of boiling, salted water for 3–5 minutes. Drain and cool. Remove hard stem from base of each leaf.

Melt the butter in a pan (skillet) and add the onion. Fry until tender but not browned. Add liver and fry for 5 minutes. Stir in tomato purée (paste), water, nutmeg, salt and pepper. Cool slightly. Divide filling between cabbage leaves, fold sides over and roll up. Place stuffed cabbage leaves in a greased, ovenproof dish, join side down. Bake in the oven for 45–50 minutes. Serve hot.

Chick pea casserole

Metric/Imperial	American
225 g./8 oz. dried chick peas, soaked overnight	1⅓ cups dried chick peas (garbanzos), soaked overnight
water to cover	water to cover
1 garlic clove, crushed	1 garlic clove, crushed
1 onion, chopped	1 onion, chopped
½ kg./1 lb. ripe tomatoes, skinned, seeded and chopped or 1 × 400 g./14 oz. can tomatoes, chopped	1 lb. ripe tomatoes, skinned, seeded and chopped or 1 × 14 oz. can tomatoes, chopped
225 g./8 oz. cabbage, shredded	2 cups shredded cabbage
½ green pepper, cored, seeded and chopped	½ green pepper, cored, seeded and chopped
1 tablespoon oil	1¼ tablespoons oil
1 teaspoon ground ginger	½ teaspoon ground ginger
pinch of ground cloves	pinch of ground cloves
1 teaspoon sea salt	1 teaspoon sea salt
freshly ground black pepper	freshly ground black pepper
100 ml./4 fl. oz. water or vegetable stock	½ cup water or vegetable stock

Serves 4–6
Oven setting: 180–190°C./350–375°F./Gas Mark 4–5
Drain the chick peas and simmer in the water for 1½–3 hours, until tender.

Meanwhile, fry the garlic and vegetables in the oil until soft. Stir in the ginger, cloves, salt and pepper. Transfer the mixture to a buttered casserole and stir in the drained chick peas and water or stock. Cook in the preheated oven for 20–30 minutes.

Potatoes dauphine

Metric/Imperial
225 g./8 oz. mashed, cooked
  potatoes
salt and pepper

Choux pastry
50 g./2 oz. butter
150 ml./¼ pint water
75 g./3 oz. plain flour
2 eggs plus 1 egg yolk
salt and pepper
oil for deep-frying

American
8 oz. sieved, cooked potatoes
salt and pepper

Choux pastry
¼ cup butter
⅔ cup water
¾ cup all-purpose flour
2 eggs plus 1 egg yolk
salt and pepper
oil for deep-frying

Serves 4–6

Beat the potatoes with salt and pepper until very smooth.

Put the butter and water into a pan and heat until the butter has melted. Remove the pan from the heat, add the flour and stir over a low heat until the flour mixture forms a dry ball. Gradually beat the eggs and egg yolk into the choux pastry then blend in the potato purée. Taste and add more seasoning if required.

Heat the oil until it is hot enough to turn a stale bread cube golden brown in 30 seconds (190°C./375°F. on a deep-fat thermometer). Either pipe or spoon small balls of the mixture into the oil and fry for a few minutes until golden brown. Drain on absorbent paper. Serve at once.

Cauliflower basket

Metric/Imperial
1 medium-sized cauliflower
salt
300 ml./½ pint hot cheese
  sauce
2 eggs, hard boiled and chopped
1 tablespoon chopped gherkins
1 teaspoon capers
1 tablespoon chopped parsley
1 tablespoon chopped chives
50 g./2 oz. Cheddar cheese,
  grated

American
1 medium-sized cauliflower
salt
1¼ cups hot cheese sauce
2 eggs, hard cooked and
  chopped
1¼ tablespoons chopped
  gherkins
1 teaspoon capers
1¼ tablespoons chopped
  parsley
1¼ tablespoons chopped chives
½ cup grated Cheddar cheese

Serves 4–6

Prepare the cauliflower, keeping it whole. Cook in boiling salted water until just tender and drain.

Blend the eggs with the hot cheese sauce together with the gherkins, capers and herbs. Scoop out the centre part of the cauliflower. Put this on to a plate, chop coarsely and add to the sauce.

Stand the cauliflower in a hot serving dish. Pile the cheese sauce mixture into the centre. Top with the cheese and brown for 1–2 minutes under a very hot grill.

Helpful hints

Use peeled prawns (shrimp) or diced, cooked ham instead of the eggs.

VEGETABLES

Lentil rissoles

Metric/Imperial	American
100 g./4 oz. brown or yellow lentils, soaked overnight and drained	2/3 cup brown or yellow lentils, soaked overnight and drained
1 large onion, grated	1 large onion, grated
2 medium-sized potatoes, boiled and mashed	2 medium-sized potatoes, boiled and mashed
75 g./3 oz. fresh breadcrumbs	1½ cup fresh breadcrumbs
100 g./4 oz. chopped almonds	1 cup chopped almonds
25 g./1 oz. sesame seeds	3 tablespoons sesame seeds
sea salt	sea salt
2 tablespoons chopped parsley	2½ tablespoons chopped parsley
1 egg, beaten	1 egg, beaten

Serves 6

Oven setting: 180°C./350°F./Gas Mark 4

Bring the lentils to the boil in a pan of cold, salted water.
Cover and simmer for 1½ hours until they are tender.
Drain and mash, then mix them with the onion, potatoes,
breadcrumbs, nuts, sesame seeds, salt, parsley and egg.
Add enough cold water to bind the mixture together.

Form the mixture into 12 rissoles and arrange them on a
greased baking sheet. Bake in the preheated oven for 25
minutes. (If preferred, fry them gently in oil for 15
minutes, or until golden on both sides, turning once.)

Crumbed potatoes and garlic beans

Metric/Imperial	American
1 × 450 g./1 lb. can new potatoes	1 × 1 lb. can new potatoes
75 g./3 oz. butter or margarine	6 tablespoons butter or margarine
2–3 tablespoons dry breadcrumbs	2½–4 tablespoons dry breadcrumbs
½ kg./1 lb. canned or frozen green beans	1 lb. canned or frozen green beans
1 garlic clove, crushed	1 garlic clove, crushed

Serves 4

Heat the potatoes in a pan, then drain thoroughly. Heat
50 g./2 oz. (4 tablespoons) of butter or margarine in the
pan and stir in the breadcrumbs. Return the potatoes to
the pan and turn in the mixture until coated. Keep hot.

Heat or cook the beans, then drain well. Heat the
remaining butter or margarine in the pan and stir in the
crushed garlic. Return the beans to the pan and blend well.

Transfer the potatoes and beans to a warmed serving
dish and mix gently before serving.

Helpful hints

Never boil canned potatoes. Heat gently to simmering
point and maintain a gentle heat until the potatoes are
warmed through.

Courgettes (zucchini) with ham

Metric/Imperial	American
½ kg./1 lb. courgettes, cut into 1½ cm./¾ inch thick slices	1 lb. zucchini, cut into ¾ inch thick slices
flour	flour
salt and pepper	salt and pepper
oil	oil
2 onions, chopped	2 onions, chopped
1 garlic clove, crushed	1 garlic clove, crushed
225 g./8 oz. cooked ham, cut into 4 pieces	8 oz. cooked ham, cut into 4 pieces
50 g./2 oz. grated Parmesan cheese	½ cup grated Parmesan cheese

Serves 4
Oven setting: 190°C./375°F./Gas Mark 5
Coat the courgette (zucchini) slices with the flour,
seasoned with salt and pepper. Heat a little oil in a pan,
add the onions and garlic and cook until they are soft. Add
the ham and brown lightly. Transfer the ham and onions
to a plate. Heat a little more oil in the pan and add the
courgette (zucchini) slices. Cook just long enough to
brown lightly and evenly.

Arrange most of the courgette (zucchini) slices in a
buttered ovenproof dish and sprinkle over half the onions
and half the grated cheese. Put the ham pieces on top,
sprinkle with the remaining onion and cheese, and top
with the remaining courgettes (zucchini). Bake in the
preheated oven for 15 minutes.

Carrots and fried almonds

Metric/Imperial	American
½ kg./1 lb. carrots, peeled and sliced	1 lb. carrots, peeled and sliced
salt	salt
50 g./2 oz. blanched almonds	⅓ cup blanched almonds
25 g./1 oz. butter	2 tablespoons butter

Serves 4
Boil the carrot slices in salted water until tender. Drain
well.

Meanwhile, fry the almonds in the butter, stirring, until
they are golden brown. Mix the carrots with the almonds
before serving.

Helpful hints
As an alternative, use whole, canned or frozen, baby
carrots.

VEGETABLES

Cabbage and tomato casserole

Metric/Imperial	American
50 g./2 oz. margarine	4 tablespoons margarine
1 onion, grated	1 onion, grated
1 small apple, peeled, cored and grated	1 small apple, peeled, cored and grated
4 large tomatoes, skinned and chopped	4 large tomatoes, skinned and chopped
150 ml./¼ pint water	⅔ cup water
salt and pepper	salt and pepper
about ½ small cooked cabbage, shredded	about ½ small cooked cabbage, shredded
75–100 g./3–4 oz. grated Cheddar cheese	¾–1 cup grated Cheddar cheese
50 g./2 oz. dry breadcrumbs	⅔ cup dry breadcrumbs

Serves 4

Heat the margarine, add the onion, apple and tomatoes
and fry for 1 minute. Pour in the water and seasoning and
bring to the boil. Simmer until the mixture is a thick purée.
Stir in the cooked cabbage and heat through for 5 minutes.
Transfer the mixture to a flameproof dish. Sprinkle with
the cheese and breadcrumbs. Put under a grill (broiler) and
brown.

Helpful hints

As an alternative to fresh, use canned tomatoes for this
dish. Drain before adding to the pan.

Harvard beets

Metric/Imperial	American
50 g./2 oz. soft brown sugar	⅓ cup light brown sugar
salt and freshly ground black pepper	salt and freshly ground black pepper
1 tablespoon cornflour	1¼ tablespoons cornstarch
100 ml./4 fl. oz. wine vinegar	½ cup wine vinegar
2 tablespoons cold water	2½ tablespoons cold water
½ kg./1 lb. cooked beetroots, skinned and sliced	2⅔ cups skinned and sliced cooked beets

Serves 4

Put the sugar, seasoning and cornflour (cornstarch) into a
pan and slowly stir in the vinegar and water. Bring to the
boil, stirring. Simmer gently for 5 minutes, stirring
constantly until the sauce thickens. Add the beetroots
(beets), cover and continue to cook for 10 minutes. Serve
piping hot with a knob of butter.

Helpful hints

Freeze without the butter. To thaw, tip the frozen beetroot
(beets) into a large saucepan, add 2–3 tablespoons water,
cover and heat through gently, stirring occasionally, for 40
minutes. After 20 minutes separate the beetroot (beet)
slices gently.

Baked potatoes with cheese and bacon

Metric/Imperial	American
4 large old potatoes, scrubbed	4 large Idaho potatoes, scrubbed
1 tablespoon corn oil	1¼ tablespoons corn oil
50 g./2 oz. butter	4 tablespoons butter
2 tablespoons grated Cheddar cheese	2½ tablespoons grated Cheddar cheese
2 teaspoons finely chopped parsley	2 teaspoons finely chopped parsley
4 rashers bacon, finely chopped	4 slices bacon, finely chopped
1 tablespoon cooking oil	1¼ tablespoons cooking oil
salt and freshly ground black pepper	salt and freshly ground black pepper

Serves 4

Oven setting: 200°C./400°F./Gas Mark 6

Place the potatoes on a baking sheet and prick them with a fork. Rub the skins with a little corn oil and bake in the preheated oven for 1–1½ hours, or until cooked.

Cut off the tops of the potatoes lengthways and scoop out the centre. Mash the potato flesh with the butter, cheese and parsley until well blended.

Fry the bacon in the oil until golden brown and crisp. Drain, then stir into the mashed potato mixture. Season to taste and spoon the mixture into the potato cases.

Vegetable casserole

Metric/Imperial	American
2 large onions, coarsely chopped	2 large onions, coarsely chopped
2 garlic cloves, crushed	2 garlic cloves, crushed
vegetable oil for frying	vegetable oil for frying
2 green peppers, cored, seeded and chopped	2 green peppers, cored, seeded and chopped
½ kg./1 lb. courgettes, thinly sliced	1 lb. zucchini, thinly sliced
2 medium-sized aubergines, chopped and dégorged	2 medium-sized eggplants, chopped and dégorged
225 g./8 oz. mushrooms, quartered	2 cups quartered mushrooms
½ kg./1 lb. ripe tomatoes, skinned, seeded and chopped	1 lb. ripe tomatoes, skinned, seeded and chopped
1 × 35 g./2¼ oz. can tomato purée	1 × 2¼ oz. can tomato paste
2 bay leaves	2 bay leaves
1 tablespoon chopped parsley	1¼ tablespoons chopped parsley
½ teaspoon dried oregano	½ teaspoon dried oregano
½ teaspoon dried thyme	½ teaspoon dried thyme
2 large potatoes, peeled and sliced	2 large potatoes, peeled and sliced
25 g./1 oz. margarine	2 tablespoons margarine

Serves 4

Oven setting: 180–190°C./350–375°F./Gas Mark 4–5

Fry the onions and garlic in the oil in a large flameproof casserole. Add the peppers, courgettes (zucchini), aubergines (eggplants) and mushrooms and cook for 5 minutes. Stir in the tomatoes, tomato purée (paste) and herbs and bring to the boil.

Cover the top completely with a layer of sliced potatoes and dot the potatoes with knobs of margarine. Cook in the preheated oven for about 1 hour, or until the potatoes are cooked through and brown on top.

VEGETABLES

Herb stuffed mushrooms

Metric/Imperial	American
½ kg./1 lb. large, cup-shaped mushrooms	4 cups large, cup-shaped mushrooms
50 g./2 oz. chopped cooked ham	⅓ cup chopped cooked ham
1 teaspoon finely chopped fresh oregano	1 teaspoon finely chopped fresh oregano
¼ teaspoon chopped fresh thyme	¼ teaspoon chopped fresh thyme
1 teaspoon chopped parsley	1 teaspoon chopped parsley
2 tablespoons grated Parmesan cheese	2½ tablespoons grated Parmesan cheese
2 tablespoons fresh breadcrumbs	2½ tablespoons fresh breadcrumbs
salt and pepper	salt and pepper
olive oil	olive oil

Serves 4

Oven setting: 180°C./350°F./Gas Mark 4

Wash the mushrooms, remove the stalks, trim as necessary and then chop them finely. Mix the chopped mushroom stalks with the ham, herbs, grated cheese and breadcrumbs. Season to taste. Put the mushrooms into an ovenproof dish and fill with the mixture. Pour a little oil on each mushroom, cover, and cook in the preheated oven for about 20–25 minutes. Add a little extra oil if necessary while the mushrooms are cooking so that they do not become dry.

Helpful hints

You really do need extra large mushrooms for this dish. Serve it as a special supper dish or as an after-dinner savoury. A light, chilled white wine will complement the rich flavour.

Cheese and potato ring

Metric/Imperial	American
½ kg./1 lb. potatoes, peeled weight	1 lb. potatoes, peeled weight
350 g./12 oz. onions, peeled weight	12 oz. onions, peeled weight
50 g./2 oz. butter	¼ cup butter
175 g./6 oz. coarsely grated cheese	1½ cups coarsely grated cheese
salt and pepper	salt and pepper
paprika	paprika
Garnish	Garnish
parsley	parsley

Serves 4–6

Oven setting: 180°C./350°F./Gas Mark 4

Grate the potatoes and onions very coarsely. Melt the butter and toss the vegetables in it with half the cheese and plenty of salt, pepper and paprika. Put a well-greased 20 cm./8 inch ring tin into the oven. When the tin is very hot remove it from the oven and spoon the potato mixture into it, pressing down well. Cover with greased foil and bake for about 45 minutes.

Turn out carefully on to a heated ovenproof dish, then gently 'pull out' the vegetables from their neat round. Sprinkle the remaining cheese over the ring and return to the oven for 5 to 10 minutes or until cheese has melted. Garnish with parsley sprigs before serving.

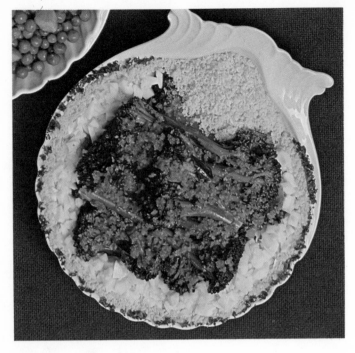

Broccoli polonaise

Metric/Imperial	American
½ kg./1 lb. frozen broccoli spears	1 lb. frozen broccoli spears
salt	salt
75 g./3 oz. butter	6 tablespoons butter
100 g./4 oz. fresh white breadcrumbs	2 cups fresh white breadcrumbs
2 hard boiled eggs, whites finely chopped and yolks sieved	2 hard cooked eggs, whites finely chopped and yolks strained
2 tablespoons chopped parsley	2½ tablespoons chopped parsley

Serves 4

Boil the broccoli in salted water for 5 minutes. Drain well, put in a heated serving dish and add one-third of the butter. Set aside and keep hot.

Fry the breadcrumbs in the remaining butter until they are crisp and golden. Sprinkle them over the broccoli. Arrange a circle of egg white around the edge of the dish, then a circle of egg yolk and then a circle of parsley.

Helpful hints

A substantial accompaniment to a light fish dish.

Boston baked beans

Metric/Imperial	American
½ kg./1 lb. dried haricot beans, soaked overnight	2⅔ cups dried white beans, soaked overnight
water to cover	water to cover
2 large tomatoes, skinned, seeded and chopped	2 large tomatoes, skinned, seeded and chopped
1–2 tablespoons black treacle	1¼–2½ tablespoons molasses
1–2 teaspoons made mustard	1–2 teaspoons made mustard
salt and pepper	salt and pepper
350 g./12 oz. fat salt pork, diced	12 oz. fat salt pork, diced
1–2 onions, thinly sliced	1–2 onions, thinly sliced
chopped parsley	chopped parsley

Serves 8

Oven setting: 120–140°C./250–275°F./Gas Mark ½–1

Drain the beans and put into a large saucepan. Just cover with water and simmer without seasoning for 10–15 minutes. Strain the beans and set aside. Reserve a generous 300 ml./½ pint (1¼ cups) of the cooking liquid, and simmer this with the tomatoes to make a thin sauce. Strain and stir in the treacle (molasses), mustard and a generous amount of seasoning.

Put the beans, salt pork and onions into a deep ovenproof casserole. Pour over the tomato sauce and mix well. Allow plenty of space for the beans to swell during cooking. Cover tightly (if the lid does not fit well, put foil around the dish) and cook in the preheated oven for about 5 hours.

Check the progress of the cooking after 2½ hours. If the beans are still very hard, increase the oven temperature slightly. If they become a little dry, add boiling water to moisten, but do not make them too wet.

Sprinkle with parsley before serving.

VEGETABLES

Sweet glazed turnips

Metric/Imperial	American
approx. 700 g./1½ lb. turnips, peeled and thickly sliced	*approx. 1½ lb. turnips, peeled and thickly sliced*
salt	*salt*
25 g./1 oz. butter	*2 tablespoons butter*
1 tablespoon soft brown sugar	*1¼ tablespoons light brown sugar*
100 ml./4 fl. oz. chicken stock	*½ cup chicken stock*
freshly ground black pepper	*freshly ground black pepper*
1 tablespoon chopped parsley	*1¼ tablespoons chopped parsley*

Serves 4

Boil the turnips in salted water for 20–25 minutes, or until almost tender. Drain and refresh under cold running water.

Heat the butter in the rinsed-out pan. Stir in the sugar until dissolved, then pour in the stock. Bring to the boil. Add the turnips, reduce the heat and simmer gently for 8–10 minutes, or until the stock is reduced and the turnips glazed.

Transfer to a hot serving dish and sprinkle with black pepper and parsley before serving.

French-fried fennel

Metric/Imperial	American
1 head of fennel	*1 head of fennel*
50 g./2 oz. flour	*½ cup flour*
1 egg	*1 egg*
6 tablespoons milk	*½ cup milk*
salt and pepper	*salt and pepper*
oil or fat for frying	*oil or fat for frying*

Serves 4

Slice the white root of the fennel and save the green leaves for garnish. Separate the root into rings.

Sift the flour into a mixing bowl, gradually add the egg and milk and beat to a smooth batter. Season well. Dip the fennel rings in the batter. Heat the oil or fat until hot. Put the coated rings into the pan and fry for 2–3 minutes, until the rings are crisp on the outside. (You can also deep-fry the fennel rings.)

Helpful hints

Fry a few at a time and drain the rings on absorbent paper as they are cooked.

Italian-style peppers

Metric/Imperial	American
butter and olive oil for frying	*butter and olive oil for frying*
1 large onion, finely chopped	*1 large onion, finely chopped*
1 garlic clove, crushed with ½ teaspoon salt	*1 garlic clove, crushed with ½ teaspoon salt*
½ kg./1 lb. red and green peppers, cored, seeded and chopped	*1 lb. red and green peppers, cored, seeded and chopped*
½ kg./1 lb. tomatoes, skinned, seeded and chopped	*1 lb. tomatoes, skinned, seeded and chopped*
freshly ground black pepper	*freshly ground black pepper*
1 teaspoon sugar	*1 teaspoon sugar*
1 teaspoon chopped fresh basil or ½ teaspoon dried basil	*1 teaspoon chopped fresh basil or ½ teaspoon dried basil*

Serves 4

Heat a knob of butter and 2 tablespoons of oil in a large pan, add the onion and garlic and fry until golden. Add the peppers and tomatoes and stir in plenty of black pepper, the sugar and basil. Fry briskly for 5 minutes, cover and reduce the heat. Simmer very gently, for 20–30 minutes, or until the peppers and tomatoes are almost a purée. If the mixture becomes too dry during cooking, add a little water. Adjust seasoning before serving.

Cauliflower with brown sauce topping

Metric/Imperial	American
1 cauliflower	*1 cauliflower*
Sauce	*Sauce*
vegetable stock	*vegetable stock*
tomato juice	*tomato juice*
25 g./1 oz. butter or margarine	*2 tablespoons butter or margarine*
25 g./1 oz. flour	*¼ cup flour*
little yeast extract	*little yeast extract*
chopped parsley	*chopped parsley*

Serves 4

Divide the cauliflower into small florets and boil in salted water for 8–10 minutes, until tender. Strain the florets and transfer to a warmed serving dish. Keep hot.

To make the sauce, strain the vegetable stock and reserve about 175 ml./6 fl. oz. (¾ cup). Add enough tomato juice to give just over 300 ml./½ pint (1¼ cups) liquid. Heat the butter or margarine in a saucepan and stir in the flour. Cook, stirring, for 1 minute. Gradually add the liquid and bring to the boil, stirring. Simmer for 3 minutes, stirring constantly, or until the sauce thickens. Stir in enough yeast extract to give the sauce a fairly pronounced flavour.

Spoon the sauce over the cauliflower and sprinkle over the chopped parsley.

Helpful hints

The vegetable stock will blend into the hot roux (fat and flour mixture) more easily if it is warm, rather than hot. Hot stock blended into a hot roux is likely to give the sauce a granular texture.

PASTA, RICE and PIZZA

Tagliatelle with bacon and tomato sauce

Metric/Imperial	American
75 g./3 oz. butter or margarine	6 tablespoons butter or margarine
225 g./8 oz. lean back bacon, diced	8 oz. lean back bacon, diced
1 carrot, peeled and diced	1 carrot, peeled and diced
4 sticks celery, chopped	4 sticks celery, chopped
1 garlic clove, chopped	1 garlic clove, chopped
4 tablespoons tomato purée	5 tablespoons tomato paste
150 ml./1/4 pint water	2/3 cup water
1 chicken stock cube	1 chicken bouillon cube
salt and pepper	salt and pepper
225–350 g./8–12 oz. tagliatelle	8–12 oz. tagliatelle
2 tablespoons grated Parmesan cheese	2 1/2 tablespoons grated Parmesan cheese

Serves 4–6

Heat two-thirds of the butter or margarine and gently fry the diced bacon for 4–5 minutes. Add the carrot, celery and garlic, cover and sauté for 5 minutes, shaking the pan occasionally. Add the tomato purée (paste), water, stock (bouillon) cube, salt and pepper. Cook gently for a further 5 minutes.

Cook the tagliatelle according to the directions on the packet, usually for 5–8 minutes.

To serve, drain the tagliatelle, return it to the pan, add the remaining butter or margarine and shake over the heat until the tagliatelle is well coated. Add Parmesan cheese, stir in gently then transfer to a warm serving dish. Pour the hot bacon and tomato sauce on top.

Tuna and pear pizza

Metric/Imperial	American
225 g./8 oz. basic pizza dough	2 cups basic pizza dough
olive oil	olive oil
1 × 200 g./7 oz. can tuna	1 × 7 oz. can tuna
1 Spanish onion, chopped	1 Bermuda onion, chopped
2 ripe dessert pears, peeled, cored and chopped	2 ripe eating pears, peeled, cored and chopped
1 × 225 g./8 oz. can tomatoes	1 × 8 oz. can tomatoes
1/2 teaspoon dried oregano	1/2 teaspoon dried oregano
salt and black pepper	salt and black pepper
anchovy fillets	anchovy fillets
pickled walnuts or black olives	pickled walnuts or black olives

Serves 4

Oven setting: 220°C./425°F./Gas Mark 7

Turn the risen dough on to a floured board and knead lightly until it is smooth. Roll out into a circle about 1/2 cm./1/4 inch thick and place on an oiled baking sheet. Brush lightly with oil.

Drain the oil from the tuna into a pan, put the onion and pears into the oil and cook for a few minutes. Add the flaked fish and tomatoes and cook slowly, uncovered, for about 25 minutes, or until most of the liquid has evaporated. Add oregano and seasoning to taste. When the filling is cool, spread it over the dough. Top with anchovy fillets and garnish with slices of pickled walnut or olives. Leave in a warm place for about 15 minutes to prove. Bake in the preheated oven for about 20–25 minutes. Serve hot.

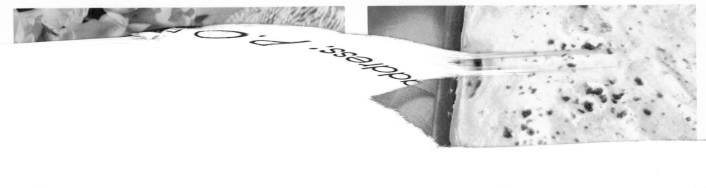

Mexican macaroni

Metric/Imperial	American
Cheese sauce	Cheese sauce
25 g./1 oz. margarine	2 tablespoons margarine
25 g./1 oz. flour	¼ cup flour
300 ml./½ pint milk	1¼ cups milk
100 g./4 oz. grated cheese	1 cup grated cheese
salt and pepper	salt and pepper
pinch cayenne pepper	pinch cayenne pepper
100 g./4 oz. macaroni	4 oz. macaroni
1–2 teaspoons made mustard	1–2 teaspoons made mustard
8 frankfurters	8 frankfurters
100–175 g./4–6 oz. cooked, frozen, or canned peas	⅔–1 cup cooked, frozen, or canned peas

Serves 4

Make the sauce with the margarine, flour and milk. When thickened, add the cheese and seasoning together with the cayenne pepper. Do not *boil* after adding the cheese, otherwise the sauce will curdle.

Meanwhile cook the macaroni according to the packet directions, usually for 8–10 minutes, drain, then add to the cheese sauce with enough mustard to give a fairly hot flavour. Chop the frankfurters, add to the sauce with the well-drained peas. Heat gently, then serve.

Helpful hints

A few diced red or green peppers will add extra flavour to the sauce.

Lasagne al forno

Metric/Imperial	American
olive oil for frying	olive oil for frying
1 large onion, chopped	1 large onion, chopped
1 garlic clove	1 garlic clove
2 sticks celery, finely chopped	2 sticks celery, finely chopped
100 g./4 oz. bacon, chopped	4 oz. bacon, chopped
½ kg./1 lb. minced beef	1 lb. ground beef
1 × 400 g./14 oz. can tomatoes	1 × 14 oz. can tomatoes
150 ml./¼ pint beef stock	⅔ cup beef stock
2 tablespoons tomato purée	2½ tablespoons tomato paste
1 teaspoon sugar	1 teaspoon sugar
2 teaspoons chopped oregano	2 teaspoons chopped oregano
salt and black pepper	salt and black pepper
175 g./6 oz. lasagne verde	6 oz. lasagne verde
50 g./2 oz. grated Parmesan	½ cup grated Parmesan
Sauce	Sauce
600 ml./1 pint hot white sauce	2½ cups hot white sauce
pinch of grated nutmeg	pinch of grated nutmeg
salt and pepper	salt and pepper
225 g./8 oz. cottage cheese, sieved	1 cup strained cottage cheese

Serves 4

Oven setting: 190°C./375°F./Gas Mark 5

Heat a tablespoon of oil in a large pan. Add the onion, garlic and celery and fry until golden. Add the bacon and continue to fry until crisp. Add the beef to the pan and fry until browned, stirring constantly. Stir in the tomatoes, stock, tomato purée (paste), sugar, oregano and salt and pepper to taste. Bring to the boil, stirring constantly, then lower heat, half cover and simmer for 20 minutes.

Cook the lasagne according to packet instructions.

Season sauce with nutmeg, salt and pepper. Allow to cool slightly, then stir in cottage cheese.

Arrange the meat, pasta and prepared sauce in layers in a buttered baking dish, starting with a layer of meat, then pasta, then sauce. Sprinkle the top layer of sauce with the Parmesan. Bake in the preheated oven for 30 minutes, or until browned and bubbling. Serve straight from the baking dish.

PASTA, RICE and PIZZA

Neapolitan pizza

Metric/Imperial	American
Basic pizza dough	Basic pizza dough
¼ teaspoon sugar	¼ teaspoon sugar
150 ml./¼ pint warm water	⅔ cup warm water
1 teaspoon dried yeast	1 teaspoon dried yeast
225 g./8 oz. plain flour	2 cups all-purpose flour
1 teaspoon salt	1 teaspoon salt
15 g./½ oz. butter	1 tablespoon butter
Filling	Filling
olive oil	olive oil
6 medium-sized tomatoes, skinned and sliced	6 medium-sized tomatoes, skinned and sliced
1 garlic clove, chopped	1 garlic clove, chopped
12 anchovy fillets	12 anchovy fillets
100 g./4 oz. Mozzarella cheese, thinly sliced	4 oz. Mozzarella cheese, thinly sliced
12 large black olives, stoned	12 large black olives, pitted
dried oregano	dried oregano
pepper	pepper

Serves 1–2 as a light meal, 4 as a starter
Oven setting: 230°C./450°F./Gas Mark 8
To make the dough, dissolve the sugar in the warm water and sprinkle the dried yeast on top. Leave the mixture in a warm place for 10–15 minutes, until frothy. Meanwhile, sift the flour and salt into a mixing bowl. Rub the butter into the flour and bind with the yeast liquid, adding a little extra flour if the dough is sticky. Knead for about 10 minutes on a lightly floured surface, until the dough is smooth and elastic, then put it in an oiled bowl. Cover with oiled paper and leave in a warm place to rise until the dough has doubled in size.

Turn the dough on to the floured surface and knead lightly until it is smooth. Roll out into a circle ½ cm./¼ inch thick and place it on an oiled baking sheet. Brush the dough with olive oil and cover it with slices of tomato. Sprinkle with garlic, then top with anchovy fillets, cheese slices and olives. Sprinkle with oregano and pepper and bake near the top of the preheated oven for 15–20 minutes.

Risotto

Metric/Imperial	American
50 g./2 oz. butter, or use 25 g./1 oz. butter and 1 tablespoon oil	4 tablespoons butter, or use 2 tablespoons butter and 1¼ tablespoons oil
1 small onion, finely chopped	1 small onion, finely chopped
1 garlic clove (optional)	1 garlic clove (optional)
225 g./8 oz. long-grain rice	1⅓ cups long-grain rice
600 ml./1 pint chicken stock	2½ cups chicken stock
good pinch of saffron or few strands of saffron	good pinch of saffron or few strands of saffron
salt and pepper	salt and pepper
grated nutmeg	grated nutmeg
1 tablespoon tomato purée	1¼ tablespoons tomato paste
grated Parmesan cheese	grated Parmesan cheese

Serves 4
Heat the butter or butter and oil in a pan. Add the onion and crushed garlic or, if a more delicate flavour is preferred, put the whole clove of garlic into the hot butter for a few minutes only, then remove. Add the rice, and turn in the butter or butter and oil until every grain is separate. (This prevents the rice from becoming sticky.) Blend the stock with the saffron, or, if using saffron strands, infuse in the stock for a while then strain. Add seasoning, nutmeg and tomato purée (paste), then add to the rice, stir well. Cook steadily until the rice has absorbed the liquid. A risotto should be pleasantly moist. Top with the cheese and serve.

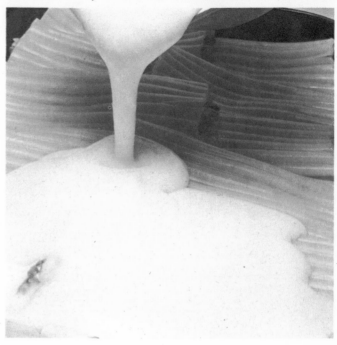

Spaghetti bolognese

Metric/Imperial	American
15 g./½ oz. butter	1 tablespoon butter
75 g./3 oz. bacon or uncooked ham, chopped	3 oz. bacon, chopped
1 onion, finely chopped	1 onion, finely chopped
1 carrot, peeled and chopped	1 carrot, peeled and chopped
1 stick celery, finely chopped	1 stick celery, finely chopped
225 g./8 oz. lean minced beef	8 oz. lean ground beef
100 g./4 oz. chicken livers, chopped	4 oz. chicken livers, chopped
1 tablespoon tomato purée	1¼ tablespoons tomato paste
100 ml./4 fl. oz. white wine	½ cup white wine
300 ml./½ pint stock or water	1¼ cups stock or water
salt, pepper and grated nutmeg	salt, pepper and grated nutmeg
50 ml./2 fl. oz. cream or milk	¼ cup cream or milk
350 g./12 oz. spaghetti	12 oz. spaghetti
2 tablespoons grated Parmesan cheese	2½ tablespoons grated Parmesan cheese

Serves 4

Heat the butter in a pan and fry the bacon, onion, carrot and celery for about 10 minutes, or until the vegetables are soft. Add the meat and when it has browned add the chicken livers. Cook for 2–3 minutes, then add tomato purée (paste), wine and stock or water. Add a little salt, pepper and nutmeg. Stir the mixture until it boils, then cover and simmer very gently for about 40 minutes, stirring occasionally. Just before serving, stir in the cream or milk and check the seasoning.

Cook the spaghetti according to the packet directions, usually for 10–12 minutes, drain and rinse with hot water. Turn it into a hot serving dish, pour the sauce over and sprinkle with Parmesan cheese.

To vary: For anchovy sauce to serve with spaghetti, fry 225 g./8 oz. mushrooms, 2 onions, garlic, 5 chopped anchovy fillets, 3 rashers (slices) bacon, olives and parsley together for 15 minutes.

Cannelloni ripieni

Metric/Imperial	American
6–8 tubes cannelloni	6–8 tubes cannelloni
Stuffing	*Stuffing*
1 tablespoon oil	1¼ tablespoons oil
25 g./1 oz. butter	2 tablespoons butter
1 onion, finely chopped	1 onion, finely chopped
100 g./4 oz. mushrooms, chopped	1 cup chopped mushrooms
1 small green pepper, cored, seeded and chopped	1 small green pepper, cored, seeded and chopped
50–100 g./2–4 oz. chopped ham	⅓–⅔ cup chopped ham
1 egg	1 egg
50 g./2 oz. grated Parmesan	½ cup grated Parmesan
salt and pepper	salt and pepper
Sauce	*Sauce*
40 g./1½ oz. butter	3 tablespoons butter
40 g./1½ oz. flour	6 tablespoons flour
450 ml./¾ pint milk	2 cups milk
salt and pepper	salt and pepper
25 g./1 oz. Parmesan cheese	¼ cup Parmesan cheese
50 g./2 oz. grated Gruyère or Cheddar cheese	½ cup grated Swiss or Cheddar cheese

Serves 3–4 as a main dish or 6–8 as a starter

Oven setting: 190°C./375°F./Gas Mark 5

To make the stuffing, heat the oil and butter, add the onion and mushrooms and cook gently until soft, then add the green pepper and ham and blend well. Stir in the egg, cheese and seasoning, do not cook again.

To make the sauce, heat the butter in a pan, stir in the flour and cook for 1 minute, stirring constantly. Gradually blend in the milk. Bring to the boil and stir until thickened. Add seasoning. Stir in cheeses, but do not cook again.

Cook the cannelloni in boiling salted water until tender. Drain, allow to cool, then put the filling into each 'tube'. Spoon 2–3 tablespoons of the cheese sauce into an ovenproof dish, add the filled cannelloni, top with the remainder of the sauce. Bake in the preheated oven for about 25 minutes or until sauce is lightly browned.

PASTA, RICE and PIZZA

Fried rice with ham and bean sprouts

Metric/Imperial	American
2 tablespoons oil	2½ tablespoons oil
2 spring onions, finely chopped	2 scallions, finely chopped
1 garlic clove, crushed	1 garlic clove, crushed
350 g./12 oz. rice, cooked	6 cups cooked rice
150 g./5 oz. ham, chopped	5 oz. ham, chopped
2 tablespoons soy sauce	2½ tablespoons soy sauce
2 eggs, beaten	2 eggs, beaten
salt and pepper	salt and pepper
225 g./8 oz. canned bean sprouts, drained	8 oz. canned bean sprouts, drained

Serves 6–8

Heat the oil in a frying pan and fry the spring onions (scallions) and garlic for 2 minutes over medium heat. Add the rice, mix well and heat through. Mix the ham with the soy sauce, add it to the rice mixture and mix well. Season the beaten eggs with salt and pepper, and pour into the rice in a thin stream, stirring constantly, until the eggs are cooked. Stir in the bean sprouts and heat through. Serve immediately.

Pizza with olives and herbs

Metric/Imperial	American
Pastry	Pastry
225 g./8 oz. plain flour	2 cups all-purpose flour
½ teaspoon salt	½ teaspoon salt
100 g./4 oz. lard	½ cup lard
2 eggs	2 eggs
Filling	Filling
3 tablespoons olive oil	4 tablespoons olive oil
2 onions, finely chopped	2 onions, finely chopped
1 garlic clove, crushed	1 garlic clove, crushed
1 × 1¼ kg./2½ lb. can tomatoes	1 × 2½ lb. can tomatoes
2 tablespoons tomato purée	2½ tablespoons tomato paste
2 teaspoons dried oregano	2 teaspoons dried oregano
2 teaspoons chopped fresh basil	2 teaspoons chopped fresh basil
1 bay leaf	1 bay leaf
2 teaspoons sugar	2 teaspoons sugar
1 teaspoon salt	1 teaspoon salt
freshly ground black pepper	freshly ground black pepper
fresh herbs, as available	fresh herbs, as available
stoned green olives	pitted green olives

Serves 4–6

Oven setting: 190°C./375°F./Gas Mark 5

Sift the flour and salt into a mixing bowl. Rub the lard into the flour until the mixture resembles fine breadcrumbs. Bind with the eggs. Knead the pastry lightly on a floured surface. Roll out and line a 20 cm./8 inch round baking pan. Put some dry beans or crusts of bread in the bottom and bake in the preheated oven for 15 minutes.

Heat the oil in a pan and cook the onions and garlic until the onions are soft. Add the chopped tomatoes and can liquid, tomato purée (paste), herbs, sugar, salt and pepper. Bring to boiling point, lower the heat and simmer very gently, uncovered, for about 45 minutes, stirring occasionally. Remove the bay leaf, check the seasoning and pour into the pastry case (pie shell). Sprinkle with coarsely chopped fresh herbs and a few drops of oil. Arrange the olives on top. Reduce the oven setting to 180°C./350°F./Gas Mark 4 and bake for 10–15 minutes.

Spaghetti à la napolitaine

Metric/Imperial
225 g./8 oz. spaghetti
50 g./2 oz. Parmesan cheese, grated
40 g./1½ oz. butter
1 × 400 g./14 oz. can tomatoes
1 tablespoon tomato purée
225 g./8 oz. smoked ham, diced
chopped parsley
salt and pepper

American
8 oz. spaghetti
½ cup grated Parmesan cheese
3 tablespoons butter
1 × 14 oz. can tomatoes
1¼ tablespoons tomato paste
8 oz. smoked ham, diced
chopped parsley
salt and pepper

Serves 4
Cook the spaghetti in boiling salted water for 10 minutes, or until tender (al dente). Strain then toss with Parmesan cheese and butter. Meanwhile heat the canned tomatoes with the tomato purée (paste). Add ham, parsley and seasoning. Spoon the spaghetti on to a hot dish and top with the tomato sauce.

Spanish rice

Metric/Imperial
1 tablespoon oil
15 g./½ oz. butter
1 small onion, chopped
225 g./8 oz. long-grain rice
600 ml./1 pint chicken stock
pinch of saffron
1 small green pepper, cored, seeded and chopped
1 canned pimiento, chopped
100 g./4 oz. prawns, shelled
salt and pepper

American
1¼ tablespoons oil
1 tablespoon butter
1 small onion, chopped
1⅓ cup long-grain rice
2½ cups chicken stock
pinch of saffron
1 small green pepper, cored, seeded and chopped
1 canned pimiento, chopped
4 oz. peeled shrimp
salt and pepper

Serves 4
Heat the oil and butter in a saucepan, add the onion and sauté until transparent. Add the rice, stir over low heat for a few minutes, then add the stock and saffron. Bring to boiling point, then cover and cook for 20 minutes or until all the liquid has been absorbed. Add the green pepper, pimiento, tomatoes and prawns (shrimp). Mix well and stir occasionally over gentle heat until the mixture is well heated through. A little extra stock may be needed if the rice is not sufficiently moist.

PASTA, RICE and PIZZA

Vegetable risotto

Metric/Imperial	American
2 tablespoons oil	2 ½ tablespoons oil
2 large onions, sliced and pushed into rings	2 large onions, sliced and pushed into rings
2 garlic cloves, crushed	2 garlic cloves, crushed
½ kg./1 lb. tomatoes, skinned and sliced	1 lb. tomatoes, skinned and sliced
175 g./6 oz. long-grain rice	1 cup long-grain rice
600 ml./1 pint water	2 ½ cups water
3 large carrots, grated	3 large carrots, grated
50 g./2 oz. peas	⅜ cup peas
salt and pepper	salt and pepper
100 g./4 oz. mushrooms, sliced	1 cup sliced mushrooms
2 tablespoons parsley	2 ½ tablespoons parsley
225 g./8 oz. Cheddar cheese, grated	2 cups grated Cheddar cheese

Serves 4–6

Heat the oil in a saucepan and add the onions and garlic. Fry for a few minutes, then remove some of the onion rings.

Stir half the tomatoes into the onion mixture, together with the rice. Add the water and bring to the boil. Add the carrots and peas. Season and cook for about 10 minutes or until the rice and vegetables are almost tender. Add the remainder of the tomatoes, mushrooms and remaining onion rings. Cook gently, stirring occasionally, until the rice is tender and the liquid absorbed. Blend in half the parsley and half the cheese. Pile on to a hot dish, top with the remainder of the parsley and cheese.

Rice casserole

Metric/Imperial	American
400 g./14 oz. long-grain rice	2 cups long-grain rice
1 onion, chopped	1 onion, chopped
2 garlic cloves, chopped	2 garlic cloves, chopped
1 green pepper, cored, seeded and chopped	1 green pepper, cored, seeded and chopped
5 tablespoons olive oil	6 tablespoons olive oil
3 carrots, diced	3 carrots, diced
225 g./8 oz. French beans, chopped	1 cup chopped green beans
1 × 225 g./8 oz. can kidney beans	1 × 8 oz. can kidney beans
1 tablespoon chopped parsley	1 ¼ tablespoons chopped parsley
900 ml./1 ½ pints vegetable stock	3 ¾ cups vegetable stock
¼ teaspoon saffron	¼ teaspoon saffron
¼ teaspoon turmeric	¼ teaspoon turmeric
¼ teaspoon crushed coriander	¼ teaspoon crushed coriander

Serves 6

Half cook the rice. Fry onion, garlic and pepper gently in olive oil until soft. Add all vegetables and parsley, together with the rice and stir in.

Heat vegetable stock to which you have added saffron, turmeric and coriander. Add slowly to the rice mixture. Bring to the boil, reduce heat, cover and cook for 20 minutes or until all liquid is absorbed. Serve hot.

Kidney omelette

Metric/Imperial
½ onion, chopped
oil
1 small can kidneys
Tabasco sauce
4 eggs
salt and pepper
1 tablespoon water
25–40 g./1–1½ oz. butter

American
½ onion, chopped
oil
1 small can kidneys
Tabasco sauce
4 eggs
salt and pepper
1¼ tablespoons water
2–3 tablespoons butter

Serves 2

Fry the onion gently in a little oil until soft, add the kidneys and heat through. Season with a little Tabasco sauce.

Beat the eggs with the seasoning and water very lightly. Heat the butter in a 15–18 cm./6–7 inch omelette pan (skillet). Pour in the eggs and leave for about ½–1 minute until set at the bottom, then loosen the eggs away from the side of the pan, tilting this at the same time. Continue working the omelette until it is just set, or even a little liquid in the centre. Add the kidney filling. Fold away from the handle and tip on to a hot plate.

Helpful hints

An omelette made with four eggs and halved is much more satisfactory than two two-egg omelettes; the eggs cook to a better consistency.

Savoury filled pancakes (crêpes)

Metric/Imperial
100 g./4 oz. plain flour
salt
1 egg
300 ml./½ pint milk
oil for frying

Sauce
1 × 215 g./7½ oz. can salmon
4 spring onions, chopped
5 cm./2 inch piece cucumber,
   chopped
600 ml./1 pint white sauce
salt and pepper
100 g./4 oz. grated Cheddar
   cheese

American
1 cup all-purpose flour
salt
1 egg
1¼ cups milk
oil for frying

Sauce
1 × 7½ oz. can salmon
4 scallions, chopped
2 inch piece cucumber, chopped
2½ cups white sauce
salt and pepper
1 cup grated Cheddar cheese

Serves 4

Oven setting: 200°C./400°F./Gas Mark 6

Sift the flour and salt into a large bowl. Add the egg and half the milk and mix to a smooth paste. Gradually beat in the remaining milk until a smooth batter.

Lightly grease a frying pan (skillet) with oil. Heat until very hot, then pour off any surplus. Pour 2–3 tablespoons (2½–4 tablespoons) of the batter into the pan and quickly tilt in all directions, so the batter thinly covers the entire base of the pan. Cook until the underside is golden. Gently turn and cook until the other side is golden. Cook the remaining batter in the same way. Pile the pancakes (crêpes) on to a plate, separating them with pieces of foil or greaseproof (waxed) paper.

Add the salmon, together with any juice from the can, the spring onions (scallions) and cucumber to half the sauce. Season well. Divide this filling between the pancakes (crêpes) and roll them up. Place in an ovenproof dish. Add the cheese to the remainder of the sauce and pour over the pancakes (crêpes). Bake, uncovered, in the preheated oven for about 30 minutes, or until heated through.

SNACKS

Crab and tomato toasts

Metric/Imperial
4 small rounds bread
50 g./2 oz. butter
½ lemon
1 × 200 g./7 oz. can crabmeat
1 tablespoon tomato purée
salt and pepper

Garnish
½ lemon
watercress or lettuce

American
4 small rounds bread
¼ cup butter
½ lemon
1 × 7 oz. can crabmeat
1 tablespoon tomato paste
salt and pepper

Garnish
½ lemon
watercress or lettuce

Serves 4
Toast the bread, then spread with half the butter. Squeeze the juice from the ½ lemon, then blend with the flaked crabmeat, tomato purée (paste) and the remaining butter. Season well and spread on to the hot toast.

Serve garnished with lemon and watercress or lettuce.

Farmhouse pie

Metric/Imperial
Savoury shortcrust pastry
350 g./12 oz. plain flour
good pinch each of salt, celery
  and garlic salts, mustard and
  dried mixed herbs
pinch of pepper
175 g./6 oz. margarine or
  cooking fat
water to bind

Filling
2 onions, chopped
3 large tomatoes, skinned and
  chopped
50 g./2 oz. margarine
½ kg./1 lb. cooked or canned
  lambs' tongues, diced
salt and pepper
1–2 tablespoons sweet pickle or
  chutney
beaten egg to glaze

American
Savoury shortcrust pastry
3 cups all-purpose flour
good pinch each of salt, celery
  and garlic salts, mustard and
  dried mixed herbs
pinch of pepper
¾ cup margarine or fat
water to bind

Filling
2 onions, chopped
3 large tomatoes, skinned and
  chopped
4 tablespoons margarine
1 lb. cooked or canned lambs'
  tongues, diced
salt and pepper
1¼–2½ tablespoons sweet
  pickle or chutney
beaten egg to glaze

Serves 6
Oven setting: 220–230°C./425–450°F./Gas Mark 7–8
Sift the flour with the seasonings and herbs into a mixing bowl. Rub the margarine or fat into the flour until the mixture resembles fine breadcrumbs. Bind with water. Knead the pastry lightly on a floured surface. Roll out and use about three-quarters to line a 1 kg./2 lb. loaf pan.

Fry the onions and tomatoes in the margarine. Blend with the tongue. Season and add the sweet pickle or chutney. Put into the pastry-lined pan. Dampen the pastry edges with a little water. Roll out the remainder of the pastry, make a 'lid' to fit on the pie and a few pastry 'leaves'. Place the lid in position, flute the edges together. Brush the top of the pie with beaten egg, put the 'leaves' in position and brush these with egg. Make 1 or 2 slits on top.

Bake the pie in the centre of the preheated oven for about 20 minutes, then lower the oven setting to 160°C./325°F./Gas Mark 3 for a further 20 minutes.

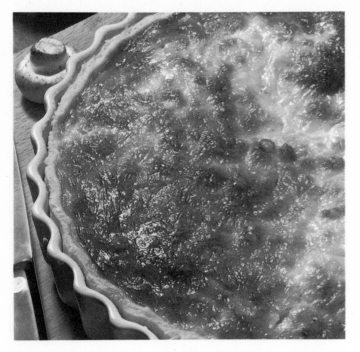

Dutch leek and mushroom flan

Metric/Imperial	American
2 medium-sized leeks	2 medium-sized leeks
25 g./1 oz. butter	2 tablespoons butter
100 g./4 oz. mushrooms, sliced	1 cup sliced mushrooms
salt and pepper	salt and pepper
20 cm./8 inch shortcrust pastry flan case, baked	8 inch shortcrust pastry pie shell, baked
2 eggs	2 eggs
150 ml./¼ pint milk	⅔ cup milk
175 g./6 oz. Edam or Gouda cheese, grated	1½ cups grated Edam or Gouda cheese

Serves 4
Oven setting: 180°C./350°F./Gas Mark 4
Trim off the top and root of the leeks. Slice the leeks into 1 cm./½ inch rings and wash thoroughly. Heat the butter in a pan, add the leeks, cover and cook gently for 10 minutes. Add the mushrooms and seasoning and cook for a further 5 minutes. Remove the vegetables from the pan with a draining spoon or fish slice, so that any liquid is left in the pan, and place vegetables in the flan case. Beat the eggs with the milk and season well with more salt and pepper. Add the cheese and spoon over the vegetables. Bake in the oven for about 30 minutes or until the top is golden brown.

Helpful hints
Omit the leeks and mushrooms and replace with 4 rashers (slices) of rinded and chopped bacon, or use 1 large, chopped onion instead.

Piroshki

Metric/Imperial	American
100 g./4 oz. flour, preferably plain	1 cup flour, preferably all-purpose
pinch of salt	pinch of salt
1 egg	1 egg
300 ml./½ pint milk	1¼ cups milk
2 egg whites	2 egg whites
oil for frying	oil for frying
Filling	Filling
225 g./8 oz. cream or cottage cheese	1 cup cream or cottage cheese
25 g./1 oz. butter, softened	2 tablespoons butter, softened
1 egg yolk	1 egg yolk
salt and pepper	salt and pepper

Serves 4
Sift the flour and salt into a bowl and add the egg and milk to make a smooth, thin batter. Use two-thirds of the batter to make 8 small pancakes (crêpes) (see recipe on page 95).

Blend the cheese, butter and egg yolk together and season well. Beat the egg whites until they are stiff and fold into the remaining one-third of the batter. Put the filling into the pancakes (crêpes), tuck in the ends to make very secure 'parcels'. Dip each 'parcel' into the remaining batter and fry in hot oil. Although shallow oil can be used, deep-frying is better. Drain on absorbent paper.

Helpful hints
To vary these, omit the seasoning and spread the pancakes with strawberry jam before filling with the cheese mixture.

SNACKS

Open sandwiches

Choose a firm type of bread — this can be white, brown, rye or crispbread.

Cut it fairly thinly and spread generously with butter or margarine.

Select the toppings with an eye to colour as well as flavour and food value.

Toppings
Sliced Danish blue cheese, topped with grapes and slices of radish. This cheese is also excellent with mayonnaise and nuts; with twists of cucumber and tomato; crisply fried or grilled (broiled) twists of bacon and/or frankfurters; ham rolls and potato salad.

Sliced Danish Danbo cheese (or Cheddar) on sliced cucumber or lettuce and thick mayonnaise, topped with grated raw carrot.

Shelled prawns (shrimp), topped with thick mayonnaise, parsley and lemon and/or cucumber twists.

Slices of salami, laid flat, or rolled, then topped with scrambled egg and chopped gherkins or a gherkin fan, or just with raw onion rings. The rolls of salami (or cooked ham) can be filled with potato or mixed vegetable salad or soft cream cheese.

Helpful hints
The secret with open sandwiches is to combine several different flavours and to make the garnishes stand up attractively. That way you achieve a miniature meal on each slice of bread.

Oeufs florentine

Metric/Imperial	American
1/2 kg./1 lb. spinach	1 lb. spinach
salt and pepper	salt and pepper
40 g./1 1/2 oz. butter	3 tablespoons butter
25 g./1 oz. flour	1/4 cup flour
300 ml./1/2 pint milk	1 1/4 cups milk
50 g./2 oz. grated Parmesan or Cheddar cheese	1/2 cup grated Parmesan or Cheddar cheese
4 eggs	4 eggs
2–3 tablespoons single cream	2 1/2–4 tablespoons light cream
Garnish	Garnish
tomato slices	tomato slices

Serves 4
Oven setting: 190°C./375°F./Gas Mark 5
Wash the spinach well, put it into a pan with a little salt and just the water that clings to the leaves. Cook for 10–15 minutes until tender, then drain well. Chop roughly and mix with 15 g./1/2 oz. (1 tablespoon) of the butter and seasoning. Put into an ovenproof dish.

Meanwhile make a cheese sauce, heat the remaining butter in a pan, blend in the flour and cook over a gentle heat for 1 minute. Gradually stir in the milk and bring to the boil, stirring constantly. Cook for 2 minutes. Stir in all but 15 g./1/2 oz. (1 tablespoon) of the cheese; do not cook again. Poach the eggs lightly and place side by side on the spinach. Add the cream to the cheese sauce and pour over the spinach and eggs; sprinkle with the remaining cheese. Put the dish in the centre of the preheated oven and bake for 10–15 minutes, until golden. Alternatively, brown under the grill (broiler). Garnish with tomato slices.

Eggs au gratin

Metric/Imperial	American
4 eggs	4 eggs
25 g./1 oz. butter or margarine	2 tablespoons butter or margarine
25 g./1 oz. flour	¼ cup flour
300 ml./½ pint milk	1¼ cups milk
salt and pepper	salt and pepper
100 g./4 oz. grated cheese	1 cup grated cheese
2 tablespoons dry breadcrumbs	2½ tablespoons dry breadcrumbs

Serves 2

Boil (cook) the eggs; these can be firmly set or hard boiled (hard cooked), according to personal taste. Plunge into cold water to cool, crack the shells, then remove these. Heat the butter or margarine in a pan, stir in the flour and cook for 1 minute. Gradually stir in the milk and bring to the boil, then cook until the sauce has thickened. Season well, stir in most of the grated cheese. Do not continue cooking after the cheese has melted. Arrange the whole or halved eggs in a dish; top with the cheese sauce. Sprinkle the remaining cheese and the breadcrumbs on top and brown under the grill (broiler).

Helpful hints

Do not freeze this dish as the eggs would be rubbery when thawed.

Pissaladière

Metric/Imperial	American
olive oil for frying	olive oil for frying
2 large onions, sliced	2 large onions, sliced
1 garlic clove, crushed with ½ teaspoon salt	1 garlic clove, crushed with ½ teaspoon salt
1 tablespoon tomato purée	1¼ tablespoons tomato paste
1 tablespoon chopped fresh basil or ½ teaspoon dried basil	1¼ tablespoons chopped fresh basil or ½ teaspoon dried basil
1 teaspoon sugar	1 teaspoon sugar
freshly ground black pepper	freshly ground black pepper
shortcrust pastry flan case	shortcrust pastry pie shell
50 g./2 oz. grated Gruyère or Cheddar cheese	½ cup grated Swiss or Cheddar cheese
1 × 50 g./2 oz. can anchovies in olive oil, drained and soaked in milk for 30 minutes	1 × 2 oz. can anchovies in olive oil, drained and soaked in milk for 30 minutes
25 g./1 oz. black olives, stoned	2 tablespoons black olives, pitted

Serves 4–6

Oven setting: 190°C./375°F./Gas Mark 5

Heat 2 tablespoons of oil in a frying pan (skillet). Add the onions and garlic and fry gently until golden. Stir in the tomato purée (paste), basil, sugar and pepper to taste. Stir well, and bring to the boil. Cool slightly, then transfer to the flan case (pie shell). Sprinkle with the cheese, then arrange drained anchovies in a lattice pattern on top. Put halved olives in each 'window' of the lattice.

Bake in the preheated oven for 25–30 minutes, or until the pastry is golden brown.

Helpful hints

A 225 g./8 oz. can of drained tomatoes may be added, with the tomato purée (paste), to accentuate the tomato flavour.

SNACKS

Cold cheese soufflé

Metric/Imperial	American
3 eggs	3 eggs
aspic jelly to set 450 ml./¾ pint	1 envelope unflavoured gelatin
300 ml./½ pint boiling water	1¼ cups boiling water
150 ml./¼ pint double cream	⅔ cup heavy cream
150 ml./¼ pint single cream (or use all double cream)	⅔ cup light cream (or use all heavy cream)
100 g./4 oz. very finely grated Cheddar or Gruyère cheese	1 cup very finely grated Cheddar or Swiss cheese
salt and pepper	salt and pepper
Garnish	Garnish
gherkins	gherkins
radishes	radishes
tomatoes	tomatoes

Serves 6–8

Tie a band of greaseproof paper round a medium soufflé dish, to stand about 5 cm./2 inches above the rim.

Separate the egg whites from the yolks and put the yolks into a bowl. Soften and then dissolve the aspic jelly (gelatin) in the water. Beat on to the egg yolks and continue beating until blended. Allow to cool and begin to stiffen slightly. Meanwhile, beat the double (heavy) cream until it is stiff, then gradually beat in the single (light) cream, cheese and seasoning. Fold into the aspic jelly (gelatin) mixture. Lastly fold in the stiffly beaten egg whites. Spoon into the prepared soufflé dish and allow to set. Remove the band of paper and garnish with pieces of gherkin, radish and tomato.

Note The amount of aspic (gelatin) gives a very lightly set soufflé which is ideal, but it must be given adequate time to set. If worried about the time then use enough aspic to set 600 ml./1 pint (2½ cups).

Store cupboard omelette

Metric/Imperial	American
1 can asparagus spears	1 can asparagus spears
1 can diced potatoes	1 can diced potatoes
1–2 tablespoons oil	1¼–2½ tablespoons oil
25–50 g./1–2 oz. Cheddar cheese, diced	¼–½ cup Cheddar cheese, diced
3 eggs	3 eggs
salt and pepper	salt and pepper
1 tablespoon water	1¼ tablespoons water
25 g./1 oz. butter	2 tablespoons butter
parsley to garnish	parsley to garnish

Serves 2

Open the cans, cut the tips from the asparagus spears. Chop the stalks. Heat the tips and put to one side for garnish. Fry the drained diced potatoes in hot oil until golden, drain. Mix the chopped asparagus stalks, fried potatoes and cheese.

Beat the eggs with the seasoning and water very lightly. Heat the butter in a 15 cm./6 inch omelette pan (skillet). Pour in the eggs and leave for about ½–1 minute until set at the bottom, then loosen the eggs from the side of the pan, tilting this at the same time. Continue working the omelette until it is just set, or even a little liquid in the centre. Add the potato mixture. Fold away from the handle and slide on to a hot plate. Garnish with hot asparagus tips and parsley.

Helpful hints

As alternatives to asparagus and potatoes, use canned diced mixed vegetables, shrimps (omitting the cheese), sliced mushrooms and a little chopped cooked meat. Heat through thoroughly and flavour with sautéed, chopped onion.

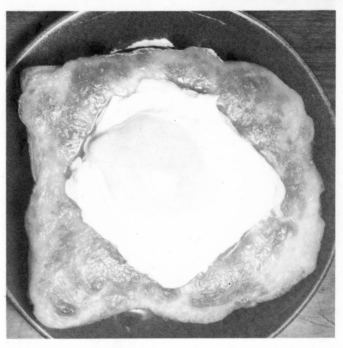

Harlequin soufflé omelette

Metric/Imperial	American
6–8 eggs	6–8 eggs
225 g./8 oz. cottage cheese	1 cup cottage cheese
salt and pepper	salt and pepper
1 tablespoon chopped parsley	1¼ tablespoons chopped
1–2 tablespoons chopped chives	parsley
or spring onions	1¼–2½ tablespoons chopped
50 g./2 oz. butter	chives or scallions
	4 tablespoons butter
Topping	
slices of red pepper or tomato	Topping
and green pepper	slices of red pepper or tomato
	and green pepper

Serves 4

Separate the egg whites from the yolks. Beat the yolks with the cottage cheese and seasoning until smooth and well blended. Add the parsley and chives or spring onions (scallions). Fold in the stiffly beaten egg whites. Heat the butter in a very large frying pan (skillet). Pour in the egg mixture. Cook steadily for about 5–6 minutes, then put the pan under a medium grill (broiler) and cook for a further 3–4 minutes until set. Slip out of the pan (do not try to fold) on to a hot plate. Top with slices of red pepper, or tomato and green pepper.

Helpful hints

A soufflé omelette is excellent served as a sweet, with a jam or fruit topping.

Buck rarebit

Metric/Imperial	American
275 g./10 oz. Cheddar cheese	10 oz. Cheddar cheese
65 g./2½ oz. butter	5 tablespoons butter
5 eggs	5 eggs
salt and pepper	salt and pepper
2 tablespoons beer or milk	2½ tablespoons beer or milk
1 teaspoon made mustard	1 teaspoon made mustard
4 slices bread	4 slices bread

Serves 4

Grate the cheese and blend with half the butter, 1 egg, the seasoning, beer or milk and the mustard. Toast the bread and spread with the rest of the butter and the cheese mixture. Toast under the grill (broiler) while poaching the remaining 4 eggs. Lift the eggs on to the cheese mixture and serve at once.

Helpful hints

For a stiffer topping, use the egg yolk only and 1 tablespoon beer or milk.

SNACKS

Piperade

Metric/Imperial
100 g./4 oz. butter
1 green pepper, cored, seeded
* and chopped*
1 red pepper, cored, seeded and
* chopped*
3 medium-sized onions, sliced
4 tomatoes, chopped
2 garlic cloves, crushed
10 eggs, beaten
salt and pepper

American
½ cup butter
1 green pepper, cored, seeded
* and chopped*
1 red pepper, cored, seeded and
* chopped*
3 medium-sized onions, sliced
4 tomatoes, chopped
2 garlic cloves, crushed
10 eggs, beaten
salt and pepper

Serves 4
Heat the butter in a pan. Add the peppers, onions, tomatoes and garlic. Cook gently, stirring occasionally for 10 minutes or until tender. Add the seasoned eggs and scramble until lightly set. Serve with crusty French bread or with crisp toast.

Cheese kebabs

Metric/Imperial
½ kg./1 lb. Edam or Gouda
* cheese*
12 small mushrooms
8 small, firm tomatoes
1 large green pepper, cored,
* seeded and chopped*
8 small onions, cooked
melted butter

American
1 lb. Edam or Gouda cheese
12 small mushrooms
8 small, firm tomatoes
1 large green pepper, cored,
* seeded and chopped*
8 small onions, cooked
melted butter

Serves 4
Cut the cheese into 2.5 cm./1 inch cubes. Thread cheese on to skewers, alternating with mushrooms, tomatoes, pepper and onions. Brush with melted butter and cook for a few minutes under a hot grill (broiler).

Helpful hints
For cheese and fruit kebabs, replace the vegetables with orange segments, banana slices and pieces of apple.

Swiss fondue

Metric/Imperial
1 garlic clove, halved
450 ml./¾ pint dry white wine
1 teaspoon lemon juice
350 g./12 oz. Emmenthal
  cheese, grated
350 g./12 oz. Gruyère cheese,
  grated
2 teaspoons cornflour
3 tablespoons Kirsch
white pepper
black pepper
cayenne
grated nutmeg
paprika

American
1 garlic clove, halved
2 cups dry white wine
1 teaspoon lemon juice
6 cups grated Swiss cheese
2 teaspoons cornstarch
4 tablespoons Kirsch
white pepper
black pepper
cayenne
grated nutmeg
paprika

Serves 4
Rub the inside of a fondue pot with garlic. Put in the wine and lemon juice and heat over a low flame. Add the cheese gradually, stirring all the time using a figure-of-eight motion. When the mixture bubbles, add the cornflour (cornstarch) blended smoothly with the Kirsch and cook for about 3 minutes. Add pepper, cayenne, nutmeg and paprika to taste. Serve with cubes of French bread.

Cheese fondue

Metric/Imperial
1 garlic clove, halved
350 ml./12 fl. oz. dry white
  wine
½ kg./1 lb. Gruyère cheese,
  grated
1 teaspoon arrowroot
2 tablespoons Kirsch
1 tablespoon butter

American
1 garlic clove, halved
1½ cups dry white wine
4 cups grated Swiss cheese
1 teaspoon arrowroot flour
2½ tablespoons Kirsch
1¼ tablespoons butter

Serves 2–3
Rub the inside of a fondue pot with the garlic. Add the wine, heat for a minute then add the cheese. Stir continuously over moderate heat until the fondue thickens. Mix the arrowroot smoothly with the Kirsch and stir into the mixture. Add the butter and stir until it has melted. Serve with cubes of French bread.

SNACKS

Fondue with herbs

Metric/Imperial	American
1 garlic clove, halved	1 garlic clove, halved
150 ml./¼ pint dry white wine	⅔ cup dry white wine
½ kg./1 lb. Gouda cheese, grated	4 cups grated Gouda cheese
3 teaspoons cornflour	3 teaspoons cornstarch
2 tablespoons Kirsch	2½ tablespoons Kirsch
1 teaspoon finely chopped parsley	1 teaspoon finely chopped parsley
½ teaspoon finely chopped tarragon	½ teaspoon finely chopped tarragon
black pepper	black pepper
pinch of grated nutmeg	pinch of grated nutmeg

Serves 4

Rub the inside of a fondue pot with garlic. Put in the wine, heat a little then add the cheese gradually and stir until it has melted and the mixture begins to bubble. Add the cornflour (cornstarch), blended smoothly with the Kirsch, parsley, tarragon, black pepper and nutmeg. Allow it to bubble for a minute or so. Serve with cubes of French bread.

Scampi fondue

Metric/Imperial	American
1 kg./2 lb. prawns, shelled	2 lb. shrimp, peeled
cornflour	cornstarch
2 eggs	2 eggs
1 teaspoon soy sauce	1 teaspoon soy sauce
breadcrumbs	breadcrumbs
vegetable oil	vegetable oil

Serves 4

Coat the prawns (shrimp) with cornflour (cornstarch), shaking off any excess. Lightly beat the eggs and stir in the soy sauce. Dip the prawns (shrimp) in the egg and coat with breadcrumbs. Press with the palm of the hand to flatten a little. Heat the oil until it is hot enough to turn a stale bread cube golden brown in 30 seconds (190°C./375°F. on a deep-fat thermometer). Spear a prawn (shrimp) on to a fork and cook for 1 minute in the oil. Serve with sauces of your choice.

Fondue bourguignonne

Metric/Imperial
1 kg./2 lb. fillet steak
vegetable oil
1 bay leaf
Bearnaise sauce
tartare sauce
curry sauce
French mustard
salt and pepper

American
2 lb. fillet steak
vegetable oil
1 bay leaf
Bearnaise sauce
tartare sauce
curry sauce
French mustard
salt and pepper

Serves 4
Remove any fat and sinew from the steak, then cut into 2.5 cm./1 inch cubes. Fill a fondue pot two thirds full of oil. Add the bay leaf. Heat the oil until it is hot enough to turn a stale bread cube golden brown in 30 seconds (190°C./375°F. on a deep-fat thermometer). Each guest spears a cube of meat on to a fork and then lowers it in the hot oil to cook it. Dip cooked meat in sauces, mustard or seasoning.

Cheese soufflé

Metric/Imperial
25 g./1 oz. butter
25 g./1 oz. flour
150 ml./¼ pint milk
½ teaspoon salt
pinch of cayenne pepper
¼ teaspoon dry mustard
4 eggs, separated
75 g./3 oz. cheese, grated

American
2 tablespoons butter
¼ cup flour
⅔ cup milk
½ teaspoon salt
pinch of cayenne pepper
¼ teaspoon dry mustard
4 eggs, separated
¾ cup grated cheese

Serves 4 as a main dish or 6 as a savoury
Oven setting: 190–200°C./375–400°F./Gas Mark 5–6
Melt the butter in a large pan, stir in the flour and cook for a minute or two. Gradually blend in the milk, stirring all the time with a wooden spoon. Cook until the sauce is thick, then add the seasonings. Remove from the heat and add the egg yolks, then the cheese. Whisk the egg whites until stiff, then fold them into the mixture. Put the mixture in a greased soufflé dish and cook in the centre of the oven for about 30 minutes. Serve immediately.

SNACKS

Cheese and tomato medley

Metric/Imperial	American
2 onions, chopped	2 onions, chopped
1 garlic clove, crushed	1 garlic clove, crushed
50 g./2 oz. butter	¼ cup butter
225 g./8 oz. bacon, chopped	8 oz. bacon, chopped
100 g./4 oz. mushrooms, sliced	1 cup sliced mushrooms
1 × 400 g./14 oz. can tomatoes	1 × 14 oz. can tomatoes
½ kg./1 lb. small potatoes, peeled, cooked and sliced	1 lb. small potatoes, peeled, cooked and sliced
salt and pepper	salt and pepper
175 g./6 oz. Edam cheese, grated	1½ cups grated Edam cheese

Serves 4

Cook the onions and garlic in the butter until quite soft. Add the bacon and mushrooms and cook, stirring for 10 minutes. Add the tomatoes, their can juice, potatoes and seasoning. Stir well and cook for a further 3 minutes. Stir in most of the cheese and as soon as it melts, it is ready to serve. Sprinkle the rest of the cheese on top.

French onion tart

Metric/Imperial	American
225 g./8 oz. shortcrust pastry dough, made with wholemeal flour	2 cups shortcrust pastry dough, made with wholemeal flour
50 g./2 oz. butter	¼ cup butter
1 tablespoon oil	1¼ tablespoons oil
1 kg./2 lb. onions, thinly sliced	2 lb. onions, thinly sliced
salt and pepper	salt and pepper
grated nutmeg	grated nutmeg
2 eggs	2 eggs
150 ml./¼ pint double cream	⅔ cup heavy cream

Serves 6

Oven setting: 190–200°C./375–400°F./Gas Mark 5–6

Line a 20 cm./8 inch flan tin (pan) with pastry.

Melt the butter and oil in a frying pan (skillet). Cook the onions, covered, until they are soft. They must not brown. Keep stirring to avoid sticking; they will take about 30 minutes. Season with salt, pepper and nutmeg.

Cool the onions then stir in the well beaten eggs and cream. Pour the filling into the pastry case (pie shell), cook in the centre of the oven for 35–45 minutes or until set. Leave to stand 5 minutes before serving.

Eggs en cocotte

Metric/Imperial
butter for greasing
salt and pepper
4 eggs
4 teaspoons melted butter
4 teaspoons single cream

American
butter for greasing
salt and pepper
4 eggs
4 teaspoons melted butter
4 teaspoons light cream

Serves 4

Oven setting: 180°C./350°F./Gas Mark 4
Use individual ovenproof cocotte dishes, 1 egg to a very small dish, or use a larger dish which will hold 2 eggs, or one good-sized ovenproof dish which will hold 4 eggs. Grease dishes liberally with butter and sprinkle with salt and pepper. Break eggs into dishes. Pour melted butter and cream over the top. Stand dishes in a baking dish of hot water and place in the oven for 8–10 minutes. Eggs continue cooking after the dishes are removed from the oven, so do not overcook.

Helpful hints

Before putting eggs into greased dishes, put in 2 teaspoons of chopped ham or lightly sautéed mushrooms per egg.

Smoked haddock and cheese flan

Metric/Imperial
225 g./8 oz. smoked haddock
150 ml./¼ pint water
juice of ½ lemon
25 g./1 oz. butter
1 small onion, finely chopped
50 g./2 oz. mushrooms, chopped
20 cm./8 inch pastry flan case, baked
2 eggs, beaten
6 tablespoons single cream
100 g./4 oz. cottage cheese
1 tablespoon chopped parsley
salt and pepper

American
8 oz. smoked haddock
⅔ cup water
juice of ½ lemon
2 tablespoons butter
1 small onion, finely chopped
½ cup chopped mushrooms
8 inch pastry pie shell, baked
2 eggs, beaten
½ cup light cream
½ cup cottage cheese
1¼ tablespoons chopped parsley
salt and pepper

Serves 4–6

Oven setting: 180–190°C./350–375°F./Gas Mark 4–5
Poach the haddock in a pan with the water and half the lemon juice. Drain, discard the skin and bones and flake the fish. Melt the butter in a pan, cook the onion for a few minutes then add the mushrooms and continue cooking for 4 minutes. Mix the fish and vegetables and spread over the base of the flan case. Beat the eggs, add the cream, cheese, remaining lemon juice and parsley. Season lightly. Pour over the fish mixture. Bake in the centre of the oven, for 30–35 minutes until set and golden.

Helpful hints

To economize use milk instead of cream, and inexpensive white fish, herrings or kippers in place of the haddock. Use leftover dry cheese, grated finely, in place of cottage cheese.

SNACKS

Spanish omelette

Metric/Imperial	American
2 tablespoons oil	2½ tablespoons oil
1 small onion, finely chopped	1 small onion, finely chopped
1 garlic clove, crushed	1 garlic clove, crushed
3 small potatoes, peeled, cooked and diced	3 small potatoes, peeled, cooked and diced
1 red pepper, cored, seeded and diced	1 red pepper, cored, seeded and diced
1 large tomato, skinned, seeded and diced	1 large tomato, skinned, seeded and diced
3 tablespoons cooked peas	4 tablespoons cooked peas
3 eggs	3 eggs
½ teaspoon Tabasco sauce	½ teaspoon Tabasco sauce
salt and pepper	salt and pepper
pinch of mixed herbs	pinch of mixed herbs

Serves 2

Heat half the oil in a pan and fry the onion and garlic until soft. Add the remaining oil, heat, then stir in the rest of the vegetables and heat thoroughly. Meanwhile, beat the eggs lightly, add Tabasco sauce and seasoning and pour into the pan over the vegetables. Stir lightly, then leave until the eggs are just set. Sprinkle with herbs just before serving.

Artichoke omelette

Metric/Imperial	American
4 canned or fresh artichoke hearts	4 canned or fresh artichoke hearts
50 g./2 oz. butter	¼ cup butter
6 eggs	6 eggs
2 tablespoons water	2½ tablespoons water
salt and pepper	salt and pepper
2 tablespoons grated Parmesan cheese	2½ tablespoons grated Parmesan cheese

Serves 1

Cut the artichoke hearts into quarters and fry gently in half the butter while preparing the omelette.

Beat the eggs lightly with water and salt and pepper to taste. Heat the rest of the butter to sizzling point in a 20 cm./8 inch omelette pan, keeping the heat fairly high. Pour in the egg mixture. Draw the edges towards the centre with a knife, at the same time tilting the pan in all directions so that the uncooked egg flows back to the edges and gets cooked (about 1 minute).

Arrange the artichoke hearts on one half of the omelette, sprinkle with cheese then fold the omelette over. Slide out on to a warm plate and serve straight away.

Kidneys with spring onions (scallions) and cauliflower

Metric/Imperial	American
4 lambs' kidneys, cored and sliced	4 lambs' kidneys, cored and sliced
2 tablespoons sherry	2½ tablespoons sherry
1 small cauliflower, in florets	1 small cauliflower, in florets
2 tablespoons oil	2½ tablespoons oil
4 spring onions, cut into lengths	4 scallions, cut into lengths
1 tablespoon cornflour	1¼ tablespoons cornstarch
1 tablespoon soy sauce	1¼ tablespoons soy sauce
1 teaspoon brown sugar	1 teaspoon brown sugar
1 teaspoon salt	1 teaspoon salt

Serves 3–4

Soak the kidneys in the sherry. Cook the cauliflower in boiling salted water for 3 minutes, then drain. Heat the oil in a frying pan (skillet) and fry the drained kidneys and cauliflower with the spring onions (scallions) for 2 minutes. Mix the cornflour (cornstarch) to a smooth paste with the soy sauce, 2 tablespoons water, the sugar, the remaining sherry and the salt. Add to the pan and cook gently for 3 minutes, stirring constantly.

Helpful hints

To prepare lambs' kidneys for cooking, first remove the membrane. Slice in half lengthwise and cut out the hard white core from the centre. Then slice or cook whole as required by the recipe.

Liver and steak casserole

Metric/Imperial	American
225 g./8 oz. lamb's liver	8 oz. lamb's liver
½ kg./1 lb. stewing steak	1 lb. chuck steak
25 g./1 oz. flour	¼ cup flour
salt and pepper	salt and pepper
50 g./2 oz. margarine or dripping	4 tablespoons margarine or dripping
600 ml./1 pint brown stock	2½ cups brown stock
1 tablespoon tomato purée	1¼ tablespoons tomato paste
2 teaspoons Worcestershire sauce	2 teaspoons Worcestershire sauce
8 small onions	8 small onions
100 g./4 oz. button mushrooms	1 cup button mushrooms
chopped parsley	chopped parsley

Serves 4–6

Cut the liver and steak into small pieces. Coat in the flour, seasoned with salt and pepper and fry in the margarine or dripping. Gradually add the stock, tomato purée (paste) and Worcestershire sauce. Cover the pan and simmer for about 1½ hours.

Add the peeled onions, and the mushrooms, then continue cooking for a further ¾–1 hour, or until the steak is tender. Top with chopped parsley.

Helpful hints

Add a little brown sugar and orange juice to the stock in this recipe for a sweeter flavour.

OFFAL

Fried sweetbreads

Metric/Imperial	American
½ kg./1 lb. lambs' or calf's sweetbreads	1 lb. lambs' or calf's sweetbreads
300 ml./½ pint chicken stock	1¼ cups chicken stock
juice of ½ lemon	juice of ½ lemon
salt and pepper	salt and pepper
25 g./1 oz. flour	¼ cup flour
1 egg	1 egg
2 tablespoons water	2½ tablespoons water
50–75 g./2–3 oz. dry breadcrumbs	⅔–1 cup dried breadcrumbs
oil, or butter and oil, see method	oil, or butter and oil, see method
lemon slices	lemon slices

Serves 4

Soak the sweetbreads in cold water for at least 1 hour. Drain, then put into a pan with fresh cold water to cover. Bring the water to the boil, drain. (This is known as 'blanching' the sweetbreads and it whitens them.) Return the sweetbreads to the pan with the stock, lemon juice and seasoning. Simmer steadily for 10–15 minutes. Lift the sweetbreads from the liquid. This could be used as the basis for a brown sauce to serve with the sweetbreads. Allow the meat to cool and drain well, remove skin and gristle. Coat in flour, seasoned with salt and pepper. Beat the egg with the water, dip the sweetbreads in this, then in the breadcrumbs to cover thoroughly. Either deep-fry in hot oil for 5–6 minutes, or shallow fry in a mixture of butter and oil (use about 50 g./2 oz. (¼ cup) butter and 1 tablespoon oil). Turn the sweetbreads as they shallow fry. Drain on absorbent paper.

Tripe French-style

Metric/Imperial	American
700 g.–1 kg./1½–2 lb. tripe	1½–2 lb. tripe
2–3 onions	2–3 onions
2–3 carrots	2–3 carrots
50–100 g./2–4 oz. mushrooms	½–1 cup mushrooms
1 garlic clove (optional)	1 garlic clove (optional)
1½–2 tablespoons oil	2–2½ tablespoons oil
1 tablespoon flour	1¼ tablespoons flour
300 ml./½ pint stock	1¼ cups stock
salt and pepper	salt and pepper
4 tablespoons cream	5 tablespoons cream
1–2 tablespoons brandy or sherry	1¼–2½ tablespoons brandy or sherry

Serves 4–6

First cut the tripe into neat pieces, wash in cold water. Put into a saucepan and cover with cold water. Bring the water to the boil, then strain the tripe and discard the liquid.

Peel and slice the vegetables and garlic. Toss in the hot oil for a few minutes. Stir in the flour and cook for 2–3 minutes, then add the stock. Bring to the boil, add the tripe and seasoning. Cover the pan tightly and simmer for 40 minutes, or until tender. Blend the cream and brandy or sherry. Add to the tripe and heat *without* boiling for 5–6 minutes.

Helpful hints

Tripe is very easy to digest. The initial blanching ensures that the meat stays a good colour.

Liver and bacon provençale

Metric/Imperial	American
½ kg./1 lb. lambs' liver, sliced	1 lb. lambs' liver, sliced
50 g./2 oz. flour	½ cup flour
salt and pepper	salt and pepper
2 tablespoons oil	2½ tablespoons oil
225 g./8 oz. streaky bacon, chopped	8 oz. fatty bacon, chopped
2 large onions, chopped	2 large onions, chopped
1 × 425 g./15 oz. can tomatoes	1 × 15 oz. can tomatoes
½ teaspoon dried marjoram	½ teaspoon dried marjoram
1 bay leaf	1 bay leaf
1 tablespoon Worcestershire sauce	1¼ tablespoons Worcestershire sauce
450 ml./¾ pint stock	2 cups stock

Serves 4

Oven setting: 150°C./300°F./Gas Mark 2

Coat the liver with the flour, seasoned with salt and pepper. Heat the oil in a frying pan (skillet) and fry the liver for about 3 minutes on each side or until golden. Remove from the pan and place in a casserole. Fry the bacon and onions in the fat remaining in the pan until golden. Stir in any remaining flour. Add the tomatoes with the juice from the can, the marjoram, bay leaf and Worcestershire sauce. Stir in the stock, then pour over the liver in the casserole and mix well. Cover and cook for 1½ hours. Taste and adjust the seasoning and remove the bay leaf before serving.

Kidney kebabs with barbecue sauce

Metric/Imperial	American
8 small onions	8 small onions
4 rashers streaky bacon	4 slices fatty bacon
4 chipolatas	4 skinless sausages
4 lambs' kidneys, cored and halved	4 lambs' kidneys, cored and halved
1 teaspoon tomato purée	1 teaspoon tomato paste
1 teaspoon Worcestershire sauce	1 teaspoon Worcestershire sauce
1 tablespoon oil	1¼ tablespoons oil
Sauce	*Sauce*
15 g./½ oz. butter	1 tablespoon butter
1 onion, finely chopped	1 onion, finely chopped
150 ml./¼ pint tomato ketchup	⅔ cup tomato ketchup
2 tablespoons clear honey	2½ tablespoons clear honey
2 tablespoons lemon juice	2½ tablespoons lemon juice
salt and pepper	salt and pepper

Serves 4

Cook the peeled onions in boiling salted water for 4 minutes, drain. Cut off any rind from the bacon and stretch the rashers (slices) on a board, using the back of a knife. Cut each rasher (slice) in half and roll up. Halve the sausages. Put the onions, bacon rolls, kidneys and sausages on 4 skewers. Mix the tomato purée (paste) with the Worcestershire sauce and oil. Brush this all over the kebabs. Put under a preheated grill (broiler) and cook for 10 minutes, turning once and brushing with the Worcestershire sauce mixture during cooking.

Heat the butter for the sauce in a pan and fry the onion for 5 minutes. Add the remaining ingredients, bring to the boil and simmer for 5 minutes. Serve the kebabs with the sauce.

OFFAL

Kidneys bordelaise

Metric/Imperial
approx. 20 lambs' kidneys,
   cored and halved
40 g./1½ oz. flour
salt and pepper
good pinch of grated nutmeg
2 medium-sized onions
2 rashers bacon
50–75 g./2–3 oz. good
   dripping or butter
1 tablespoon chopped parsley
300 ml./½ pint brown stock
150 ml./¼ pint red wine
approx. 700 g./1½ lb. creamed
   potatoes
parsley

American
approx. 20 lambs' kidneys,
   cored and halved
6 tablespoons flour
salt and pepper
good pinch of grated nutmeg
2 medium-sized onions
2 slices bacon
4–6 tablespoons good dripping
   or butter
1¼ tablespoons chopped
   parsley
1¼ cups brown stock
⅔ cup red wine
approx. 1½ lb. creamed
   potatoes
parsley

Serves 5–6
Coat the kidneys in the flour, seasoned with salt, pepper and nutmeg. Slice the onions into thin rings, cut the bacon into narrow strips. Heat the dripping or butter in a pan, fry the onion rings and bacon gently for a few minutes, then add the kidneys and cook gently for 5 minutes, stirring well. Add the parsley, mix thoroughly, then gradually blend in the stock and wine. Bring the sauce to the boil, stir and cook until thickened. Cover the pan and simmer for about 15 minutes.

   Meanwhile, pipe the creamed potatoes on to a heatproof serving dish, brown under the grill (broiler). Spoon the kidney mixture into the centre of the potatoes and garnish with parsley. Sliced pigs' kidneys may be used instead.

Sweet and sour liver

Metric/Imperial
½ kg./1 lb. lambs' liver
50 g./2 oz. butter
150 ml./¼ pint stock
1–2 tablespoons chutney
25 g./1 oz. raisins
½ tablespoon vinegar
salt and pepper

American
1 lb. lambs' liver
4 tablespoons butter
⅔ cup stock
1¼–2½ tablespoons chutney
2 tablespoons raisins
½ tablespoon vinegar
salt and pepper

Serves 4
Cut the liver into strips. Fry in the hot butter for 3 minutes only, then add the rest of the ingredients and simmer gently for 6–8 minutes.

Helpful hints
Liver is rich in iron and vitamins as well as protein — a valuable food — and cheap too.

Liver Normandy

Lemon garlic kidneys

Metric/Imperial
½ kg./1 lb. lambs' liver
25 g./1 oz. flour
salt and pepper
75 g./3 oz. butter
2 dessert apples, cored
1 large onion, thinly sliced
300 ml./½ pint dry cider
cooked rice or creamed potatoes

Garnish
black and green olives

American
1 lb. lambs' liver
¼ cup flour
salt and pepper
6 tablespoons butter
2 eating apples, cored
1 large onion, thinly sliced
1 ¼ cups dry cider
cooked rice or creamed potatoes

Garnish
black and green olives

Serves 4
Cut the liver into strips, coat with the flour, seasoned with salt and pepper. Heat half the butter in a pan and fry the liver for a few minutes only, put on one side. Heat the remainder of the butter and fry rings of apple and onion until golden brown. Add the cider and simmer until the apple and onion mixture is tender. Replace the liver and heat through. Serve in a border of cooked rice or creamed potatoes (instant mashed potato is very quick and ideal for this purpose). Garnish with a few black and green olives.

Helpful hints
To vary, use sliced tomatoes instead of apples and blend 1–2 teaspoons of paprika with the flour and seasoning. Serve with noodles.

Metric/Imperial
6 lambs' kidneys
salt and pepper
1 garlic clove, crushed
1 tablespoon olive oil
juice of ½ lemon

American
6 lambs' kidneys
salt and pepper
1 garlic clove, crushed
1 ¼ tablespoons olive oil
juice of ½ lemon

Serves 2
Skin and core the kidneys and cut into 1 cm./½ inch slices. Season with salt and pepper.
  Fry the kidneys and garlic in hot oil quickly, moving them around all the time, for 3–4 minutes. Do not overcook. Squeeze the lemon juice over the kidneys and remove from heat. Serve immediately on a bed of boiled rice.

OFFAL

Liver ragoût sicilienne

Metric/Imperial	American
550 g./1¼ lb. ox liver	1¼ lb. beef liver
25 g./1 oz. flour	¼ cup flour
salt and pepper	salt and pepper
3 medium-sized onions	3 medium-sized onions
50 g./2 oz. dripping or fat	4 tablespoons dripping or fat
1–2 garlic cloves, crushed	1–2 garlic cloves, crushed
300 ml./½ pint stock	1¼ cups stock
300 ml./½ pint cider or inexpensive red wine	1¼ cups cider or inexpensive red wine
generous tablespoon redcurrant jelly	1½ tablespoons redcurrant jelly
½ teaspoon grated lemon rind	½ teaspoon grated lemon rind
2–3 tablespoons green olives	2½–4 tablespoons green olives

Serves 4–5

Cut the liver into strips. Coat the strips in the flour, seasoned with salt and pepper. Cut the onions into rings. Heat the dripping or fat in a pan, toss the liver in this, lift out and fry the onion rings and garlic for a few minutes. Gradually blend in the stock and cider or wine, bring to the boil and cook until slightly thickened. Add the jelly and lemon rind. Replace the strips of liver, put a lid on the pan and simmer very slowly for about 2 hours. Add the olives just before serving.

Helpful hints

Choose calves' liver for the most delicate flavour; lambs' or pigs' liver for tenderness. Ox liver is coarser and needs longer, slower cooking, as in this ragoût.

Veal kidney with Marsala

Metric/Imperial	American
½ kg./1 lb. veal kidney, cored	1 lb. veal kidney, cored
1 tablespoon flour	1¼ tablespoons flour
salt and pepper	salt and pepper
butter	butter
1 onion, finely chopped	1 onion, finely chopped
1 garlic clove, crushed	1 garlic clove, crushed
100 g./4 oz. bacon, cut into fairly thick pieces	⅔ cup bacon, cut into fairly thick pieces
8–10 button mushrooms, sliced	8–10 button mushrooms, sliced
6 tablespoons Marsala	scant ½ cup Marsala
1 tablespoon brandy	1¼ tablespoons brandy

Serves 4

Wash the kidney and pat dry. Coat well with the flour, seasoned with salt and pepper.

Heat some butter in a pan, cook the onion and garlic until the onion is soft. Add the kidney and brown on both sides. Add the bacon and mushrooms, cook for a few minutes, then add any remaining flour and the Marsala. Bring to boiling point, then reduce the heat and cook very slowly until the kidney is tender — about 25-30 minutes. Add brandy and correct the seasoning before serving.

Helpful hints

Marsala, the famous fortified wine from Sicily, makes this a typically Italian dish.

Kidney kebabs with orange sauce

Metric/Imperial
8–12 skinned whole lambs'
  kidneys
salt and pepper
pinch of dried mixed herbs
12 mushrooms
12 small onions
4 rashers bacon
50 g./2 oz. butter, melted

American
8–12 skinned whole lambs'
  kidneys
salt and pepper
pinch of dried mixed herbs
12 mushrooms
12 small onions
4 slices bacon
¼ cup melted butter

Sauce
2 oranges
300 ml./½ pint brown stock
25 g./1 oz. cornflour
25 g./1 oz. butter
salt and pepper
½ teaspoon sugar

Sauce
2 oranges
1¼ cups brown stock
2 tablespoons cornstarch
2 tablespoons butter
salt and pepper
½ teaspoon sugar

Serves 4
First make the sauce. Thinly pare the rind from the oranges and simmer this in half the stock for about 5 minutes. Strain, return to the pan. Blend the cornflour (cornstarch) with the rest of the stock, add to the liquid in the pan with the juice of the oranges, butter, seasoning and sugar. Bring to the boil, cook gently and stir until thick and smooth.

Meanwhile, roll the kidneys in seasoning and herbs, put on to 4 metal skewers with the mushrooms, onions and halved bacon rashers (slices) in neat rolls. Brush with the melted butter and cook under a hot grill (broiler) for about 10 minutes. Turn several times during cooking, so the food cooks evenly. Serve on a bed of boiled rice with the orange sauce.

Chicken livers with prawns (shrimp) and broccoli

Metric/Imperial
225 g./8 oz. chicken livers
2 tablespoons cornflour
2 tablespoons oil
75 g./3 oz. mushrooms, sliced
1 spring onion, finely chopped
salt and pepper
350 g./12 oz. broccoli
100 g./4 oz. prawns, shelled
1 teaspoon cornflour
1 tablespoon soy sauce

American
8 oz. chicken livers
2½ tablespoons cornstarch
2½ tablespoons oil
¾ cup sliced mushrooms
1 scallion, finely chopped
salt and pepper
12 oz. broccoli
4 oz. peeled shrimp
1 teaspoon cornstarch
1¼ tablespoons soy sauce

Serves 2
Wash and dry the chicken livers, slice thinly and toss in the cornflour (cornstarch). Heat the oil and fry the livers for 1 minute. Wash and dry the mushrooms, add to the pan and cook for 1 minute. Add the onion to the pan with the salt and pepper. Mix well. Cook the broccoli in salted boiling water for 5 minutes. Drain and add to the pan with the prawns (shrimp).

Mix the cornflour (cornstarch) to a smooth paste with the soy sauce and 5 tablespoons (6 tablespoons) water. Add to the pan. Bring to the boil, stirring until slightly thickened. Cook for 3 minutes. Serve immediately.

LAMB

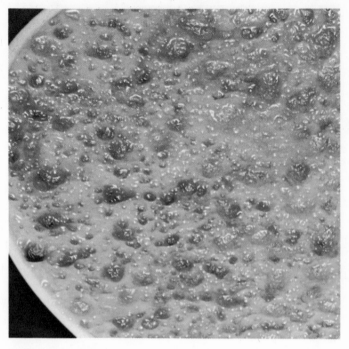

Cutlets indienne

Metric/Imperial
25 g./1 oz. margarine
1–2 teaspoons curry powder
pinch of cayenne pepper
8 lamb cutlets

Garnish
watercress or parsley

American
2 tablespoons margarine
1–2 teaspoons curry powder
pinch of cayenne pepper
8 lamb cutlets

Garnish
watercress or parsley

Serves 2
Melt the margarine, add the curry powder and pepper.
Brush the cutlets with the mixture and grill (broil) for 15
minutes, turning once during cooking. Garnish with
watercress or parsley.

Helpful hints
If you have no curry powder, blend your own from
coriander, cumin, turmeric, ginger, mace and pepper.

Moussaka

Metric/Imperial
1 kg./2 lb. aubergines, sliced
salt and pepper
100 ml./4 fl. oz. oil
½ kg./1 lb. boned lamb
 shoulder, minced
2 medium-sized onions,
 chopped
1 garlic clove, crushed
25 g./1 oz. flour
1 × 400 g./14 oz. can tomatoes
¼ teaspoon dried mixed herbs
2 tablespoons chopped parsley

Cheese sauce
25 g./1 oz. butter
25 g./1 oz. flour
300 ml./½ pint milk
100 g./4 oz. grated cheese
½ teaspoon made mustard
salt and pepper

American
2 lb. eggplants, sliced
salt and pepper
½ cup oil
1 lb. boned lamb shoulder,
 ground
2 medium-sized onions,
 chopped
1 garlic clove, crushed
¼ cup flour
1 × 14 oz. can tomatoes
¼ teaspoon dried mixed herbs
2½ tablespoons chopped
 parsley

Cheese sauce
2 tablespoons butter
¼ cup flour
1¼ cups milk
1 cup grated cheese
½ teaspoon made mustard
salt and pepper

Serves 4
Oven setting: 200°C./400°F./Gas Mark 6
Sprinkle the aubergines (eggplants) with salt and leave for
30 minutes. Drain and dry. Fry in three quarters of the oil
until brown on both sides. Remove from the pan and drain
well. Put the remaining oil in the pan, add the lamb and
brown. Add the onions and garlic and cook for 10 minutes.
Blend in the flour, about 1 teaspoon salt, pepper, tomatoes
and herbs. Arrange the aubergines (eggplants) and lamb
in layers in a buttered shallow ovenproof dish.
  To make the cheese sauce, heat the butter in a saucepan
and stir in the flour. Cook, stirring, for 1 minute.
Gradually add the milk, stirring constantly. Bring to the
boil, stirring, and simmer for 3 minutes or until the sauce
has thickened. Stir in three quarters of the cheese, the
mustard and seasoning. Pour the sauce into the dish and
sprinkle with the remaining cheese. Put into the preheated
oven for 20 minutes, or until the top is golden and bubbly.

Turkish lamb shanks

Metric/Imperial
2 lamb shanks
flour
4 tablespoons olive oil
1 onion, chopped
1 garlic clove, crushed
1 green pepper, cored, seeded
* and chopped*
1 teaspoon cumin seeds
1 teaspoon black peppercorns
1 × 425 ml./15 fl. oz. can
* tomato juice*
salt and pepper
juice of ½ lemon

American
2 lamb shanks
flour
5 tablespoons olive oil
1 onion, chopped
1 garlic clove, crushed
1 green pepper, cored, seeded
* and chopped*
1 teaspoon cumin seeds
1 teaspoon black peppercorns
1 × 15 fl. oz. can tomato juice
salt and pepper
juice of ½ lemon

Serves 4
Ask your butcher to chop through the bone in the lamb
shanks. Roll the shanks in a little flour. Heat the oil in a
heavy-based pan and lightly brown the lamb. Add the
onion and cook gently until the onion is soft. Add the
remaining ingredients. Cover the pan and simmer as
slowly as possible for at least 3 hours or until the meat is
falling off the bone.
   Serve hot, garnished with lemon wedges, accompanied
with boiled brown rice.

Simple cassoulet

Metric/Imperial
350 g./12 oz. stewing lamb
1 onion, sliced
1 tablespoon bacon fat
300 ml./½ pint stock
1 × 150 g./5 oz. can tomato
* purée*
175 g./6 oz. dried haricot
* beans, soaked overnight*
1 carrot, peeled and sliced
1 parsnip, peeled and sliced
1 stick celery, sliced
1 parsley sprig
pinch of dried thyme
1 bay leaf
freshly ground black pepper
salt

American
12 oz. stewing lamb
1 onion, sliced
1¼ tablespoons bacon fat
1¼ cups stock
1 × 5 oz. can tomato paste
1 cup dried white beans, soaked
* overnight*
1 carrot, peeled and sliced
1 parsnip, peeled and sliced
1 stick celery, sliced
1 parsley sprig
pinch of dried thyme
1 bay leaf
freshly ground black pepper
salt

Serves 4
Remove any excess fat from the meat and cut the meat into
cubes or serving portions, if chops or cutlets. Sauté the
lamb and onion in the heated fat in a heavy-based pan
until the meat is lightly browned and the onion is soft.
Pour in a little stock, then stir in the tomato purée (paste).
Add the remaining stock, the drained beans, carrot,
parsnip, celery, herbs, and a few grinds of black pepper.
Bring gently to the boil, cover and simmer gently for about
2 hours, or until the meat is very tender. Add salt to taste
and simmer gently for a further 30 minutes uncovered.
Serve hot.

LAMB

Crown roast of lamb

Metric/Imperial
2 × 8-chop best end of necks of lamb

Stuffing
350 g./12 oz. fresh breadcrumbs
6 tablespoons chopped fresh parsley
175 g./6 oz. shredded suet
6 teaspoons chopped fresh thyme
grated rind and juice of 3 lemons
3 eggs, beaten
salt and pepper

American
2 × 8-chop racks of lamb

Stuffing
6 cups fresh breadcrumbs
7 tablespoons chopped fresh parsley
1 cup shredded suet
6 teaspoons chopped fresh thyme
grated rind and juice of 3 lemons
3 eggs, beaten
salt and pepper

Serves 6–8
Oven setting: 200°C./400°F./Gas Mark 6
First make the stuffing. Blend together the breadcrumbs, parsley, suet and thyme. Stir in the lemon rind and juice and bind together with the eggs. Season with salt and pepper and mix well. Set aside. Cut off the chine bones from the meat. Trim meat and fat off the tips of the bones, leaving about 2.5 cm./1 inch of the bone exposed. Place the two best ends (racks) back to back, forming a circle with the fat in the middle, and tie with string. Put foil on the ends of the bones to stop them scorching. Spoon stuffing into the centre. Weigh and calculate cooking time; allow 35 minutes per ½ kg./1 lb. plus 35 minutes. Put into a roasting tin and cook for 20 minutes. Reduce oven temperature to 160°C./325°F./Gas mark 3 and continue cooking.

French lamb casserole

Metric/Imperial
700 g./1½ lb. stewing lamb
2 onions, quartered
25 g./1 oz. dripping
40 g./1½ oz. flour
600 ml./1 pint stock
1 teaspoon salt
¼ teaspoon white pepper
4 tablespoons tomato purée
1 garlic clove, finely chopped
1 bouquet garni
8 small pickling onions
25 g./1 oz. butter or margarine
100 g./4 oz. green peas
chopped parsley

American
1½ lb. stewing lamb
2 onions, quartered
2 tablespoons drippings
6 tablespoons flour
2½ cups stock
1 teaspoon salt
¼ teaspoon white pepper
5 tablespoons tomato paste
1 garlic clove, finely chopped
1 bouquet garni
8 small pearl onions
2 tablespoons butter or margarine
⅔ cup green peas
chopped parsley

Serves 4
Oven setting: 160–180°C./325–350°F./Gas Mark 3–4
Remove any excess fat from the meat and cut the meat into cubes or serving portions, if chops or cutlets. Gently fry the onions in the heated dripping in a heavy-based pan, until golden. Add the meat and fry until brown on all sides. Sprinkle the flour over the meat, stir and cook gently for 1 minute. Gradually blend in the stock, salt and pepper and bring to the boil, stirring occasionally. Add the tomato purée (paste), garlic and bouquet garni. Transfer to a casserole, cover with a tight-fitting lid and cook in the preheated oven for 1–1½ hours, or until the meat is tender.

Fry the onions, whole, in the butter or margarine until golden brown and add, with the peas, 20 minutes before the end of the cooking time. Serve sprinkled with chopped parsley.

Lemon and ginger chops

Metric/Imperial	American
4 tablespoons oil	5 tablespoons oil
grated rind of 1 lemon	grated rind of 1 lemon
2 tablespoons lemon juice	2 ½ tablespoons lemon juice
1 tablespoon brown sugar	1 ¼ tablespoons brown sugar
1 ½ teaspoons ground ginger	1 ½ teaspoons ground ginger
salt and pepper	salt and pepper
2 large or 4 small chump or loin chops	2 large or 4 small rib chops

Serves 2
Mix the oil, lemon rind, lemon juice, sugar, ginger and seasoning together. Place the chops in a shallow dish and pour the marinade over them. Leave for 2–3 hours, or up to 36 hours, turning occasionally. Remove the chops and place under a hot grill (broiler). Cook for 15 minutes, turning the chops once and basting them with the marinade.

Helpful hints
If using frozen chops, allow them to thaw in the marinade, in the refrigerator. They will absorb the flavour as they thaw.

Lamb in pastry

Metric/Imperial	American
2 kg./4 lb. leg of lamb	4 lb. leg of lamb
50 g./2 oz. butter	4 tablespoons butter
salt and pepper	salt and pepper
Pastry	Pastry
275 g./10 oz. plain flour	2 ½ cups all-purpose flour
¾ teaspoon salt	¾ teaspoon salt
65 g./2 ½ oz. butter	5 tablespoons butter
65 g./2 ½ oz. lard	5 tablespoons lard
approx. 10 teaspoons water	approx. 10 teaspoons water
Glaze	Glaze
1 egg, beaten with 1 teaspoon water	1 egg, beaten with 1 teaspoon water

Serves 8
Oven setting: 220°C./425°F./Gas Mark 7
Have the bone of the joint cut short and trim off any excess fat. Rub the joint with the butter and sprinkle it with salt and pepper. Place it in a roasting pan and roast in the preheated oven for 1¼ hours. Remove it from the oven and leave to cool.

Sift the flour and salt into a mixing bowl. Rub the fats into the flour until the mixture resembles fine breadcrumbs. Bind with the water to make a firm dough. Knead the pastry lightly on a floured surface. Roll out to a rectangle large enough to cover the lamb.

Wrap the lamb in the pastry with the join underneath. Return the joint to the roasting pan and decorate it with small leaves made from the pastry trimmings. Prick the pastry all over with a fork. Brush the pastry with the beaten egg. Reduce the oven setting to 190°C./375°F./Gas Mark 5 and bake the joint for a further 45 minutes.

LAMB

Grilled (broiled) lamb chops with apricots

Metric/Imperial	American
6 lamb chops	6 lamb chops
1 × 400 g./14 oz. can apricot halves	1 × 14 oz. can apricot halves
Marinade	Marinade
3 tablespoons oil	4 tablespoons oil
1 tablespoon red wine vinegar	1¼ tablespoons red wine vinegar
syrup from canned apricots	syrup from canned apricots
salt and pepper	salt and pepper
2 spring onions, coarsely chopped	2 scallions, coarsely chopped
parsley sprigs	parsley sprigs

Serves 6

Combine all the marinade ingredients and mix well. Pour the marinade into a shallow dish and add lamb chops. Marinate for 1 hour, basting occasionally.

Lift chops from marinade on to a rack in a grill (broiler) pan. Brush chops with the marinade. Arrange the apricot halves around the chops. Grill (broil) lamb under hot grill (broiler) for 5 minutes on both sides. Reduce the heat and cook for a further 5 minutes on each side or until tender. Serve chops with apricots.

Lamb cutlets in pastry case

Metric/Imperial	American
6 large lamb cutlets	6 large lamb cutlets
50 g./2 oz. butter	¼ cup butter
salt and pepper	salt and pepper
2 tomatoes, peeled, seeded and chopped	2 tomatoes, peeled, seeded and chopped
175 g./6 oz. mushrooms, finely chopped	1½ cups finely chopped mushrooms
100 g./4 oz. cooked ham, finely chopped	1 cup finely chopped cooked ham
1 tablespoon chopped parsley	1¼ tablespoons chopped parsley
400 g./14 oz. puff pastry dough	3½ cups puff pastry dough
2 egg yolks	2 egg yolks
2 tablespoons water	2½ tablespoons water

Serves 6

Oven setting: 220°C./425°F./Gas Mark 7

Dot the cutlets with half the butter, season with salt and pepper and grill (broil) on both sides until tender. Put tomatoes into a basin. Add the mushrooms, ham, parsley and seasoning. Melt the remaining butter, add to the mixture and blend well.

Roll out the pastry and cut out 6 rectangles, large enough to completely cover the cutlets. Put a spoonful of the ham mixture on each piece of pastry and place a cutlet on top. Top with another spoonful of ham mixture. Beat the egg yolks with the water and use to brush the edges of the pastry. Fold the pastry over so that each cutlet is completely enclosed. Place the cutlets, with the joins underneath, on a baking tray. Any trimmings left from the pastry can be rolled out and cut into diamond-shaped leaves for decoration. Brush all over the pastry with beaten egg and bake in the oven for about 20 minutes or until golden brown.

Stewed lamb with orange

Metric/Imperial	American
1 kg./2 lb. lamb	2 lb. lamb
1 tablespoon soy sauce	1¼ tablespoons soy sauce
1 tablespoon sherry	1¼ tablespoons sherry
1 teaspoon ground ginger	1 teaspoon ground ginger
2 tablespoons finely grated orange rind	2½ tablespoons finely grated orange rind
1 teaspoon salt	1 teaspoon salt
1¼ l./2 pints stock	5 cups stock
1 tablespoon cornflour	1¼ tablespoons cornstarch

Serves 4–6

Wipe the meat, then cut into dice. Mix the soy sauce, sherry, ginger, orange rind and salt together, add to the lamb and mix well. Put the lamb into a pan with the flavourings and stock. Bring to the boil, remove the scum, cover and simmer for 2 hours.

Mix the cornflour (cornstarch) to a smooth paste with a little cold water and add to the pan, bring back to the boil, stirring until slightly thickened. Serve immediately.

Speedy moussaka

Metric/Imperial	American
2 onions, chopped	2 onions, chopped
75 g./3 oz. fat	6 tablespoons fat
25 g./1 oz. flour	¼ cup flour
300 ml./½ pint stock	1¼ cups stock
½ kg./1 lb. minced beef or lamb	1 lb. ground beef or lamb
salt and pepper	salt and pepper
good pinch dried mixed herbs	good pinch dried mixed herbs
3 potatoes, peeled	3 potatoes, peeled
1 aubergine	1 eggplant
300 ml./½ pint full cream evaporated milk	1¼ cups full cream evaporated milk
175 g./6 oz. grated cheese	1½ cups grated cheese

Serves 4–6

Oven setting: 180–190°C./350–375°F./Gas Mark 4–5
Toss the onions in half the fat for a few minutes, then add the flour and cook for 2–3 minutes. Gradually blend in the stock, bring to the boil and cook until thickened. Add the meat, stirring very well to break up the lumps that form. Season, add the herbs; then bring the mixture to the boil. Lower the heat, cover the pan and allow to simmer for 35–40 minutes, stirring occasionally. Meanwhile, boil the potatoes in salted water, drain and slice fairly thickly. Slice the unpeeled aubergine (eggplant) thinly and toss in the remaining fat until tender. Put half the potatoes and half the sliced aubergine (eggplant) into a casserole, top with a third of the evaporated milk, cheese and seasoning. Add the meat mixture, another third of the milk, cheese and seasoning, then the rest of the aubergine (eggplant) and potato slices. Pour the remainder of the milk over the top very carefully and sprinkle with the last of the cheese. Season the mixture and put into the centre of the preheated oven for 30 minutes.

LAMB

Citrus lamb cutlets

Metric/Imperial	American
15 g./½ oz. melted butter	1 tablespoon melted butter
4 lamb cutlets	4 lamb cutlets
2 large oranges	2 large oranges

Serves 4

Brush the lamb cutlets all over with the melted butter.
Place the cutlets under the grill (broiler) and grill (broil) for
10–15 minutes or until tender.

While the cutlets are cooking, prepare the oranges. Peel
and remove any pith from the oranges. Using a sharp
knife, carefully cut into slices. A few minutes before the
meat is cooked, put the orange slices in the bottom of the
grill (broiler) pan to warm them through. Arrange the
lamb cutlets on a serving dish, with orange slices on top.

Lamb in yogurt sauce

Metric/Imperial	American
¾ kg./1½ lb. boned leg or shoulder of lamb	1½ lb. boned leg or shoulder of lamb
25 g./1 oz. butter	2 tablespoons butter
1 tablespoon oil	1¼ tablespoons oil
1 large onion, chopped	1 large onion, chopped
25 g./1 oz. flour	¼ cup flour
300 ml./½ pint stock	1¼ cups stock
salt and pepper	salt and pepper
1 tablespoon capers	1¼ tablespoons capers
2 pickled dill cucumbers, sliced	2 pickled dill cucumbers, sliced
grated rind of 1 lemon	grated rind of 1 lemon
1 tablespoon chopped parsley	1¼ tablespoons chopped parsley
300 ml./½ pint natural yogurt	1¼ cups plain yogurt

Serves 4

Oven setting: 160°C./325°F./Gas Mark 3

Cut the lamb into 2.5 cm./1 inch cubes. Heat the butter and
oil in a flameproof casserole and fry the onion gently for 5
minutes. Add the lamb to the casserole and fry for 3
minutes, stirring occasionally. Add the flour and cook for 1
minute. Add the stock and bring to the boil, stirring all the
time. Season with salt and pepper and add the capers, dill,
cucumbers, lemon rind and parsley. Cover the casserole
and cook for 1½ hours. Take the casserole out of the oven,
allow it to cool slightly, then stir in the yogurt. Put over a
very gentle heat to heat the yogurt, but do not allow the
sauce to boil. Taste and adjust the seasoning before
serving.

Barbecued beef satay

Metric/Imperial
1 kg./2 lb. rump steak
2 tablespoons soy sauce
1 tablespoon honey
2 garlic cloves, crushed
1 teaspoon ground coriander
1 teaspoon caraway seeds
¼ teaspoon chilli powder
2 tablespoons vegetable oil

American
2 lb. rump steak
2½ tablespoons soy sauce
1¼ tablespoons honey
2 garlic cloves, crushed
1 teaspoon ground coriander
1 teaspoon caraway seeds
¼ teaspoon chili powder
2½ tablespoons vegetable oil

Serves 6
Cut steak into 2.5 cm./1 inch cubes and place in a large bowl. Mix remaining ingredients together and pour over meat. Marinate for 1 hour, stirring occasionally. Thread meat on to six skewers. Cook under a hot grill (broiler), turning occasionally, for 10 minutes or until cooked to desired taste. Baste with marinade during cooking.

Meat loaf

Metric/Imperial
1 tablespoon margarine
50 g./2 oz. dried breadcrumbs
1 kg./2 lb. lean minced beef, or a mixture of beef and pork
1 medium-sized onion, finely chopped
1 teaspoon seasoned salt
½ teaspoon seasoned pepper
pinch of garlic salt
¼ teaspoon dried mixed herbs
2 tablespoons tomato purée
1 egg

American
1¼ tablespoons margarine
⅔ cup dried breadcrumbs
2 lb. lean ground beef, or a mixture of beef and pork
1 medium-sized onion, finely chopped
1 teaspoon seasoned salt
½ teaspoon seasoned pepper
pinch of garlic salt
¼ teaspoon dried mixed herbs
2½ tablespoons tomato paste
1 egg

Serves 6–8
Oven setting: 190°C./375°F./Gas Mark 5
Grease a 1 kg./2 lb. loaf pan with the margarine, then coat with some of the breadcrumbs. Put the remaining ingredients into a mixing bowl and mix well. Pack the mixture into the loaf pan. Bake in the preheated oven for 1¼ hours. Serve either hot or cold. If serving hot, allow to stand for 10 minutes before slicing.

Helpful hints
If you do not have any seasoned salt and pepper, use ordinary salt and pepper and add half a stock (bouillon) cube dissolved in 1 tablespoon boiling water to the beef.

BEEF

Pepperpot beef

Metric/Imperial
25 g./1 oz. flour
salt and pepper
½ teaspoon ground ginger
1 kg./2 lb. braising steak,
 cubed
50 g./2 oz. dripping
1 small red pepper, cored,
 seeded and sliced
1 × 425 g./15 oz. can red
 kidney beans

Sauce
1 teaspoon chilli sauce
1 × 225 g./8 oz. can tomatoes
100 g./4 oz. mushrooms, sliced
1 tablespoon Worcestershire
 sauce
2 tablespoons wine vinegar
2 garlic cloves, crushed
1 bay leaf

American
4 tablespoons flour
salt and pepper
½ teaspoon ground ginger
2 lb. chuck steak, cubed
¼ cup drippings
1 small red pepper, cored,
 seeded and sliced
1 × 15 oz. can red kidney beans

Sauce
1 teaspoon chili sauce
1 × 8 oz. can tomatoes
1 cup sliced mushrooms
1¼ tablespoons Worcestershire
 sauce
2½ tablespoons wine vinegar
2 garlic cloves, crushed
1 bay leaf

Serves 6
Oven setting: 160°C./325°F./Gas Mark 3
Mix together the flour, seasonings and ginger and use to
coat the beef. Heat the dripping in a large pan, add the beef
and fry quickly until browned, turning once. Drain on
kitchen paper then transfer to a 1.6 l./3 pint (7½ cup)
ovenproof dish.
   Combine all the ingredients for the sauce and pour over
the meat. Cover and cook for about 2 hours or until the
meat is tender. Add the red pepper and kidney beans 30
minutes before the end of the cooking time.

Stuffed fillet of beef

Metric/Imperial
3 onions, sliced
beef dripping
4 anchovy fillets, chopped
2 tablespoons finely chopped
 bacon
pinch of pepper
pinch of dried thyme
pinch of finely chopped parsley
1 egg yolk
1 kg./2 lb. beef fillet
watercress sprigs to garnish

American
3 onions, sliced
beef dripping
4 anchovy fillets, chopped
2½ tablespoons finely chopped
 bacon
pinch of pepper
pinch of dried thyme
pinch of finely chopped parsley
1 egg yolk
2 lb. beef fillet
watercress sprigs to garnish

Serves 4
Oven setting: 160°C./325°F./Gas Mark 3
Fry the onions in about 1 tablespoon dripping until golden
brown. Remove them from the pan and place them in a
mixing bowl. Add the anchovy fillets, bacon, pepper,
herbs and egg yolk to the onions and mix well. Cut the
fillet in about six places, but not right through. Put some of
the stuffing into each cavity and tie the fillet in shape with
string or secure with wooden cocktail sticks (picks). Wrap
in greased foil or place in a covered roasting pan with a
little dripping. Cook in the preheated oven for 1½ hours,
or until tender. Cut into thick slices to serve and garnish
with watercress sprigs.

Beef and vegetable stew

Metric/Imperial	American
25 g./1 oz. flour	¼ cup flour
salt and pepper	salt and pepper
800 g./1¾ lb. braising steak, cubed	1¾ lb. chuck steak, cubed
8 small onions	8 small onions
8 small carrots	8 small carrots
2 sticks celery	2 sticks celery
100 g./4 oz. small mushrooms	4 oz. small mushrooms
50 g./2 oz. dripping	¼ cup drippings
600 ml./1 pint brown stock	2½ cups brown stock
bouquet garni	bouquet garni
chopped parsley	chopped parsley

Serves 4

Blend the flour, salt and pepper. Roll the meat in the seasoned flour. Peel the onions and carrots but leave whole. Cut the celery into neat pieces. Wash the mushrooms but do not peel.

Heat the fat in a large pan. Toss the onions and meat in this for a few minutes, turning over and round until the meat is well coated with the fat. Stir in the liquid gradually. Bring to the boil and stir well until the liquid is smooth and slightly thickened. Add the rest of the vegetables, herbs and season to taste. Cover with a well-fitting lid. Simmer for 2¼–2½ hours.

Serve in a hot dish or casserole. Remove the bouquet garni and sprinkle with chopped parsley.

Forfar bridies

Metric/Imperial	American
550–700 g./1¼–1½ lb. stewing steak	1¼–1½ lb. chuck steak
butter	butter
salt and pepper	salt and pepper
3 large onions, diced	3 large onions, diced
½ kg./1 lb. flour	4 cups flour
pinch of salt	pinch of salt
175 g./6 oz. shredded suet	1 cup shredded suet
water	water

Serves 4

Oven setting: 220–230°C./425–450°F./Gas Mark 7–8

Cut the meat into thin strips about 2.5 cm./1 inch in length and 1 cm./½ inch wide. Spread a little butter on each strip and season well. Mix the diced onions with the meat strips, do not add stock or water.

Sift the flour and salt together, add the suet and mix to a soft rolling consistency with cold water. Roll out the pastry and cut it into four large ovals or rectangles. Divide the filling between these. Dampen the pastry edges, fold one half over, seal the edges and flute them. Bake in the preheated oven for 15 minutes then lower the oven setting to 160–180°C./325–350°F./Gas Mark 3–4 for just over 1 hour.

Helpful hints

Open freeze Forfar Bridies uncooked and wrap individually. Thaw for about 12 hours in the refrigerator before cooking.

BEEF

Beef stroganoff

Metric/Imperial	American
½ kg./1 lb. good quality stewing steak	1 lb. lean chuck steak
50 g./2 oz. butter	4 tablespoons butter
2 small onions, finely chopped	2 small onions, finely chopped
100 g./4 oz. mushrooms, sliced	1 cup sliced mushrooms
salt, black pepper and grated nutmeg	salt, black pepper and grated nutmeg
½ teaspoon dried basil	½ teaspoon dried basil
150 ml./¼ pint beef stock	⅔ cup beef stock
300 ml./½ pint soured cream	1¼ cups sour cream
2 tablespoons finely chopped parsley or chives	2½ tablespoons finely chopped parsley or chives

Serves 4

Cut the meat into thin slices and then into strips. Heat the butter in a pan, add the onions and sauté until soft. Add the meat and brown over fairly high heat. Reduce the heat and add the mushrooms, salt, pepper and nutmeg, basil and stock. Bring to the boil, then cover and simmer for about 45 minutes. Add the cream, check the seasoning and reheat but do not allow the mixture to boil at this stage. Sprinkle with parsley or chives.

Helpful hints

This is an excellent dish for entertaining as it can be prepared in advance and left simmering. Add the cream at the last minute and serve with rice and a salad.

Beef risotto milanese

Metric/Imperial	American
2 tablespoons oil	2½ tablespoons oil
2 onions, sliced and pushed into rings	2 onions, sliced and pushed into rings
2 garlic cloves, crushed	2 garlic cloves, crushed
½ kg./1 lb. minced beef	1 lb. ground beef
1 × 400 g./14 oz. can tomatoes	1 × 14 oz. can tomatoes
4 carrots, roughly chopped	4 carrots, roughly chopped
1 tablespoon tomato purée	1¼ tablespoons tomato paste
salt and pepper	salt and pepper
1 bay leaf	1 bay leaf
225 g./8 oz. long-grain rice	1 cup long-grain rice
water	water
salt	salt
parsley	parsley

Serves 4

Heat the oil in a pan. Toss the onions and garlic in the oil until the onions are transparent. Put a few rings on one side for garnish. Add the beef to the pan and stir well to break up any lumps. Add the tomatoes and their can juice, carrots, tomato purée (paste), seasoning and bay leaf. Cook gently in a covered pan for 45 minutes, stirring once or twice.

Put the rice and enough cold water to just cover into a saucepan with salt to taste. Bring to the boil, stir briskly then cover the pan. Lower the heat and cook for approximately 15 minutes until the rice is tender and the liquid absorbed. Fork the rice on to a hot dish. Spoon the beef mixture in the centre and garnish with onion rings and a sprig of parsley.

Corned beef plate tart

Metric/Imperial	American
2 × 350 g./12 oz. cans corned beef	2 × 12 oz. cans corned beef
2 medium-sized onions, chopped	2 medium-sized onions, chopped
1 tablespoon oil	1¼ tablespoons oil
salt and pepper	salt and pepper
1 teaspoon Tabasco sauce	1 teaspoon Tabasco sauce
1 egg	1 egg
2–3 diced cooked carrots	2–3 diced cooked carrots
100 g./4 oz. cooked peas	⅔ cup cooked peas
225 g./8 oz. shortcrust pastry, made with 225 g./8 oz. plain flour, etc.	2 cups shortcrust pastry, made with 2 cups all-purpose flour, etc.
1 egg, to glaze	1 egg, to glaze
parsley to finish	parsley to garnish

Serves 6

Oven setting: 200–220°C./400–425°F./Gas Mark 6–7
Flake the corned beef and put into a bowl. Toss the onions in the hot oil until soft, blend with the corned beef, add seasoning, Tabasco sauce, egg and vegetables. Roll out the pastry, use half to cover an 18–20 cm./7–8 inch pie plate or tin (deep pie plate or dish). Cover with the filling and the rest of the pastry. Decorate with leaves of pastry, made from the trimmings, and glaze with the beaten egg. Bake for 25–30 minutes in the centre of the preheated oven, then lower the oven setting to 180°C./350°F./Gas Mark 4 for a further 20–25 minutes. Serve hot or cold, garnished with parsley.

Boiled salt beef

Metric/Imperial	American
1 kg./2 lb. salt brisket	2 lb. corned beef
cold beef stock	cold beef stock
2 onions, chopped	2 onions, chopped
4 carrots, sliced	4 carrots, sliced
1 turnip, chopped	1 turnip, chopped
1 teaspoon black peppercorns	1 teaspoon black peppercorns
2 teaspoons dried mixed herbs	2 teaspoons dried mixed herbs

Serves 6

Cover the meat with cold water and soak overnight. Drain and discard the soaking water. Put meat in a pan and pour in enough cold stock to cover the meat. Choose a large pan, so the liquid can surround the meat; if the meat fits too tightly, the outside tends to be dry and the meat does not cook as evenly as it should. Add vegetables and seasonings. Cover pan and bring to simmering point. Reduce heat to very low and cook for 1½ hours. If serving hot, lift meat from the pan with the vegetables and serve with unthickened liquid. If serving the meat cold, allow it to cool in the liquid.

BEEF

Beef and ham pâté

Metric/Imperial	American
700 g./1½ lb. rump steak	1½ lb. round steak
225–350 g./8–12 oz. calf's liver	8–12 oz. calf's liver
½ kg./1 lb. cooked ham	2⅔ cups cooked ham
50 g./2 oz. butter or margarine	4 tablespoons butter or margarine
50 g./2 oz. flour	½ cup flour
150 ml./¼ pint brown stock	⅔ cup brown stock
300 ml./½ pint milk	1¼ cups milk
4–5 tablespoons double cream	5–6½ tablespoons heavy cream
2–3 tablespoons dry sherry	2½–4 tablespoons dry sherry
5 eggs	5 eggs
salt and pepper	salt and pepper
1–2 teaspoons chopped fresh herbs	1–2 teaspoons chopped fresh herbs

Serves 10–12
Oven setting: 160°C./325°F./Gas Mark 3
Mince (grind) the steak, liver and ham very finely. Make a fairly thick sauce with the butter or margarine, flour, stock and milk. Add the cream, sherry, 2 beaten eggs, plenty of seasoning and the herbs. Add all the meats and blend well. Hard boil (cook) 3 remaining eggs; shell. Put half the meat mixture into a large buttered mould, arrange the eggs on this, cover with the rest of the meat mixture, then with well buttered foil or greaseproof (waxed) paper. Stand in a pan of cold water and bake in the preheated oven for 1½ hours. Cool in the mould, then turn out just before serving.

Helpful hints
If you freeze this loaf, slice it first and divide the portions with waxed paper or foil — then just thaw as many portions as are required for eating and return the rest to the freezer.

Hamburgers

Metric/Imperial	American
1 kg./2 lb. minced rump or other good quality beef	2 lb. ground beef
2 eggs or 4 egg yolks	2 eggs or 4 egg yolks
salt and pepper	salt and pepper
pinch of mixed herbs	pinch of mixed herbs
flour	flour
fat for frying	fat for frying
rolls	rolls

Makes about 24
Oven setting: 200°C./400°F./Gas Mark 6
Mix the meat, eggs or egg yolks, seasoning and herbs together and form into about 24 small flat cakes. (If you flour your hands you can handle the meat mixture more easily.) Fry in a little hot fat for about 3 minutes on either side or bake on well greased baking sheets in the preheated oven for about 12 minutes. Serve on small toasted round rolls.

Helpful hints
The more finely hamburger meat is minced (ground) the better. Use the finest cutters and mince (grind) twice.

Braised beef whirls

Metric/Imperial	American
4 slices beef topside	4 slices round or rump steak
3 onions	3 onions
175 g./6 oz. ox kidney, cored	6 oz. beef kidney, cored
1 tablespoon chopped parsley	1¼ tablespoons chopped parsley
25 g./1 oz. margarine or shredded suet	2 tablespoons margarine or shredded suet
salt and pepper	salt and pepper
6 large carrots	6 large carrots
50 g./2 oz. fat	4 tablespoons fat
25 g./1 oz. flour	¼ cup flour
300 ml./½ pint brown stock or water and 1 beef stock cube	1¼ cups brown stock or water and 1 beef bouillon cube
Garnish	
chopped parsley	Garnish
	chopped parsley

Serves 4

Oven setting: 150°–160°C./300°–325°F./Gas Mark 2–3
Halve the slices of beef, chop 1 onion and the kidney finely. Mix the onion, kidney, chopped parsley, margarine or suet and seasoning together. Divide between the pieces of meat and roll up firmly. Secure with wooden cocktail sticks (picks) or string. Peel and slice the remaining onions and the carrots. Put into a casserole. Heat the fat in a pan. Coat the meat whirls in flour, seasoned with salt and pepper and toss in the hot fat until golden. Lift on top of the vegetables. Blend the brown stock or water and stock cube with the fat in the pan. Pour round the beef whirls. Cover the casserole and cook in the preheated oven for about 2 hours. Sprinkle with chopped parsley before serving.

Beef with celery and cabbage

Metric/Imperial	American
½ kg./1 lb. rump steak	1 lb. rump steak
1 teaspoon cornflour	1 teaspoon cornstarch
2 tablespoons oil	2½ tablespoons oil
2 sticks celery, finely chopped	2 sticks celery, finely chopped
4 spring onions, finely chopped	4 scallions, finely chopped
100 g./4 oz. white cabbage, finely shredded	1 cup finely shredded white cabbage
1 tablespoon soy sauce	1¼ tablespoons soy sauce
salt and pepper	salt and pepper

Serves 3–4

Wipe the meat and cut into paper thin slices. Mix the cornflour (cornstarch) to a smooth paste with about 2 tablespoons (2½ tablespoons) water, add to the beef and mix well until the beef is completely coated with the mixture. Heat the oil and fry the meat over a fierce heat, stirring all the time, for 3 minutes. Remove from the pan.

Add the vegetables to the remaining fat in the pan and fry gently for 5 minutes, stirring occasionally. Add the meat, soy sauce, salt and pepper, mix well and cook for 2–3 minutes. Serve immediately.

BEEF

Beef curry

Metric/Imperial
1 tablespoon ground coriander
1 teaspoon ground turmeric
½ teaspoon ground cumin
¼ teaspoon chilli powder
pinch of ground cinnamon
2 cloves
3 tablespoons vinegar
2 tablespoons vegetable oil
1 onion, chopped
1 garlic clove, crushed
½ kg./1 lb. beef topside, cubed
1 teaspoon salt
150 ml./¼ pint beef stock
1 bay leaf
orange wedges to garnish
boiled rice to serve

American
1¼ tablespoons ground
   coriander
1 teaspoon ground turmeric
½ teaspoon ground cumin
¼ teaspoon hot chili powder
pinch of ground cinnamon
2 cloves
4 tablespoons vinegar
2½ tablespoons vegetable oil
1 onion, chopped
1 garlic clove, crushed
1 lb. top round of beef, cubed
1 teaspoon salt
⅔ cup beef stock
1 bay leaf
orange wedges to garnish
boiled rice to serve

Serves 4
Mix and pound the spices with the vinegar to form a paste.
Heat the oil in a heavy pan and fry the onion and garlic
gently for 5 minutes. Add the curry paste and fry for 2–3
minutes, stirring constantly. Add the beef and cook
gently, stirring occasionally, until it browns. Add salt,
stock and bay leaf, cover and simmer for 1 hour. Remove
the bay leaf, taste the curry and adjust the seasoning if
necessary. Garnish with orange wedges. Serve with
boiled rice and chutney.

Helpful hints
For last minute adjustments to a curry dish, buy
ready-made curry sauce. Stir it in, a little at a time, to
strengthen the flavour as necessary.

Individual steak and kidney pies

Metric/Imperial
350 g./12 oz. stewing steak,
   cut into small cubes
100 g./4 oz. ox kidney, cut into
   small cubes
2 tablespoons flour
salt and pepper
25 g./1 oz. lard
1 large onion, finely chopped
300 ml./½ pint beef stock
350 g./12 oz. shortcrust
   pastry, made with
   350 g./12 oz. plain flour,
   etc.
milk or egg, beaten, for glazing

American
12 oz. lean chuck steak, cut into
   small cubes
4 oz. beef kidney, cut into small
   cubes
2½ tablespoons flour
salt and pepper
2 tablespoons lard
1 large onion, finely chopped
1¼ cups beef stock
3 cups shortcrust pastry, made
   with 3 cups all-purpose
   flour, etc.
milk or egg, beaten, for glazing

Serves 6
Oven setting: 200°C./400°F./Gas Mark 6
Coat the meat in the flour, seasoned with salt and pepper.
Heat the lard in a pan, add the onion and fry for 2–3
minutes. Add the meat and fry until browned. Stir in the
stock and seasoning and bring to boiling point. Cover and
simmer for about 2 hours until the meat is tender. Cool.

Roll out two-thirds of the pastry and cut into six circles.
Use the pastry to line 10 cm./4 inch diameter patty pans.
Roll out the remaining pastry and cut six 10 cm./4 inch
circles for lids. Divide the filling between the patty pans.
Dampen the pastry edges and cover with lids. Seal the
edges and flute. Make a hole in centre of each pie. Roll out
the pastry trimmings and cut three leaves to decorate each
pie. Glaze with beaten egg or milk. Bake in the preheated
oven for 30–35 minutes.

Roast beef

Pepper steak

Roast beef is one of the most delicious roast joints. When buying the beef see there is a good 'marbling' of fat, as this makes sure it will be moist when cooked. If you add fat to beef use very little, since an excess of fat is inclined to harden the meat. You can use an open roasting tin or cover with foil, put into a roasting bag or into a covered tin. If using either of these last three methods allow about 15–20 minutes extra cooking time. Good quality aitch-bone, fillet, rib, rump, sirloin and topside are all excellent joints to choose.

If using the quick roasting method, allow 15 minutes per ½ kg./1 lb. and 15 minutes over for under-done meat, 20 minutes per ½ kg./1 lb. and 20 minutes over for medium to well-done. If using the slower method then allow 25 minutes per ½ kg./1 lb. and 25 minutes over. For well-done beef add 15–20 minutes to the total time. Serve with thin gravy, horseradish sauce and Yorkshire pudding.

Metric/Imperial
2 slices fillet or rump steak,
*   100–225 g./4–8 oz. each*
3 teaspoons whole black
*   peppercorns*
50 g./2 oz. butter
1 tablespoon olive oil
2 teaspoons brandy
1 teaspoon butter

American
2 slices fillet or round steak,
*   4–8 oz. each*
3 teaspoons whole black
*   peppercorns*
4 tablespoons butter
1¼ tablespoons olive oil
2 teaspoons brandy
1 teaspoon butter

Serves 2
Trim the steaks neatly and beat with a rolling pin. Crush the peppercorns coarsely with a rolling pin, or in a mortar with a pestle. Press these into the steaks on both sides and allow to stand for about 1 hour. Heat the butter and oil in a heavy-based frying pan (skillet) and cook the steaks quickly on both sides to seal in the juices. Complete the cooking according to taste — rare, medium or well-done. Remove from the pan and keep hot.

Stir the brandy into the pan juices and bring to the boil, scraping the sediment from the pan. Remove from heat and stir in the extra butter. Pour this sauce over the steaks.

Helpful hints
For a change, try canned green peppers instead of black pepper.

BEEF

Bobotie

Metric/Imperial	American
1 tablespoon oil	1 ¼ tablespoons oil
1 large onion, chopped, or 225 g./8 oz. small onions	1 large onion, chopped, or 2 cups small onions
½ kg./1 lb. lean minced beef	1 lb. lean ground beef
1 tablespoon flour	1 ¼ tablespoons flour
150 ml./¼ pint water	⅔ cup water
1 beef stock cube	1 beef bouillon cube
2 tablespoons soy sauce	2 ½ tablespoons soy sauce
1 teaspoon curry powder	1 teaspoon curry powder
½ teaspoon dried mixed herbs	½ teaspoon dried mixed herbs
salt and pepper	salt and pepper
3–4 bay leaves	3–4 bay leaves
2 eggs	2 eggs
300 ml./½ pint milk	1 ¼ cups milk
350 g./12 oz. long-grain rice	2 cups long-grain rice
900 ml./1 ½ pints water	3 ¾ cups water
½ teaspoon salt	½ teaspoon salt
pinch of saffron powder (optional)	pinch of saffron powder (optional)
100 g./4 oz. seedless raisins	⅔ cup seedless raisins

Serves 4

Oven setting: 160°C./325°F./Gas Mark 3

Heat the oil in a pan and fry the onion for about 5 minutes. Add the beef and fry for a further 5 minutes, stirring once or twice. Add the flour and cook for 2 minutes, then gradually stir in the water. Bring to the boil, stirring, then add the stock (bouillon) cube, soy sauce, curry powder, mixed herbs and seasoning. Cover and simmer for 20 minutes. Turn the mixture into a casserole and add the bay leaves. Beat the eggs with the milk and pour over the meat. Bake in the preheated oven for about 30 minutes or until the top is golden.

Put the rice, water, salt and saffron, if using, into a saucepan. Bring to the boil and stir once. Lower the heat, cover and simmer for 15 minutes, or until the rice is tender and the liquid absorbed. Stir in the raisins just before the rice is cooked. Serve with the Bobotie.

German beef rolls

Metric/Imperial	American
1 ½ kg./3 lb. silverside of beef, very thinly sliced	3 lb. beef heel or round, very thinly sliced
German mustard	German mustard
50–100 g./2–4 oz. speck (fat ham)	2–4 oz. speck (fat ham)
1 dill pickled cucumber	1 dill pickled cucumber
2 onions, finely chopped	2 onions, finely chopped
salt and pepper	salt and pepper
1 carrot, peeled and sliced	1 carrot, peeled and sliced
50 g./2 oz. dripping	4 tablespoons dripping
50 g./2 oz. flour	½ cup flour
600 ml./1 pint water	2 ½ cups water

Serves 8

Oven setting: 180–190°C./350–375°F./Gas Mark 4–5

Beat the meat slices with a meat mallet or rolling pin to make them very thin and cut out eight 10 × 20 cm./4 × 8 inch rectangles. (Use the remaining meat in a stew or casserole or soup.) Spread the slices with mustard. Cut the speck into eight long strips. Cut the dill pickled cucumber lengthways into eight segments. Place one piece of speck and cucumber across the centre of each piece of meat, sprinkle with 1 chopped onion, salt and pepper, roll up tightly and secure with thread or wooden cocktail sticks (picks). Fry the remaining chopped onion and sliced carrot in heated dripping in a shallow heavy-based pan, until golden. Coat the meat with flour and fry with the vegetables until evenly browned. Add the water and bring to the boil, stirring occasionally. Transfer to a casserole and cook in the preheated oven for 1 hour, or until the meat is tender.

Serve on a bed of creamed potatoes. Strain the gravy, reheat and pour a little over the rolls and serve the remainder in a sauceboat.

Argentine beef stew

Metric/Imperial	American
100 g./4 oz. dried butter beans, soaked overnight	⅔ cup dried lima beans, soaked overnight
2 onions	2 onions
1 large red pepper, cored and seeded	1 large red pepper, cored and seeded
700 g./1½ lb. chuck steak	1½ lb. chuck steak
2 tablespoons olive or other oil	2½ tablespoons olive or other oil
1¼ l./2 pints brown stock	5 cups brown stock
2 teaspoons paprika	2 teaspoons paprika
few rashers bacon	few slices bacon
225 g./8 oz. chorizo or garlic sausage	8 oz. chorizo or garlic sausage
salt and pepper	salt and pepper
225 g./8 oz. sweetcorn	1⅓ cups sweetcorn

Serves 6

Drain the soaked beans, peel and chop the onions and dice the pepper. Cut the meat into small neat pieces. Heat the oil in a large pan, toss the onions, pepper and beef in this for a few minutes. Blend the stock with the paprika, add this to the pan together with the beans, diced bacon, sliced sausage and seasoning. Bring the liquid just to boiling point, lower the heat, cover tightly and simmer gently for about 2 hours. Add the sweetcorn and any extra seasoning desired. Simmer for a further 30 minutes.

Steak and kidney pie

Metric/Imperial	American
25 g./1 oz. lard or dripping	2 tablespoons lard or dripping
1 large onion, chopped	1 large onion, chopped
700 g./1½ lb. mixed steak and kidney	1 lb. chuck steak, cut into cubes
25 g./1 oz. flour	8 oz. lamb's kidney, cored and cut into cubes
scant 300 ml./½ pint water	¼ cup flour
salt and pepper	scant 1¼ cups water
1 × 400 g./14 oz. packet frozen puff pastry, thawed	salt and pepper
	1 × 14 oz. packet frozen puff pastry, thawed

Serves 4–5

Oven setting: 230°C./450°F./Gas Mark 8

Heat the lard or dripping in a pan, add the onion and fry for 5 minutes. Add the steak and kidney and cook, stirring, for 5 minutes. Stir in the flour, lower the heat and cook, stirring two or three times, for a further 10 minutes. Gradually stir in the water and add seasoning. Cover the pan and simmer gently, stirring occasionally, for about 2 hours, or until the meat is tender. Remove the pan from the heat and allow the meat to cool. When cold, turn the meat into a pie dish with a wide rim.

Roll out the pastry to an oval, just a little bit bigger than the pie dish. Cut a strip of the pastry about 1 cm./½ inch wide. Dampen the rim of the pie dish and place this strip all the way round. Dampen the pastry strip and carefully place the rolled-out pastry over the top of the pie dish. Trim off the edges of the pastry with a sharp knife. 'Knock up' (seal) and flute the edges. Roll out the pastry trimmings and cut into strips about 4 cm./1½ inches wide. Cut out diamond shapes for leaves, and mark on veins with the tip of the knife. Dampen the leaves and arrange in the centre of the pie. If you like, the pie can be brushed with a little egg or milk before baking to give it a good golden shine. Bake the pie in the preheated oven for 5 minutes, then lower the oven setting to 220°C./425°F./Gas Mark 7 for a further 15–20 minutes.

BEEF

Chilli con carne

Metric/Imperial	American
225 g./8 oz. dried red kidney beans, soaked overnight	1 1/3 cups dried red kidney beans, soaked overnight
4 tablespoons corn oil	5 tablespoons corn oil
2 onions, chopped	2 onions, chopped
2 garlic cloves, crushed	2 garlic cloves, crushed
1 kg./2 lb. lean minced beef	2 lb. lean ground beef
1 green pepper, cored, seeded and chopped	1 green pepper, cored, seeded and chopped
1–2 tablespoons mild chilli powder	1 1/4–2 1/2 tablespoons chili powder
1 teaspoon paprika	1 teaspoon paprika
1 teaspoon ground cumin	1 teaspoon ground cumin
1 tablespoon tomato purée	1 1/4 tablespoons tomato paste
1 tablespoon flour	1 1/4 tablespoons flour
salt	salt
2 × 400 g./14 oz. cans tomatoes	2 × 14 oz. cans tomatoes

Serves 8

Drain the kidney beans and cook gently in boiling salted water for 45 minutes or until almost tender. Drain and reserve about 150 ml./1/4 pint (2/3 cup) of the water. Heat the oil in a pan, add the onions and garlic and fry until golden. Add the beef and green pepper and fry for 5–6 minutes, stirring constantly to break up the meat. Stir in the chilli powder, paprika, cumin, tomato purée (paste), flour and salt to taste, and cook for 2 minutes. Add the undrained tomatoes and the beans, mix thoroughly and bring to the boil. Then lower the heat, cover and simmer for 1 1/2 hours, stirring occasionally, to prevent the meat sticking. If it gets rather dry, add the reserved bean water. Taste and adjust the seasoning.

Beef and prune ragoût

Metric/Imperial	American
600 ml./1 pint brown stock	2 1/2 cups brown stock
about 18 prunes	about 18 prunes
550 g./1 1/4 lb. chuck steak	1 1/4 lb. chuck steak
salt and pepper	salt and pepper
25 g./1 oz. flour	1/4 cup flour
50 g./2 oz. cooking fat or dripping	4 tablespoons cooking fat or dripping
1 tablespoon tomato purée	1 1/4 tablespoons tomato paste
2 bay leaves	2 bay leaves
4–5 tomatoes	4–5 tomatoes

Serves 4

Heat the stock, pour over the prunes and soak for about 12 hours, unless using tenderized prunes which need soaking for 1 hour only. Dice the meat, coat in the flour, seasoned with salt and pepper and cook in the hot cooking fat or dripping for a few minutes. Strain the stock from the prunes and add to the meat. Bring to the boil and cook until thickened. Add the tomato purée (paste), about 6 finely chopped prunes and the bay leaves. Cover the pan and simmer for 1 3/4 hours. Add the rest of the prunes and cook for a further 15 minutes. Skin the tomatoes if wished, add to the ragoût and cook for 15 minutes.

Helpful hints

To vary this recipe, try raisins or dried apricots instead of prunes; if using raisins, add them half way through the cooking so they do not become too soft.

Carpet bag steaks

Burgundy beef

Carpet bag steaks

Metric/Imperial
6 thick pieces of fillet or rump
   steak
approx. 24 prepared mussels or
   6–12 oysters
100 g./4 oz. butter
3 teaspoons chopped parsley
lemon juice
salt and pepper

Garnish
cooked tomatoes, mushrooms,
   parsley

American
6 thick pieces of fillet or round
   steak
approx. 24 prepared mussels or
   6–12 oysters
½ cup butter
3 teaspoons chopped parsley
lemon juice
salt and pepper

Garnish
cooked tomatoes, mushrooms,
   parsley

Serves 6
Split the steaks to make 'pockets'. Mix the mussels or
sliced oysters with 50 g./2 oz (¼ cup) melted butter, the
chopped parsley, a squeeze of lemon juice and seasoning.
Put into the steak 'pockets'. Skewer firmly or sew with fine
string or cotton. Brush the steaks with remainder of
melted butter and grill (broil) to personal taste until
tender. Remove the skewers, string or cotton and serve
garnished with tomatoes, mushrooms and parsley.

Helpful hints
If fresh shellfish are out of season use canned smoked
oysters.

Burgundy beef

Metric/Imperial
700 g./1½ lb. chuck steak
25 g./1 oz. bacon fat
175 g./6 oz. unsmoked streaky
   bacon, cut into strips
15 g./½ oz. flour
300 ml./½ pint beef stock
150 ml./¼ pint red wine
1 bay leaf
½ teaspoon dried mixed herbs
1 parsley sprig
½ teaspoon salt
pinch of pepper
100 g./4 oz. small, even-sized
   onions
50 g./2 oz. button mushrooms

American
1½ lb. chuck steak
2 tablespoons bacon fat
6 oz. unsmoked fatty bacon,
   cut into strips
2 tablespoons flour
1¼ cups beef stock
⅔ cup red wine
1 bay leaf
½ teaspoon dried mixed herbs
1 parsley sprig
½ teaspoon salt
pinch of pepper
1 cup small, even-sized onions
½ cup button mushrooms

Serves 6
Oven setting: 160°C./325°F./Gas Mark 3
Cut the steak into 4 cm./1½ inch squares. Heat the bacon
fat in a fairly large pan and fry the bacon for a few minutes
until it begins to turn brown. Lift the bacon out of the pan
and into a 1¾ l./3 pint (2 quart) casserole, then fry the
steak in the fat remaining in the pan until it is brown all
over. Add the steak to the bacon in the casserole and pour
off all but 2 tablespoons of the fat. Blend the flour with the
fat and continue to cook until it has browned. Remove the
pan from the heat and stir in stock and wine. Return the
pan to the heat and bring the liquor to boiling point.
Simmer until it has thickened. Add the bay leaf, herbs,
parsley and seasoning, adding only a little of the salt, as
the bacon may be salty. Pour the liquor over the meat,
cover the casserole and cook in the preheated oven for 1½
hours.

Add the onions and mushrooms to the casserole and
cook for a further 1 hour, or until the meat is really tender.
Check seasoning and add more salt and pepper if
necessary. Skim off any fat on the surface.

BEEF

Boeuf bourguignonne

Metric/Imperial	American
1 kg./2 lb. topside beef, cubed	2 lb. top round beef, cubed
25 g./1 oz. flour	¼ cup flour
2 tablespoons olive oil	2½ tablespoons olive oil
50 g./2 oz. butter	¼ cup butter
100 g./4 oz. bacon, diced	4 oz. bacon, diced
2 carrots, chopped	2 carrots, chopped
1 leek, sliced	1 leek, sliced
1 onion, chopped	1 onion, chopped
1 garlic clove, crushed	1 garlic clove, crushed
bouquet garni	bouquet garni
salt and pepper	salt and pepper
300 ml./½ pint red wine	1¼ cups red wine
300 ml./½ pint beef stock	1¼ cups beef stock
1 tablespoon cornflour	1¼ tablespoons cornstarch
12 button onions	12 button onions
12 button mushrooms	12 button mushrooms
extra oil and butter for frying	extra oil and butter for frying
juice of ½ lemon	juice of ½ lemon
chopped parsley	chopped parsley

Serves 6

Oven setting: 160°C./325°F./Gas Mark 3

Roll beef in flour. Heat oil and butter in a large heavy pan and fry bacon until crisp. Transfer to a large casserole. Fry meat until it changes colour on all sides. Transfer all meat and juices to casserole. Add carrots, leek, onion and garlic to pan and fry until golden then add to casserole. Add bouquet garni, salt, pepper and red wine to casserole. Add stock to pan and heat, stirring continuously to loosen meat sediment, then add to casserole. Cover and cook for 1½–2 hours. Blend cornflour (cornstarch) with 1 tablespoon (1¼ tablespoons) cold water to a smooth paste. Add to casserole and bring back to boiling point, stirring occasionally. Sauté button onions and mushrooms in extra oil and butter, add lemon juice and simmer until tender. Add to casserole and serve hot, sprinkled with chopped parsley.

Curried meatballs

Metric/Imperial	American
700 g./1½ lb. beef	1½ lb. beef
25 g./1 oz. butter	2 tablespoons butter
2 medium-sized onions, finely chopped	2 medium-sized onions, finely chopped
½ teaspoon ground ginger	½ teaspoon ground ginger
1–2 teaspoons curry powder	1–2 teaspoons curry powder
50 g./2 oz. fresh breadcrumbs	1 cup fresh breadcrumbs
2 egg yolks	2 egg yolks
3–4 tablespoons double cream	4–5 tablespoons heavy cream
75 g./3 oz. fat or butter	6 tablespoons fat or butter
1–2 green peppers, cored and seeded	1–2 green peppers, cored and seeded
3–4 tomatoes	3–4 tomatoes
cooked rice	cooked rice
Sauce	Sauce
25 g./1 oz. flour	¼ cup flour
1–2 teaspoons curry powder	1–2 teaspoons curry powder
300 ml./½ pint white stock	1¼ cups white stock
150 ml./¼ pint single cream	⅔ cup light cream
salt and pepper	salt and pepper

Serves 5–6

Mince (grind) the meat very finely. Heat the butter in a pan, stir in the onions and cook gently until nearly soft. Add the ginger and curry powder, then the meat. Blend very thoroughly, then stir in the breadcrumbs and egg yolks and mix well. Gradually add enough cream to give a soft creamy texture. Put into a cool place for about 30 minutes to stiffen slightly. Make into walnut-sized balls.

Heat the fat or butter in a large frying pan (skillet). Put in the balls and brown. Remove balls from pan (skillet).

Blend the flour with the fat remaining in the pan and cook for 1–2 minutes. Add the curry powder, then blend in the stock and bring to the boil. Cook gently until thickened, stir in the cream or milk and seasoning. Replace the meatballs and simmer gently for about 10 minutes. Spoon the balls and sauce on to a heated dish, garnish with rings of pepper, slices of tomato and cooked rice.

Topside slices in red wine

Metric/Imperial
4 slices topside beef, cut into
   1 cm./½ inch thick slices
150 ml./¼ pint red wine
1 onion, chopped
1 bay leaf
1 parsley sprig
1 thyme sprig
1 marjoram sprig
25 g./1 oz. beef dripping
25 g./1 oz. flour
300 ml./½ pint beef stock
salt and pepper
225 g./8 oz. carrots, sliced
225 g./8 oz. button onions
1 tablespoon chopped parsley

American
4 slices top round beef, cut into
   ½ inch thick slices
⅔ cup red wine
1 onion, chopped
1 bay leaf
1 parsley sprig
1 thyme sprig
1 marjoram sprig
2 tablespoons beef dripping
¼ cup flour
1¼ cups beef stock
salt and pepper
2 cups sliced carrots
8 oz. button onions
1¼ tablespoons chopped
   parsley

Serves 4
Oven setting: 150°C./300°F./Gas Mark 2
Lay the beef slices in a shallow dish. Pour over the wine and add the onion and herbs. Leave to marinate in a cool place for 5–6 hours, turning occasionally. Drain the meat and strain and reserve the marinade. Melt the dripping in a large pan, add the meat and cook on both sides until brown. Remove from the pan and place in a casserole. Add the flour to the fat remaining in the pan and cook over a low heat until the flour is browned, but not burnt. Stir in the stock and reserved marinade and bring to the boil, stirring all the time. Season and pour over the meat in the casserole. Cover and cook for 1½ hours. Add the carrots and onions to the casserole and cook for a further 1 hour. Taste and adjust the seasoning and sprinkle with chopped parsley.

Stuffato di Manzo

Metric/Imperial
1 teaspoon salt
freshly ground black pepper
1 bay leaf, crushed
2 teaspoons chopped fresh
   thyme
2 medium-sized onions,
   chopped
2 garlic cloves, crushed
3 sticks celery, chopped
300 ml./½ pint red wine
1 kg./2 lb. braising steak, cut
   into cubes
1 tablespoon olive oil
4 bacon rashers, chopped
2 tablespoons tomato purée
300 ml./½ pint beef stock
1 tablespoon chopped parsley

American
1 teaspoon salt
freshly ground black pepper
1 bay leaf, crushed
2 teaspoons chopped fresh
   thyme
2 medium-sized onions,
   chopped
2 garlic cloves, crushed
3 sticks celery, chopped
1¼ cups red wine
2 lb. chuck steak, cut into cubes
1¼ tablespoons olive oil
4 bacon slices, chopped
2½ tablespoons tomato paste
1¼ cups beef stock
1¼ tablespoons chopped
   parsley

Serves 4–6
Oven setting: 150°C./300°F./Gas Mark 2
Put the salt, pepper, bay leaf, thyme, 1 onion, the garlic, 1 stick celery and the wine into a bowl. Mix together, then add the cubes of meat. Cover and leave to marinate in a cool place for 5–6 hours, turning occasionally.

Drain the meat well and strain and reserve the marinade. Heat the oil in a flameproof casserole. Add the remaining onion and celery and the bacon and fry gently until soft and pale golden. Add the beef cubes and fry fairly quickly until browned on all sides. Add the marinade, tomato purée (paste) and stock. Cover and cook in the oven for 2½ hours. Taste and adjust the seasoning before serving sprinkled with parsley.

VEAL

Wiener schnitzel

Metric/Imperial	American
4 slices (escalopes) of veal	4 slices (scaloppini) of veal
juice of 2 lemons	juice of 2 lemons
salt and freshly ground black pepper	salt and freshly ground black pepper
1 large egg, beaten	1 large egg, beaten
100 g./4 oz. dried breadcrumbs	1⅓ cups dried breadcrumbs
butter for frying	butter for frying
lemon slices	lemon slices

Serves 4

Beat the veal on a wooden board with a meat mallet or rolling pin until very thin. Sprinkle with the lemon juice and salt and pepper to taste, and leave to marinate for about 1 hour. Dip the veal in the egg, then in the breadcrumbs, ensuring that they are thoroughly covered. Chill in the refrigerator for 10 minutes.

Melt a knob of butter in a large frying pan (skillet) and, when foaming, add two of the veal slices. Fry over high heat for about 2–3 minutes on each side, or until tender and golden brown. Drain on absorbent paper, then transfer to a hot serving platter. Keep hot while you cook the remaining slices in the same way. Garnish with lemon slices.

Helpful hints

This can be turned into a Schnitzel Holstein by adding a garnish of chopped hard boiled (hard cooked) eggs or a whole fried egg, anchovy fillets and stoned olives or capers.

Veal and bean stew

Metric/Imperial	American
225 g./8 oz. dried white haricot beans, soaked overnight	1⅓ cups dried white beans, soaked overnight
2 tablespoons oil	2½ tablespoons oil
15 g./½ oz. butter	1 tablespoon butter
1 onion, chopped	1 onion, chopped
700 g./1½ lb. pie veal, cut into small cubes	1½ lb. lean veal, cut into small cubes
3 tablespoons flour	4 tablespoons flour
salt and pepper	salt and pepper
75 ml./3 fl. oz. dry white wine	⅜ cup dry white wine
4–5 tomatoes, skinned, seeded and chopped	4–5 tomatoes, skinned, seeded and chopped
½ teaspoon dried oregano	½ teaspoon dried oregano
stock	stock
chopped parsley	chopped parsley

Serves 4

Drain the soaked beans and set aside. Heat the oil and butter in a pan, add the onion and cook until soft. Coat the veal with the flour seasoned with salt and pepper, put into the pan and brown on all sides. Add the wine, let it bubble for a few minutes then add the tomatoes, oregano and beans. Add a little stock, bring to boiling point, then cover and simmer gently for 1½–2 hours, until the meat and beans are tender, adding a little extra stock if necessary. Correct the seasoning and sprinkle with chopped parsley.

Veal with mushrooms

Metric/Imperial	American
150 g./5 oz. butter	⅔ cup butter
2 small onions, finely chopped	2 small onions, finely chopped
4 tablespoons chopped parsley	5 tablespoons chopped parsley
1 teaspoon dried marjoram	1 teaspoon dried marjoram
1 teaspoon dried basil	1 teaspoon dried basil
pinch of dried thyme	pinch of dried thyme
225 g./8 oz. fresh breadcrumbs	4 cups fresh breadcrumbs
salt and pepper	salt and pepper
1 egg, beaten	1 egg, beaten
12 small slices (escalopes) of veal	12 small slices (scaloppini) of veal
1 large onion, sliced	1 large onion, sliced
100 g./4 oz. mushrooms, sliced	1 cup sliced mushrooms
1 tablespoon flour	1¼ tablespoons flour
300 ml./½ pint chicken stock	1¼ cups chicken stock
100 ml./4 fl. oz. dry white wine	½ cup dry white wine
1 bay leaf	1 bay leaf

Serves 6
Oven setting: 160°C./325°F./Gas Mark 3
Melt 50 g./2 oz. (¼ cup) butter in a pan and add the chopped onions, fry gently until soft. Remove from the heat and stir in the herbs, breadcrumbs and seasoning. Add enough egg to bind.
   Beat the veal on a wooden board with a meat mallet or rolling pin until very thin. Spread a little of the herb mixture on each veal slice, roll up tightly and secure with string or a cocktail stick (pick). Heat the remaining butter in a pan, add the veal and fry over a moderate heat until golden brown on all sides, remove and place in a casserole. Add the sliced onion to the pan and fry until soft, then add the mushrooms and fry for 3 minutes. Sprinkle in the flour and cook for 1 minute. Gradually stir in the stock and wine, season to taste and add the bay leaf. Bring to the boil, stirring constantly, then cook until thickened and pour over the veal. Cover the casserole and cook in the preheated oven for 1 hour, or until the veal is tender. Remove the bay leaf and string.

Escalopes Turin-style

Metric/Imperial	American
4 thin slices (escalopes) of veal	4 thin slices (scaloppini) of veal
2 tablespoons flour	2½ tablespoons flour
salt and pepper	salt and pepper
1 egg, beaten	1 egg, beaten
50 g./2 oz. fresh white breadcrumbs	1 cup fresh white breadcrumbs
25 g./1 oz. grated Parmesan cheese	¼ cup grated Parmesan cheese
50 g./2 oz. butter	4 tablespoons butter
1 tomato, sliced	1 tomato, sliced
4 anchovy fillets	4 anchovy fillets
lemon wedges and parsley to garnish	lemon wedges and parsley to garnish

Serves 4
Beat the veal on a wooden board with a meat mallet or rolling pin until very thin. Coat the veal with the flour seasoned with salt and pepper. Dip in the beaten egg, then in a mixture of the breadcrumbs and grated Parmesan. Heat the butter and fry the veal until golden, turning once. Top each slice with a slice of tomato and an anchovy fillet, serve with lemon wedges and garnish with parsley.

Helpful hints
Freeze the coated veal slices uncooked. To cook, thaw for 3–4 hours at room temperature and fry as above. Or fry from frozen, allowing about 10 minutes.

VEAL

Osso bucco

Metric/Imperial	American
6 pieces of knuckle of veal, about 1 kg./2 lb.	6 pieces of knuckle of veal, about 2 lb.
25 g./1 oz. flour	¼ cup flour
1 tablespoon oil	1¼ tablespoons oil
50 g./2 oz. butter	4 tablespoons butter
1 onion, chopped	1 onion, chopped
1 garlic clove, crushed	1 garlic clove, crushed
100 g./4 oz. carrots, peeled and diced	⅔ cup diced carrots
100 g./4 oz. celery, diced	⅔ cup diced celery
150 ml./¼ pint chicken stock	⅔ cup chicken stock
150 ml./¼ pint dry white wine	⅔ cup dry white wine
½ kg./1 lb. tomatoes, skinned, seeded and chopped	1 lb. tomatoes, skinned, seeded and chopped
50 g./2 oz. black olives	¼ cup black olives
salt and freshly ground black pepper	salt and freshly ground black pepper
grated rind of ½ lemon	grated rind of ½ lemon
1 tablespoon chopped parsley	1¼ tablespoons chopped parsley

Serves 4

Oven setting: 180°C./350°F./Gas Mark 4

Coat the veal pieces with the flour, shaking off the excess and reserving any left over.

Heat the oil and butter in a pan and fry the veal briskly on all sides. When lightly brown, place the veal, bones upright, in a casserole dish. Add the onion, garlic, carrots and celery to the pan and fry until golden brown. Sprinkle over any leftover flour and fry for 1 minute. Gradually stir in the stock and wine, then add the tomatoes, olives and seasoning and bring to the boil, stirring constantly. Pour over the veal. Cover the casserole dish and cook in the preheated oven for 1½–2 hours, or until tender. Adjust the seasoning and sprinkle over the grated lemon rind and chopped parsley.

Veal mornay

Metric/Imperial	American
4 thin slices (escalopes) of veal	4 thin slices (scaloppini) of veal
4 small slices cooked ham	4 small slices cooked ham
little flour	little flour
salt and pepper	salt and pepper
1 egg	1 egg
2–3 tablespoons dry breadcrumbs	2½–4 tablespoons dry breadcrumbs
50 g./2 oz. butter	4 tablespoons butter
1 tablespoon olive oil	1¼ tablespoons olive oil
cooked small new potatoes	cooked small new potatoes
chopped parsley	chopped parsley
lemon	lemon
cooked peas or asparagus tips	cooked peas or asparagus tips
Sauce	*Sauce*
25 g./1 oz. butter	2 tablespoons butter
25 g./1 oz. flour	¼ cup flour
150 ml./¼ pint milk	⅔ cup milk
150 ml./¼ pint white wine	⅔ cup white wine
1 teaspoon French mustard	1 teaspoon French mustard
salt and pepper	salt and pepper
2 tablespoons double cream	2½ tablespoons heavy cream
100 g./4 oz. grated Cheddar or Gruyère cheese	1 cup grated Cheddar or Swiss cheese

Serves 4

Beat the veal on a wooden board with a meat mallet or rolling pin until very thin. Cover half of each fillet with a slice of ham, then fold the meat to cover the ham. Coat in the flour, seasoned with salt and pepper, dip in the beaten egg and then the breadcrumbs. Heat the butter and oil in a large pan and fry the veal quickly on both sides until crisp and golden brown. Lower the heat and continue cooking until tender. Lift out of the pan, drain on absorbent paper.

Heat the butter, stir in the flour and cook for 1 minute. Gradually blend in the milk and stir until thickened, lower heat and add wine, mustard and seasoning. Stir cream and cheese into sauce just before serving. Do not boil.

Arrange the veal on a dish. Garnish with potatoes tossed in parsley, sauce, lemon and peas or asparagus.

Veal paupiettes

Metric/Imperial
½ kg./1 lb. slices (escalopes) of
  veal
2 rashers bacon, chopped
1 tablespoon chopped parsley
1 small garlic clove, crushed
50 g./2 oz. fresh white
  breadcrumbs
1 egg
25 g./1 oz. butter
1 tablespoon flour
150 ml./¼ pint water or stock
150 ml./¼ pint dry white wine
salt and pepper
100 g./4 oz. mushrooms,
  halved
4 tomatoes, skinned and
  quartered
few stuffed green olives

American
1 lb. slices (scaloppini) of veal
2 slices bacon, chopped
1¼ tablespoons chopped
  parsley
1 small garlic clove, crushed
1 cup fresh white breadcrumbs
1 egg
2 tablespoons butter
1¼ tablespoons flour
⅔ cup water or stock
⅔ cup dry white wine
salt and pepper
1 cup halved mushrooms
4 tomatoes, skinned and
  quartered
few stuffed green olives

Serves 4
Oven setting: 160°C./325°F./Gas Mark 3
Beat the veal on a wooden board with a meat mallet or
rolling pin until very thin. Mix together the bacon, parsley,
garlic, breadcrumbs and egg and use to stuff the slices of
veal. Roll up each slice tightly and secure with string or a
cocktail stick (pick). Melt the butter in a pan, add the veal
and fry quickly until browned. Remove the veal from the
pan and place in a 1½ l./2½ pint (1½ quart) ovenproof
dish.
   Add the flour to the pan and cook for 1 minute. Stir in
the water or stock and wine, bring to the boil, add
seasoning and pour over the veal. Cover and cook for 1
hour in the preheated oven. Half an hour before the end of
the cooking time, add the remaining ingredients.

Piquant veal escalopes

Metric/Imperial
4 thin slices (escalopes) of veal
salt and pepper
flour
50 g./2 oz. butter
6 spring onions
1 lemon, sliced
2 teaspoons rosemary
¼ teaspoon Tabasco sauce
150 ml./¼ pint Vermouth
1 tablespoon chopped parsley

American
4 thin slices (scaloppini) of veal
salt and pepper
flour
¼ cup butter
6 scallions
1 lemon, sliced
2 teaspoons rosemary
¼ teaspoon Tabasco sauce
⅔ cup Vermouth
1¼ tablespoons chopped
  parsley

Serves 4
Coat the veal with seasoned flour, shaking off any excess.
   Melt the butter and fry the veal until golden, turning
once. Remove from the pan and keep hot. Add a little
more butter to the pan if necessary and fry the chopped
white part of the spring onions (scallions) until soft.
Replace the veal, add the lemon, rosemary, Tabasco and
Vermouth. Simmer for 2–3 minutes, then check the
seasoning and sprinkle with the chopped green part of the
onions and chopped parsley.

VEAL

Hungarian veal goulash

Metric/Imperial
dripping or lard for frying
1 large onion, finely chopped
1 garlic clove, crushed with ½
*   teaspoon salt*
1 kg./2 lb. pie veal, cut into
*   cubes*
½ teaspoon caraway seeds
2 tablespoons paprika
1 teaspoon dried mixed herbs
freshly ground black pepper
1 red pepper and 1 green
*   pepper, cored, seeded and*
*   sliced into rings*
1 × 400 g./14 oz. can tomatoes
150 ml./¼ pint chicken stock
225 g./8 oz. button
*   mushrooms, sliced*
150 ml./¼ pint soured cream

American
dripping or lard for frying
1 large onion, finely chopped
1 garlic clove, crushed with ½
*   teaspoon salt*
2 lb. lean veal, cut into cubes
½ teaspoon caraway seeds
2½ tablespoons paprika
1 teaspoon dried mixed herbs
freshly ground black pepper
1 red pepper and 1 green
*   pepper, cored, seeded and*
*   sliced into rings*
1 × 14 oz. can tomatoes
⅔ cup chicken stock
2 cups sliced button
*   mushrooms*
⅔ cup sour cream

Serves 4
Oven setting: 150°C./300°F./Gas Mark 2
Melt the dripping or lard in a flameproof casserole. Add
the onion and garlic and fry gently for 5 minutes or until
golden. Add the veal to the casserole and fry briskly until
browned on all sides. Stir in the caraway seeds, paprika,
herbs and black pepper to taste. Continue cooking for 1–2
minutes, stirring constantly. Add the peppers, tomatoes
and stock, cover and transfer to the preheated oven. Cook
for about 2–2½ hours, or until the veal is quite tender,
adding the mushrooms 30 minutes before the end of
cooking time. Before serving, adjust seasoning. Transfer
to a hot serving dish and spoon the cream on top.

Swiss veal

Metric/Imperial
1½ kg./3 lb. boned leg of veal
75 g./3 oz. flour
salt and pepper
175 g./6 oz. butter or
*   margarine*
2 onions, finely chopped
450 ml./¾ pint dry white wine
225–350 g./8–12 oz.
*   mushrooms, chopped*
450 ml./¾ pint cream
1 tablespoon chopped parsley
¼ teaspoon paprika

American
3 lb. boned leg of veal
¾ cup flour
salt and pepper
¾ cup butter or margarine
2 onions, finely chopped
2 cups dry white wine
2–3 cups chopped mushrooms
2 cups cream
1¼ tablespoons chopped
*   parsley*
¼ teaspoon paprika

Serves 8
Oven setting: 180–190°C./350–375°F./Gas Mark 4–5
Cut the veal into narrow strips, 5 cm./2 inches long and
½ cm./¼ inch thick. Coat the strips in the flour, seasoned
with salt and pepper. Heat two-thirds of the butter or
margarine in a frying pan (skillet) and fry the veal and
onions until lightly browned, stirring occasionally. Add
the wine and cook over a medium heat, stirring to a
smooth consistency. Fry the mushrooms in the remaining
butter or margarine for 5 minutes. Stir in the cream,
parsley and paprika. Mix the veal and the mushrooms
together in a casserole and season to taste with salt and
pepper. Reheat in the preheated oven, without allowing it
to boil.

Blanquette de veau

Metric/Imperial	American
700 g./1½ lb. pie veal, cut into cubes	1½ lb. lean veal, cut into cubes
2 onions, quartered	2 onions, quartered
2 large carrots, peeled and quartered	2 large carrots, peeled and quartered
3 bay leaves	3 bay leaves
1 parsley sprig	1 parsley sprig
1 tablespoon lemon juice	1¼ tablespoons lemon juice
salt and pepper	salt and pepper
1¼ l./2 pints water	5 cups water
175 g./6 oz. small mushrooms	1½ cups small mushrooms
40 g./1½ oz. butter	3 tablespoons butter
40 g./1½ oz. flour	scant ½ cup flour
150 ml./¼ pint single cream	⅔ cup light cream

Serves 4

Put the veal in a pan, cover with cold water and bring to boiling point. Drain the veal and rinse off scum. Return the veal to the pan with the onions, carrots, herbs, lemon juice and seasoning. Add the water and bring to boiling point. Cover and simmer for 1½–2 hours, or until tender. Half an hour before the end of the cooking time add the mushrooms. Put the veal and vegetables into a hot serving dish and keep warm. Reduce the cooking liquor to 600 ml./1 pint (2½ cups) by boiling rapidly.

Melt the butter in a pan, add the flour and cook for 1 minute. Add the reduced cooking liquor to the roux and simmer for 5 minutes. Check seasoning. Add cream and simmer for 1 more minute. Pour over the veal and vegetables.

Veal escalopes milanese

Metric/Imperial	American
1 egg, beaten	1 egg, beaten
salt and pepper	salt and pepper
4 thin slices (escalopes) veal	4 thin slices (scaloppini) veal
100 g./4 oz. dry breadcrumbs	1⅓ cups dry breadcrumbs
50 g./2 oz. butter	¼ cup butter
1 tablespoon olive oil	1¼ tablespoons olive oil

Garnish	Garnish
1 hard boiled egg, chopped	1 hard cooked egg, chopped
1 lemon, sliced	1 lemon, sliced
parsley	parsley

Serves 4

Season the egg with salt and pepper. Dip the veal slices in the egg, then in the breadcrumbs, pressing them on well with a knife.

Melt the butter with the oil in a frying pan (skillet). When it is foaming, fry the veal slices for 4 to 5 minutes on each side. Arrange the veal slices on a hot serving dish and garnish with the chopped egg, lemon slices and parsley.

PORK

Apricot-stuffed pork

Metric/Imperial
approx. 2¼ kg./4½ lb. loin of
  pork
100 g./4 oz. fresh
  breadcrumbs, preferably
  wholemeal
50 g./2 oz. margarine, melted
generous 100 g./4 oz. chopped
  canned or cooked apricots
75 g./3 oz. raisins
1–2 tablespoons flaked almonds
  (optional)
salt and pepper
1 tablespoon chopped parsley
little apricot syrup
little oil

American
approx. 4½ lb. loin of pork
2 cups fresh breadcrumbs,
  preferably wholewheat
4 tablespoons margarine,
  melted
generous ⅔ cup chopped
  canned or cooked apricots
½ cup raisins
1¼–2½ tablespoons slivered
  almonds (optional)
salt and pepper
1¼ tablespoons chopped
  parsley
little apricot syrup
little oil

Serves 6
Oven setting: 220–230°C./425–450°F./Gas Mark 7–8
Have the pork boned so it can be rolled round the stuffing.
Blend the breadcrumbs with the margarine, apricots,
raisins, almonds, seasoning, parsley and apricot syrup.
Lay the pork out flat and spread over the filling. Roll up
tightly and secure with string. Brush the pork with a little
oil. Cooking time includes the weight of the stuffing so
allow about 2 hours. Cook in the preheated oven for about
45 minutes, then reduce the oven setting to
200°C./400°F./Gas Mark 6 for the remainder of the cooking
time.

Squab pie

Metric/Imperial
½ kg./1 lb. pork chump chops,
  or middle neck of lamb chops,
  trimmed of excess fat and cut
  into small cubes
1 large onion, sliced
½ kg./1 lb. cooking apples,
  peeled, cored and thickly
  sliced
½ teaspoon mixed spice
2 teaspoons soft brown sugar
salt and freshly ground black
  pepper
1 tablespoon cornflour
300 ml./½ pint beef stock
225 g./8 oz. shortcrust pastry,
  made with 225 g./8 oz. plain
  flour, etc.

American
1 lb. pork loin chops, or middle
  neck of lamb chops, trimmed
  of excess fat and cut into
  small cubes
1 large onion, sliced
1 lb. cooking apples, peeled,
  cored and thickly sliced
½ teaspoon ground allspice
2 teaspoons light brown sugar
salt and freshly ground black
  pepper
1¼ tablespoons cornstarch
1¼ cups beef stock
2 cups shortcrust pastry made
  with 2 cups all-purpose
  flour, etc.

Serves 4
Oven setting: 190°C./375°F./Gas Mark 5
Fill a 1¼ l./2 pint (1½ quart) ovenproof pie dish with
alternate layers of meat, onion and apples, finishing with a
layer of meat and sprinkling each layer with the mixed
spice, brown sugar and seasoning. Blend the cornflour
(cornstarch) until smooth with a little stock, add the
remaining stock and pour over the pie.
  Roll out the pastry 2½ cm./1 inch larger all round than
the top of the pie dish. Cut off a 2½ cm./1 inch wide strip
round the edge of the pastry. Dampen the rim of the pie
dish and place this strip all the way round. Dampen the
pastry strip and carefully place the rolled-out pastry over
the top of the pie dish. Press down firmly to seal the edges
and trim off the edges of the pastry with a sharp knife.
Knock up (seal) the edges of the pastry using the back of a
knife and use any pastry trimmings to decorate the top.
Make a slit in the centre of the lid. Bake in the preheated
oven for about 1 hour, reducing the oven setting if the
pastry starts to brown too quickly.

Hungarian pork

Metric/Imperial	American
800 g./1¾ lb. pork fillet	1¾ lb. pork tenderloin
2 tablespoons oil	2½ tablespoons oil
25 g./1 oz. butter	2 tablespoons butter
1 onion, chopped	1 onion, chopped
1 tablespoon paprika	1¼ tablespoons paprika
1 tablespoon flour	1¼ tablespoons flour
300 ml./½ pint beef stock	1¼ cups beef stock
5 tablespoons sherry	6 tablespoons sherry
1 teaspoon tomato purée	1 teaspoon tomato paste
salt and pepper	salt and pepper
175 g./6 oz. small button mushrooms	1½ cups small button mushrooms
150 ml./¼ pint soured cream	⅔ cup sour cream

Serves 4

Cut the pork into 4 cm./1½ inch pieces. Fry quickly in the oil and butter until just beginning to turn brown. Remove the pork from the pan and drain on absorbent paper. Fry the onion and paprika in the fat remaining in the pan for 2 minutes, stirring. Blend in the flour and cook for 1 minute. Gradually blend in the stock, sherry and tomato purée (paste). Bring to the boil and simmer until the mixture has thickened, stirring constantly.

Return the meat to the pan with seasoning to taste, cover and simmer for 30–40 minutes, or until the pork is tender. Stir in the mushrooms and simmer for 2 minutes. Just before serving, stir in the cream.

Sweet and sour pork with lychees

Metric/Imperial	American
3 tablespoons soy sauce	4 tablespoons soy sauce
1 tablespoon dry sherry	1¼ tablespoons dry sherry
1 teaspoon chopped root ginger	1 teaspoon chopped root ginger
pinch of monosodium glutamate	pinch of monosodium glutamate
½ kg./1 lb. spring or shoulder pork, cubed	1 lb. picnic shoulder pork, cubed
25 g./1 oz. flour	¼ cup flour
25 g./1 oz. cornflour	¼ cup cornstarch
pinch of salt	pinch of salt
2 eggs, beaten	2 eggs, beaten
oil for deep frying	oil for deep frying
½ red pepper, cored, seeded and cut into wedges	½ red pepper, cored, seeded and cut into wedges
½ green pepper, cored, seeded and cut into wedges	½ green pepper, cored, seeded and cut into wedges
2 apples, peeled, cored and quartered	2 apples, peeled, cored and quartered
1 tablespoon brown sugar	1¼ tablespoons brown sugar
150 ml./¼ pint syrup from canned lychees	⅔ cup syrup from canned lychees
2 tablespoons vinegar	2½ tablespoons vinegar
4 spring onions, finely chopped	4 scallions, finely chopped
1 × 300 g./11 oz. can lychees, drained	1 × 11 oz. can lychees, drained
extra 1 tablespoon cornflour	extra 1¼ tablespoons cornstarch
extra 1 tablespoon soy sauce	extra 1¼ tablespoons soy sauce

Serves 4–6

In a bowl, mix the soy sauce, sherry, ginger and monosodium glutamate. Add the pork cubes, stir to coat them and marinate for 1–2 hours.

Sift the flour, cornflour (cornstarch) and salt into a bowl. Add the eggs gradually, beating well to make a smooth batter. Coat the pork cubes in the batter and deep fry them in hot oil until golden. Drain and keep hot.

Mix all the remaining ingredients in a small pan. Bring to the boil, stirring constantly, and simmer for 2–3 minutes. Put the pork on a serving dish and pour over the sauce.

PORK

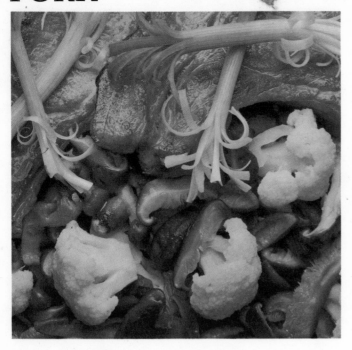

Pork with mushrooms

Metric/Imperial	American
1 kg./2 lb. pork chops	2 lb. pork chops
100 g./4 oz. dried mushrooms	1 cup dried mushrooms
4 tablespoons soy sauce	5 tablespoons soy sauce
3 tablespoons sherry	4 tablespoons sherry
4 spring onions	4 scallions
1 teaspoon brown sugar	1 teaspoon brown sugar
1 teaspoon salt	1 teaspoon salt
1 cauliflower	1 cauliflower

Serves 4

Wipe the chops and put them into a large pan with
600 ml./1 pint (2½ cups) water. Bring to the boil, remove
the scum, cover the pan with a tight fitting lid and simmer
for 30 minutes.

Soak the mushrooms in hot water for 20 minutes, drain
and chop finely. Add to the pan with the soy sauce,
sherry, whole onions, sugar and salt. Cover and simmer
for a further 45 minutes. Wash the cauliflower and break
into florets. Add to the pan, mix well and cook for a further
15 minutes.

Serve immediately.

Normandy pork

Metric/Imperial	American
5–6 pork chops, or thick slices pork	5–6 pork chops, or thick slices pork
2–3 onions, chopped	2–3 onions, chopped
300 ml./½ pint white wine	1¼ cups white wine
1 tablespoon Calvados (optional)	1¼ tablespoons Calvados (optional)
pinch of fresh or dried sage	pinch of fresh or dried sage
2–3 dessert apples, peeled, cored and chopped	2–3 eating apples, peeled, cored and chopped
salt and pepper	salt and pepper
little olive oil	little olive oil

Serves 5–6

Oven setting: 180–190°C./350–375°F./Gas Mark 4–5

Fry the chops in a large pan for about 5–8 minutes until
lightly browned. Lift out of the pan. Toss the onions in any
fat left in the pan until soft. Add the wine, Calvados, sage,
apples and seasoning. Spoon into a large shallow
casserole. Arrange the chops on top. Try to keep the skin
above the wine so it crisps, and brush this with the oil. Do
not cover the dish. Cook for 40–45 minutes in the centre of
the preheated oven.

Helpful hints

If Calvados is not available, ordinary brandy may be used
instead.

Country pork casserole

Metric/Imperial	American
½ kg./1 lb. pork fillet, cut into slices	1 lb. pork tenderloin, cut into slices
50 g./2 oz. flour	½ cup flour
salt and freshly ground black pepper	salt and freshly ground black pepper
50 g./2 oz. butter	4 tablespoons butter
2 onions, sliced	2 onions, sliced
1 large leek, washed and sliced	1 large leek, washed and sliced
4 sticks celery, diced	4 sticks celery, diced
1 small green pepper, cored, seeded and sliced	1 small green pepper, cored, seeded and sliced
225 g./8 oz. tomatoes, skinned, seeded and chopped	8 oz. tomatoes, skinned, seeded and chopped
1 tablespoon white wine vinegar	1¼ tablespoons white wine vinegar
150 ml./¼ pint tomato juice	⅔ cup tomato juice

Serves 4
Oven setting: 180°C./350°F./Gas Mark 4
Coat the pork slices in the flour, seasoned with salt and pepper. Heat the butter and fry the pork briskly on both sides until golden brown, remove and place in a casserole dish. Add the onions, leek and celery to the pan and fry for 10 minutes, then spoon on to the pork, together with the green pepper and tomatoes. Season to taste and pour over the vinegar and tomato juice. Cover the casserole and bake in the preheated oven for 40–50 minutes, or until just tender.

Sautéed pork and orange

Metric/Imperial	American
550 g./1¼ lb. pork fillet, cut into cubes	1¼ lb. pork tenderloin, cut into cubes
flour	flour
salt and pepper	salt and pepper
3 oranges	3 oranges
2 tablespoons butter	2½ tablespoons butter
1 small onion, chopped	1 small onion, chopped
1 green pepper, cored, seeded and cut into strips	1 green pepper, cored, seeded and cut into strips
grated rind of ½ orange	grated rind of ½ orange
1 tablespoon Worcestershire sauce	1¼ tablespoons Worcestershire sauce
150 ml./¼ pint stock	⅔ cup stock

Serves 4
Coat the pork with the flour seasoned with salt and pepper. Peel one of the oranges, remove all the white pith and cut into segments. Set them aside.
Heat the butter in a pan, add the onion and green pepper and sauté for 3 minutes. Add the meat and cook for 5 minutes, turning frequently. Add the juice of 2 oranges and the grated orange rind, then the Worcestershire sauce and stock. Bring to boiling point and simmer for 20 minutes, stirring occasionally. Check the seasoning and add the orange segments just before serving.

Helpful hints
If using a less expensive cut of pork for this recipe, add extra stock and extend the cooking time. Allow about 50 minutes — 1 hour for leg.

PORK

Sweet and sour pork spareribs

Metric/Imperial	American
1 kg./2 lb. pork spareribs, American cut	2 lb. pork spareribs
1 tablespoon corn oil	1¼ tablespoons corn oil
1 onion, chopped	1 onion, chopped
1 small carrot, peeled and cut into thin strips	1 small carrot, peeled and cut into thin strips
150 ml./¼ pint pineapple juice	⅔ cup pineapple juice
75 ml./3 fl. oz. white wine vinegar	6 tablespoons white wine vinegar
1 tablespoon Worcestershire sauce	1¼ tablespoons Worcestershire sauce
1 teaspoon soy sauce	1 teaspoon soy sauce
50 g./2 oz. soft brown sugar	⅓ cup light brown sugar
1 tablespoon cornflour	1¼ tablespoons cornstarch
4 tablespoons water	5 tablespoons water
juice and grated rind of ½ lemon	juice and grated rind of ½ lemon
salt and black pepper	salt and black pepper
1 small red pepper, cored, seeded and chopped	1 small red pepper, cored, seeded and chopped
4 canned pineapple rings, chopped	4 canned pineapple rings, chopped

Serves 4
Oven setting: 220°C./425°F./Gas Mark 7
Cook spareribs in a roasting pan, uncovered, in the oven for 20 minutes. Drain off any fat.

Heat the corn oil in a pan, add the onion and carrot and fry for 5 minutes. Pour in the pineapple juice, vinegar, Worcestershire sauce, soy sauce and brown sugar, and stir until the sugar has dissolved. Lower the heat and simmer for 20 minutes, stirring occasionally. Blend the cornflour (cornstarch) and water together until smooth and add to the sauce, together with the lemon juice, rind and seasoning to taste. Bring to the boil, stirring constantly, then simmer until thick. Add red pepper and pineapple pieces. Pour the sauce over the spareribs. Reduce the oven setting to 180°C./350°F./Gas Mark 4, cover the pan and cook for 40 minutes basting ribs with sauce.

Pork chops in ginger beer

Metric/Imperial	American
25 g./1 oz. butter	2 tablespoons butter
4 pork chops, trimmed of excess fat	4 pork chops, trimmed of excess fat
1 large onion, sliced into rings	1 large onion, sliced into rings
4 sticks celery, diced	4 sticks celery, diced
2 carrots, peeled and thinly sliced	2 carrots, peeled and thinly sliced
25 g./1 oz. flour	¼ cup flour
450 ml./¾ pint ginger beer	2 cups ginger beer
1 beef stock cube dissolved in 4 tablespoons hot water	1 beef bouillon cube dissolved in 5 tablespoons hot water
dash of Worcestershire sauce	dash of Worcestershire sauce
juice of ½ lemon	juice of ½ lemon
225 g./8 oz. tomatoes, skinned, seeded and chopped	8 oz. tomatoes, skinned, seeded and chopped
salt and freshly ground black pepper	salt and freshly ground black pepper

Serves 4
Oven setting: 180°C./350°F./Gas Mark 4
Heat the butter in a heavy pan and cook the chops quickly over a moderate heat until they are golden brown, remove and place in a casserole.

Add the onion, celery and carrots to the pan and fry until soft, sprinkle in the flour and cook, stirring constantly, for 1 minute. Gradually blend in the ginger beer and dissolved stock (bouillon) cube and bring to the boil, stirring constantly. When the sauce has thickened, stir in the Worcestershire sauce, lemon juice, tomatoes and seasoning to taste. Pour the sauce over the chops, cover the casserole and cook in the preheated oven for 45 minutes, or until the pork is tender.

Pork with barbecue sauce

Metric/Imperial	American
2 tablespoons oil	2½ tablespoons oil
4–6 spare rib pork chops	4–6 pork slices
2 medium-sized onions, chopped	2 medium-sized onions, chopped
2 tablespoons tomato purée	2½ tablespoons tomato paste
2 tablespoons water	2½ tablespoons water
2 tablespoons soft brown sugar	2½ tablespoons light brown sugar
2 tablespoons vinegar	2½ tablespoons vinegar
1 teaspoon Worcestershire sauce	1 teaspoon Worcestershire sauce
1–2 teaspoons made mustard	1–2 teaspoons made mustard
pinch of dried mixed herbs	pinch of dried mixed herbs
salt and pepper	salt and pepper

Serves 4–6

Heat the oil in a pan and fry the meat on both sides until lightly browned. Remove from the pan and put on a plate. Add the onions to the pan, fry gently for 5 minutes; then stir in the remaining ingredients and bring to the boil. Replace the meat in the pan, cover and simmer for 15 minutes.

Helpful hints

To economize, use lean diced belly pork instead of chops. Serve with a green salad.

Sweet and sour pork in batter

Metric/Imperial	American
225 g./8 oz. lean pork, cut in 1 cm./½ inch pieces	8 oz. lean pork, cut in ½ inch pieces
25 g./1 oz. seasoned flour	¼ cup seasoned flour
oil for deep-frying	oil for deep-frying

Batter	Batter
100 g./4 oz. self-raising flour	1 cup self-rising flour
½ teaspoon salt	½ teaspoon salt
150 ml./¼ pint water	⅔ cup water

Sweet and sour sauce	Sweet and sour sauce
1 × 350 g./12 oz. can pineapple chunks	1 × 12 oz. can pineapple chunks
3 tablespoons malt vinegar	4 tablespoons cider vinegar
1 tablespoon tomato purée	1¼ tablespoons tomato paste
2 teaspoons soft brown sugar	2 teaspoons light brown sugar
2 teaspoons cornflour	2 teaspoons cornstarch
1 tablespoon water	1¼ tablespoons water
1 spring onion, cut in 2.5 cm./1 inch pieces	1 scallion, cut in 1 inch pieces
1 green pepper, cored, seeded and sliced	1 green pepper, cored, seeded and sliced
oil for frying	oil for frying

Serves 3

Sift the flour and salt into a mixing bowl, gradually add the water and beat to a smooth batter. Set aside for 15 minutes.

Drain the pineapple chunks, reserving 4 tablespoons (5 tablespoons) juice. Put the juice in a saucepan with the vinegar, tomato purée (paste), sugar, cornflour (cornstarch) and water. Simmer for 2 minutes, stirring. Meanwhile, fry the spring onion (scallion) and green pepper in 1 tablespoon oil for 30 seconds. Add to the saucepan with the pineapple and mix well.

Toss the pork in the flour, seasoned with salt and pepper. Heat the oil until it is hot enough to turn a stale bread cube golden in 30 seconds (190°C./375°F on a deep-fat thermometer). Dip the pork pieces in the batter, then fry in the hot oil for 5 minutes, or until pale golden. Drain, place on serving dish and pour over the sauce.

PORK

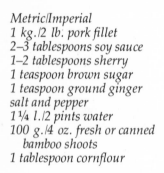

Pork and bamboo shoots

Metric/Imperial	American
1 kg./2 lb. pork fillet	2 lb. pork tenderloin
2–3 tablespoons soy sauce	2½–4 tablespoons soy sauce
1–2 tablespoons sherry	1¼–2½ tablespoons sherry
1 teaspoon brown sugar	1 teaspoon brown sugar
1 teaspoon ground ginger	1 teaspoon ground ginger
salt and pepper	salt and pepper
1¼ l./2 pints water	5 cups water
100 g./4 oz. fresh or canned bamboo shoots	4 oz. fresh or canned bamboo shoots
1 tablespoon cornflour	1¼ tablespoons cornstarch

Serves 6–8

Cut the pork into small cubes. Mix the soy sauce, sherry, sugar, ginger, salt and pepper together. Add the pork, toss well and leave for 10 minutes. Place the pork and flavourings into a large pan, add most of the water and bring to the boil. Cover and simmer for 1 hour.

Wash and drain fresh or canned bamboo shoots and shred finely. Add to the pan and simmer for another 10 minutes. Blend the cornflour (cornstarch) with the remaining water, stir into the juices in the pan and continue cooking for 10 minutes, stirring occasionally. Serve with extra soy sauce.

Somerset pork

Metric/Imperial	American
½ kg–550 g./1–1¼ lb. pork fillet	1–1¼ lb. pork tenderloin
2 tablespoons flour	2½ tablespoons flour
50 g./2 oz. butter	4 tablespoons butter
1 large onion, finely chopped	1 large onion, finely chopped
175 g./6 oz. mushrooms, sliced	1½ cups sliced mushrooms
300 ml./½ pint dry cider	1¼ cups dry cider
salt and pepper	salt and pepper
4 tablespoons double cream	5 tablespoons heavy cream
chopped parsley to garnish	chopped parsley to garnish

Serves 4

Cut the pork into eight pieces. Place each piece between two sheets of greaseproof (waxed) paper, and beat with a meat mallet or rolling pin until ½ cm./¼ inch thick. Coat the pork lightly with the flour, reserving any left over. Heat the butter and fry the pork slowly for about 4 minutes on each side. Remove from the pan, drain well and keep warm. Add the onion and mushrooms to the pan and cook gently until soft. Stir in the remaining flour, and cook for 1 minute. Gradually blend in the cider and bring to the boil, stirring constantly. Add the pork and seasoning, then stir in the cream. Heat for a further 2–3 minutes *without boiling*. Serve garnished with chopped parsley.

Toad in the hole

Metric/Imperial
8 large pork or beef sausages
25 g./1 oz. pork or beef
   dripping or lard
100 g./4 oz. flour
¼ teaspoon salt
2 eggs, beaten
300 ml./½ pint milk
1 teaspoon dried mixed herbs
freshly ground black pepper

American
8 large pork or beef sausages
2 tablespoons pork or beef
   dripping or lard
1 cup flour
¼ teaspoon salt
2 eggs, beaten
1¼ cups milk
1 teaspoon dried mixed herbs
freshly ground black pepper

Serves 4
Oven setting: 220°C./425°F./Gas Mark 7
Put the sausages in a shallow ovenproof dish or baking pan with the dripping or lard and bake in the preheated oven for 5–10 minutes, turning the sausages occasionally to brown on all sides.

Meanwhile, make the batter. Sift the flour and salt into a mixing bowl. Make a well in the centre and put in the beaten eggs and half the milk. Gradually mix the flour into the liquid. Stir in remaining milk and beat vigorously with a wooden spoon or wire whisk to make the batter smooth. Stir in the dried herbs and pepper to taste.

Pour the batter into the dish or pan with the sausages and continue to bake for a further 40–45 minutes, or until the batter has risen and is brown and crisp.

Helpful hints
To vary, use mushrooms and small tomatoes as well as sausages.

Sweet and sour ham

Metric/Imperial
40 g./1½ oz. butter or
   margarine
25 g./1 oz. brown sugar
3 tablespoons vinegar
3 tablespoons redcurrant or
   apple jelly
1–2 teaspoons made mustard
pepper
4 slices cooked ham, about
   ½–1 cm./¼–½ inch thick

American
3 tablespoons butter or
   margarine
2 tablespoons brown sugar
4 tablespoons vinegar
4 tablespoons redcurrant or
   apple jelly
1–2 teaspoons made mustard
pepper
4 slices cooked ham, about
   ¼–½ inch thick

Serves 4
Put the butter or margarine, brown sugar, vinegar and redcurrant or apple jelly into a frying pan (skillet). Stir over a gentle heat until the mixture forms a smooth sauce. Add the mustard and pepper; a little salt can be added if the ham is mild in flavour. Put in the slices of ham, baste well and heat gently until the ham is heated through.

Helpful hints
Serve with pasta for a quickly prepared but substantial meal.

BACON and SAUSAGES

Ham and sweet peppers

Metric/Imperial
3 red peppers, cored, seeded and
  finely sliced
1 tablespoon cornflour
2 tablespoons soy sauce
1 tablespoon sherry
1 teaspoon sugar
2 tablespoons stock or water
350 g./12 oz. ham, cubed
2 tablespoons oil

American
3 red peppers, cored, seeded and
  finely sliced
1¼ tablespoons cornstarch
2½ tablespoons soy sauce
1¼ tablespoons sherry
1 teaspoon sugar
2½ tablespoons stock or water
12 oz. ham, cubed
2½ tablespoons oil

Serves 4
Cover the peppers with boiling water and leave for 1
minute to blanch, then drain. Mix the cornflour
(cornstarch), soy sauce, sherry, sugar and stock or water.
Pour the mixture over the ham and mix well so that the
meat is coated. Heat the oil in a frying pan (skillet) and
fry the peppers for 2 minutes over fierce heat, stirring
constantly. Remove the peppers from the pan. Put the
ham into the pan, with the liquid and cook for 1 minute,
stirring constantly, over medium heat. Add the peppers,
cook for another minute, then serve.

Mexican frankfurters

Metric/Imperial
75 g./3 oz. shell or other
  shaped macaroni
salt
300 ml./½ pint canned or
  home-made consommé
few drops chilli sauce
4 tomatoes, skinned and sliced
6–8 frankfurters

Garnish
2 pineapple rings
1 tomato
parsley

American
3 oz. shell or other shaped
  macaroni
salt
1¼ cups canned or home-made
  consommé
few drops chili sauce
4 tomatoes, skinned and sliced
6–8 frankfurters

Garnish
2 pineapple rings
1 tomato
parsley

Serves 4
Cook the macaroni in boiling salted water, drain and mix
with the consommé, chilli (chili) sauce, tomatoes and
frankfurters. Simmer steadily for 20 minutes. Transfer to a
serving dish and top with pineapple rings, sliced tomato
and parsley.

Helpful hints
A good light dish for lunch or a late supper. Serve with a
crisp, fresh salad.

Cider casserole

Metric/Imperial	American
4 large onions or 4–5 medium-sized leeks	4 large onions or 4–5 medium-sized leeks
75 g./3 oz. margarine	6 tablespoons margarine
300 ml./½ pint cider	1¼ cups cider
salt and pepper	salt and pepper
pinch of dried or fresh sage	pinch of dried or fresh sage
2–3 dessert apples	2–3 eating apples
4 thick rashers rather fat bacon or pork belly	4 thick slices rather fat bacon

Serves 4

Oven setting: 160–180°C./325–350°F./Gas Mark 3–4
Peel and cut the onions into slices then separate into rings. (If using leeks, wash thoroughly and cut into 1 cm./½ inch lengths.) Heat 50 g./2 oz. (¼ cup) of the margarine in a large pan, toss the onion rings or leek slices in this until pale golden brown. Put into a casserole with the cider, seasoning and herbs. Cover and cook for approximately 40 minutes in the centre of the preheated oven. Core and slice the apples, but do not peel, toss in the remaining margarine. Remove the casserole from the oven, arrange the apples over the top of the onion and cider mixture. Top with the uncooked rashers (slices) of bacon or pork belly. Do not put the lid back on the dish. Return to the oven for a further 25–30 minutes.

Helpful hints

Vary this by using slices of pork belly. This is a cheap, rather fatty cut but goes well with the apples, onions and cider mixture. Serve with baked potatoes.

Frankfurters with white cabbage

Metric/Imperial	American
1 kg./2 lb. white cabbage, finely shredded	2 lb. white cabbage, finely shredded
salt and pepper	salt and pepper
25 g./1 oz. butter	2 tablespoons butter
1 large onion, chopped	1 large onion, chopped
1 garlic clove, crushed	1 garlic clove, crushed
1 large tart apple, peeled, cored and grated	1 large tart apple, peeled, cored and grated
4 streaky bacon rashers	4 fatty bacon slices
8 frankfurters	8 frankfurters
150 ml./¼ pint stock	⅔ cup stock

Serves 4

Oven setting: 180°C./350°F./Gas Mark 4
Cook the cabbage in boiling salted water for 5 minutes, drain well and turn into a bowl. Melt the butter in a frying pan and fry the onion and garlic for 5 minutes. Add to the cabbage with the cooking apple, season with salt and pepper and mix well. Put half the cabbage mixture into a casserole. Stretch the bacon rashers (slices) on a board with the back of a knife and cut each in half. Wrap a piece of bacon round each frankfurter. Lay the frankfurters on top of the cabbage in the casserole and cover with the remaining cabbage. Pour over the stock. Cover and cook for 1½ hours.

BACON and SAUSAGES

Stuffed ham rolls

Metric/Imperial
2 sticks celery, chopped
2 apples, peeled, cored and
  chopped
50 g./2 oz. chopped walnuts
1 tablespoon chopped chives
1 tablespoon lemon juice
150 ml./¼ pint mayonnaise
salt and pepper
8 slices ham
100 g./4 oz. pâté

Garnish
parsley sprigs
lemon slices

American
2 sticks celery, chopped
2 apples, peeled, cored and
  chopped
½ cup chopped walnuts
1¼ tablespoons chopped chives
1¼ tablespoons lemon juice
⅔ cup mayonnaise
salt and pepper
8 slices ham
4 oz. pâté

Garnish
parsley sprigs
lemon slices

Serves 4
Mix together the celery, apples, walnuts, chives and
lemon juice. Add the mayonnaise, then taste and adjust
seasoning. Spread each slice of ham with pâté. Divide the
mayonnaise mixture between the slices and roll them up.
Garnish with parsley and lemon.

Helpful hints
Choose a smooth, lightly flavoured pâté or liver sausage to
complement the chunky, nutty mayonnaise filling.

Cheese and bacon kebabs

Metric/Imperial
4–5 rashers bacon
225–275 g./8–10 oz. firm
  Cheddar cheese
1–2 ripe dessert apples and/or
  ½ green pepper cored and
  seeded
few small mushrooms
parboiled onions (see method)

American
4–5 slices bacon
8–10 oz. firm Cheddar cheese
1–2 ripe dessert apples and/or
  ½ green pepper cored and
  seeded
few small mushrooms
parboiled onions (see method)

Serves 3–4
Cut any rind from the bacon and cut each rasher (slice) in
half. Cut the cheese into cubes, then roll the bacon round
the cheese. Put the bacon rolls on to a metal skewer.

Add segments of apple and/or pieces of green pepper,
small mushrooms and tiny onions (brushed with melted
fat).

Cook under the grill (broiler), turning occasionally, until
the bacon is evenly cooked. Do not overcook the cheese as
it then becomes less easy to digest.

Helpful hints
A good meal for a family with young children. Vary the
'extras' on the skewers to suit the varying tastes of adults
and children.

Ham en croûte

Metric/Imperial
2 kg./4 lb. middle joint
  gammon or ham
½ kg./1 lb. shortcrust pastry
  dough
1 egg, beaten

American
4 lb. middle joint gammon or
  ham
4 cups shortcrust pastry dough
1 egg, beaten

Serves 8–10
Oven setting: 190°C./375°F./Gas Mark 5
Soak the gammon or ham for 12 hours in cold water unless
green or sweetcure. If very salty, soak for 24 hours. Lift out
of the water, dry thoroughly and cut away the skin.

Roll the pastry out to about 2 cm./¾ inch in thickness
and cut off about two thirds. Place the gammon or ham on
the larger piece of pastry, and bring up the pastry to encase
the sides of the meat. Roll out the remaining pastry for the
lid and place over the meat. Cut away any surplus pastry,
brush the edges with beaten egg and pinch together very
firmly. Lift on to a baking tray. Brush with beaten egg. Cut
a slit in the top to allow the steam to escape. Make small
leaves of pastry for decoration and press on top of the
croûte and brush with beaten egg. Bake in the centre of the
oven for 30 minutes, then reduce the heat to
160°C./325°F./Gas Mark 3, for the remainder of the time.
Allow 25 minutes per ½ kg./1 lb. and 25 minutes over, so a
2 kg./4 lb. joint will take 2 hours 5 minutes. Serve hot or
cold, cut into thin slices.

Helpful hints
For ham with pineapple, soak the ham as above but do not
remove the skin. Cook as above. When cooked, remove
skin. Allow to cool slightly, then press browned
breadcrumbs into the fat. Garnish with pineapple rings,
attached with wooden cocktail sticks (picks), through the
holes. Spear a maraschino cherry on the end of the stick
(pick) and a clove in the centre of the cherry.

Gammon with pineapple

Metric/Imperial
4 slices lean gammon
50 g./2 oz. melted butter
4 canned pineapple rings,
  halved

Sauce
25 g./1 oz. butter
25 g./1 oz. flour
300 ml./½ pint milk
1 onion, finely chopped
salt and pepper
4 tablespoons sweetcorn
2 teaspoons chopped parsley
2 tablespoons pineapple syrup
  from can

Garnish
watercress

American
4 slices lean gammon
¼ cup melted butter
4 canned pineapple rings,
  halved

Sauce
2 tablespoons butter
¼ cup flour
1¼ cups milk
1 onion, finely chopped
salt and pepper
5 tablespoons sweetcorn
2 teaspoons chopped parsley
2½ tablespoons pineapple
  syrup from can

Garnish
watercress

Serves 4
Snip the edges of the gammon, to prevent it from curling.
Brush with melted butter and cook for several minutes on
one side, turn, brush with more butter and continue
cooking. Meanwhile, make the sauce. Heat the butter in a
pan, stir in the flour and cook for several minutes.
Gradually blend in the milk, then add the onion. Bring to
the boil and cook until thickened, stirring all the time.
Season the sauce then add the sweetcorn and parsley. At
the last minute, whisk in the pineapple syrup. When the
gammon is nearly ready add the pineapple to the grill pan.
Brush with butter and heat thoroughly. Place the gammon
and pineapple on a plate and garnish with watercress.
Serve the sauce separately.

Sausage twists

Metric/Imperial
½ kg./1 lb. small chipolata
  sausages
225 g./8 oz. puff pastry dough
beaten egg

American
1 lb. skinless sausages
2 cups puff pastry dough
beaten egg

Serves 8 as an hors d'oeuvre.
Oven setting: 230°C./450°F./Gas Mark 8
Grill (broil) or fry the sausages for about 6 minutes, until
partially cooked. Allow to cool. Roll out the pastry until
wafer thin. Cut into strips and roll round the sausages. Put
on a baking tray. Brush with beaten egg. Bake for 15
minutes towards the top of the oven. Reduce the heat after
7–8 minutes if necessary. Serve with mustard or a sauce of
your choice.

Candied ham with fried eggs

Metric/Imperial
15 g./½ oz. butter
2 tablespoons pineapple juice
2 slices cooked ham, ½ cm./¼
  inch thick
1 tablespoon brown sugar
3 tablespoons vegetable oil
4 eggs

American
1 tablespoon butter
2½ tablespoons pineapple juice
2 slices cooked ham, ¼ inch
  thick
1¼ tablespoons brown sugar
4 tablespoons vegetable oil
4 eggs

Serves 2
Oven setting: 200°C./400°F./Gas Mark 6
Melt butter in an ovenproof dish. Add pineapple juice. Put
ham slices in dish and sprinkle with brown sugar. Put into
the oven to heat for 10 minutes. When ham is almost
ready, heat the oil in a frying pan (skillet). Break eggs into
oil, keeping them apart if possible. Baste while they cook
by spooning hot oil over until a film of white is set over the
egg yolk. Lift eggs from oil with an egg slice and drain
well. Serve with hot candied ham.

Chicken curry with yellow rice

Metric/Imperial
40 g./1½ oz. butter
1 large onion, chopped
1 green pepper, cored, seeded
   and sliced
1 garlic clove, crushed
about 1 tablespoon Madras
   curry powder
1 teaspoon chilli powder
salt
4 chicken portions
4 tomatoes, skinned and
   chopped
2 tablespoons natural yogurt

Rice
25 g./1 oz. butter
225 g./8 oz. long-grain rice
1 teaspoon turmeric
few cloves
1 teaspoon ground cumin
salt
600 ml./1 pint water

American
3 tablespoons butter
1 large onion, chopped
1 green pepper, cored, seeded
   and sliced
1 garlic clove, crushed
about 1¼ tablespoons Madras
   curry powder
1 teaspoon chili powder
salt
4 chicken portions
4 tomatoes, skinned and
   chopped
2½ tablespoons plain yogurt

Rice
2 tablespoons butter
1⅓ cups long-grain rice
1 teaspoon turmeric
few cloves
1 teaspoon ground cumin
salt
2½ cups water

Serves 4
Heat the butter in a pan and fry the onion, pepper and garlic for about 5 minutes. Add the curry powder, chilli (chili) powder and salt, and mix well. Add the chicken portions and brown quickly over a high heat. Lower the heat, cover and simmer gently for 1 hour. If using frozen chicken, you will probably not need to add any water at all, but if using fresh, add 2–3 tablespoons (2½–4 tablespoons) before lowering the heat. Add the tomatoes to the pan 5 minutes before the end of the cooking time. Stir in the yogurt just before serving.

    Heat the butter for the rice in a pan, and toss the rice gently in this for 5 minutes. Add the spices and salt and mix well. Pour in the water. Cover and simmer gently for about 15 minutes or until the rice is tender and all the liquid absorbed. Put the rice on the bottom of a serving dish and spoon over the chicken mixture.

Hare in Madeira sauce

Metric/Imperial
4 joints young hare
15 g./½ oz. flour
1 teaspoon chopped sage
75 g./3 oz. butter
100 g./4 oz. mushrooms
225 ml./8 fl. oz. Madeira
½ teaspoon fresh chopped
   herbs
salt and pepper

American
4 joints young hare
2 tablespoons flour
1 teaspoon chopped sage
⅜ cup butter
4 oz. mushrooms
1 cup Madeira
½ teaspoon fresh chopped
   herbs
salt and pepper

Serves 4
Oven setting: 190°C./375°F./Gas Mark 5
Sprinkle the hare with flour, mixed with a little chopped sage. Melt half the butter and brown the hare in this. Lift the hare out of the pan and put into a casserole. Melt the rest of the butter and cook the mushrooms in this. Add to the casserole with the Madeira, herbs and seasoning. Cover the casserole and cook in the oven for 1 hour. Garnish with chopped parsley, if liked.

POULTRY and GAME

Stuffed roast turkey

Metric/Imperial	American
1 × 6 kg./12 lb. turkey	1 × 12 lb. turkey
several rashers fat bacon, or enough bacon fat to cover the bird	several slices fat bacon, or enough bacon fat to cover the bird
1 tablespoon flour	1¼ tablespoons flour
300–600 ml./½–1 pint stock (made from the giblets)	1¼–2½ cups stock (made from the giblets)
Stuffing	*Stuffing*
100 g./4 oz. lean ham, chopped	4 oz. lean ham, chopped
225 g./8 oz. sausage meat	8 oz. sausage meat
1 teaspoon chopped parsley	1 teaspoon chopped parsley
grated rind of 1 lemon	grated rind of 1 lemon
50 g./2 oz. sultanas	½ cup seedless raisins
1 egg, beaten	1 egg, beaten
salt and pepper	salt and pepper
Garnish	*Garnish*
225 g./8 oz. streaky bacon rashers	8 oz. fatty bacon slices
½ kg./1 lb. small sausages	1 lb. small sausages
watercress sprig	watercress sprig

Serves 14–16

Oven setting: 230°C./450°F./Gas Mark 8

Combine all the ingredients for the stuffing and season well. Lift the skin of the neck of the turkey and place stuffing under it. Pull the skin gently over the stuffing and fasten it with a skewer. Put any remaining stuffing inside the bird. Cross the legs over the vent and secure them with string. Cover the bird with the bacon or bacon fat. Place the turkey in a roasting pan and cook for 30 minutes. Reduce the heat to 190°C./375°F./Gas Mark 5 and cook for a further 3½–4 hours, basting occasionally.

To make the garnish, remove the bacon rind and cut the rashers (slices) in half. Stretch each slice on a board with the back of a knife, then roll up and secure with a wooden or metal skewer. Grill (broil) the bacon rolls and sausages and place round the cooked turkey. Garnish with watercress. Serve with cranberry sauce.

Ragoût of duckling

Metric/Imperial	American
50 g./2 oz. fat	4 tablespoons fat
2 onions, chopped	2 onions, chopped
25 g./1 oz. flour	¼ cup flour
450 ml./¾ pint duck stock or water and 1 chicken stock cube	2 cups duck stock or water and 1 chicken bouillon cube
salt and pepper	salt and pepper
½–1 teaspoon chopped fresh or pinch of dried sage	½–1 teaspoon chopped fresh or pinch of dried sage
2 large carrots, peeled and diced	2 large carrots, peeled and diced
175–225 g./6–8 oz. cooked or canned chestnuts or diced Chinese water chestnuts	1–1⅓ cups cooked or canned chestnuts or diced Chinese water chestnuts
3 tablespoons port wine	4 tablespoons port wine
enough cooked duckling for 4	enough cooked duckling for 4
Garnish	*Garnish*
1–2 oranges	1–2 oranges

Serves 4

Heat the fat and fry the onion for 4–5 minutes. Blend in the flour, then stir over a low heat for 2–3 minutes. Add the stock or water and stock (bouillon) cube. Bring to the boil and cook until thickened. Add the seasoning, sage and carrots. Cover the pan, simmer for 40 minutes, then add the chestnuts, port wine and portions of duckling. Heat gently, but thoroughly. Garnish with orange slices.

Helpful hints

Use this recipe for game birds or rabbit, hare, goose, chicken, turkey, sliced cooked meat, cooked pork or lamb chops.

Sweet and sour chicken salad

Metric/Imperial	American
1 × 2 kg./4 lb. cooked chicken	1 × 4 lb. cooked chicken
8 small gherkins, sliced	8 small gherkins, sliced
4 canned pineapple rings, diced	4 canned pineapple rings, diced
1 tablespoon raisins	1¼ tablespoons raisins
2 tablespoons flaked almonds	2½ tablespoons flaked almonds

Marinade	Marinade
2 teaspoons French mustard	2 teaspoons French mustard
4 tablespoons white wine vinegar	5 tablespoons white wine vinegar
6 tablespoons salad oil	7½ tablespoons salad oil
2 garlic cloves	2 garlic cloves
1 teaspoon soy sauce	1 teaspoon soy sauce
1 tablespoon honey	1¼ tablespoons honey
salt and pepper	salt and pepper

Garnish	Garnish
endive or lettuce	chicory or lettuce
sliced beetroot	sliced beets
sliced, cooked potatoes	sliced, cooked potatoes

Serves 6

For the marinade blend the mustard with the white wine vinegar, then add the oil, crushed garlic, soy sauce, honey and seasoning.

Cut the chicken into small neat pieces. Add chicken, gherkins, pineapple and raisins to the marinade. Allow to stand for only 15 minutes. If the chicken has not absorbed all the marinade then spoon this out of the bowl and sprinkle over the salad at the last minute. Stir the almonds into the mixture just before serving. Arrange the endive (chicory) or lettuce on a dish, pile the chicken mixture in the centre and the sliced beetroot (beets) and potatoes around the edge of the dish.

Chicken and avocado casserole

Metric/Imperial	American
6 young chicken portions	6 young chicken portions
25 g./1 oz. flour	¼ cup flour
salt and pepper	salt and pepper
1 teaspoon chopped fresh or ¼ teaspoon dried thyme	1 teaspoon chopped fresh or ¼ teaspoon dried thyme
1 lemon	1 lemon
75 g./3 oz. butter	6 tablespoons butter
2 onions, sliced	2 onions, sliced
300 ml./½ pint dry white wine	1¼ cups dry white wine
150 ml./¼ pint chicken stock or water and ½ chicken stock cube	⅔ cup chicken stock or water and ½ chicken bouillon cube
1 tablespoon flour	1¼ tablespoons flour
150 ml./¼ pint double cream	⅔ cup heavy cream
2 ripe avocados	2 ripe avocados
little oil	little oil

Serves 6

Oven setting: 190–200°C./375–400°F./Gas Mark 5–6

Coat the portions of chicken in the flour, seasoned with salt, pepper, fresh or dried thyme and very finely grated lemon rind. Brown in two-thirds of the butter then put into a casserole. Add the remaining butter to the saucepan. Toss the onions in this for a few minutes, add the white wine and chicken stock or water and stock (bouillon) cube, blended with the flour. Bring to the boil and cook until thickened. Pour over the chicken. Cover and cook for about 1 hour in the preheated oven. Remove from the oven, cool slightly so the liquid is no longer boiling, and stir in the cream. Peel and slice the avocados and sprinkle with the lemon juice. Put on top of the chicken and brush with a little oil. Return to the coolest part of the oven for 10 minutes.

POULTRY and GAME

Cnicken cacciatore

Metric/Imperial	American
1 × 2 kg./4 lb. chicken	1 × 4 lb. chicken
flour	flour
50 g./2 oz. butter	¼ cup butter
1 tablespoon olive oil	1 ¼ tablespoons olive oil
1 large onion, chopped	1 large onion, chopped
2 garlic cloves, chopped	2 garlic cloves, chopped
8 tomatoes, skinned and chopped	8 tomatoes, skinned and chopped
3 tablespoons tomato purée	4 tablespoons tomato paste
1 teaspoon sugar	1 teaspoon sugar
150 ml./¼ pint chicken stock	⅔ cup chicken stock
salt and pepper	salt and pepper
225 g./8 oz. button mushrooms, sliced	2 cups sliced button mushrooms
4 tablespoons Marsala	5 tablespoons Marsala

Serves 4

Cut the chicken into joints and coat with flour. Heat the butter and olive oil together in a large pan. Add the chicken joints and fry until crisp and golden all over. Remove from the pan and keep hot. Add the onion and garlic to the pan and fry gently until pale gold. Stir in the tomatoes, tomato purée (paste), sugar and stock; season well with salt and pepper. Bring to the boil, then replace the chicken. Reduce the heat, cover the pan and simmer slowly for 30–45 minutes. Add the mushrooms and Marsala and continue to cook for 10–15 minutes. Serve with pasta.

Casserole of duck

Metric/Imperial	American
1 large duck	1 large duck
stuffing, see method	stuffing, see method
about 12 very small onions, peeled and left whole	about 12 very small onions, peeled and left whole
1–2 garlic cloves, crushed	1–2 garlic cloves, crushed
4–5 carrots, peeled and quartered	4–5 carrots, peeled and quartered
450 ml./¾ pint duck stock, made by simmering giblets	2 cups duck stock, made by simmering the giblets
salt and pepper	salt and pepper
25 g./1 oz. flour	¼ cup flour
4 large potatoes, peeled and roughly sliced	4 large potatoes, peeled and roughly sliced
Garnish	Garnish
parsley	parsley

Serves 4

Oven setting: 220–230°C./425–450°F./ Gas Mark 7–8
This is an excellent way of cooking a rather fat duck. The duck can be stuffed with sage and onion or chestnut stuffing, or with whole peeled apples and soaked, but not cooked, prunes. Roast the duck in the preheated oven for about 30 minutes, until really crisp and brown and until most of the fat has run out. While the duck is cooking, simmer the onions, garlic and carrots in 300 ml./½ pint (1¼ cups) stock for 30 minutes, season well. Blend the flour with the remaining stock, stir into the pan, and then cook until a smooth thickened sauce. Transfer to a casserole with the sliced potatoes. Place the duck on top and cover the casserole. Cook for 1½ hours in the oven reduced to 160–180°C./325–350°F./Gas Mark 3–4. Garnish with parsley.

Roast stuffed duck with orange sauce

Metric/Imperial
1 duck, about
* 2–2½ kg./4–5 lb.*
salt and pepper
1 garlic clove (optional)
juice of 1 orange
orange slices to garnish

Stuffing
25 g./1 oz. chicken fat
1 small onion, chopped
50 g./2 oz. raisins, soaked in 2
* tablespoons hot stock*
225 g./8 oz. long-grain rice,
* cooked*
1 apple, peeled and chopped
salt

Orange sauce
1 tablespoon flour
juice and rind of 1 orange
juice and rind of ½ lemon
150 ml./¼ pint stock
salt and pepper

American
1 duck, about 4–5 lb.
salt and pepper
1 garlic clove (optional)
juice of 1 orange
orange slices to garnish

Stuffing
2 tablespoons chicken fat
1 small onion, chopped
⅓ cup raisins, soaked in 2½
* tablespoons hot stock*
1⅓ cups long-grain rice,
* cooked*
1 apple, peeled and chopped
salt

Orange sauce
1¼ tablespoons flour
juice and rind of 1 orange
juice and rind of ½ lemon
⅔ cup stock
salt and pepper

Serves 5–6
Oven setting: 220°C./425°F./Gas Mark 7
Heat the fat for the stuffing in a pan and fry the onion until soft. Mix in the raisins, rice, apple and seasoning. Rub the duck with the seasoning and garlic clove. Stuff the bird and place it on a rack in a roasting pan. Pour the orange juice over and cover the breast with foil. Cook in the preheated oven. After 15 minutes, reduce the oven setting to 190°C./375°F./Gas Mark 5. Remove the foil 30 minutes before the end of the cooking time (about 1½–2 hours).

Remove the duck from the oven, garnish with orange slices and keep it hot. Pour off the fat except for 1 tablespoon. Add the flour for the sauce and cook until brown. Add the fruit juice and rinds and stock. Cook until thick, stirring constantly. Adjust seasoning and strain the sauce into a sauceboat.

Jugged hare

Metric/Imperial
1 hare, jointed
flour
salt and freshly ground black
* pepper*
beef dripping for frying
dry cider or water to cover
blood from hare (if available)
2 medium-sized onions, stuck
* with a few cloves*
1 bouquet garni

American
1 hare, jointed
flour
salt and freshly ground black
* pepper*
beef dripping for frying
hard cider or water to cover
2 medium-sized onions, stuck
* with a few cloves*
1 bouquet garni

Serves 4–6
Oven setting: 160°C./325°F./Gas Mark 3
Coat the hare pieces with the flour, seasoned with salt and pepper. Heat a knob of dripping in a large flameproof casserole. Fry the hare pieces in the dripping until browned on all sides. Stir in cider or water to cover, or a mixture of both. If using the blood, add it now. Bring to the boil, and add the onions and bouquet garni. Cover, transfer to the preheated oven and cook for 3–4 hours, or until the hare is tender. (The cooking time will vary depending on the age of the hare.)

Remove the hare pieces and onions from the casserole. Discard the bouquet garni. Remove the meat from the bones, discard the cloves from the onions and cut the onions into slices. Return the hare and onions to the casserole to heat through. Adjust seasoning before serving.

POULTRY and GAME

Chicken Hawaiian salad

Metric/Imperial
100 g./4 oz. almonds
1 cooked roasting chicken,
    about 1–1¼ kg./2–2½ lb.
    trussed
1 fresh pineapple
1 green pepper, cored, seeded
    and diced
1 head of chicory or few sticks
    celery, chopped
150–300 ml./¼–½ pint
    mayonnaise
lettuce

Garnish
tomatoes
cucumber or extra chicory

American
1 cup almonds
1 cooked roasting chicken,
    about 2–2½ lb. trussed
1 fresh pineapple
1 green pepper, cored, seeded
    and diced
1 head of endive or few sticks
    celery, chopped
⅔–1¼ cups mayonnaise
lettuce

Garnish
tomatoes
cucumber or extra endive

Serves 4
Blanch the almonds and brown the nuts under the grill
(broiler) or in the oven. Dice the cooked chicken. Cut the
top off the pineapple (keep this if the leaves are pleasantly
green). Cut the pineapple into rings, cut away the skin and
core the rings. Do this over a bowl so the juice is not
wasted. Dice the pineapple. Blend most of the almonds,
the chicken, pineapple, green pepper and chicory (endive)
or celery. Blend enough mayonnaise with any pineapple
juice to make a sauce. Toss the chicken mixture in this. Pile
on to a bed of lettuce, sprinkle with the remaining
almonds. Garnish with quartered tomatoes and sliced
cucumber or chicory (endive) leaves. Top the salad with
the pineapple leaves if retained.

To vary: Use 2 large oranges in place of the pineapple.
Remove all the skin, pith and pips.

Coq au vin

Metric/Imperial
1 tablespoon corn oil
50 g./2 oz. butter
100 g./4 oz. streaky bacon,
    chopped
75 g./6 oz. button onions or
    shallots, peeled and left
    whole
1 garlic clove, crushed
6 chicken portions
4 tablespoons brandy
3 tablespoons flour
300 ml./½ pint red wine
150 ml./¼ pint beef stock
1 small bay leaf
½ teaspoon dried thyme
1 parsley sprig
pinch of sugar
salt and freshly ground black
    pepper

American
1¼ tablespoons corn oil
4 tablespoons butter
⅔ cup chopped fatty bacon
6 oz. button onions or shallots,
    peeled and left whole
1 garlic clove, crushed
6 chicken portions
5 tablespoons brandy
4 tablespoons flour
1¼ cups red wine
⅔ cup beef stock
1 small bay leaf
½ teaspoon dried thyme
1 parsley sprig
pinch of sugar
salt and freshly ground black
    pepper

Serves 6
Oven setting: 180°C./350°F./Gas Mark 4
Heat the oil and butter in a large pan. Add the bacon,
onions, and garlic and fry briskly for 2–3 minutes until
lightly brown. Remove from the pan and place in a
casserole dish. Add the chicken to the pan and fry until
golden brown. Pour in the brandy, remove the pan from
the heat and flame the chicken, by igniting the brandy
with a match; shake the pan to encourage the flaming.
Remove the chicken and place in the casserole. Return the
pan to the heat, sprinkle in the flour and cook, stirring
constantly, for 1 minute. Gradually stir in the red wine and
stock and bring to the boil, stirring constantly. Add the bay
leaf, herbs, sugar and seasoning and pour over the
chicken.

Cover the casserole and cook in the preheated oven for 1
hour, or until just tender. Taste and adjust the seasoning.

Creamed turkey duchesse

Chicken charlotte

Metric/Imperial
½ kg./1 lb. mashed potatoes
2 eggs or 2 egg yolks
50 g./2 oz. butter
salt and pepper
100 g./4 oz. button mushrooms
1 green pepper, cored, seeded and diced
300 ml./½ pint turkey stock
25 g./1 oz. flour
150 ml./¼ pint milk
few drops of Tabasco sauce
½ kg./1 lb. diced cooked turkey
2–3 tablespoons single cream
chopped parsley to garnish

American
2⅔ cups mashed potatoes
2 eggs or 2 egg yolks
4 tablespoons butter
salt and pepper
1 cup button mushrooms
1 green pepper, cored, seeded and diced
1¼ cups turkey stock
¼ cup flour
⅔ cup milk
few drops of Tabasco sauce
2⅔ cups diced cooked turkey
2½–4 tablespoons light cream
chopped parsley to garnish

Serves 4–6
Oven setting: 180°C./350°F./Gas Mark 4
Mix the mashed potatoes with 1 egg or egg yolk and half the butter; season well. Form the potato into a border round an ovenproof dish. Brush with the second egg or egg yolk, diluted with a few drops of water, and brown in the preheated oven.

Meanwhile, simmer the mushrooms and green pepper in the stock for 10 minutes. Strain off the liquid and put it aside for the sauce.

Heat the remainder of the butter in a pan, stir in the flour and cook for 1 minute, stirring. Gradually stir in the milk, then the stock. Bring to the boil and cook until the sauce thickens, stirring constantly. Season well and flavour with Tabasco. Put the vegetables and turkey in the sauce and heat gently for a few minutes. Stir in the cream. Put the turkey mixture inside the potato border and garnish with parsley.

Metric/Imperial
5–6 slices of bread
75 g./3 oz. white cooking fat
25 g./1 oz. butter
25 g./1 oz. flour
generous 300 ml./½ pint milk
350 g./12 oz. diced cooked chicken
100 g./4 oz. diced cooked lean ham
chopped fresh or dried chives
chopped fresh or dried thyme
parsley

American
5–6 slices of bread
⅜ cup shortening
2 tablespoons butter
¼ cup flour
generous 1¼ cups milk
12 oz. diced cooked chicken
½ cup diced cooked lean ham
chopped fresh or dried chives
chopped fresh or dried thyme
parsley

Serves 4
Cut the slices of bread into fingers. Do not cut away the crusts. Melt the fat (shortening) and fry the bread fingers until crisp and golden. Drain on absorbent paper. Make a white sauce with the butter, flour and milk. Add the diced chicken, ham, chives and thyme. Put half the bread fingers into an oven-proof dish, top with the sauce mixture, then the rest of the fried bread fingers. Heat in the oven for a few minutes. Garnish with parsley.

Helpful hints
For variation, try using ½ kg./1 lb. flaked, cooked white fish instead of chicken and ham.

POULTRY and GAME

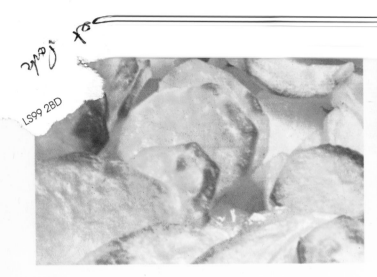

Chicken hotpot

Metric/Imperial
½ kg./1 lb. potatoes, peeled
    and sliced
350 g./12 oz. onions, sliced
3 tomatoes, skinned and sliced
salt and pepper
4 chicken portions
about 150 ml./¼ pint stock
chopped fresh or dried rosemary
margarine

American
1 lb. potatoes, peeled and sliced
3 cups sliced onions
3 tomatoes, skinned and sliced
salt and pepper
4 chicken portions
scant ½ cup stock
chopped fresh or dried rosemary
margarine

Serves 4
Oven setting: 160–180°C./325–350°F./Gas Mark 3–4
Put a layer of potatoes into a casserole, cover with a layer of
onions and tomatoes. Season each layer well. Put the
chicken portions over the vegetables, add well seasoned
stock, a light sprinkling of rosemary, then a layer of
tomatoes, onions, and a topping of potato slices. Season
well, put small pieces of margarine over the potatoes.
Cover the casserole and cook near the centre of the
preheated oven for approximately 1¼–1½ hours. Remove
the lid for the last 20–30 minutes if wished, to brown the
potatoes.

Helpful hints
When there are lots of vegetables to slice, as here, a
mandoline slicer is invaluable. It should have an
adjustable blade that allows you to vary the thickness of
the slices.

Hare with prunes

Metric/Imperial
175 g./6 oz. prunes
300 ml./½ pint red wine
1 hare, with the liver, cut into
    serving pieces
4 tablespoons water
40 g./1½ oz. flour
salt and pepper
75 g./3 oz. dripping
3 onions, chopped
2 garlic cloves, crushed
600 ml./1 pint brown stock
juice of ½ lemon
2 tablespoons redcurrant jelly
1 bouquet garni
3 slices white bread
25 g./1 oz. butter

American
1 cup prunes
1¼ cups red wine
1 hare, with the liver, cut into
    serving pieces
5 tablespoons water
⅜ cup flour
salt and pepper
⅜ cup drippings
3 onions, chopped
2 garlic cloves, crushed
2½ cups brown stock
juice of ½ lemon
2½ tablespoons redcurrant
    jelly
1 bouquet garni
3 slices white bread
2 tablespoons butter

Serves 6–8
Oven setting: 160°C./325°F./Gas Mark 3
Soak the prunes in the red wine overnight. Put the hare
liver into a saucepan with the water and simmer gently for
20 minutes or until tender. Mash with the cooking liquid.
Coat hare with flour, seasoned with salt and pepper.

Heat the dripping in a large flameproof casserole and fry
the hare quickly on all sides until golden. Remove from the
casserole and put on one side. Fry the onions and garlic in
the fat remaining in the casserole for about 5 minutes or
until soft. Stir in any remaining flour, then gradually stir in
the stock. Bring slowly to the boil, stirring all the time. Add
the lemon juice, mashed liver mixture, redcurrant jelly,
prunes, with the wine, and bouquet garni. Season well.
Replace the hare in the casserole, cover and cook in the
oven for 3 hours.

Remove the crusts from the bread and cut into triangles.
Melt the butter in a frying pan (skillet) and fry the bread
until golden on both sides. Taste the hare casserole, adjust
the seasoning and remove the bouquet garni. Turn into a
serving dish and garnish with the croûtes.

Sesame chicken

Metric/Imperial
100 g./4 oz. butter, melted
2 tablespoons soy sauce
2 tablespoons white wine
1 teaspoon chopped tarragon
1 teaspoon mustard powder
4 chicken breasts, boned
sesame seeds

American
½ cup butter, melted
2½ tablespoons soy sauce
2½ tablespoons white wine
1 teaspoon chopped tarragon
1 teaspoon mustard powder
4 chicken breasts, boned
sesame seeds

Serves 4
Mix the butter, soy sauce, wine, tarragon and mustard together. Marinate the chicken in this mixture for 3 hours. Drain and keep the marinade.

Grill the chicken for 4–6 minutes on each side. Remove from heat, brush with the marinade, roll in sesame seeds and return to heat until sesame seeds are golden brown.

Serve immediately.

Cyprus chicken salad in rice ring

Metric/Imperial
175 g./6 oz. long-grain rice
600 ml./1 pint very well clarified chicken stock
150 ml./¼ pint fresh orange juice
salt and pepper
2–3 tablespoons olive oil
1–1½ tablespoons white wine vinegar
finely shredded peel of 2–3 oranges
1 cooked chicken, about 2½ kg./5 lb.
150 ml./¼ pint mayonnaise
4 tablespoons white wine
1 tablespoon olive oil
salt and pepper
1 green pepper, cored and seeded
2 teaspoons fresh herbs
about 225 g./8 oz. grapes
2–4 tablespoons blanched almonds

American
1 cup long-grain rice
2½ cups very well clarified chicken stock
⅔ cup fresh orange juice
salt and pepper
2½–4 tablespoons olive oil
1¼–2 tablespoons white wine vinegar
finely shredded peel of 2–3 oranges
1 cooked chicken, about 5 lb.
⅔ cup mayonnaise
5 tablespoons white wine
1¼ tablespoons olive oil
salt and pepper
1 green pepper, cored and seeded
2 teaspoons fresh herbs
about 8 oz. grapes
2½–5 tablespoons blanched almonds

Serves 6–8
Put the rice into a pan with the stock, orange juice and seasoning. Bring to the boil, lower the heat, cover and simmer gently for about 15 minutes until the rice is just tender and the liquid has evaporated. Blend the oil and vinegar and soak the shredded peel in this to soften. Drain the peel well, then blend enough oil and vinegar into the rice, with extra seasoning, to make it slightly moist. Form into a ring on serving dish, cool, then top with peel.

To make the salad, cut the chicken meat from the bones, save some of the best pieces of breast for garnish. Blend the mayonnaise with the white wine and oil, season well. Cut green pepper into neat pieces. Blend diced chicken, pepper and herbs into the dressing, pile into the centre of the rice ring. Garnish with the reserved chicken breast, grapes and the browned almonds.

POULTRY and GAME

Roast pheasant

Metric/Imperial
1 young pheasant
oil or melted butter
salt and pepper
4 rashers unsmoked streaky
  bacon
approx. 600 ml./1 pint giblet
  stock

Garnish
225 g./8 oz. button
  mushrooms, cooked
bread sauce

American
1 young pheasant
oil or melted butter
salt and pepper
4 slices unsmoked fatty bacon
approx. 2½ cups giblet stock

Garnish
8 oz. button mushrooms,
  cooked
bread sauce

Serves 3–4; if appetites are large, roast 2 pheasants.
Oven setting: 200°C./400°F./Gas Mark 6
Wash the pheasant and dry thoroughly with absorbent paper. Brush all over with the oil or butter, then sprinkle liberally with salt and pepper. Stretch the bacon rashers (slices) with the blade of a sharp knife and use to cover the pheasant.

Put the pheasant on a rack in a roasting pan and pour 450 ml./¾ pint (2 cups) of the stock into the pan. Roast in the preheated oven for 40–45 minutes, or until the bird is tender. Baste occasionally during the roasting. Remove the bacon rashers (slices) covering the breast for the last 10 minutes to brown the skin.

When the pheasant is ready, remove from the oven and transfer to a hot serving platter. Arrange the mushrooms around the pheasant. Keep hot while you quickly make a gravy in the roasting pan, using the cooking juices. Add the remaining stock if the gravy is too thick. Serve the gravy and bread sauce separately.

Country chicken pie

Metric/Imperial
25 g./1 oz. butter
25 g./1 oz. flour
300 ml./½ pint milk
salt and pepper
juice of ½ lemon
225 g./8 oz. cooked chicken
  meat, diced
100 g./4 oz. cooked ham or
  bacon, cut into small pieces
2–3 cooked carrots, diced
1 × 200 g./7 oz. packet frozen
  puff pastry, thawed

American
2 tablespoons butter
¼ cup flour
1¼ cups milk
salt and pepper
juice of ½ lemon
1⅓ cups diced cooked chicken
  meat
½ cup diced cooked ham or
  bacon
2–3 cooked carrots, diced
1 × 7 oz. packet frozen puff
  pastry, thawed

Serves 4
Oven setting: 220°C./425°F./Gas Mark 7
Melt the butter in a pan and stir in the flour. Cook, stirring, for 1 minute. Gradually add the milk, stirring constantly. Bring to the boil, stirring, and simmer for 2 minutes. Add all the remaining pie ingredients and mix well. Turn into an ovenproof pie dish. Roll out the pastry and cover the pie. Use the trimmings to decorate the top.

Bake in the preheated oven for 15 minutes. Reduce the oven setting to 180°C./350°F./Gas Mark 4 and bake for a further 15 minutes.

Helpful hints
This pie freezes well unbaked. To cook, either thaw completely then cook as above or cook from frozen for 30 minutes at 220°C./425°F./Gas Mark 7 and a further 20 minutes at 180°C./350°F./Gas Mark 4.

Turkey escalopes

Metric/Imperial
butter for frying
8 thick slices of roast turkey
  breast or 4 fresh turkey
  escalopes, beaten
225 g./8 oz. button
  mushrooms, sliced
4 tablespoons cranberry sauce
little chicken stock
salt and freshly ground black
  pepper

American
butter for frying
8 thick slices of roast turkey
  breast or 4 fresh turkey
  scaloppini, beaten
2 cups sliced button
  mushrooms
5 tablespoons cranberry sauce
little chicken stock
salt and freshly ground black
  pepper

Serves 4

Melt a knob of butter in a large frying pan (skillet). Add the turkey and fry gently for a few minutes on both sides. (If using fresh turkey escalopes (scaloppini) they will take about 5 minutes on each side before they are tender, depending on thickness.)

Add the mushrooms to the pan and fry for 1–2 minutes, then stir in the cranberry sauce and a few spoonfuls of chicken stock to make a thin sauce. Season to taste with salt and pepper and transfer to a hot serving platter.

Helpful hints

Look for turkey portions now on sale in some shops. They make an economical meal and are more meaty than chicken.

Chicken cordon bleu

Metric/Imperial
4 chicken breasts
4 slices ham
4 slices Gruyère cheese
15 g./½ oz. flour
salt and pepper

To coat
1 egg
50 g./2 oz. fresh breadcrumbs
oil or fat for deep-frying

American
4 chicken breasts
4 slices ham
4 slices Swiss cheese
2 tablespoons flour
salt and pepper

To coat
1 egg
1 cup fresh breadcrumbs
oil or fat for deep-frying

Serves 4

Dry well, then slit each breast to make a pocket. Insert the slices of ham and cheese into the pockets. Coat the chicken in the flour seasoned with salt and pepper. Dip in beaten egg then the breadcrumbs to cover thoroughly. Heat the oil until it is hot enough to turn a stale bread cube golden in 30 seconds (190°C./375°F. on a deep-fat thermometer). Fry the parcels for 12–15 minutes, or until crisp and golden brown. Drain on absorbent paper.

Helpful hints

For speed, use ready-cooked chicken breasts. Insert the ham and cheese, coat and fry for 2–3 minutes only.

POULTRY and GAME

Chicken with apricots

Metric/Imperial
½ kg./1 lb. raw chicken meat
3 tablespoons oil
1 teaspoon flour
225 g./8 oz. dried apricots,
    soaked overnight
about 600 ml./1 pint apricot
    juice (from soaked fruit)
1 tablespoon chopped onion
1 teaspoon sugar
salt and pepper

American
1 lb. raw chicken meat
4 tablespoons oil
1 teaspoon flour
8 oz. dried apricots, soaked
    overnight
about 2½ cups apricot juice
    (from soaked fruit)
1¼ tablespoons chopped onion
1 teaspoon sugar
salt and pepper

Serves 2

Cut the chicken into bite-sized pieces and fry in oil in a
saucepan until golden. Remove from pan and keep warm.
Pour off all the oil except for 1 tablespoon (1¼
tablespoons). Stir the flour into the oil and gradually add
half the liquid from the soaked apricots, stirring
continuously. Add the onion and cook for another 5
minutes.

Return chicken pieces to the pan, add the sugar, salt and
pepper to taste, half the apricots and sufficient apricot
juice to cover the chicken well. Cover and simmer gently
for 30 minutes or until the chicken is tender.

Just before serving, add the remainder of the apricots
and apricot juice and reheat. Serve hot.

This dish improves if it is cooked the day before and
reheated.

Partridge-in-a-pear-tree

Metric/Imperial
butter for frying
2–4 partridges, according to
    size, jointed if large, and
    skinned
1 tablespoon redcurrant jelly
150 ml./¼ pint chicken stock
150 ml./¼ pint red wine
    (Burgundy-type)
salt and freshly ground black
    pepper
4 small dessert pears, peeled
    and quartered
beurre manié, made with 2
    tablespoons butter, mixed
    with 1 tablespoon flour
4 tablespoons double cream
1 bunch of watercress (to
    garnish)

American
butter for frying
2–4 partridges, according to
    size, cut into serving pieces if
    large, and skinned
1¼ tablespoons redcurrant
    jelly
⅔ cup chicken stock
⅔ cup red wine
    (Burgundy-type)
salt and freshly ground black
    pepper
4 small eating pears, peeled and
    quartered
beurre manié, made with 2½
    tablespoons butter, mixed
    with 1¼ tablespoons flour
5 tablespoons heavy cream
1 bunch of watercress (to
    garnish)

Serves 4

Melt a knob of butter in a large flameproof casserole. Add
the partridges and brown on all sides. Stir in the
redcurrant jelly, stock, wine and seasoning to taste. Bring
to the boil, then reduce the heat. Add the pears to the
casserole. Cover and simmer gently for 40 minutes, or
until the partridges are tender, and the pears are nicely
coloured.

Remove the pears and partridges from the casserole and
keep hot on a serving platter. Add the beurre manié, in
small pieces, to the cooking liquid, stirring constantly, and
simmer gently until the sauce thickens. Adjust seasoning.
Stir in the cream and heat gently. Do not allow to boil or
the cream will curdle. Pour some of the sauce over the
partridges and put the rest in a sauceboat. Garnish with
sprigs of watercress.

Chicken Maryland

Metric/Imperial
4 chicken portions, skinned
flour
salt and pepper
1–2 eggs, beaten
100 g./4 oz. dried breadcrumbs
butter and cooking oil

Garnish
4 bananas
juice of ½ lemon
flour
4 rashers bacon
1 bunch of watercress

American
4 chicken portions, skinned
flour
salt and pepper
1–2 eggs, beaten
1⅓ cups dried breadcrumbs
butter and cooking oil

Garnish
4 bananas
juice of ½ lemon
flour
4 slices bacon
1 bunch of watercress

Serves 4
Oven setting: 180°C./350°F./Gas Mark 4
Coat the chicken in the flour, seasoned with salt and
pepper. Dip in the beaten egg and then the breadcrumbs,
ensuring the chicken is thoroughly covered.

Melt a knob of butter and 2 tablespoons of oil in a large
frying pan (skillet). Put in the chicken portions and fry
gently until golden brown on both sides. Transfer to a
casserole dish, cover and bake in the preheated oven for
about 45 minutes, or until the chicken is tender.

Peel the bananas, sprinkle with lemon juice and coat in
flour. Add to the frying pan (skillet), with more butter if
necessary, and fry on both sides until golden brown. Keep
warm.

To make the bacon rolls, stretch the bacon rashers
(slices) with the blade of a sharp knife, then roll up and
pierce on to a skewer. Cook under a preheated hot grill
(broiler) until crisp and golden brown, turning
occasionally.

Transfer the chicken to a hot serving platter and garnish
with fried bananas and bacon rolls. Decorate the platter
with sprigs of watercress and serve immediately.
Sweetcorn fritters are the traditional accompaniment.

Paprikascsirke

Metric/Imperial
1 chicken
little grated lemon rind
900 ml./1½ pints water
1 onion, chopped
4–5 peppercorns
little salt
1 bouquet garni

Sauce
75 g./3 oz. butter
100 g./4 oz. button
    mushrooms
25 g./1 oz. flour
1–2 tablespoons paprika
600 ml./1 pint stock (see
    method)
150 ml./¼ pint double cream
salt and pepper

American
1 chicken
little grated lemon rind
3¾ cups water
1 onion, chopped
4–5 peppercorns
little salt
1 bouquet garni

Sauce
6 tablespoons butter
1 cup button mushrooms
4 tablespoons flour
1¼–2½ tablespoons paprika
2½ cups stock (see method)
⅔ cup heavy cream
salt and pepper

Serves 4–6
Divide the chicken into 4 portions (or buy in portions). Put
the lemon rind, chicken, water and onion into a pan with
the peppercorns, salt and bouquet garni. Simmer until the
chicken is tender (about 45 minutes to 1 hour if young). Lift
the chicken from the stock, strain the stock and keep
600 ml./1 pint (2½ cups) for the sauce. Either dice the
chicken or keep in the 4 portions.

Heat the butter in a pan. Toss the mushrooms in the hot
butter for a few minutes, lift out on to a plate. Add the flour
and paprika, stir well for 2–3 minutes over a low heat, then
gradually blend in the stock, bring to the boil and cook,
stirring, until thickened. Put the pieces or portions of
chicken and mushrooms into the sauce. Simmer until
thoroughly heated. Add some of the cream and seasoning,
and simmer for 4–5 minutes; do not boil. Top with the
remainder of the cream.

POULTRY and GAME

Chicken in wine Italian-style

Metric/Imperial	American
1 chicken, about 2 kg./4 lb.	1 chicken, about 4 lb.
flour	flour
salt and pepper	salt and pepper
50 g./2 oz. butter	4 tablespoons butter
4 tablespoons olive oil	5 tablespoons olive oil
1 medium-sized onion, chopped	1 medium-sized onion, chopped
2 medium-sized carrots, peeled and thinly sliced	2 medium-sized carrots, peeled and thinly sliced
2 sticks celery, thinly sliced	2 sticks celery, thinly sliced
1 chicken liver, chopped	1 chicken liver, chopped
150 ml./¼ pint chicken stock	⅔ cup chicken stock
150 ml./¼ pint dry red wine	⅔ cup dry red wine
1 teaspoon dried basil	1 teaspoon dried basil
100 g./4 oz. mushrooms, sliced	1 cup sliced mushrooms
2 teaspoons finely chopped parsley	2 teaspoons finely chopped parsley
3 tablespoons Marsala	4 tablespoons Marsala
watercress to garnish	watercress to garnish

Serves 4

Divide the chicken into portions (or buy in portions) and coat them with flour, seasoned with salt and pepper. Heat the butter and oil in a large pan. Add the chicken and fry until golden brown all over. Remove the portions from the pan and keep hot. Add the onion, carrots, celery and chicken liver to the butter and oil remaining in the pan and cook slowly until the onion is golden. Add the stock, wine, basil and mushrooms, then replace the chicken portions. Cover and cook gently for 30 minutes. Then add seasoning, parsley and Marsala and continue to simmer until the chicken is tender. Garnish with watercress.

Duck with orange

Metric/Imperial	American
1 duck, about 2 kg./4 lb.	1 duck, about 4 lb.
1 onion	1 onion
salt and freshly ground black pepper	salt and freshly ground black pepper
coarsely grated rind and juice of 2 oranges	coarsely grated rind and juice of 2 oranges
coarsely grated rind and juice of 1 lemon	coarsely grated rind and juice of 1 lemon
1 tablespoon flour	1¼ tablespoons flour
2 tablespoons red wine	2½ tablespoons red wine
250 ml./8 fl. oz. chicken stock	1 cup chicken stock
1 tablespoon redcurrant jelly	1¼ tablespoons redcurrant jelly
1 orange, peeled and segmented	1 orange, peeled and segmented
watercress	watercress

Serves 4

Oven setting: 180°C./350°F./Gas Mark 4

Sprinkle the duck inside and out with salt and pepper and insert the onion into the body cavity. Prick the skin all over with a fork and stand the duck on a grid or rack in a roasting pan. Bake in the centre of the preheated oven for 25 minutes per ½ kg./1 lb. Do not baste or cover. When cooked, discard the onion, and put the duck on a large serving dish. Drain and reserve 1 tablespoon of the pan juices.

Blanch the orange and lemon rind in boiling water for 2 minutes and drain.

Melt the reserved tablespoon of the duck fat in a pan, stir in the flour and cook for 1 minute, stirring constantly. Add the blanched rind, the juice of the oranges and lemon and gradually stir in the wine, stock and jelly. Bring slowly to the boil, stirring constantly, season to taste and cook, stirring constantly until the sauce is smooth and thick. Taste and adjust the seasoning. Arrange orange slices over duck and pour sauce over. Garnish with watercress.

Chicken pilau

Metric/Imperial	American
2 onions	2 onions
1 garlic clove (optional)	1 garlic clove (optional)
2 tablespoons chicken fat or oil	2 1/2 tablespoons chicken fat or oil
225 g./8 oz. long-grain rice	1 1/3 cups long-grain rice
600 ml./1 pint chicken stock, made by simmering chicken carcass or giblets	2 1/2 cups chicken stock, made by simmering chicken carcass or giblets
25–50 g./1–2 oz. sultanas	1/6–1/3 cup seedless raisins
few pine or other nuts (optional)	few pine or other nuts (optional)
350 g./12 oz. cooked chicken, diced	2 cups diced cooked chicken
salt and pepper	salt and pepper
Garnish	Garnish
few nuts or dry breadcrumbs	few nuts or dry breadcrumbs

Serves 4–5
Peel and chop the onions, crush the garlic. Fry in the hot fat or oil for a few minutes, and then add the rice, turning in the fat or oil. Add the stock, bring to the boil, and stir; then simmer in an open pan for about 10 minutes. Add the rest of the ingredients and cook for a further 10–15 minutes until the liquid has just been absorbed. Pile on to a hot dish and top with the nuts or crumbs.

Helpful hints
If preparing this dish in advance add extra stock as the rice will absorb more liquid while standing.

Normandy chicken

Metric/Imperial	American
25 g./1 oz. butter	2 tablespoons butter
1 tablespoon oil	1 1/4 tablespoons oil
4–6 young chicken portions	4–6 young chicken portions
1 onion, chopped	1 onion, chopped
1 garlic clove, crushed	1 garlic clove, crushed
3 rashers streaky bacon, chopped	3 slices fatty bacon, chopped
25 g./1 oz. flour	1/4 cup flour
450 ml./3/4 pint dry cider	2 cups dry cider
2 dessert apples	2 eating apples
150 ml./1/4 pint single cream	2/3 cup light cream
1 tablespoon chopped parsley	1 1/4 tablespoons chopped parsley

Serves 4–6
Heat the butter and oil in a large pan. Fry the chicken on both sides until golden brown. Remove from the pan and put on a plate. Add the onion, garlic and bacon to the fat in the pan and cook for 5 minutes, or until the onion is golden. Stir in the flour and cook for 1 minute. Gradually stir in the cider and bring to the boil; cook until a smooth sauce. Return the chicken to the pan, cover and simmer gently for 30 minutes. Core and dice the apples, but do not remove the peel. Stir into the chicken mixture with the cream. Heat for 2–3 minutes *without* boiling, turn into a heated serving dish and sprinkle with chopped parsley.

Helpful hints
To make an even more luxurious dish, use a little less cider and add a small amount of Calvados (apple brandy).

POULTRY and GAME

Rabbit chasseur

Metric/Imperial	American
1 tender rabbit, jointed	1 tender rabbit, cut into serving
juice of ½ lemon	pieces
50 g./2 oz. flour	juice of ½ lemon
50 g./2 oz. butter	½ cup flour
1 tablespoon corn or olive oil	4 tablespoons butter
1 onion, chopped	1¼ tablespoons corn or olive oil
2 carrots, peeled and sliced	1 onion, chopped
100 g./4 oz. button	2 carrots, peeled and sliced
mushrooms, left whole	1 cup whole button mushrooms
250 ml./8 fl. oz. dry white	1 cup dry white wine
wine	1 cup chicken stock
250 ml./8 fl. oz. chicken stock	2 teaspoons tomato paste
2 teaspoons tomato purée	1 teaspoon dried thyme
1 teaspoon dried thyme	1 bay leaf
1 bay leaf	salt and freshly ground black
salt and freshly ground black	pepper
pepper	

Serves 4

Put the rabbit in a bowl, cover with cold water and the
lemon juice and leave overnight. Drain, rinse under cold
water and dry on absorbent paper. Coat the rabbit pieces
in half the flour.

Heat the butter and oil in a large pan, add the rabbit and
fry until browned on all sides. Remove the rabbit and
reserve. Add the onion, carrots and mushrooms and cook
for 2 minutes. Sprinkle in the remaining flour and cook,
stirring constantly, until it starts to brown. Gradually stir
in the wine, stock and tomato purée (paste) and bring to
the boil, stirring constantly. Add the thyme, bay leaf and
seasoning to taste. Return the rabbit to the pan, cover,
reduce the heat and simmer for 40–50 minutes, or until
rabbit is tender. Skim off any excess fat. Taste and adjust
the seasoning.

Chicken suprême

Metric/Imperial	American
25 g./1 oz. butter	2 tablespoons butter
few finely chopped mushrooms	few finely chopped mushrooms
or mushroom stalks	or mushroom stalks
2 parsley sprigs	2 parsley sprigs
1 small onion, finely chopped	1 small onion, finely chopped
25 g./1 oz. flour	¼ cup flour
300 ml./½ pint chicken stock	1¼ cups chicken stock
2 teaspoons lemon juice	2 teaspoons lemon juice
350 g./12 oz. cooked chicken,	2 cups sliced cooked chicken
sliced	1 egg yolk
1 egg yolk	5 tablespoons heavy cream
4 tablespoons double cream	salt and pepper
salt and pepper	
	Rice
Rice	1⅓ cups long-grain rice
225 g./8 oz. long-grain rice	2½ cups water
600 ml./1 pint water	1 teaspoon salt
1 teaspoon salt	2½ tablespoons chopped
2 tablespoons chopped parsley	parsley

Serves 4

Melt the butter in a pan. Add the mushrooms, parsley and
onion and fry very gently for 5 minutes. Stir in the flour
and cook for 1 minute. Gradually stir in the stock and bring
to the boil, stirring all the time. Reduce the heat, cover the
pan and simmer very gently for 30 minutes. Strain the
sauce and add the lemon juice and sliced chicken. Heat the
chicken through for about 5 minutes. Mix the egg yolk
with the cream, then stir in 3 tablespoons (4 tablespoons)
of the hot chicken sauce. Pour the cream mixture into the
pan and heat *without boiling*.

Put the rice, water, salt and parsley into a saucepan.
Bring to the boil and stir once. Cover and simmer for 15
minutes or until the rice is tender and all the liquid is
absorbed. Put the rice round the edge of the serving dish
and spoon the chicken and sauce into the centre.

Chicken in wine

Metric/Imperial
1½–2 kg./3–4 lb. chicken
40 g./1½ oz. butter
1 tablespoon oil
100 g./4 oz. piece smoked
   streaky bacon, cubed
12 pickling onions
2 sticks celery, chopped
175 g./6 oz. mushrooms,
   quartered
1 garlic clove, crushed
2 tablespoons flour
450 ml./¾ pint red Burgundy
150 ml./¼ pint water
1 bay leaf
¼ teaspoon dried thyme
salt and pepper
the chicken giblets, washed
small triangles of fried bread

American
3–4 lb. chicken
3 tablespoons butter
1¼ tablespoons oil
⅔ cup cubed smoked fatty
   bacon
12 pearl onions
2 sticks celery, chopped
1½ cups quartered mushrooms
1 garlic clove, crushed
2½ tablespoons flour
2 cups red Burgundy
⅔ cup water
1 bay leaf
¼ teaspoon dried thyme
salt and pepper
the chicken giblets, washed
small triangles of fried bread

Serves 6
Oven setting: 160°C./325°F./Gas Mark 3
Divide the chicken into portions. Heat 25 g./1 oz. (2 tablespoons) of butter in a pan with the oil and fry the bacon cubes until golden brown. Remove the bacon from the pan and drain. Fry the chicken until brown all over. Put the portions, with the bacon, into a 2 l./3 pint (2 quart) casserole. Fry the onions and celery in the fat remaining in the pan until soft, then add to the casserole. Heat the remaining butter in the pan, add the mushrooms and cook for 2 minutes, then put to one side. Blend the garlic and flour with the fat remaining in the pan. Cook gently until browned, stirring frequently. Add the wine, water, herbs and seasoning to taste. Simmer until thickened. Pour over the chicken and add the giblets. Cover and cook in the preheated oven for about 2 hours.

When almost tender, remove the giblets and bay leaf. Stir in the mushrooms and cook for a further 10 minutes. Skim off any excess fat with absorbent paper. Check the seasoning and garnish with fried bread triangles.

Roast duck with Marsala

Metric/Imperial
2 fresh sage leaves, or ¼
   teaspoon dried sage
1 garlic clove, halved
1 × 2 kg./4 lb. duck
salt and pepper
5 tablespoons Marsala

American
2 fresh sage leaves, or ¼
   teaspoon dried sage
1 garlic clove, halved
1 × 4 lb. duck
salt and pepper
6 tablespoons Marsala

Serves 4
Oven setting: 190°C./375°F./Gas Mark 5
Put the sage and garlic in the body cavity of the duck and place it on a rack in a large roasting pan. Prick the skin all over with a fork and then sprinkle with salt and pepper. Pour the Marsala into the pan. Roast in the centre of the oven for 1½ hours, basting at least twice.

PRESERVES

Grapefruit marmalade

Metric/Imperial
1 kg./2¼ lb. grapefruit
3 lemons
3½ l./6 pints water
2½ kg./6 lb. sugar

American
2¼ lb. grapefruit
3 lemons
15 cups water
12 cups sugar

Yields about 4½ kg./10 lb.
Scrub the grapefruit and lemons thoroughly in warm
water. Cut the grapefruit in half, squeeze out the juice,
remove the pips (seeds) and reserve them. Cut excess pith
off the skins and put to one side. Cut the grapefruit skins
into match-stick strips.

Cut the lemons in half and squeeze out the juice. Slice
the lemon skins thinly and tie them loosely in a muslin or
cheesecloth bag with the lemon pips (seeds), grapefruit
pips (seeds) and grapefruit pith.

Place the strips of grapefruit skin in a preserving pan
with the grapefruit and lemon juices, the muslin or
cheesecloth bag and the water. Bring to the boil, reduce
the heat and simmer until the grapefruit peel is tender,
about 2 hours. Remove the muslin or cheesecloth bag.
Add the sugar and bring to the boil again, stirring until the
sugar has dissolved. Boil rapidly until setting point is
reached (see Greengage jam). Skim. Allow the marmalade
to cool slightly before pouring it into hot sterilized jars.
Cover.

Fig and apple jam

Metric/Imperial
1½ kg./3 lb. slightly
   under-ripe fresh figs, sliced
300 ml./½ pint water
juice of 4 lemons
rind and pith of 2 lemons
½ kg./1 lb. cooking apples
1½ kg./3 lb. sugar

American
3 lb. slightly under-ripe fresh
   figs, sliced
1¼ cups water
juice of 4 lemons
rind and pith of 2 lemons
1 lb. cooking apples
6 cups sugar

Yields about 2¼ kg./5 lb.
Put the figs in a preserving pan with half the water and
lemon juice, and the lemon rind and pith, tied loosely in a
muslin or cheesecloth bag. Bring to the boil, reduce the
heat and simmer until the figs are tender. Meanwhile,
peel, core and slice the apples and cook in the remaining
water in a separate pan until soft.

Remove the muslin or cheesecloth bag. Mix the two
cooked fruits together. Add the sugar and stir until it has
dissolved. Boil rapidly until setting point is reached (see
Greengage jam), about 20 minutes. Skim. Pour the hot jam
into hot sterilized jars. Cover.

Helpful hints
The lemon rind and pith contain a high proportion of
pectin, which helps the jam to set.

Tomato, apple and raisin chutney

Metric/Imperial
1¾ kg./4 lb. ripe tomatoes, skinned and chopped
½ kg./1 lb. cooking apples, peeled, cored and chopped
225 g./8 oz. onions, chopped
450 ml./¾ pint white malt vinegar
225 g./8 oz. sultanas
1 tablespoon salt
¼ teaspoon each ground cinnamon, ground allspice, ground ginger, paprika and cayenne
350 g./12 oz. sugar

American
4 lb. ripe tomatoes, skinned and chopped
1 lb. tart apples, peeled, cored and chopped
2 cups chopped onions
2 cups white cider vinegar
1⅓ cups seedless raisins
1¼ tablespoons salt
¼ teaspoon each ground cinnamon, ground allspice, ground ginger, paprika and cayenne
1½ cups sugar

Yields about 1½ kg./3½ lb.
Put the fruit and vegetables in a preserving pan with a little of the vinegar, the sultanas (raisins), salt and ground spices. Simmer gently until just boiling then cook, uncovered, for 1½–1¾ hours. Dissolve the sugar in the remaining vinegar, add to the pan and simmer until the chutney has thickened. Pour into hot sterilized jars and seal with vinegar-proof tops.

Brandied peaches

Metric/Imperial
peaches
sugar
brandy

American
peaches
sugar
brandy

Wipe the peaches if necessary and halve them if you wish. Prick them to the stone (pit) all over with a cocktail stick (pick). Pack the peaches into clean dry jars with about 100 g./4 oz. (½ cup) sugar for each pound of fruit. Pour in enough brandy to cover the fruit well. Seal the jars and store in a cool dark place for at least 4 months before using.

Helpful hints
Skin the peaches if you prefer. Plunge them first into boiling water then gently peel off the skins.

PRESERVES

Dark shred marmalade

Metric/Imperial
1½ kg./3 lb. Seville oranges
3½ l./6 pints water
juice of 2 lemons
2½ kg./6 lb. sugar
1 tablespoon black treacle

American
3 lb. bitter oranges
15 cups water
juice of 2 lemons
12 cups sugar
1¼ tablespoons molasses

Yields about 4½ kg./10 lb.

Scrub the oranges thoroughly in warm water. Cut in half, squeeze out the juice, remove the pips (seeds) and reserve them. Cut the peel into thin match-stick strips, remove excess pith if necessary and tie the pith and pips (seeds) loosely in a muslin or cheesecloth bag. Place the cut orange peel, juice and muslin or cheesecloth bag in a preserving pan with the water and lemon juice. Bring slowly to the boil, stirring occasionally, reduce the heat and simmer gently until the peel is very tender, about 2 hours. Remove the muslin or cheesecloth bag. Add the sugar and treacle (molasses) and bring to the boil, stirring until the sugar has dissolved. Boil rapidly until setting point is reached (see Greengage jam). Skim. Allow the marmalade to cool slightly before pouring it into hot sterilized jars. Cover.

Pear and ginger chutney

Metric/Imperial
1¾ kg./4 lb. cooking pears, peeled, cored and chopped
225 g./8 oz. onions, finely chopped
900 ml./1½ pints brown malt vinegar
700 g./1½ lb. sugar
175 g./6 oz. chopped preserved ginger
225 g./8 oz. sultanas
½ teaspoon each mixed spice, dry mustard and ground cinnamon
1 teaspoon salt

American
4 lb. cooking pears, peeled, cored and chopped
2 cups finely chopped onions
3¾ cups brown cider vinegar
3 cups sugar
1 cup chopped preserved ginger
1⅓ cups seedless raisins
½ teaspoon each ground allspice, dry mustard and ground cinnamon
1 teaspoon salt

Yields about 2¾ kg./6 lb.

Put the pears in a preserving pan with the onions and half the vinegar. Bring to the boil and simmer until the pears and onions are very soft and pulpy. Add the remaining vinegar, the sugar, ginger, sultanas (raisins), spices and salt and bring to the boil, stirring until the sugar has dissolved. Simmer, stirring occasionally and uncovered, until the chutney has thickened. Pour into hot sterilized jars and seal with vinegar-proof tops.

Helpful hints

Use best quality vinegar for pickles, of at least 5% acetic acid content. Malt (cider) vinegar gives the best flavour; white distilled vinegar gives a rather better colour.

Tomato relish

Metric/Imperial
1½ kg./3 lb. ripe tomatoes,
   skinned and chopped
225 g./8 oz. onions, finely
   chopped
3 sticks celery, finely chopped
cooking salt
½ tablespoon curry powder
1 tablespoon flour
½ teaspoon dry mustard
600 ml./1 pint white malt
   vinegar
350 g./12 oz. sugar

American
3 lb. ripe tomatoes, skinned
   and chopped
2 cups finely chopped onions
3 sticks celery, finely chopped
cooking salt
½ tablespoon curry powder
1¼ tablespoons flour
½ teaspoon dry mustard
2½ cups white cider vinegar
1½ cups sugar

Yields about 1¾ kg./4 lb.
Put the vegetables in a bowl and sprinkle them with salt.
Cover the bowl with a clean towel and leave for 24 hours.
   Meanwhile, mix the curry powder, flour and mustard in
a bowl. Add enough of the vinegar to make a paste. Drain
the vegetables, rinse off excess salt and place them in a
preserving pan. Simmer gently until just boiling, then
cook for 5 minutes. Dissolve the sugar in the remaining
vinegar and add to the pan; simmer for about 30 minutes.
Add the flour paste and cook for 2–3 minutes, stirring
constantly. Pour into hot sterilized jars and seal with
vinegar-proof tops.

Greengage jam

Metric/Imperial
1½ kg./3 lb. greengages,
   halved and stoned
150–450 ml./¼–¾ pint water
1½ kg./3 lb. sugar

American
3 lb. greengage plums, halved
   and pitted
⅔–2 cups water
6 cups sugar

Yields about 2¼ kg./5 lb.
Put the fruit in a preserving pan with 150 ml./¼ pint (⅔
cup) of water. Crack some of the stones (pits), remove the
kernels and blanch them in boiling water for 1 minute;
then remove the skins and split in half. Add the kernels to
the pan, bring to the boil and simmer until the greengages
are tender and the contents of the pan well reduced. Add
extra water if necessary.
   Add the sugar, stirring until it has dissolved. Boil
rapidly until setting point is reached (see below). Skim.
Pour the hot jam into hot sterilized jars. Cover.

To test for setting point
Flake Test: When you think that the setting point of the
jam, jelly or marmalade has been reached, dip a wooden
spoon into the pan and spoon up about a teaspoonful of
the mixture. Holding the spoon over the pan, allow the hot
preserve to cool slightly. If setting point has been reached,
the jam, jelly or marmalade will not run off the spoon but
will drop off cleanly in clots or 'flakes'.
Wrinkle Test: Spoon about a teaspoonful of the preserve
on to a cold plate and put aside in a cold place for a few
minutes. If setting point has been reached, the surface will
have set and will wrinkle when pushed gently with a
finger.
   NOTE: Remove the cooking pan from the heat while
doing this test as it takes a little time to cool and the jam,
jelly or marmalade may become overcooked in the
meantime.

PRESERVES

Tomato chutney

Metric/Imperial
1 kg./2 lb. red or green
    tomatoes, skinned and
    chopped
1 large onion, chopped
1 large apple, peeled, cored and
    chopped
1 garlic clove, crushed
    (optional)
300 ml./½ pint white or brown
    malt vinegar
1–2 teaspoons mixed pickling
    spices
50–75 g./2–3 oz. sultanas or
    raisins
½ teaspoon salt
275 g./10 oz. sugar

American
2 lb. red or green tomatoes,
    skinned and chopped
1 large onion, chopped
1 large apple, peeled, cored and
    chopped
1 garlic clove, crushed
    (optional)
1¼ cups white or brown cider
    vinegar
1–2 teaspoons mixed pickling
    spices
⅓–½ cup seedless or other
    raisins
½ teaspoon salt
1¼ cups sugar

Put the fruit, vegetables and garlic, if used, into a
preserving pan with about half the vinegar and the
pickling spices, tied up in a muslin or cheesecloth bag.
Simmer steadily until just soft. Gradually add the
remaining vinegar. Remove the bag of pickling spices. Put
in the remaining ingredients, stirring until the sugar has
dissolved. Cook steadily until the mixture is the
consistency of jam. Pour into hot sterilized jars and seal
with vinegar-proof tops.

Helpful hints
For chutneys use an aluminium or stainless steel
preserving pan. Copper and brass react with vinegar to
produce toxic substances and should not be used.

Apple ginger jam

Metric/Imperial
1½ kg./3 lb. apples
600 ml./1 pint water
2 lemons
50 g./2 oz. root ginger, or
    15 g./½ oz. ground ginger
1½ kg./3 lb. sugar

American
3 lb. apples
2½ cups water
2 lemons
2 oz. root ginger, or 1
    tablespoon ground ginger
6 cups sugar

Yields about 2¼ kg./5 lbs.
Peel, core and chop the apples. Reserve the peel and cores.
Place the apples with the water, lemon juice and ground
ginger (if used) in a preserving pan. Pare the lemon rind
thinly with a sharp knife or potato peeler to remove all the
pith. Tie the apple peel and cores, lemon rind and bruised
root ginger (if used) in a muslin or cheesecloth bag and add
to the pan. Bring to the boil, reduce the heat and simmer
until the apple is tender. Remove the muslin or
cheesecloth bag. Add the sugar and stir until it has
dissolved. Boil rapidly until setting point is reached (see
Greengage jam). Skim. Pour the hot jam into hot sterilized
jars. Cover.

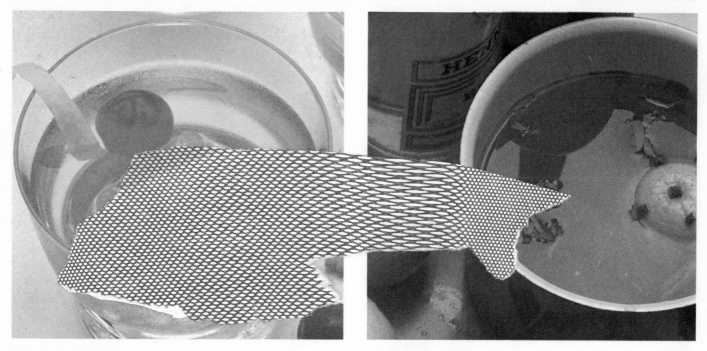

Manhattan

Metric/Imperial	American
35 ml./1⅓ fl. oz. Scotch or rye whisky	1½ tablespoons Scotch or bourbon
20 ml./⅔ fl. oz. dry vermouth	1 tablespoon dry vermouth
1 dash Angostura bitters	1 dash Angostura bitters
crushed ice	crushed ice
cherry (to garnish)	cherry (to garnish)
twist of lemon peel (to garnish)	twist of lemon peel (to garnish)

Serves 1
Stir the whisky, vermouth and bitters with crushed ice in a mixing glass. Strain to serve and garnish with a cherry and lemon peel twist.

Helpful hints
To vary, substitute 2 teaspoons each dry and sweet vermouth for the 4 teaspoons dry vermouth. The crushed ice can be replaced by a large ice cube, if preferred.

Glühwein

Metric/Imperial	American
3 standard bottles dry red wine	3 standard bottles dry red wine
250 ml./8 fl. oz. brandy	1 cup brandy
300 ml./½ pint water	1¼ cups water
300 ml./½ pint orange juice	1¼ cups orange juice
juice of 2 lemons	juice of 2 lemons
thinly pared rind of 1 lemon and 1 orange	thinly pared rind of 1 lemon and 1 orange
6 cinnamon sticks	6 cinnamon sticks
1 orange, stuck with 24 cloves	1 orange, stuck with 24 cloves

Serves 20
Put all the ingredients in a large pan and simmer over low heat. Serve in mugs.

Helpful hints
Never allow glühwein to boil — it must simmer gently for about 15 minutes to extract the flavour from the spices.

DRINKS

Cream mull

Metric/Imperial	American
2 oranges	*2 oranges*
few cloves	*few cloves*
1 lemon	*1 lemon*
1¾ l./3 pints ale	*2 quarts ale*
1 miniature bottle brandy	*¼ cup brandy*
1–2 tablespoons sugar	*1¼–2½ tablespoons sugar*
1–2 cinnamon sticks	*1–2 cinnamon sticks*
grated nutmeg	*grated nutmeg*
good pinch of ground allspice	*good pinch of ground allspice*
little double or single cream	*little heavy or light cream*

Serves 12
Oven setting: 180°C./350°F./Gas Mark 4
Stud the oranges with the cloves and bake in the preheated oven for about 25 minutes, or until golden. Slice the oranges and the lemon and put into a pan with the ale, brandy, sugar and cinnamon sticks. Heat steadily, stirring well to dissolve the sugar. Remove the cinnamon sticks. Pour into a hot punch bowl. Top with the nutmeg and allspice. Put a hot poker (if available) into the hot drink just before ladling into well heated glasses. Top each portion with a little cream. Serve at once.

Helpful hints
Mulled ale can equally well be served without the cream. This is a delightful Christmas drink.

Summer Sauternes

Metric/Imperial	American
1 standard bottle Sauternes (or other sweet white dessert wine)	*1 standard bottle Sauternes (or other sweet white dessert wine)*
100 ml./4 fl. oz. Cointreau	*½ cup Cointreau*
100 ml./4 fl. oz. brandy	*½ cup brandy*
juice of 1 lemon	*juice of 1 lemon*
crushed ice	*crushed ice*
600 ml./1 pint tonic water	*2½ cups tonic water*
mint sprigs (to garnish)	*mint sprigs (to garnish)*
orange and lemon slices (to garnish)	*orange and lemon slices (to garnish)*

Serves 8–10
Mix the wine, Cointreau, brandy and lemon juice in a punch bowl. Add several handfuls of crushed ice and pour in the tonic water. Serve in tall glasses garnished with a sprig of mint and a slice each of orange and lemon.

Helpful hints
For a party, mix the wine, liqueur and brandy with the ice and leave time for the mixture to chill. Add the tonic water immediately before serving.

Wine cup

Grenadine grape

Metric/Imperial	American
2 lemons	2 lemons
1–2 oranges	1–2 oranges
300 ml./½ pint water	1¼ cups water
50–75 g./2–3 oz. sugar	4–6 tablespoons sugar
ice cubes	ice cubes
2 standard bottles white wine	2 standard bottles white wine
1 miniature bottle brandy	¼ cup brandy
Garnish	Garnish
cucumber slices	cucumber slices
orange slices	orange slices
borage or mint sprigs (optional)	borage or mint sprigs (optional)

Metric/Imperial	American
300 ml./½ pint grape juice	1¼ cups grape juice
1 tablespoon grenadine	1¼ tablespoons grenadine
1 egg white	1 egg white
crushed ice	crushed ice
soda	soda

Serves 2
Thoroughly shake the grape juice, grenadine and egg white with crushed ice in a cocktail mixer. Strain into two tall glasses and fill with soda.

Helpful hints
This is a sophisticated, non-alcoholic cocktail suitable for young people. Add a measure of vodka for adults.

Serves about 16
Thinly pare the rind from the lemons and oranges. Squeeze out the juice and put on one side. Simmer the rind in the water for about 5 minutes. Add the sugar and stir until dissolved. Strain and allow to cool, then blend with the fruit juices.

Put the ice into a serving bowl, add the fruit mixture, wine and brandy. Stir gently to mix, then garnish with the cucumber, orange slices and herbs.

Helpful hints
Use a light, medium-dry wine for Wine cup for best results.

DRINKS

Whisky cola

Metric/Imperial
50 ml./2 fl. oz. Scotch whisky
15 ml./½ fl. oz. curaçao
15 ml./½ fl. oz. lemon juice
2 dashes Angostura bitters
crushed ice
cola
twist of orange peel

American
¼ cup Scotch whisky
1 tablespoon curaçao
1 tablespoon lemon juice
2 dashes Angostura bitters
crushed ice
cola
twist of orange peel

Serves 1
Mix whisky, curaçao, lemon juice and Angostura bitters in a glass. Add a heaped spoon of crushed ice, and fill with cola. Garnish with orange peel.

Champagne julep

Metric/Imperial
lump sugar
crushed ice
mint sprigs
1 bottle champagne
strawberries

American
loaf sugar
crushed ice
mint sprigs
1 bottle champagne
strawberries

Serves 6
Put 1 tablespoon (1¼ tablespoons) crushed ice into each 100 ml./4 fl. oz. (½ cup) wine glass with 1 sugar lump.
Add 2 crushed or bruised sprigs of mint to each glass.
Fill with champagne and top with 2 or 3 strawberries or other fruit in season.

White sauce

Metric/Imperial	American
25 g./1 oz. butter	2 tablespoons butter
25 g./1 oz. flour	¼ cup flour
300 ml./½ pint hot milk	1¼ cups hot milk
pinch of grated nutmeg	pinch of grated nutmeg
salt and freshly ground black pepper	salt and freshly ground black pepper

Makes 300 ml./½ pint (1¼ cups)

Heat the butter in a saucepan and stir in the flour. Cook, stirring, for 1 minute. Gradually add the hot milk, stirring constantly. Bring to the boil, stirring. Reduce the heat, add the seasonings and simmer gently for 3 minutes or until the sauce has thickened.

Italian mushroom sauce

Metric/Imperial	American
4 tablespoons corn or olive oil	5 tablespoons corn or olive oil
175 g./6 oz. onions, sliced	1½ cups sliced onions
1 garlic clove, crushed	1 garlic clove, crushed
225 g./8 oz. mushrooms, sliced	2 cups sliced mushrooms
600 ml./1 pint beef stock	2½ cups beef stock
2 teaspoons cornflour	2 teaspoons cornstarch
150 ml./¼ pint dry white wine	⅔ cup dry white wine
4 tomatoes, skinned, seeded and chopped	4 tomatoes, skinned, seeded and chopped
2 tablespoons tomato purée	2½ tablespoons tomato paste
1 teaspoon dried oregano	1 teaspoon dried oregano
1 teaspoon dried marjoram	1 teaspoon dried marjoram
salt and freshly ground black pepper	salt and freshly ground black pepper
1 tablespoon chopped parsley	1¼ tablespoons chopped parsley

Makes 1 l./1¾ pints (4¼ cups)

Heat the oil in a pan, add the onions and garlic and fry until soft. Stir in the mushrooms and cook gently for 5 minutes.

Gradually add the stock, the cornflour (cornstarch) smoothly blended with the wine, tomatoes, tomato purée (paste), herbs and seasoning to taste. Bring to the boil, stirring, and simmer, uncovered, for 20 minutes, stirring occasionally. Add the chopped parsley, taste and adjust the seasoning.

Serve with liver or pour over pasta and serve with grated Parmesan cheese.

SAUCES

Cumberland sauce

Metric/Imperial
2 small oranges
1 lemon
150 ml./¼ pint water
2 teaspoons cornflour
150 ml./¼ pint white stock
2 teaspoons made mustard
2 tablespoons port or red wine
4 tablespoons redcurrant jelly
salt and pepper

American
2 small oranges
1 lemon
⅔ cup water
2 teaspoons cornstarch
⅔ cup white stock
2 teaspoons made mustard
2½ tablespoons port or red
  wine
5 tablespoons redcurrant jelly
salt and pepper

Serves 4
Cut the peel from the oranges. Remove the white pith, then cut peel into matchstick strips. Cut the peel from ¼ of the lemon and treat in the same way. Squeeze the juice from oranges and lemon. Put the rind into a pan with cold water and soak for 1 hour. Place the pan on the heat and simmer very gently, covered, for 15–20 minutes or until nearly tender. Remove the lid towards the end of the cooking time so that the liquid in the pan is reduced to 3 tablespoons (4 tablespoons).

Blend the cornflour (cornstarch) with the white stock. Stir into the pan with the fruit juice, mustard, port or red wine and jelly. Stir over a low heat until thickened and clear. Season well. Serve hot or cold.

Apple sauce

Metric/Imperial
½ kg./1 lb. cooking apples,
  peeled, cored and sliced
50 ml./2 fl. oz. water
25 g./1 oz. butter
salt and freshly ground black
  pepper, or sugar

American
1 lb. tart apples, peeled, cored
  and sliced
¼ cup water
2 tablespoons butter
salt and freshly ground black
  pepper, or sugar

Put the apples, water and butter into a pan and bring to the boil. Cover, reduce the heat, and simmer, stirring occasionally, for about 15 minutes or until the apples are soft. Beat with a wooden spoon until completely smooth. Season with salt and pepper, or sugar, to taste.

Serve with roast, grilled (broiled) or fried pork, roast duck or goose.

Helpful hints
Keep frozen apple purée in small containers in the freezer. To make apple sauce, thaw the purée and beat in butter and seasoning or sugar over a gentle heat.

Tomato sauce

Metric/Imperial
4 tablespoons corn oil
225 g./8 oz. onions, chopped
2 garlic cloves, crushed
1½ kg./3 lb. ripe tomatoes,
   skinned and chopped or 3 ×
   450 g./1 lb. cans tomatoes,
   drained
2 teaspoons sugar
salt and freshly ground black
   pepper
2 tablespoons tomato purée
2 teaspoons dried thyme
2 bay leaves
300 ml./½ pint beef stock or
   white wine

American
5 tablespoons corn oil
2 cups chopped onions
2 garlic cloves, crushed
3 lb. ripe tomatoes, skinned
   and chopped or 3 × 1 lb.
   cans tomatoes, drained
2 teaspoons sugar
salt and freshly ground black
   pepper
2½ tablespoons tomato paste
2 teaspoons dried thyme
2 bay leaves
1¼ cups beef stock or white
   wine

Makes 1¼ l./2 pints (5 cups)
Heat the oil in a pan, add the onions and garlic and fry
until soft. Add the tomatoes and all the remaining
ingredients and bring to the boil. Cover, reduce the heat
and simmer gently for 30 minutes, stirring occasionally.
Remove the bay leaves and purée the sauce in a blender.
Return it to the pan and simmer gently, uncovered, for
about 20 minutes, or until reduced. Taste and adjust the
seasoning.
   Use in recipes as required or serve with pasta.

Cheese sauce

Metric/Imperial
25 g./1 oz. butter
25 g./1 oz. flour
300 ml./½ pint milk
50 g./2 oz. grated Cheddar
   cheese
½ teaspoon made mustard
salt and pepper

American
2 tablespoons butter
¼ cup flour
1¼ cups milk
½ cup grated Cheddar cheese
½ teaspoon made mustard
salt and pepper

Makes 300 ml./½ pint (1¼ cups)
Melt the butter in a pan, stir in the flour and cook for 2
minutes. Remove the pan from the heat and gradually stir
in the milk. Return the pan to the heat and bring to
simmering point. Lower the heat and cook, stirring
constantly, until the sauce thickens. Stir in the cheese,
mustard, salt and pepper.
   Gruyère, Emmenthal (Swiss) or Parmesan cheese may
be used in place of Cheddar.

Helpful hints
For cauliflower au gratin, pour cheese sauce over cooked
cauliflower. Sprinkle with Parmesan cheese and fresh
breadcrumbs. Grill (broil) until browned.

SAUCES

Curry sauce

Metric/Imperial	American
100 g./4 oz. lard	½ cup lard
2 Spanish onions, chopped	2 Bermuda onions, chopped
225 g./8 oz. cooking apples, peeled, cored and chopped	8 oz. cooking apples, peeled, cored and chopped
75 g./3 oz. medium strength curry powder	¾ cup medium strength curry powder
50 g./2 oz. cornflour	½ cup cornstarch
1 l./1 ¾ pints beef stock	4 ¼ cups beef stock
2 tomatoes, skinned, seeded and chopped	2 tomatoes, skinned, seeded and chopped
grated rind and juice of ½ lemon	grated rind and juice of ½ lemon
2 teaspoons soft brown sugar	2 teaspoons light brown sugar
2 tablespoons mango chutney	2 ½ tablespoons mango chutney
salt	salt

Makes 1¼ l./2 pints (5 cups)

Melt the lard in a pan, add the onions and apples and fry until golden brown. Stir in the curry powder and cornflour (cornstarch) and cook, stirring, for 2–3 minutes. Gradually add the stock, stirring constantly until blended. Add the remaining ingredients and bring to the boil, stirring constantly. Cover, reduce the heat and simmer for 30 minutes, stirring occasionally. Taste and adjust seasoning. For a smoother sauce, rub the mixture through a strainer.

Pour over hard boiled (cooked) eggs, or add cooked meat or vegetables and serve with rice.

Piquant gherkin sauce

Metric/Imperial	American
50 g./2 oz. butter	4 tablespoons butter
1 onion, finely chopped	1 onion, finely chopped
2 tablespoons cornflour	2 ½ tablespoons cornstarch
1 tablespoon tomato purée	1 ¼ tablespoons tomato paste
75 g./3 oz. gherkins, thinly sliced	½ cup thinly sliced gherkins
600 ml./1 pint brown stock	2 ½ cups brown stock
2 tablespoons lemon juice	2 ½ tablespoons lemon juice
1 teaspoon sugar	1 teaspoon sugar
salt and freshly ground black pepper	salt and freshly ground black pepper

Makes 600 ml./1 pint (2½ cups)

Heat the butter in a pan, add the onion and fry until golden brown. Stir in the cornflour (cornstarch) and cook, stirring, for 1 minute. Add the tomato purée (paste) and gherkins. Gradually add the stock, stirring constantly. Bring to the boil, stirring, and simmer gently, uncovered, for 5 minutes, or until the sauce has thickened. Season with the lemon juice, sugar and seasoning to taste.

Serve with grilled (broiled) meat or fish.

Cranberry sauce

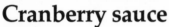

Metric/Imperial	American
300 ml./½ pint water	1¼ cups water
100 g./4 oz. sugar	½ cup sugar
225 g./8 oz. fresh cranberries, washed	8 oz. fresh cranberries, washed
25 g./1 oz. butter, softened	2 tablespoons butter, softened

Put the water and sugar in a pan and heat gently until the sugar dissolves, stirring occasionally. Add the cranberries and cook briskly for 2–3 minutes, or until the skins pop open. Reduce the heat and simmer, uncovered, stirring occasionally for 15–20 minutes, or until soft and reduced. Remove from the heat and beat in the butter. For a smoother sauce, rub the mixture through a strainer.

Serve with chicken, duck, turkey, game and lamb.

Helpful hints
Freeze in small quantities in rigid containers. To serve cold, thaw at room temperature for 3–4 hours. To serve hot, tip the frozen sauce into a saucepan and reheat, stirring occasionally, over a low heat.

Mayonnaise

Metric/Imperial	American
2 egg yolks	2 egg yolks
½ teaspoon dry mustard	½ teaspoon dry mustard
½ teaspoon salt	½ teaspoon salt
pepper	pepper
300 ml./½ pint oil	1¼ cups oil
2 tablespoons wine vinegar or lemon juice	2½ tablespoons wine vinegar or lemon juice

Makes 300 ml./½ pint (1¼ cups)
If possible have all the ingredients at room temperature. (You can make mayonnaise with eggs straight from the refrigerator but there is a much greater chance of it curdling.) Beat the egg yolks with the mustard, salt and pepper. Using either a balloon whisk or a wooden spoon, whichever you find easier, gradually beat in half the oil, drop by drop, until the sauce is thick and shiny. Beat in 1 tablespoon (1¼ tablespoons) of the vinegar or lemon juice then beat in the remaining oil. At this stage the oil can be added a little more quickly. Add the remaining vinegar or lemon juice when all the oil has been incorporated.

If you want to thin the mayonnaise down a little, you can add some lemon juice, a little single (light) cream or 1–2 teaspoons hot water.

The thick mayonnaise can be put into a screw-top jar or other suitable container and kept in the refrigerator for about 2 weeks. If you add the oil too quickly at the beginning and the mixture curdles, beat another egg yolk in a clean bowl and beat in the curdled mixture, a teaspoon at a time.

Helpful hints
For egg mayonnaise to use as a sandwich filler, mash 4 hard boiled (hard cooked) eggs with 150 ml./¼ pint (⅔ cup) mayonnaise. Season well.

SAUCES

Barbecue sauce

Metric/Imperial	American
4 tablespoons oil	5 tablespoons oil
1 large onion, finely chopped	1 large onion, finely chopped
2 garlic cloves, crushed	2 garlic cloves, crushed
2 tablespoons tomato purée	2½ tablespoons tomato paste
100 g./4 oz. soft brown sugar	⅔ cup light brown sugar
2 tablespoons wine vinegar	2½ tablespoons wine vinegar
1 teaspoon Tabasco or chilli sauce	1 teaspoon Tabasco or chili sauce
4 teaspoons cornflour	4 teaspoons cornstarch
300 ml./½ pint water	1¼ cups water
salt	salt

Makes 450 ml./¾ pint (2 cups)

Heat the oil in a pan, add the onion and garlic and fry until soft. Add the tomato purée (paste), sugar, vinegar and Tabasco or chilli sauce, and stir well. Blend the cornflour (cornstarch) to a smooth paste with a little of the water. Stir in the paste and cook, stirring, for 1 minute. Gradually add the remaining water and bring to the boil, stirring. Add salt to taste.

Use to brush kebabs, hamburgers, sausages or lamb cutlets during grilling (broiling) or barbecuing.

French dressing

Metric/Imperial	American
150 ml./¼ pint olive, corn or nut oil	⅔ cup olive, corn or nut oil
3 tablespoons red or white wine or tarragon vinegar	4 tablespoons red or white wine or tarragon vinegar
1 garlic clove, crushed with ½ teaspoon salt	1 garlic clove, crushed with ½ teaspoon salt
freshly ground black pepper	freshly ground black pepper

Put the oil and vinegar in a bowl and beat until quite thick. Beat in the garlic and black pepper to taste. If the dressing seems too oily add more salt.

Helpful hints

For vinaigrette dressing, add 1 tablespoon chopped fresh parsley, thyme or basil to French dressing. To make tomato and mushroom vinaigrette, arrange sliced tomatoes in dish. Spoon vinaigrette dressing over, add sliced mushrooms and sprinkle with chopped parsley.

Hot melon and ginger

Metric/Imperial
1 ripe melon, sliced and seeded
5–6 tablespoons fresh orange
 juice
little ground ginger

American
1 ripe melon, sliced and seeded
6–7½ tablespoons fresh orange
 juice
little ground ginger

Serves 4
Oven setting: 180°C./350°F./Gas Mark 4
Moisten the melon slices with the orange juice, sprinkle with a little ground ginger and warm in the preheated oven.

Helpful hints
To tell a ripe melon, press firmly round the stem end of the fruit — it should be soft there but still firm over the rest of the fruit.

Apple and mincemeat flan

Metric/Imperial
350 g./12 oz. digestive
 biscuits, crushed
75 g./3 oz. butter, melted
2 tablespoons golden syrup
600 ml./1 pint thick custard
2 dessert apples
lemon juice
2½ tablespoons mincemeat
2 tablespoons apricot jam
 (optional)

American
2 cups crushed graham crackers
6 tablespoons butter, melted
2½ tablespoons light corn
 syrup
2½ cups egg custard or vanilla
 pudding
2 eating apples
lemon juice
3 tablespoons mincemeat
2½ tablespoons apricot jam
 (optional)

Serves 4–6
Mix the biscuits (crackers), butter and syrup together until combined, then use to line a 20–23 cm./8–9 inch flan ring or loose-bottomed sandwich tin (layer pan). Chill in the refrigerator for 30 minutes.

Make up the custard (or vanilla pudding), cover with a circle of damp greaseproof (waxed) paper and allow to cool; the paper will prevent a skin from forming on top.

Remove the crust from the flan ring or tin (pan) and spoon the custard into the centre. Core and slice the apples and dip in lemon juice to preserve the colour, then arrange around the top of the flan as shown in the picture. Heat the mincemeat for a few minutes to melt the suet, cool and spoon into the centre of the flan. If liked, the apples can be brushed with warmed apricot jam.

DESSERTS

Mocha pots

Metric/Imperial
6 eggs, separated
25 g./1 oz. butter
175 g./6 oz. plain chocolate
1½ tablespoons rum
3 tablespoons coffee essence
3 tablespoons double cream

American
6 eggs, separated
2 tablespoons butter
6 squares semi-sweet chocolate
2 tablespoons rum
4 tablespoons coffee extract
4 tablespoons heavy cream

Serves 8
Put the egg yolks, butter and chocolate in a heatproof bowl set over a pan of hot water. Cook gently, stirring occasionally, until the chocolate has melted. Remove from the heat and beat in the rum and coffee essence (extract). Beat the egg whites until stiff and fold into the coffee mixture until thoroughly mixed. Pour into eight small ramekin dishes or pots and leave to set in a cool place. Beat the cream until thick and use to decorate.

Helpful hints
Freeze the pots undecorated. Thaw at room temperature for 1 hour.

Blackberry mille feuilles

Metric/Imperial
1 × 400 g./14 oz. packet frozen
  puff pastry, thawed
½ kg./1 lb. blackberries
sugar to taste
150 ml./¼ pint double cream
150 ml./¼ pint single cream
icing sugar

American
1 × 14 oz. packet frozen puff
  pastry, thawed
1 lb. blackberries
sugar to taste
⅔ cup heavy cream
⅔ cup light cream
confectioners' sugar

Serves 5–6
Oven setting: 230°C./450°F./Gas Mark 8
Roll out the pastry very thinly on a floured surface. Cut into 3 equal-sized rounds and 1 ring to fit over the top. Put on to a baking sheet and bake in the preheated oven for about 5 minutes. Then reduce the heat to 200°C./400°F./Gas Mark 6 for about 10 minutes. Leave to cool.

Mash about half the blackberries with sugar. Beat the double (heavy) cream, add the single (light) cream and beat again. Spread the first layer of pastry with mashed fruit and cream, put on the second layer of pastry, spread with cream, add a third layer, spread with cream and top with the pastry circle. Fill the centre with the whole fruit and dust the edge with icing (confectioners') sugar.

Lemon soufflé

Metric/Imperial
finely grated rind of 2 lemons
4 tablespoons lemon juice
3 eggs, separated
100–175 g./4–6 oz. caster
  sugar
¾ tablespoon gelatine
4 tablespoons water
300 ml./½ pint double cream
small ratafia biscuits (to
  decorate)

American
finely grated rind of 2 lemons
5 tablespoons lemon juice
3 eggs, separated
½–¾ cup superfine sugar
¾ tablespoon gelatin
5 tablespoons water
1¼ cups heavy cream
small macaroons (to decorate)

Serves 5–6
Tie a deep band of doubled greased greaseproof (waxed) paper around a medium-sized soufflé dish, to stand about 5 cm./2 inches above the rim. Put the lemon rind, juice, egg yolks and sugar into a heatproof bowl set over a pan of very hot water and beat until thick and pale.

Sprinkle the gelatine (gelatin) over the water, in a small heatproof bowl and leave until spongy, then add to the egg yolk mixture and stir over low heat until dissolved. Cool and allow to stiffen slightly.

Beat the cream lightly and fold into the jellied mixture. Beat the egg whites until stiff and fold into the mixture with a metal spoon. Spoon into the prepared soufflé dish and chill in the refrigerator for at least 4 hours, or until set.

Before serving, carefully remove the paper. Press some finely crushed ratafia biscuits (macaroons) on to the sides and decorate the top with whole ratafias (macaroons).

Orange pancakes (crêpes)

Metric/Imperial
100 g./4 oz. plain flour
pinch of salt
1 egg
300 ml./½ pint milk or milk
  and water
3 oranges
fat for frying
little caster sugar

American
1 cup all-purpose flour
pinch of salt
1 egg
1¼ cups milk or milk and water
3 oranges
fat for frying
little superfine sugar

Serves 4
Sift the flour and salt into a mixing bowl, gradually add the egg and liquid and beat to a smooth batter. Grate the rind from the oranges and mix into the batter to flavour it.

Cook the pancakes (crêpes) as in Cinnamon apple pancakes (crêpes) and keep hot.

Remove all the pith from the oranges and slice them. Fill the pancakes (crêpes) with most of the orange slices and roll up. Dust with a little sugar, decorate with any remaining orange slices and serve at once.

DESSERTS

Easy ice cream

Metric/Imperial	American
1 tablespoon custard powder	1¼ tablespoons vanilla
50 g./2 oz. caster sugar	pudding mix
1 teaspoon vanilla essence	¼ cup superfine sugar
1 egg, separated	1 teaspoon vanilla extract
600 ml./1 pint milk	1 egg, separated
15 g./½ oz. gelatine	2½ cups milk
2 tablespoons water	½ oz. gelatin
150 ml./¼ pint double cream	2½ tablespoons water
	⅔ cup double cream

Serves 4

Turn the refrigerator to its coldest setting. Put the custard powder (vanilla pudding), sugar, vanilla essence (extract) and egg yolk in a mixing bowl and stir in a little of the milk. Mix to a smooth cream. Scald (bring to just under boiling point) the remaining milk and pour on to the custard mixture, stirring constantly. Return to the rinsed-out pan and heat gently until thick, stirring constantly.

Sprinkle the gelatine (gelatin) over the water in a small heatproof bowl and leave until spongy, then set the bowl over a pan of hot water and stir over low heat until dissolved. Remove from the heat and stir into the custard mixture. Leave to cool, then chill in the refrigerator, stirring occasionally for about 1 hour. Beat the egg white until stiff and fold into the custard mixture with a metal spoon. Pour into a shallow polythene (plastic) container that will fit into the freezing compartment of the refrigerator. Freeze for about 30 minutes or until mushy. Turn into an ice-cold mixing bowl and beat vigorously. Beat the cream until thick and fold into the ice cream. Return to the freezing compartment and freeze until quite firm. This could take several hours, depending on the refrigerator.

Before serving, the ice cream should be transferred to the body of the refrigerator to allow it to soften. Leave for about 1 hour, then scoop into serving bowls and serve immediately.

Brigade pudding

Metric/Imperial	American
Suetcrust pastry	Suetcrust pastry
225 g./8 oz. self-raising flour	2 cups self-rising flour or
or plain flour with 2	all-purpose flour with 2
teaspoons baking powder	teaspoons baking powder
pinch of salt	pinch of salt
100 g./4 oz. chopped or	½ cup chopped or shredded beef
shredded beef suet	suet
water to mix	water to mix
Filling	Filling
2 tablespoons golden syrup	2½ tablespoons light corn
225 g./8 oz. mincemeat	syrup
3 large cooking apples, peeled,	1 cup mincemeat
cored and grated	3 large tart apples, peeled, cored
	and grated

Serves 6

Grease a 1¾ l./3 pint (7½ cup) pudding basin. Sift the flour and salt into a bowl. Add the suet and bind with water to a soft dough. Turn out the dough on to a floured surface and divide into four pieces of graduating sizes. Roll out the pieces individually, the smallest to fit the bottom of the basin, the largest to fit the top. Put the syrup into the basin and add the first round of pastry. Cover with one-third of the mincemeat blended with the apples. Continue making layers in this way until the ingredients are used up, finishing with the final round of pastry. Cover with greased foil or greaseproof (waxed) paper. Make a pleat in the centre and tie on with string around the rim.

Place the basin in a large pan of boiling water, cover and steam for 2½ hours. Remove the basin from the heat, discard the foil or paper and turn the pudding out on to a warmed serving dish. Serve with cream or custard sauce.

Orange and pear caprice

Metric/Imperial
75 g./3 oz. sugar
150 ml./¼ pint water
1 × 175 ml./6 fl. oz. can
  concentrated frozen orange
  juice, thawed
1 egg white
2 oranges
1 pear
lemon juice

American
⅜ cup sugar
⅔ cup water
1 × 6 fl. oz. can concentrated
  frozen orange juice, thawed
1 egg white
2 oranges
1 pear
lemon juice

Serves 4
Put the sugar and water into a saucepan and heat slowly until the sugar has dissolved. Remove from the heat and allow to cool. Stir in the orange juice (do not dilute this) and mix well. Turn into a small container and freeze in the ice-making compartment of the refrigerator for about 2 hours, or until it is barely firm.

Remove from the refrigerator, turn into a bowl and mash with a fork so that no large lumps remain. Stiffly whisk the egg white in a separate bowl and fold into the orange mixture. Spoon back into the container and return to the refrigerator. Freeze until firm; this will take about 6 hours.

Remove the peel from the oranges, using a sharp knife, and divide into segments, leaving the orange segments free from skin.

Peel, core and slice the pear and sprinkle with lemon juice to preserve the colour.

Scoop the water ice into glasses and decorate with the orange and pear segments.

Helpful hints
If you are in a hurry, use commercially made water ice — either orange or tangerine flavour.

Baked apples with orange filling

Metric/Imperial
4 large cooking apples
2–3 tablespoons orange
  marmalade
finely grated rind of 1–2
  oranges
approx. 2 tablespoons orange
  juice

American
4 large tart apples
2½–4 tablespoons orange
  marmalade
finely grated rind of 1–2
  oranges
approx. 2½ tablespoons orange
  juice

Serves 4
Oven setting: 180–190°C./350–375°F./Gas Mark 4–5
Wash the apples and, using a knife or corer, hollow out the centres and remove the cores. Score the skin of each apple. Place the apples in a shallow baking dish. Blend together the marmalade, grated rind and orange juice and use to fill the centre of each apple. Bake for about ¾ hour in the centre of the preheated oven. Decorate with strips of orange rind. Serve with custard sauce, cream or ice cream.

Helpful hints
A dash of cointreau in whipped cream served with this dish adds luxury.

DESSERTS

Honey cheesecake

Italian lemon water ice

Metric/Imperial	American
Crust	Crust
225 g./8 oz. wheatmeal biscuits, crushed	2 cups crushed wheatmeal cookies
50 g./2 oz. butter or margarine, melted	4 tablespoons butter or margarine, melted
Filling	Filling
350 g./12 oz. cottage cheese	1½ cups cottage cheese
100 g./4 oz. clear honey	½ cup clear honey
2 teaspoons sugar	2 teaspoons sugar
2 eggs	2 eggs
pinch of salt	pinch of salt
ground cinnamon	ground cinnamon

Serves 8–12

Oven setting: 140–150°C./275–300°F./Gas Mark 1–2

Mix the biscuits (cookies) and melted butter or margarine together and use to line a 20 cm./8 inch sandwich tin (layer pan). Chill in the refrigerator for 30 minutes.

Beat the cheese, honey, sugar, eggs and salt together until smooth. Spoon into the biscuit (cookie) case, sprinkle liberally with cinnamon and cook in the centre of the preheated oven for 35–45 minutes. Leave to cool in the oven with the heat turned off. (An electric oven holds the heat, so allow only 35–40 minutes.) Serve cold.

Metric/Imperial	American
6 large lemons	6 large lemons
225 g./8 oz. sugar	1 cup sugar
600 ml./1 pint water	2½ cups water
1 egg white, stiffly beaten (optional)	1 egg white, stiffly beaten (optional)

Serves 6

Thinly pare the rind from 2 lemons. Squeeze the juice from all the lemons to make 300 ml./½ pint (1¼ cups). Place sugar and water in a saucepan and heat gently, stirring until sugar dissolves. Add lemon rind and boil gently for 10 minutes. Leave to cool. Add the lemon juice and strain into an ice-cube tray.

Place in the freezing compartment of the refrigerator and leave until half frozen, about 1 hour. Turn mixture into a bowl and fold in egg white, if desired. Return to ice-cube tray and re-freeze. Serve in glasses or in the empty lemon shells. Cut a slice from the bottom of each lemon shell so that it will stand firmly.

Honey banana creams

Metric/Imperial	American
3 large ripe bananas	3 large ripe bananas
juice and rind of 1 large lemon	juice and rind of 1 large lemon
2–3 tablespoons clear honey	2½–4 tablespoons clear honey
300 ml./½ pint milk	1¼ cups milk
15 g./½ oz. gelatine	½ oz. gelatin
150 ml./¼ pint water	⅔ cup water
2–3 tablespoons double cream, whipped	2½–4 tablespoons heavy cream, whipped
ice cream or cream	ice cream or cream

Serves 4–6

Mash the bananas with the lemon juice. Heat the honey in the milk and stir into the banana. Soften the gelatine (gelatin) in 3 tablespoons (4 tablespoons) of the cold water. Simmer the lemon rind in the remainder of the water for about 5–6 minutes to extract the maximum flavour, then blend the liquid with the softened gelatine (gelatin). When quite clear add to the banana mixture. Allow to cool and stiffen very slightly then fold in the lightly whipped cream. Spoon into glasses, top with ice cream or cream.

Helpful hints

Decorate with chopped walnuts or toasted, flaked almonds.

Cinnamon apple pancakes (crêpes)

Metric/Imperial	American
Batter	Batter
100 g./4 oz. plain flour	1 cup all-purpose flour
¼ teaspoon salt	¼ teaspoon salt
1 egg	1 egg
1 tablespoon salad oil	1¼ tablespoons salad oil
300 ml./½ pint milk	1¼ cups milk
oil for frying	oil for frying
Filling	Filling
4 very large Bramley apples, peeled, cored and sliced	4 very large tart apples, peeled, cored and sliced
¼ teaspoon ground cinnamon	¼ teaspoon ground cinnamon
175 g./6 oz. demerara sugar	1 cup light brown sugar
100 g./4 oz. butter	½ cup butter
about 65 g./2½ oz. butter for frying	about 5 tablespoons butter for frying
extra demerara sugar mixed with cinnamon for sprinkling	extra light brown sugar mixed with cinnamon for sprinkling

Serves 5–6

Sift the flour and salt into a mixing bowl, gradually add the egg, salad oil and enough milk to beat to a smooth, fairly thin batter. Heat a very little oil in an 18 cm./7 inch frying pan (crêpe pan). Drop 2 tablespoons (2½ tablespoons) of the batter into the centre of the pan and tilt to spread the batter. Cook for 1 minute, then turn the pancake (crêpe) over and cook the other side for 1 minute. Turn the pancake (crêpe) out of the pan and make nine or ten more in the same way, keeping them hot.

For the filling, put the apples, cinnamon, sugar and butter in a saucepan and simmer gently for about 20 minutes, or until the apple is tender, stirring occasionally. Divide the filling between the pancakes (crêpes) and roll them up. Pile on a warm serving dish and sprinkle with the sugar and cinnamon mixture. Serve with cream or ice cream.

DESSERTS

Pineapple ice cream

Metric/Imperial
1 medium-sized fresh pineapple
juice of 1½ lemons
175 g./6 oz. caster sugar
150 ml./¼ pint water
300 ml./½ pint double cream,
  lightly whipped

American
1 medium-sized fresh pineapple
juice of 1½ lemons
¾ cup superfine sugar
⅔ cup water
1¼ cups heavy cream, lightly
  whipped

Serves 6
Cut the pineapple in half lengthways, and cut out the hard core down the centre of each side. Keep the pineapple shells. With a grapefruit knife or a sharply pointed spoon, scoop out all flesh and chop finely, saving the juice. Mix the chopped pineapple, juice, and lemon juice together. Put the sugar and water in a pan and dissolve the sugar slowly over gentle heat. Leave to cool. Add the syrup to the pineapple and pour into a rigid container. Cover and freeze until almost set, then turn into a bowl and beat until broken up and light. Fold in the cream and return to the container. Cover and freeze. When required, thaw at room temperature for 15 minutes.

Scoop out the ice cream with a metal spoon dipped in boiling water. Serve in pineapple shells.

Rich cheesecake

Metric/Imperial
225 g./8 oz. digestive type
  biscuits, crushed
100 g./4 oz. butter, melted
¾ kg./1½ lb. cream cheese
175 g./6 oz. caster sugar
2 eggs
2 teaspoons lemon juice
½ teaspoon vanilla essence

American
1⅓ cups crushed graham
  crackers
½ cup butter, melted
3 cups cream cheese
¾ cup superfine sugar
2 eggs
2 teaspoons lemon juice
½ teaspoon vanilla extract

Serves 8–10
Oven setting: 150°C./300°F./Gas Mark 2
Put the crumbs into a basin and blend with the melted butter. Line the base and sides of a 20 cm./8 inch baking tin (pan) with a loose base, with the crumb mixture. Refrigerate for 30 minutes. Cream the cheese with the sugar and eggs. Spread the cheese mixture over the crumbs and bake in the centre of the oven for 30–40 minutes until set. Turn off the heat, but keep the cheesecake in the oven until cold; this prevents it 'wrinkling'. Chill overnight before removing from the tin. If liked, decorate with fresh fruit as in the picture, or with cream.

Helpful hints
Instead of flavouring the cheesecake with vanilla and lemon, use ½ teaspoon mixed spice, or before filling with the cheese mixture, put firm, fresh fruit — strawberries, diced pineapple or halved apricots — over crumb mixture.

Oranges in rum sauce

Metric/Imperial
12 medium-sized oranges
300 ml./½ pint water
225 g./8 oz. sugar
4–5 tablespoons rum

American
12 medium-sized oranges
1¼ cups water
1 cup sugar
5–6 tablespoons rum

Serves 10–12

Cut away the peel from the oranges so you remove all the
pith as well. Cut the orange part of some of the peel into
very narrow strips, as shown in the picture. Soak in half
the water for 1 hour, then simmer in this water in a covered
pan for about 20 minutes. Leave in the liquid until ready to
add this to the caramel.

Put the sugar and remaining water into a pan and
dissolve the sugar over gentle heat. Increase the heat and
boil until the syrup turns rich brown. Strain the liquid
from the orange peel into the caramel, stir over the heat
until blended, then add the rum. Put the oranges into a
dish, pour the syrup over slowly so it soaks into the fruit,
and top with the peel.

Kissel

Metric/Imperial
2½ tablespoons cornflour
pinch of salt
2 tablespoons white wine
1 tablespoon lemon juice
450 ml./¾ pint fruit purée,
* sweetened to taste*

American
3¼ tablespoons cornstarch
pinch of salt
2½ tablespoons white wine
1¼ tablespoons lemon juice
2 cups fruit purée, sweetened to
* taste*

Serves 4

Blend together the cornflour (cornstarch), salt, wine and
juice. Bring the fruit purée to the boil and pour over the
blended cornflour (cornstarch). Return to the pan and
cook, stirring all the time, until thick. Pour into individual
serving dishes, chill, and decorate with cream, if liked.
Redcurrants, cherries, strawberries or any other fruit can
be used.

DESSERTS

Fresh fruit salad

Metric/Imperial	American
300 ml./½ pint water	1¼ cups water
2 oranges	2 oranges
1 lemon	1 lemon
75–100 g./3-4 oz. sugar	⅓–½ cup sugar
1 kg./2 lb. mixed prepared fresh fruit	2 lb. mixed prepared fresh fruit

Serves 8–10

Put the water, with thin strips of orange and lemon rind, into a pan; take just the top 'zest' from the fruit, as the white pith would make the sauce bitter. Simmer for 5 minutes. Add the sugar, stir until dissolved then add the orange and lemon juice. Strain over the prepared fruit, and leave until cold.

Helpful hints

For a luxury salad add a little sherry, kirsch, cointreau or maraschino to the syrup.

Apple strudel

Metric/Imperial	American
175 g./6 oz. strong flour	1½ cups all-purpose flour
pinch of salt	pinch of salt
1 tablespoon oil	1¼ tablespoons oil
1 egg	1 egg
4 tablespoons warm water	5 tablespoons warm water
oil for glazing	oil for glazing
icing sugar	confectioners' sugar
Filling	*Filling*
50 g./2 oz. breadcrumbs	1 cup breadcrumbs
50 g./2 oz. sultanas	⅓ cup seedless raisins
½ kg./1 lb. tart apples, peeled, cored and chopped	1 lb. tart apples, peeled, cored and chopped
50 g./2 oz. sugar	¼ cup sugar
grated rind and juice of ½ lemon	grated rind and juice of ½ lemon
1 teaspoon cinnamon	1 teaspoon cinnamon

Serves 6

Oven setting: 220°C./425°F./Gas Mark 7

Mix together the flour and salt. Add the oil, egg and water to make a soft dough. Knead well until smooth. Leave covered in a warm bowl for 30 minutes. Roll out half the pastry at a time on floured greaseproof (waxed) paper. Roll until paper thin. Brush with oil, and sprinkle with breadcrumbs. Mix the remaining filling ingredients and spread half the mixture to within 1 cm./½ inch of edge of the pastry. Wet the edges and roll up using the greaseproof (waxed) paper to help. Seal the edges. Place on a well oiled baking sheet. Brush with oil. Repeat process with rest of pastry. Bake for 40 minutes. Cut into pieces and sprinkle with icing (confectioners') sugar.

Other fruits, such as apricots and strawberries, may be used instead of apples.

Brandied strawberries

Metric/Imperial	American
½ kg./1 lb. strawberries	3 cups strawberries
2 tablespoons icing sugar	2½ tablespoons confectioners' sugar
6 tablespoons brandy or grand marnier	½ cup brandy or grand marnier

Serves 6

Place fresh strawberries in a bowl and sprinkle with the sugar and brandy. Leave to stand at room temperature for at least 1 hour. Serve in individual glasses with cream, if desired.

Iced Christmas pudding

Metric/Imperial	American
150 ml./¼ pint milk	⅔ cup milk
100 g./4 oz. marshmallows	4 oz. marshmallows
1 teaspoon cocoa powder	1 teaspoon unsweetened cocoa powder
1 teaspoon instant coffee powder	1 teaspoon instant coffee powder
50 g./2 oz. raisins	⅓ cup raisins
25 g./1 oz. sultanas	2 tablespoons seedless raisins
25 g./1 oz. currants	2 tablespoons currants
2 tablespoons sherry	2½ tablespoons sherry
50 g./2 oz. maraschino cherries, chopped	½ cup chopped maraschino cherries
50 g./2 oz. chopped nuts	½ cup chopped nuts
300 ml./½ pint double cream, stiffly whipped	1¼ cups heavy cream, stiffly whipped
25 g./1 oz. icing sugar, sifted (optional)	2½ tablespoons confectioners' sugar, sifted (optional)
maraschino cherries (to decorate)	maraschino cherries (to decorate)

Serves 4

Put the milk, marshmallows, cocoa and coffee into a pan. Heat gently until the marshmallows are nearly melted. Leave to cool.

Meanwhile, mix the dried fruit with the sherry. Leave for 30 minutes then add to the marshmallow mixture with the cherries and nuts. Freeze for a short time until slightly thickened. Fold the cream into this mixture and pack into a chilled bowl. Freeze until firm. Turn out, decorate with cherries if liked, and serve with more whipped cream (flavoured with brandy and sweetened with icing (confectioners') sugar) or with brandy butter. You can also serve crisp biscuits (cookies) with the ice cream, if wished.

DESSERTS

Banana lemon cream

Metric/Imperial	American
1 packet lemon-flavoured jelly	1 packet lemon-flavoured
450 ml./¾ pint boiling water	gelatin
2 teaspoons lemon juice	2 cups boiling water
1 tablespoon sugar	2 teaspoons lemon juice
300 ml./½ pint double cream,	1¼ tablespoons sugar
stiffly whipped	1¼ cups heavy cream, stiffly
2 egg whites, stiffly beaten	whipped
3 small bananas, sliced	2 egg whites, stiffly beaten
	3 small bananas, sliced

Decoration
sponge finger biscuits
whipped double cream
sliced bananas
glacé cherries

Decoration
sponge finger cookies
whipped heavy cream
sliced bananas
candied cherries

Serves 4–6

Dissolve the jelly (gelatin) in the water and add lemon juice and sugar. Chill until beginning to set.

When jelly is firm, whip until frothy, then whisk in cream. Fold in the egg whites and bananas. Spoon into a 1¼ l./2 pint (5 cup) mould (rinsed in cold water). Leave until set.

Turn out and decorate. Press sponge fingers round the edge, top with cream, sliced bananas and cherries.

Caramel apples

Metric/Imperial	American
6 apples, peeled, cored and	6 apples, peeled, cored and
quartered	quartered
40 g./1½ oz. plain flour	6 tablespoons all-purpose flour
15 g./½ oz. cornflour	1 tablespoon cornstarch
2 egg whites	2 egg whites
oil for deep frying	oil for deep frying
100 g./4 oz. sugar	½ cup sugar
1 tablespoon oil	1¼ tablespoons oil
1 tablespoon sesame seeds	1¼ tablespoons sesame seeds

Serves 4–6

Dust apples lightly with some of the flour. Sift the remaining flour with the cornflour (cornstarch) into a mixing bowl. Add the egg whites and mix to a paste. Add the apples and stir to coat in paste. Heat the oil until it is hot enough to turn a stale bread cube golden brown in 30 seconds (190°C./375°F. on a deep-fat thermometer). Deep fry until golden. Drain on absorbent kitchen paper. Place the sugar in a small saucepan with 2 tablespoons (2½ tablespoons) water. Heat, stirring, until the sugar has dissolved. Add the oil and continue heating slowly until the sugar has caramelized and is a light golden brown. Stir in the apple and sesame seeds. Serve immediately in individual, lightly oiled serving dishes. Dip into cold water (to harden the caramel) before eating.

Baked Alaska

Metric/Imperial	American
100 g./4 oz. trifle sponges	4 oz. sponge jelly roll
2 tablespoons sweet sherry	2½ tablespoons sweet sherry
3 egg whites	3 egg whites
175 g./6 oz. caster sugar	¾ cup superfine sugar
600 ml./1 pint vanilla ice cream	2½ cups vanilla ice cream

Serves 6
Oven setting: 220°C./425°F./Gas Mark 7
Halve the sponges and use them to line a shallow
ovenproof dish. Moisten with the sherry. Beat the egg
whites until stiff. Beat in half the sugar and continue to
beat for 1 minute. Fold in the remaining sugar.

Pile the ice cream on to the sponge cakes, leaving a
1 cm./½ inch margin around the edge. Swirl the meringue
completely over the ice cream and cake, to cover it
completely and thickly. Bake in the preheated oven for 4–5
minutes, or until brown and crisp. Serve immediately.

Fresh fruit meringue cake

Metric/Imperial	American
4 egg whites	4 egg whites
225 g./8 oz. caster sugar or icing sugar, sifted	1 cup superfine sugar or 2 cups confectioners' sugar, sifted
300 ml./½ pint double cream	1¼ cups heavy cream
about ½ kg./1 lb. fresh fruit e.g. raspberries, strawberries, cherries or mixed fruit or 1 × 800 g./1 lb. 12 oz. can fruit, drained	about 1 lb. fresh fruit e.g. raspberries, strawberries, cherries or mixed fruit or 1 × 1 lb. 12 oz. can fruit, drained
extra sugar	extra sugar

Serves 6
Oven setting: 110°C./225°F./Gas Mark ¼
Draw a 20 cm./8 inch circle on a sheet of oiled greaseproof
(waxed) paper. Beat the egg whites until they are very stiff
and you can turn the bowl upside down. Gradually beat in
half the sugar, a teaspoon at a time, then fold in the
remainder. Spread half the meringue over the circle,
taking it right to the edges. Using a tablespoon, pile
spoonfuls of meringue all round the edge to make a case.
Bake in the preheated oven for about 6 hours, or until the
meringue has completely dried out and the paper can be
easily removed. The meringue case can be left in the oven
to dry out overnight; turn the oven down as low as
possible and cook for about 10 hours.

Beat the cream lightly until just stiff. Spread over the
base of the meringue case. Top with the fruit; fresh fruit
will probably need to be sprinkled with a little sugar before
serving. If using fruits which discolour, such as apples,
pears and peaches, they should first be dipped in a little
lemon juice to preserve the colour.

DESSERTS

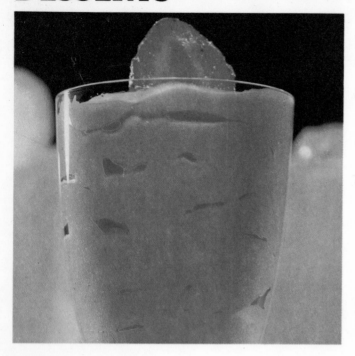

Yogurt whip

Metric/Imperial	American
approx. 300 ml./½ pint thick sweetened fruit purée	approx. 1¼ cups thick sweetened fruit purée
150 ml./¼ pint natural yogurt	⅔ cup plain yogurt
1 egg white	1 egg white
fruit (to decorate)	fruit (to decorate)

Serves 3–4

The purée can be obtained in various ways. If using ripe strawberries or other soft fruit just mash, strain or use a blender and add sugar to taste. Hard fruit should be cooked in the minimum of water (or omit water if possible) with sugar to taste, then mashed, strained or blended. If using canned or defrosted frozen fruit, strain off the syrup (this can be used in a fruit salad or jelly), mash, strain or blend. Add extra sugar if required.

Chill the yogurt well then beat into the cold purée. Beat the egg white until stiff and fold into the mixture with a metal spoon. Spoon into glasses, decorate with fruit and serve at once. The mixture tends to separate if left standing.

Chocolate sponge pudding

Metric/Imperial	American
100 g./4 oz. butter	½ cup butter
100 g./4 oz. caster sugar	½ cup superfine sugar
2 large eggs, beaten	2 large eggs, beaten
75 g./3 oz. self-raising flour	¾ cup self-rising flour
pinch of salt	pinch of salt
15 g./½ oz. cornflour	2 tablespoons cornstarch
15 g./½ oz. cocoa powder	2 tablespoons unsweetened cocoa powder
50 g./2 oz. plain chocolate, melted with 1 tablespoon warm milk	2 squares semi-sweet chocolate, melted with 1¼ tablespoons warm milk

Serves 4

Cream the butter and sugar together until fluffy. Add the eggs, one at a time. Sift the flour, salt, cornflour (cornstarch) and cocoa powder together and fold into the creamed mixture. Add the melted chocolate to make a soft mixture that will fall easily from a spoon. Grease a 900 ml./1½ pint (3¾ cup) pudding basin and spoon in the mixture. Cover with greased foil or greaseproof (waxed) paper. Make a pleat in the centre and tie on with string around the rim.

Place the basin in a large pan with boiling water one third up the sides, cover and steam for 1½–2 hours. Remove from the pan, discard the foil or paper and turn the pudding out on to a warmed serving plate. Serve with hot chocolate sauce.

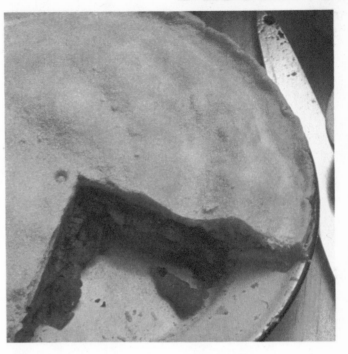

Crêpes Suzette

Metric/Imperial
175 g./6 oz. plain flour
pinch of salt
2 eggs
450 ml./¾ pint milk
oil or fat for frying

Filling
50–75 g./2–3 oz. butter
finely grated rind of 2 oranges
* or 4 tangerines*
75 g./3 oz. icing sugar, sifted
little orange or tangerine juice

Sauce
50 g./2 oz. caster or granulated
* sugar*
juice of 2 oranges or 4
* tangerines*
juice of 1 small lemon
2–3 tablespoons Curaçao

American
1½ cups all-purpose flour
pinch of salt
2 eggs
2 cups milk
oil or fat for frying

Filling
4–6 tablespoons butter
finely grated rind of 2 oranges
* or 4 tangerines*
¾ cup confectioners' sugar,
* sifted*
little orange or tangerine juice

Sauce
¼ cup superfine or granulated
* sugar*
juice of 2 oranges or 4
* tangerines*
juice of 1 small lemon
2½–4 tablespoons Curaçao

Serves 6
Sift the flour and salt into a mixing bowl, gradually add the eggs and milk and beat to a smooth batter. Cook the pancakes (crêpes) as in Cinnamon apple pancakes (crêpes) (page 195) to make about 12. Keep hot. Blend all the filling ingredients together, adding just enough fruit juice to give the consistency of thick cream. Put some of the filling into the centre of each cooked pancake (crêpe), then fold in four. Put the sugar into a large pan and heat over low heat until it just begins to turn golden brown. Add the fruit juice and blend with the sugar. Heat the pancakes (crêpes) very gently in the hot sauce. Add the Curaçao just before serving. Ignite if wished.

Blackberry and apple pie

Metric/Imperial
225 g./8 oz. sweet shortcrust
* pastry dough*
½ kg./1 lb. tart apples
225 g./8 oz. blackberries
2 tablespoons sugar
¼ teaspoon ground cinnamon
extra sugar

American
2 cups sweet shortcrust pastry
* dough*
1 lb. tart apples
8 oz. blackberries
2½ tablespoons sugar
¼ teaspoon ground cinnamon
extra sugar

Serves 6–8
Oven setting: 220°C./425°F./Gas Mark 7
Roll out half the pastry into a round and line a 20 cm./8 inch plate. Peel, core and slice the apples. Pick the blackberries clean. Place apple and blackberries into pie plate and sprinkle with sugar and cinnamon. Brush edge of pastry with cold water. Roll out remaining pastry to a round, to fit pie plate and place on top of fruit. Seal edges, trim neatly, and decorate edge. Make a neat hole in the centre of pastry to allow steam to escape.

Sprinkle pastry with a little sugar and bake towards the top of the oven for 30–40 minutes, or until pastry is cooked and golden brown. Serve hot or cold with cream.

DESSERTS

Pineapple mousse

Metric/Imperial	American
3 eggs, separated	3 eggs, separated
juice of 1 lemon	juice of 1 lemon
50 g./2 oz. caster sugar	¼ cup superfine sugar
15 g./½ oz. gelatine	½ oz. gelatin
300 ml./½ pint canned pineapple juice	1¼ cups canned pineapple juice
150 ml./¼ pint double cream	⅔ cup heavy cream

Serves 6

Place the egg yolks, lemon juice and sugar in a heatproof bowl set over a pan of simmering water and beat until thick and pale. Remove from the heat and continue to beat occasionally until cool.

Sprinkle the gelatine (gelatin) over 4 tablespoons of the pineapple juice in a small heatproof bowl and leave until spongy, then set the bowl over a pan of hot water and stir over low heat until dissolved. Add to the remaining pineapple juice and stir into the egg yolk mixture. Leave in a cool place until just beginning to set, stirring frequently.

Beat the cream until thick, and fold it into the pineapple mixture. Beat the egg whites until stiff and fold into the mixture with a metal spoon. Turn into a serving dish and leave to set in a cool place. Decorate with whipped cream rosettes.

Jellied fruit snow

Metric/Imperial	American
300 ml./½ pint thick apple purée, sweetened	1¼ cups thick apple purée, sweetened
few drops green food colouring	few drops green food colouring
1 teaspoon gelatine	1 teaspoon gelatin
2 tablespoons water or fruit juice	2½ tablespoons water or fruit juice
150 ml./¼ pint double cream, lightly whipped	⅔ cup heavy cream, lightly beaten
3 egg whites	3 egg whites
Decoration	**Decoration**
lemon slices (optional)	lemon slices (optional)

Serves 4–6

Warm the purée gently. Add a few drops of the green food colouring. Soften the gelatine in cold water or fruit juice. Mix with the warm purée and stir until dissolved. Allow to cool, then fold in half the cream and 2 stiffly beaten egg whites. Spoon into 4–6 serving glasses and allow to set lightly. Whip the remainder of the cream and the third egg white in separate basins, fold together and pile on top of the dessert. Decorate with lemon slices if wished.

Peach gâteau

Metric/Imperial	American
peach halves and raspberries	peach halves and raspberries
Confectioners' custard	*Confectioners' custard*
50 g./2 oz. sugar	¼ cup sugar
25 g./1 oz. flour	¼ cup flour
2 egg yolks	2 egg yolks
½ teaspoon grated lemon rind	½ teaspoon grated lemon rind
300 ml./½ pint milk	1¼ cups milk
15 g./½ oz. butter	1 tablespoon butter
Marsala	Marsala
Sponge	*Sponge*
3 eggs, separated	3 eggs, separated
75 g./3 oz. sugar	6 tablespoons sugar
½ teaspoon grated lemon rind	½ teaspoon grated lemon rind
65 g./2½ oz. plain flour, sifted	½ cup plus 2 tablespoons
pinch of salt	all-purpose flour, sifted
	pinch of salt

Serves 4–6

Oven setting: 190°C./375°F./Gas Mark 5

Put the sugar, flour, egg yolks and lemon rind into a bowl, add a little of the milk and beat well. Bring the remaining milk to the boil, and beat into the egg mixture. Return to the pan and beat until mixture thickens. Stir in butter and 1 tablespoon Marsala; cover and leave until cold.

Grease and line a 20 cm./8 inch sandwich tin (layer pan) with greased greaseproof (waxed) paper. Beat the egg yolks, sugar and lemon rind together until thick and light. Beat the egg whites until stiff and fold lightly into the yolks with a metal spoon. Fold in the flour and salt. Pour into the prepared tin (pan) and bake in the preheated oven for 15–20 minutes. Turn on to wire rack. Remove paper.

When cold, cut into three slices horizontally. Spread bottom with half the custard and arrange some peach halves and raspberries on top. Sprinkle with a few drops of Marsala. Cover with the second slice of sponge, spread with the rest of the custard and add more peaches and raspberries. Top with the third slice of sponge, sprinkle with Marsala and arrange the rest of the peaches and raspberries on top.

Chilled raspberry cheesecake

Metric/Imperial	American
1 packet lemon-flavoured jelly	1 packet lemon-flavoured gelatin
175 g./6 oz. digestive biscuits, crushed	1 cup crushed graham crackers
25 g./1 oz. demerara sugar	2 tablespoons light brown sugar
75 g./3 oz. butter, melted	6 tablespoons butter, melted
150 ml./¼ pint double cream	⅔ cup heavy cream
350 g./12 oz. rich cream cheese	1½ cups rich cream cheese
juice of 2 lemons	juice of 2 lemons
100 g./4 oz. caster sugar	½ cup superfine sugar
Topping	*Topping*
225 g./8 oz. raspberries, frozen or fresh	8 oz. raspberries, frozen or fresh
4 tablespoons redcurrant jelly	5 tablespoons redcurrant jelly

Serves 6

Dissolve the jelly (gelatin) in 150 ml./¼ pint (⅔ cup) boiling water. Make up to 300 ml./½ pint (1¼ cups) with cold water, and leave until cold, thick and nearly set.

Mix the biscuits (crackers), brown sugar and melted butter together and use to line the bottom of a 20–23 cm./8–9 inch spring mould. Chill in the refrigerator for 30 minutes.

Beat the cream until thick. Mash the cream cheese, then gradually beat in the thickened jelly (gelatin), lemon juice, cream and sugar. Turn into the prepared mould and put in the refrigerator to chill.

Thirty minutes before serving, arrange the raspberries around the edge of the cheesecake. Melt the redcurrant jelly over low heat and spoon over the cheesecake. If necessary, thin the jelly with a little water.

DESSERTS

Cherry compote

Metric/Imperial
150 ml./¼ pint red wine
approx. 50 g./2 oz. caster sugar
700 g./1½ lb. fresh cherries,
   stoned
1 cinnamon stick
2 teaspoons arrowroot

American
⅔ cup red wine
approx. ¼ cup superfine sugar
1½ lb. fresh cherries, pitted
1 cinnamon stick
2 teaspoons arrowroot

Serves 6
Put the wine and sugar in a pan and dissolve the sugar slowly over gentle heat. Add the cherries to the pan, with the cinnamon stick and a little water if the syrup does not quite cover the cherries. Simmer the cherries very gently for 8–10 minutes, or until just soft, being careful not to overcook. Remove the pan from the heat. Taste for sweetness and add more sugar if necessary.

Blend the arrowroot with a little water, until smooth then stir into the pan. Bring slowly to the boil, stirring constantly. The juices should be thick and syrupy. Discard the cinnamon stick and transfer the compote to a serving bowl. Serve hot or cold.

Fruit meringue trifle

Metric/Imperial
550–700 g./1¼–1½ lb.
   dessert fruit*
sugar to taste
450 ml./¾ pint double cream
up to 150 ml./¼ pint white
   wine
about 8 medium-sized
   home-made or bought
   meringue shells

American
1¼–1½ lb. dessert fruit*
sugar to taste
2 cups heavy cream
up to ⅔ cup white wine
about 8 medium-sized
   home-made or bought
   meringue shells

Serves 6–8
Prepare the fruit, put into a bowl and sprinkle with sugar. Beat the cream until just stiff. Put a little on one side for decoration. Gradually blend up to 150 ml./¼ pint (⅔ cup) white wine with the remaining cream. Sweeten to taste. Break the meringue shells into fairly large pieces. Put a layer at the bottom of a dish. Add half the fruit, then the cream and wine layer then nearly all the remaining fruit (save a little for decoration). Top with meringue pieces, piped cream and fruit.

This must be served within an hour of preparation so the meringue pieces will still be crisp.

*The picture shows raspberries, but sliced fresh peaches, apricots, pears or a mixture of fruit may be used. Add a little white wine (extra to the 150 ml./¼ pint (⅔ cup) in the ingredients) or lemon juice to peaches, apricots or pears to prevent them from discolouring. White wine can also be added to the berry fruit.

Treacle tart

Metric/Imperial
175 g./6 oz. shortcrust pastry
    made with 175 g./6 oz. plain
    flour, etc.
grated rind of ½ lemon
1 tablespoon lemon juice
4 tablespoons golden syrup
breadcrumbs or crushed
    cornflakes

American
1½ cups shortcrust pastry
    made with 1½ cups
    all-purpose flour, etc.
grated rind of ½ lemon
1¼ tablespoons lemon juice
5 tablespoons light corn syrup
breadcrumbs or crushed
    cornflakes

Serves 4–6
Oven setting: 200°C./400°F./Gas Mark 6
Roll out the pastry on a floured surface and use to line a
20–23 cm./8–9 inch pie plate. Prick the base of the pastry
shell with a fork. Fill the pastry with greased greaseproof
(waxed) paper and beans or crusts of bread and bake blind
towards the top of the preheated oven for 10 minutes.
Remove the beans and paper.

    Meanwhile, mix the grated lemon rind with the lemon
juice, syrup and enough breadcrumbs or cornflakes to give
the mixture a soft consistency. Spoon into the partially
cooked pastry case (pie shell). Move to a cooler part of the
oven, or reduce the heat slightly, and bake for a further
15–20 minutes, or until the pastry is golden brown. Serve
hot with cream, or leave to cool and serve cold.

Fruit flan

Metric/Imperial
175 g./6 oz. shortcrust pastry,
    made with 175 g./6 oz. plain
    flour, etc.
100 g./4 oz. sugar
300 ml./½ pint water
½ kg./1 lb. grapes, halved and
    seeded
100 g./4 oz. strawberries
arrowroot or cornflour

American
1½ cups shortcrust pastry,
    made with 1½ cups
    all-purpose flour, etc.
½ cup sugar
1¼ cups water
1 lb. grapes, halved and pitted
4 oz. strawberries
arrowroot or cornstarch

Serves 4
Oven setting: 220°C./425°F./Gas Mark 7
Roll out the pastry on a floured surface and line a
20–23 cm./8–9 inch fluted flan case (pie shell). Fill pastry
with greased greaseproof (waxed) paper and beans or
crusts of bread and bake blind in the preheated oven for
20–25 minutes, removing the beans and paper about
halfway through cooking to allow the pastry to brown.
Leave to cool.

    Put the sugar and water in a pan and dissolve the sugar
slowly over gentle heat. Increase the heat slightly and boil
for 5 minutes, then remove from the heat. Put the grapes
in the warm syrup for 2–3 minutes, then strain them and
arrange in flan case (pie shell). Put strawberries in syrup
for 2–3 minutes, strain and add to the centre of the flan.

    Measure the remaining syrup and allow 1 teaspoon
arrowroot or cornflour (cornstarch) to each 150 ml./¼ pint
(⅔ cup). Blend with the syrup and boil until thickened and
clear. Cool slightly then brush over the fruit.

DESSERTS

Strawberry soufflé

Metric/Imperial	American
350 g./12 oz. fresh strawberries	12 oz. fresh strawberries
150 g./5 oz. caster sugar	⅔ cup superfine sugar
3 eggs, separated	3 eggs, separated
15 g./½ oz. gelatine	½ oz. gelatin
2 tablespoons lemon juice	2½ tablespoons lemon juice
150 ml./¼ pint double cream	⅔ cup heavy cream
25 g./1 oz. finely chopped hazelnuts or walnuts	¼ cup finely chopped hazelnuts or walnuts

Serves 4

Tie a deep band of doubled greased greaseproof (waxed) paper around the outside of a 600 ml./1 pint (2½ cup) soufflé dish, to stand about 5 cm./2 inches above the rim. Purée the strawberries in a blender or work through a sieve (strainer), reserving a few for decoration. Stir in 50 g./2 oz. (¼ cup) of the sugar. Place the egg yolks and remaining sugar in a heatproof bowl set over a pan of simmering water and beat until thick and pale. Remove from the heat and continue beating until cold. Fold in the strawberry purée.

Sprinkle the gelatine (gelatin) over the lemon juice in a small heatproof bowl and leave until spongy, then set the bowl over a pan of hot water and stir over low heat until dissolved. Leave to cool slightly, then stir into the strawberry mixture. Beat the cream until thick and stir into the strawberry mixture, making sure it is thoroughly blended. Beat the egg whites until stiff then fold into the strawberry mixture with a metal spoon. Spoon into the prepared soufflé dish and chill in the refrigerator for at least 4 hours, or until set.

Before serving, carefully remove the greaseproof (waxed) paper. Decorate the top of the soufflé with the reserved strawberries and press the nuts around the edge.

Fruit fritters

Metric/Imperial	American
200 g./7 oz. plain flour	1¾ cups all-purpose flour
25 g./1 oz. caster sugar	2 tablespoons superfine sugar
250 ml./8 fl. oz. white wine	1 cup white wine
1 tablespoon olive oil	1¼ tablespoons olive oil
grated rind of ½ lemon	grated rind of ½ lemon
3 eggs, separated	3 eggs, separated
3 dessert apples, peeled, cored and finely chopped	3 eating apples, peeled, cored and finely chopped
25 g./1 oz. dried apricots, finely chopped	2 tablespoons finely chopped dried apricots
25 g./1 oz. sultanas	2 tablespoons seedless raisins
40 g./1½ oz. blanched almonds, finely chopped	¼ cup finely chopped blanched almonds
1 tablespoon rum	1¼ tablespoons rum
oil for deep-frying	oil for deep-frying
extra caster sugar	extra superfine sugar

Serves 4–6

Sift the flour into a mixing bowl and add the sugar. Gradually add the wine, olive oil, lemon rind, then the egg yolks and beat to a smooth batter. Set aside in a cool place until required.

Put the apples, apricots, sultanas (raisins) and almonds in a bowl with the rum and leave to macerate for 1 hour. Beat the egg whites until stiff, then fold them into the batter with the fruit mixture with a metal spoon. Heat the oil until it is hot enough to turn a stale bread cube golden brown in 30 seconds (190°C./375°F. on a deep-fat thermometer). Put tablespoons of the mixture carefully into the oil and fry for a few seconds until golden brown. Drain on absorbent paper, sprinkle liberally with sugar and serve at once.

French apple tart

Metric/Imperial	American
Sweet flan pastry	Sweet flan pastry
150 g./5 oz. plain flour	1¼ cups plain flour
pinch of salt	pinch of salt
65 g./2½ oz. butter	5 tablespoons butter
1 tablespoon caster sugar	1¼ tablespoons superfine
2 teaspoons ground almonds	sugar
1 egg yolk	2 teaspoons ground almonds
2–3 tablespoons cold water	1 egg yolk
	2½–4 tablespoons cold water
Filling	
50 g./2 oz. sugar	Filling
grated rind of ½ lemon	¼ cup sugar
½ kg./1 lb. cooking apples,	grated rind of ½ lemon
cooked and puréed	1 lb. tart apples, cooked and
2 cooking apples, peeled, cored	puréed
and thinly sliced	2 cooking apples, peeled, cored
	and thinly sliced
Glaze	
1 tablespoon apricot jam, sieved	Glaze
2 teaspoons water	1¼ tablespoons apricot jam,
1 teaspoon lemon juice	strained
	2 teaspoons water
	1 teaspoon lemon juice

Serves 4–6

Oven setting: 200°C./400°F./Gas Mark 6

Sift the flour and salt into a mixing bowl. Rub the butter into the flour until the mixture resembles fine breadcrumbs. Stir in the sugar and almonds. Bind with the egg yolk and enough cold water to make a stiff dough. Knead until smooth. Wrap in foil and chill in the refrigerator for 30 minutes. Roll out the pastry on the floured surface and use to line a 20 cm./8 inch flan ring, placed on a baking sheet. Add the sugar and lemon rind to the apple purée and spoon into the flan case (pie shell). Arrange sliced apples neatly over the surface. Bake in the preheated oven for 25–30 minutes. Leave to cool slightly.

    Put the jam, water and lemon juice in a pan and heat, stirring occasionally, until syrupy. Brush over tart.

Empress rice

Metric/Imperial	American
100 g./4 oz. round-grain rice	½ cup round-grain rice
900 ml./1½ pints milk	3¾ cups milk
¼ teaspoon vanilla essence	¼ teaspoon vanilla extract
100 g./4 oz. sugar	½ cup sugar
25 g./1 oz. butter	2 tablespoons butter
100 g./4 oz. glacé fruits	½ cup candied fruits
3 tablespoons Kirsch	4 tablespoons Kirsch
300 ml./½ pint double cream	1¼ cups heavy cream
4 egg yolks, lightly beaten	4 egg yolks, lightly beaten
15 g./½ oz. gelatine	1 tablespoon gelatin
fruit or fruit sauce	fruit or fruit sauce

Serves 4–6

Lightly grease a large decorative mould or charlotte tin. Put the rice in a saucepan and cover with water. Bring to the boil, simmer 2–3 minutes and drain the rice. Return the rice to the saucepan, add two-thirds of the milk and the vanilla essence (extract), bring to the boil and simmer, covered, stirring occasionally, until the rice is tender and the milk absorbed. Stir in half of the sugar and butter. Allow the rice to cool.

    Chop the glacé (candied) fruit into small pieces and soak them in Kirsch. Whip the cream until stiff and fold into the rice. Mix the egg yolks and remaining sugar together in a bowl. Put remaining milk into a saucepan and heat it until bubbles begin to rise to the surface (do not allow it to boil). Pour the milk on to the egg yolks, add the gelatine and stir until the gelatine is dissolved. Cool. Strain the custard on to the rice, add the soaked glacé (candied) fruits and stir together well. Spoon the prepared mixture into the greased mould. Put in a cool place, preferably the refrigerator, until set. Turn out of the mould on to a chilled serving plate and serve decorated with fruit or with a fruit sauce, and cream if liked.

DESSERTS

Apple jalousie

Metric/Imperial	American
½ kg./1 lb. cooking apples, peeled, cored and sliced	1 lb. tart apples, peeled, cored and sliced
2 tablespoons water	2½ tablespoons water
25 g./1 oz. butter	2 tablespoons butter
50 g./2 oz. sugar	¼ cup sugar
1 × 400 g./14 oz. packet frozen puff pastry, thawed	1 × 14 oz. packet frozen puff pastry, thawed
1 egg white	1 egg white

Serves 6–8
Oven setting: 200°C./400°F./Gas Mark 6
Place the apples in a pan with the water, butter and sugar, cover and simmer slowly until the apples are tender. Remove the lid and continue to cook the apples, mashing them with a wooden spoon as they simmer. Cook until the apple is a thick purée. Put on one side to cool.

Roll out the pastry on a floured surface to a rectangle 20 × 30 cm./8 × 12 inches, then cut into two strips each 10 × 30 cm./4 × 12 inches long. Lay one strip on a baking dish. Brush the edges with water and spoon the cold apple purée down the centre. Fold the second strip of pastry in half lengthways and cut with a sharp knife across the fold at 5 cm./2 inch intervals, leaving 2.5 cm./1 inch of pastry uncut at the sides. Unfold and place on top of the filling, press on firmly and knock up (flake) the edges with the back of a knife.

Lightly beat the egg white and brush over the top. Bake in the centre of the preheated oven for 20–30 minutes, or until the pastry is well risen and golden brown. Remove from the oven and brush again with egg white.

Christmas pudding

Metric/Imperial	American
225 g./8 oz. dark molasses sugar	1 cup dark molasses sugar
400 g./14 oz. fresh breadcrumbs	7 cups fresh breadcrumbs
225 g./8 oz. shredded beef suet	1 cup shredded beef suet
½ teaspoon salt	½ teaspoon salt
1 teaspoon mixed spice	1 teaspoon ground allspice
350 g./12 oz. sultanas	2 cups seedless raisins
350 g./12 oz. raisins	2 cups raisins
225 g./8 oz. currants	1⅓ cups currants
100 g./4 oz. candied peel, chopped	⅔ cup chopped candied peel
50 g./2 oz. blanched almonds, finely chopped	½ cup finely chopped blanched almonds
2 large cooking apples, peeled, cored and finely chopped	2 large tart apples, peeled, cored and finely chopped
finely grated rind and juice of ½ lemon	finely grated rind and juice of ½ lemon
2 eggs, beaten	2 eggs, beaten
300 ml./½ pint stout	1¼ cups milk stout
approx. 150 ml./¼ pint milk	approx. ⅔ cup milk

Serves 12
Put the dry ingredients, fruit, peel and nuts in a large mixing bowl and stir well. Add the apples with the lemon rind and juice, eggs and stout. Stir well. Stir in enough milk to give the batter a soft, dropping consistency. Pour the mixture into two greased 1¼ l./2 pint (5 cup) basins. Cover with circles of greased greaseproof (waxed) paper, then with foil. Make a pleat in the centre and tie on with string around the rim. Leave overnight.

Place the basins in the top of a steamer or double boiler, or in a large pan of gently bubbling water, cover and steam for 4–5 hours, topping up the water level from time to time. Remove carefully from the pan and leave until quite cold. Discard the foil and paper and replace with fresh greaseproof (waxed) paper and foil before storing. Steam again for about 2 hours before serving.

Stuffed peaches

Metric/Imperial	American
75 g./3 oz. sultanas	1/2 cup seedless raisins
3 tablespoons brandy	4 tablespoons brandy
5 large ripe peaches	5 large ripe peaches
100 g./4 oz. macaroons	1 cup macaroons
icing sugar	confectioners' sugar
whipped cream	whipped cream
almonds	almonds

Serves 4

Put the sultanas (raisins) into a pan with the brandy, bring slowly to boiling point, then leave until cold.

Peel one of the peaches, remove the stone (pit) and put the peach into a bowl with the macaroons. Pound well together, add sultanas (raisins) and brandy and a little icing (confectioners') sugar to taste. If mixture is too stiff, add a little more brandy.

Halve the remaining peaches, remove the stones (pits) and sandwich the halves together again with the filling between. Put a whirl of whipped cream on top and finish with a blanched toasted almond.

Glazed apples

Metric/Imperial	American
300 ml./1/2 pint water	1 1/4 cups water
juice of 1 lemon	juice of 1 lemon
strip of lemon rind	strip of lemon rind
100 g./4 oz. sugar	1/2 cup sugar
4 medium-sized cooking apples, peeled	4 medium-sized tart apples, peeled
1 tablespoon Curaçao	1 1/4 tablespoons Curaçao
2 tablespoons butter	2 1/2 tablespoons butter

Serves 4

Put the water, lemon juice, lemon rind and sugar into a pan and bring to boiling point. Poach the apples very carefully in the syrup until tender. Add the curaçao and butter, and baste the apples with the syrup until well glazed.

Helpful hints

Use sweet, firm, cooking pears instead, if in season.

DESSERTS

Crème caramel

Metric/Imperial	American
Custard	*Custard*
600 ml./1 pint milk	*2½ cups milk*
2 eggs, beaten	*2 eggs, beaten*
2 egg yolks, beaten	*2 egg yolks, beaten*
2 tablespoons caster sugar	*2½ tablespoons superfine*
150 ml./¼ pint evaporated	* sugar*
* milk*	*⅔ cup evaporated milk*
Caramel	*Caramel*
100 g./4 oz. sugar	*½ cup sugar*
150 ml./¼ pint water	*⅔ cup water*

Serves 4

Oven setting: 180°C./350°F./Gas Mark 4

Put the milk in a pan and heat gently until lukewarm. Meanwhile, put the remaining ingredients for the custard in a bowl and stir until the sugar dissolvès. Stir in the warmed milk and set aside. To prepare the caramel, put the sugar and water in a pan and dissolve the sugar slowly over gentle heat. Increase the heat and boil until the syrup turns a rich brown, caramel colour. Immediately pour the caramel into a warm 600 ml./1 pint (2½ cup) cake tin (pan) or mould. Tip the tin (pan) or mould from side to side to ensure that the base and sides are thoroughly coated with the caramel.

Strain in the custard mixture. Cover with foil, then put in a roasting pan half full of hot water. Bake in the preheated oven for 50 minutes–1 hour, or until the custard is set. Test by shaking it gently from side to side. When set, remove from the oven and leave to cool. Chill in the refrigerator for several hours, preferably overnight, then carefully turn out on to a flat serving dish.

Grape meringue flan

Metric/Imperial	American
10–12 small home-made or	*10–12 small home-made or*
* bought meringues*	* bought meringues*
50 g./2 oz. butter	*4 tablespoons butter*
75 g./3 oz. soft brown sugar	*1 cup light brown sugar*
75 g./3 oz. demerara sugar	*½ cup light corn syrup*
100 ml./4 fl. oz. golden syrup	*1⅓ cups crushed graham*
225 g./8 oz. bran buds	* crackers*
Filling	*Filling*
225 g./8 oz. white grapes	*8 oz. white grapes*
50–100 g./2–4 oz. black grapes	*2–4 oz. black grapes*
4 tablespoons sieved apricot jam	*5 tablespoons strained apricot*
3 tablespoons water	* jam*
	4 tablespoons water

Serves 5–6

If making meringues prepare these first. Heat the butter, sugars and syrup in a large pan. Remove from the heat and add the bran buds (crushed crackers). Mix well then use to line a 20 cm./8 inch flan ring placed on a serving plate. Leave in a cool place for 2–3 hours.

Halve the grapes and remove the pips. Heat the jam and water until a smooth glaze. Arrange the grapes in the flan and brush with the warm glaze. Leave to cool, then put the meringues around the edge. Serve with cream.

Summer pudding

Metric/Imperial
6 slices white bread, crusts
   removed
225 g./8 oz. rhubarb, prepared
100 g./4 oz. redcurrants
100 g./4 oz. blackberries
100 g./4 oz. blackcurrants
175 g./6 oz. sugar
2 tablespoons water
225 g./8 oz. strawberries
100 g./4 oz. raspberries

American
6 slices white bread, crusts
   removed
2 cups prepared rhubarb
4 oz. redcurrants
4 oz. blackberries
4 oz. blackcurrants
¾ cup sugar
2½ tablespoons water
8 oz. strawberries
4 oz. raspberries

Serves 4
Cut a slice of bread to fit the base of a 1¼ 1./2 pint (5 cup)
pudding basin. Reserve a slice of bread for the top. Cut the
remaining bread into fingers. Line the base and side of the
basin with the bread fingers. Put all the fruit (except the
strawberries and raspberries) and sugar in a pan with the
water. Cover and simmer gently until the fruit is almost
soft, then add the strawberries and raspberries and cook
for a further 2 minutes. Put the mixture in the prepared
basin, top with the remaining slice of bread, pressing it
down firmly. Cover the basin with a plate. Press down
with weights overnight.

   Turn out just before serving and serve with whipped
cream.

Pears in red wine

Metric/Imperial
100 g./4 oz. sugar
150 ml./¼ pint red wine
   (Burgundy-type)
150 ml./¼ pint water
strip of lemon rind
¼ teaspoon ground cinnamon
8–10 small dessert pears
50 g./2 oz. blanched almonds,
   split and toasted (to decorate)

American
½ cup sugar
⅔ cup red wine
   (Burgundy-type)
⅔ cup water
strip of lemon rind
¼ teaspoon ground cinnamon
8–10 small dessert pears
⅓ cup blanched almonds, split
   and toasted (to decorate)

Serves 4–5
Put the sugar, wine, water, lemon rind and cinnamon in a
large pan and dissolve the sugar slowly over gentle heat.
Peel the pears, cutting off the core at the base and leaving
the stalks on. Add to the pan, cover and simmer gently for
20–25 minutes, or until soft and coloured. Remove the
pears carefully from the pan and place, standing upright,
in a heatproof glass serving bowl. Set aside.

   Increase the heat and boil the liquid in the pan rapidly
until it thickens and is syrupy. Take off the heat and allow
to cool slightly. Remove the lemon rind, then pour over
the pears. When the pears and syrup are quite cold, chill in
the refrigerator for several hours, spooning the syrup over
the pears from time to time. Just before serving, sprinkle
over the almonds.

DESSERTS

Stuffed figs

Metric/Imperial	American
4 ripe, even-sized figs	4 ripe, even-sized figs
225 g./8 oz. Ricotta, cottage or cream cheese	1 cup Ricotta, cottage or cream cheese
1 large egg, separated	1 large egg, separated
50 g./2 oz. sugar	¼ cup sugar
1–2 tablespoons kirsch or brandy	1¼–2½ tablespoons kirsch or brandy
almonds	almonds

Serves 4

Cut the figs into quarters, just enough to be able to open out the fruit — be careful not to cut right through. If using cottage cheese, it should be strained. Add the egg yolk and sugar to the cheese and beat until light. Add the kirsch or brandy. Beat the egg white until stiff, then fold lightly into the cheese mixture with a metal spoon.

Spoon the cheese mixture into the centre of the figs and, if liked, arrange an almond on top. Chill before serving.

Helpful hints

Ricotta is an Italian cheese, smooth and delicate flavoured, suitable for cooking in both sweet and savoury dishes.

Pacific delight

Metric/Imperial	American
1 ripe, medium-sized pineapple	1 ripe, medium-sized pineapple
900 ml./1½ pints ice cream	3¾ cups ice cream
Meringue	*Meringue*
4 egg whites, stiffly beaten	4 egg whites, stiffly beaten
100 g./4 oz. caster sugar	½ cup superfine sugar

Serves 4–6

Oven setting: 240°C./475°F./Gas Mark 9

Cut the top from the pineapple very carefully. Put this on one side to be used for decoration. Cut the pineapple into 4–6 rings and then remove the skin from each slice with a sharp knife or kitchen scissors. Take out the centre core with an apple corer, or sharp knife. Make sure the ice cream is firm. Gradually whisk half the sugar into the egg whites, then fold in the remainder.

Put the bottom slice of pineapple on to an oven-proof serving dish. Fill the centre hole of the pineapple with ice cream. Top with a second slice of fruit and ice cream, continue like this until the pineapple is put together. Put the meringue mixture into a cloth piping bag fitted with a ½ cm./¼ inch nozzle, and pipe over the fruit to look like the original shape of the pineapple. Put into the oven and leave for about 3 minutes only, until the meringue is tinged golden brown. Remove from the oven. Put the pineapple leaves into position, on the top of the meringue shape. Serve at once.

This dessert will stand for about 25–30 minutes without the ice cream melting.

Biscuit crumb flan

Metric/Imperial	American
50 g./2 oz. butter or margarine	4 tablespoons butter or margarine
50 g./2 oz. caster sugar	1/4 cup superfine sugar
2 teaspoons golden syrup	2 teaspoons light corn syrup
100 g./4 oz. plain or semi-sweet biscuits, crushed	2/3 cup crushed graham crackers
Filling	Filling
fruit	fruit

Serves 4
Oven setting: 180°C./350°F./Gas Mark 4
Cream the butter or margarine until fluffy. Stir in the sugar and syrup and add the crushed biscuits (crackers). Use to line a fluted flan case. Either set in a cool place for a short time or brown for 10 minutes in the preheated oven. Fill with fruit and serve with cream.

Fruit tarts

Metric/Imperial	American
225 g./8 oz. sweet shortcrust pastry dough	2 cups sweet shortcrust pastry dough
Filling	Filling
selection of fruit such as pears, apples, grapes	selection of fruit such as pears, apples, grapes
lemon juice	lemon juice
175 g./6 oz. apricot jam	3/4 cup apricot jelly
glacé cherries	candied cherries

Makes 20–24
Oven setting: 200°C./400°F./Gas Mark 6
Roll out the dough on a lightly floured board. Cut it into rounds and line 20–24 patty tins. Place small rounds of greased greaseproof (waxed) paper in the patty cases and fill each with some dry beans. Bake the cases in the preheated oven for about 20 minutes, or until cooked and golden. Cool on a rack.

Meanwhile, prepare the fruit. Peel, core and slice the pears thinly and dip each slice in lemon juice. Do the same with apples, but leave the peel on if it is red. Halve and seed the grapes.

Heat the apricot jam (jelly) in a small pan with a few drops of lemon juice. Stir until blended, then sieve (strain). Fill the cooked pastry cases with the fruit and brush with the apricot glaze. Decorate with cherries, if desired.

DESSERTS

Cream cheesecake

Chocolate mousse

Metric/Imperial
1 sponge cake (approximately
 15 × 7.5 cm./6 × 3 inches
 deep)
550 g./1¼ lb. Ricotta or cream
 cheese
175 g./6 oz. sugar
1 tablespoon Curaçao or apricot
 brandy
50 g./2 oz. plain chocolate, cut
 into small pieces
100 g./4 oz. candied peel,
 finely chopped

American
1 sponge cake (approximately
 6 × 3 inches deep)
2½ cups Ricotta or cream
 cheese
¾ cup sugar
1¼ tablespoons Curaçao or
 apricot brandy
2 squares semi-sweet chocolate,
 cut into small pieces
⅔ cup finely chopped candied
 peel

Serves 4–6
Cut the cake into three layers horizontally. If Ricotta
cheese is used, rub it through a strainer, then mix the
cheese and sugar together and add the Curaçao or brandy.
Divide the mixture in two and put half of it aside in the
refrigerator for coating. Add chocolate and candied peel to
the other half and mix well. Put the bottom layer of sponge
on to a serving dish and spread with half the cheese
mixture. Cover with the second slice and repeat the
process, then cover with the top piece of sponge and press
all lightly together. Leave to chill for as long as possible.

Spread the top and sides of the cake with the reserved
chilled cheese mixture and decorate as liked with whirls of
cream cheese and strips of candied peel.

Metric/Imperial
175 g./6 oz. plain chocolate,
 broken into pieces
2 tablespoons strong black coffee
4 eggs, separated
1 tablespoon rum

Garnish
150 ml./¼ pint double cream
1 tablespoon grated chocolate

American
6 squares semi-sweet chocolate,
 broken into pieces
2½ tablespoons strong black
 coffee
4 eggs, separated
1¼ tablespoons rum

Garnish
⅔ cup heavy cream
1¼ tablespoons grated
 chocolate

Serves 4
Put the chocolate pieces and coffee in a heatproof bowl set
over a pan of hot water and heat gently until the chocolate
melts, stirring occasionally. Remove from the heat and
leave to cool for 1–2 minutes. Beat the egg yolks and
gradually stir into the chocolate mixture. Stir in the rum.
Beat the egg whites until stiff, then carefully fold into the
chocolate mixture until thoroughly combined with a metal
spoon. Spoon into a serving dish and chill in the
refrigerator for several hours, preferably overnight.

Before serving, beat the cream until thick, then pipe
rosettes of cream to decorate. Sprinkle with the grated
chocolate.

Rice pudding

Metric/Imperial	American
50 g./2 oz. round-grain rice	1/3 cup round-grain rice
25–50 g./1–2 oz. sugar	1/8–1/4 cup sugar
600 ml./1 pint milk	2 1/2 cups milk
small knob butter	small knob butter
little grated nutmeg	little grated nutmeg

Serves 4
Oven setting: 140–160°C./275–300°F./Gas Mark 1–2
Put all the ingredients into a pie dish and cook in the centre of the preheated oven for 1½ hours. Stir the pudding once or twice during cooking if possible. Serve hot by itself or with fruit.

Helpful hints
This may be cooked in a saucepan on top of the stove if you prefer.

Profiteroles

Metric/Imperial	American
Choux pastry	Choux pastry
50 g./2 oz. butter	4 tablespoons butter
150 ml./1/4 pint milk and water	2/3 cup milk and water
65 g./2½ oz. plain flour, sifted	good ½ cup all-purpose flour, sifted
2 eggs, beaten	2 eggs, beaten
Filling and icing	Filling and icing
300 ml./½ pint double cream, lightly whipped	1¼ cups heavy cream, lightly whipped
225 g./8 oz. icing sugar, sifted	2 cups confectioners' sugar, sifted
1 tablespoon cocoa powder	1¼ tablespoons unsweetened cocoa powder
1 tablespoon rum	1¼ tablespoons rum
1–2 tablespoons warm water	1¼–2½ tablespoons warm water

Serves 6
Oven setting: 220°C./425°F./Gas Mark 7
Put the butter, milk and water into a small pan and bring to the boil. Remove the pan from the heat, add the flour all at once and beat the mixture until the dough comes away from the sides. Gradually beat in the eggs until the mixture is thick and glossy. Put the mixture into a large piping bag (forcing bag) fitted with a 1 cm./½ inch plain nozzle. Pipe 20 blobs on to a greased baking sheet. Bake in the preheated oven for 10 minutes, then reduce the heat to 190°C./375°F./Gas Mark 5 for a further 15–20 minutes, or until golden brown. Split one side of each bun so the steam can escape. Leave to cool on a wire rack.

Fill each bun with whipped cream. Sift the icing (confectioners') sugar and cocoa into a bowl. Stir in the rum and sufficient warm water to make a thick glacé icing. Spear each bun with a fork and dip the tops in icing. Pile up in a pyramid as each one is finished. Serve the same day.

DESSERTS

Melon and grapes

Metric/Imperial	American
1 small melon	1 small melon
1 tablespoon caster sugar	1¼ tablespoons superfine
juice of 1 lemon	sugar
1 small bunch seedless grapes	juice of 1 lemon
	1 small bunch seedless grapes

Serves 4

Remove skin and seeds carefully from melon and cut melon flesh into cubes. Place in a serving bowl, sprinkle with sugar and squeeze lemon juice over. Add washed, slightly crushed grapes. Serve chilled.

Yogurt California

Metric/Imperial	American
225 g./8 oz. prunes, stoned	1⅓ cups pitted prunes
water	water
1 orange	1 orange
300 ml./½ pint natural yogurt	1¼ cups plain yogurt

Serves 4

Cover the prunes with cold water, add a little grated orange rind and fresh orange juice. Leave to soak overnight, then simmer until tender, unless using tenderized prunes which will become quite soft with soaking alone. Chill and serve with yogurt.

Helpful hints

Add a little honey to the prunes for a sweeter flavour.

Apple pan dowdy

Metric/Imperial	American
3 good-sized cooking apples, peeled, cored and sliced	3 good-sized tart apples, peeled, cored and sliced
1–2 tablespoons brown sugar	1¼–2½ tablespoons brown sugar
1–2 tablespoons golden syrup	1¼–2½ tablespoons light corn syrup
grated nutmeg	grated nutmeg
ground cinnamon	ground cinnamon
100 g./4 oz. self-raising flour or plain flour and 1 teaspoon baking powder	1 cup self rising flour or all-purpose flour and 1 teaspoon baking powder
pinch of salt	pinch of salt
50 g./2 oz. sugar	¼ cup sugar
1 egg	1 egg
50 ml./2 fl. oz. milk	4 tablespoons milk
50 g./2 oz. butter or margarine, melted	4 tablespoons butter or margarine, melted
extra sugar	extra sugar

Serves 4

Oven setting: 180°C./350°F./Gas Mark 4

Put the apples into a greased 900 ml./1½ pint (3¾ cup) pie dish with the brown sugar, syrup and a sprinkling of nutmeg and cinnamon. Do not add any water. Cover the dish and bake in the centre of the preheated oven for 15–20 minutes, or until the apples are nearly soft.

Meanwhile, sift the flour, salt and sugar into a mixing bowl, gradually add the egg, milk and butter or margarine and beat to a smooth, thick batter. Spoon the batter over the apples, sprinkle lightly with extra sugar and bake in the centre of the preheated oven for 30–35 minutes. Turn out the pudding, upside-down, on to a serving dish and serve with cream, brandy butter or vanilla-flavoured sweet white sauce.

Apricot lemon soufflé

Metric/Imperial	American
1 × 700 g./1½ lb. can apricot halves	1 × 1½ lb. can apricot halves
juice of 2 lemons	juice of 2 lemons
25 g./1 oz. gelatine	1 oz. gelatin
5 eggs, separated	5 eggs, separated
75 g./3 oz. caster sugar	6 tablespoons superfine sugar
450 ml./¾ pint double cream, stiffly whipped	2 cups heavy cream, stiffly whipped
chocolate vermicelli	chocolate shot

Serves 6–8

Tie a deep band of greased greaseproof (waxed) paper around the outside of a medium-sized soufflé dish. Drain the fruit from the syrup, put eight halves on one side for decoration. Sieve (or emulsify) the remaining fruit, add the lemon juice and enough syrup to give 450 ml./¾ pint (2 cups). Soften the gelatine (gelatin) in a little of the cold apricot mixture. Heat the remainder, stir in the softened gelatine (gelatin), and continue stirring until thoroughly dissolved. Beat the egg yolks with the sugar, then beat in the warm apricot mixture. Leave until cool and beginning to stiffen slightly, then fold in 300 ml./½ pint (1¼ cups) cream and the stiffly beaten egg whites. Spoon into the prepared soufflé dish and leave to set.

Remove the band of paper from the mixture and press chocolate vermicelli (chocolate shot) against the sides. Top with remaining piped cream and the reserved apricots.

DESSERTS

Apricot fool

Metric/Imperial
225 g./8 oz. dried apricots,
  soaked overnight in
  300 ml./½ pint water and
  the juice of 1 lemon
sugar to taste
150 ml./¼ pint double cream
  or natural yogurt
flaked browned almonds to
  decorate

American
8 oz. dried apricots, soaked
  overnight in 1¼ cups water
  and the juice of 1 lemon
sugar to taste
⅔ cup heavy cream or plain
  yogurt
flaked browned almonds to
  decorate

Serves 4
Simmer the apricots in the soaking water and lemon juice until they are tender. Sieve or purée in a blender and sweeten with sugar to taste. Blend the apricot purée with the whipped cream or yogurt. Spoon into four glasses and top with almonds.

Cherry pie

Metric/Imperial
550–700 g./1¼–1½ lb. black
  cherries
75 g./3 oz. caster sugar
1 tablespoon brandy
225 g./8 oz. plain flour
pinch of salt
3 eggs, separated
300 ml./½ pint milk and water
15 g./½ oz. butter

American
1¼–1½ lb. black cherries
6 tablespoons superfine
  sugar
1¼ tablespoons brandy
2 cups all-purpose flour
pinch of salt
3 eggs, separated
1¼ cups milk and water
1 tablespoon butter

Serves 6
Oven setting: 190°C./375°F./Gas Mark 5
Grease a 1¾ l./3 pint (7½ cup) ovenproof dish. Sprinkle the unstoned cherries with 25 g./1 oz. (2 tablespoons) of the sugar and brandy and leave for about 30 minutes.

Sift the flour and salt into a mixing bowl, gradually add the egg yolks and enough of the milk and water to beat to a smooth batter. Beat the egg whites with the remaining sugar until stiff, then fold into the batter with a metal spoon. Pour the batter into the prepared dish and spoon the cherry mixture over. Dot with butter.

Bake in the preheated oven for about 40 minutes, or until well risen and firm and golden brown.

Crème brûlée

Metric/Imperial
600 ml./1 pint double cream
4 egg yolks
75 g./3 oz. caster sugar
1 teaspoon vanilla essence
almonds

American
2½ cups heavy cream
4 egg yolks
6 tablespoons superfine sugar
1 teaspoon vanilla extract
almonds

Serves 4
Oven setting: 150°C./300°F./Gas Mark 2
Put the cream in the top of a double boiler or in a heatproof bowl set over a pan of hot water and bring to just below boiling point.

Meanwhile, put the egg yolks, 50 g./2 oz. (¼ cup) of the sugar and the vanilla essence (extract) in a bowl and beat thoroughly. Pour in the cream and stir to mix. Pour the mixture into a shallow baking dish and place in a roasting pan half full of hot water. Bake in the preheated oven for 1 hour, or until set.

When set, remove from the pan and leave until cold. Chill in the refrigerator for several hours, preferably overnight. Sprinkle the top of the Crème brûlée with the remaining sugar and put under a preheated hot grill (broiler) until the sugar turns to caramel. Leave to cool before serving, and sprinkle with almonds.

Apples with Calvados

Metric/Imperial
40 g./1½ oz. butter
2 tablespoons vanilla sugar or sugar with vanilla essence
4 large Granny Smith apples*, peeled, cored and sliced
2 tablespoons Calvados
*or use any other dessert apple that can be cooked

American
3 tablespoons butter
2½ tablespoons vanilla sugar or sugar with vanilla extract
4 large crisp eating apples, peeled, cored and sliced
2½ tablespoons Calvados

Serves 4
Heat the butter in a large frying pan (skillet), stir in the vanilla sugar, then add the apple slices. Turn in the butter mixture until pale golden and transparent; when turning the apple slices, do so gently to avoid breaking them. When the apples are tender, warm the Calvados over a flame in a soup ladle or spoon, ignite and pour over the apples. Serve as soon as the flames go out.

Helpful hints
Vanilla sugar is caster (superfine) sugar flavoured with a vanilla pod (bean). Place the pod (bean) in a jar of sugar and leave for the flavours to combine. Or buy ready prepared vanilla sugar.

DESSERTS

Banana rum mousse

Metric/Imperial
1 packet lemon-flavoured jelly
2 large bananas, mashed
225 ml./8 fl. oz. double cream,
  stiffly whipped
2 tablespoons rum

Decoration
extra whipped cream
blanched almonds
chocolate flakes

American
1 packet lemon-flavoured
  gelatin
2 large bananas, mashed
1 cup heavy cream, stiffly
  whipped
2½ tablespoons rum

Decoration
extra whipped cream
blanched almonds
chocolate flakes

Serves 6–8
Make lemon jelly (gelatin) and chill until half set. Add mashed bananas, whipped cream and rum and beat until smooth. Pour into a serving dish and refrigerate until set. Serve chilled, topped with whipped cream, almonds and chocolate.

Chestnut and rum Swiss gâteau

Metric/Imperial
Cake
3 large eggs
100 g./4 oz. caster sugar
75 g./3 oz. flour, plain or
  self-raising, sifted
50 g./2 oz. butter, melted

Filling
1 × 225 g./8 oz. can
  unsweetened chestnut purée
1 egg yolk
100 g./4 oz. icing sugar, sifted
1–2 tablespoons rum

Coating
1 egg white
275 g./10 oz. icing sugar,
  sifted
50–75 g./2–3 oz. plain
  chocolate

American
Cake
3 large eggs
½ cup superfine sugar
¾ cup flour, all-purpose or
  self-rising, sifted
4 tablespoons butter, melted

Filling
1 × 8 oz. can unsweetened
  chestnut purée
1 egg yolk
1 cup confectioners' sugar,
  sifted
1¼–2½ tablespoons rum

Coating
1 egg white
2½ cups confectioners' sugar,
  sifted
2–3 squares semi-sweet
  chocolate

Serves 6–8
Oven setting: 190–200°C./375–400°F./Gas Mark 5–6
Line a medium-sized Swiss roll tin (jelly roll pan) with greased greaseproof (waxed) paper. Beat the eggs and sugar until thick. Fold the flour, then the butter into the mixture. Pour into the prepared tin (pan) and bake for 12–13 minutes. Turn out on to sugared paper, roll up in the paper and leave to cool.
   Beat the chestnut purée, egg yolk, sugar and enough rum together to give a soft creamy consistency. Unroll the cold sponge, spread with the filling and re-roll. Beat the egg white lightly, add the icing (confectioners') sugar and enough warm water to give an icing soft enough to flow. Smooth over the roll and 'swirl' slightly, then leave to set. Melt the chocolate in a heatproof bowl set over a pan of hot water. Arrange several well washed and dried leaves on a flat dish, spread the melted chocolate over these, allow to set. Lift chocolate off leaves. Arrange on top of cake.

Cherry layer pudding

Metric/Imperial	American
15 g./½ oz. butter	1 tablespoon butter
50 g./2 oz. demerara sugar	⅓ cup light brown sugar
175 g./6 oz. self-raising flour, or plain flour and 1½ teaspoons baking powder	1½ cups self-rising flour, or all-purpose flour and 1½ teaspoons baking powder
pinch of salt	pinch of salt
75 g./3 oz. shredded beef suet	⅓ cup shredded beef suet
2 × 400 g./14 oz. cans cherry pie filling	2 × 14 oz. cans cherry pie filling

Serves 4–6

Butter a 1¼ l./2 pint (5 cup) pudding basin and sprinkle round 40 g./1½ oz. (3 tablespoons) of the sugar. Mix the flour with the remaining sugar, salt and suet and add enough cold water to make a soft dough. Turn out on to a floured surface and divide into four pieces of graduating sizes. Roll out the pieces individually, the smallest to fit the bottom of the basin, the largest to fit the top. Place the smallest piece in the bowl. Drain off most of the sauce from the cherries and reserve. Put the cherries and pastry in layers in the basin, finishing with the largest piece of pastry. Cover with greased foil or greaseproof (waxed) paper. Make a pleat in the centre and tie on with string around the rim.

Place the basin in a large pan of boiling water, cover and steam for 1 hour with the water boiling briskly. Then reduce the heat so the water bubbles steadily, and cook for a further 2 hours. Serve hot with custard or with the reserved cherry juice.

Peach madrilène

Metric/Imperial	American
12 grapes	12 grapes
1 orange	1 orange
150 ml./¼ pint double cream	⅔ cup heavy cream
sugar	sugar
4 large or 8 small peach halves	4 large or 8 small peach halves

Serves 4

Halve and seed the grapes, skin if wished. Remove the skin, pith and pips (seeds) from the orange and cut into neat pieces. Beat the cream until just stiff. Sweeten to taste. Add the grapes and orange segments and pile into the peach halves.

Helpful hints

Use thick custard or natural (plain) yogurt in place of cream.

DESSERTS

Lime meringue pie

Metric/Imperial
Crust
100 g./4 oz. butter
50 g./2 oz. caster sugar
225 g./8 oz. cream crackers,
   crushed

Filling
2 fresh limes
water
2½ tablespoons cornflour
175–225 g./6–8 oz. caster
   sugar
15–25 g./½–1 oz. butter
2 eggs, separated

American
Crust
½ cup butter
¼ cup superfine sugar
1⅓ cups crushed graham
   crackers

Filling
2 fresh limes
water
3 tablespoons cornstarch
¾–1 cup superfine sugar
1–2 tablespoons butter
2 eggs, separated

Serves 4
Oven setting: 160–180°C./325–350°F./Gas Mark 3–4
Cream the butter and sugar together until fluffy and mix in
the crumbs. Use to line a 20 cm./8 inch fluted flan dish. Set
in a cool place.

Grate the zest from the limes, squeeze out the juice,
measure and add water to give 300 ml./½ pint (1¼ cups).
Blend the cornflour (cornstarch) with the lime juice and
water, put into a pan with the grated rind, 50–100 g./2–4
oz. (¼–½ cup) sugar (depending on personal taste) and
the butter. Stir over gentle heat until thickened. Remove
from the heat and add the beaten egg yolks. Cook very
gently for several minutes. Taste and add a little more
sugar if required. Pour into the crumb crust. Beat the egg
whites until stiff, beat in 50 g./2 oz. (¼ cup) sugar, then
fold in the remaining 50 g./2 oz. (¼ cup). Spoon the
meringue over the lime mixture, so that it touches the
crumb crust. Bake in the centre of the preheated oven for
20 minutes. Serve hot.

Soufflé omelette

Metric/Imperial
3–4 eggs, separated
1 tablespoon sugar
1 tablespoon milk or cream
25–40 g./1–1½ oz. butter
100 g./4 oz. strawberries,
   halved
2 tablespoons strawberry jam,
   warmed

American
3–4 eggs, separated
1¼ tablespoons sugar
1¼ tablespoons milk or cream
2–3 tablespoons butter
4 oz. strawberries, halved
2½ tablespoons strawberry
   jam, warmed

Serves 2
Beat the egg yolks, sugar and milk or cream together. Beat
the egg whites until stiff, then fold them into the yolks
with a metal spoon. Heat the butter in a 15–18 cm./6–7 inch
omelette pan (skillet). Pour in the egg mixture and cook
over a low to moderate heat until just set at the bottom.
Meanwhile preheat the grill (broiler) to medium. Place the
pan under the grill (broiler). When the omelette is just set,
mark across the centre with a knife (this makes it easier to
fold). Spread with the halved strawberries and warmed
jam, fold and tip on to a warmed dish.

Beignets aux cerises

Metric/Imperial	American
Sauce	Sauce
½ kg./1 lb. black or Morello cherries	1 lb. black or Bing cherries
150 ml./¼ pint water	⅔ cup water
50–100 g./2–4 oz. sugar	¼–½ cup sugar
1 teaspoon arrowroot	1 teaspoon arrowroot
3–4 tablespoons cherry brandy	4–5 tablespoons cherry brandy
Choux pastry	Choux pastry
150 ml./¼ pint water	⅔ cup water
25 g./1 oz. butter	2 tablespoons butter
75 g./3 oz. flour	¾ cup flour
pinch of sugar	pinch of sugar
2 eggs	2 eggs
1 egg yolk	1 egg yolk
oil for deep-frying	oil for deep-frying

Serves 6–8

Put the cherries, water and sugar into a pan and simmer for about 5 minutes. Blend the arrowroot with the cherry brandy, stir into the cherry mixture and boil steadily, stirring well, until thickened. Keep hot.

Heat the water and the butter in a pan. When the butter has melted add the flour, sifted with sugar. Stir over low heat until the dough comes away from the sides. Remove the pan from the heat and gradually add the beaten eggs and egg yolk until the mixture is thick and glossy. Heat the oil until it is hot enough to turn a stale bread cube golden brown in 30 seconds (190°C./375°F. on a deep-fat thermometer). Put spoonfuls of the mixture into the hot oil and fry steadily for 6–8 minutes until golden brown. Drain on absorbent paper. To serve, pile into a pyramid and serve with the hot sauce.

Old-fashioned gingerbread

Metric/Imperial	American
225 g./8 oz. plain flour	2 cups all-purpose flour
¾ teaspoon bicarbonate of soda	¾ teaspoon baking soda
½–1 teaspoon ground cinnamon	½–1 teaspoon ground cinnamon
1½–2 teaspoons ground ginger	1½–2 teaspoons ground ginger
100 g./4 oz. butter or cooking fat	½ cup butter or shortening
100 g./4 oz. moist brown sugar	⅔ cup moist brown sugar
150 g./5 oz. black treacle	⅔ cup molasses
2 eggs	2 eggs
4 tablespoons milk	5 tablespoons milk
Apple sauce	Apple sauce
½ kg./1 lb. apples, peeled, cored and chopped	1 lb. apples, peeled, cored and chopped
little water	little water
sugar	sugar

Serves 5–6

Oven setting: 150–160°C./300–325°F./Gas Mark 2–3

Grease and line an 18–20 cm./7–8 inch square tin (pan) with greased greaseproof (waxed) paper. Sift the dry ingredients into a bowl. Melt the butter or cooking fat (shortening) with the sugar and treacle (molasses) and add to the flour. Beat in the eggs and milk.

Put into the prepared tin (pan) and bake in the preheated oven for 1¼ hours, or until a skewer inserted into the centre of the loaf comes out clean. Leave to cool in the tin (pan).

Simmer the apples in a little water with sugar to taste. Sieve (or emulsify) until a smooth purée. Cut the gingerbread into portions and spoon over the apple sauce.

DESSERTS

Apple fritters

Metric/Imperial	American
100 g./4 oz. plain flour	1 cup all-purpose flour
pinch of salt	pinch of salt
2 eggs	2 eggs
150 ml./¼ pint milk or milk and water	⅔ cup milk or milk and water
1–2 teaspoons melted butter or oil	1–2 teaspoons melted butter or oil
4 good-sized cooking apples	4 good-sized tart apples
1 tablespoon flour	1¼ tablespoons flour
oil for deep-frying or 75–100 g./3–4 oz. fat for shallow-frying	oil for deep-frying or ⅓–½ cup fat for shallow-frying
sugar to coat	sugar to coat

Serves 4

Sift the flour and salt into a mixing bowl, gradually add the eggs and liquid and beat to a smooth batter. Add butter or oil just before cooking. For a lighter texture separate the eggs. Add the yolks to the flour, then the milk and butter or oil. Fold the stiffly beaten egg whites into the mixture just before coating the fruit.

Peel and core apples and cut into 1 cm./½ inch rings. Coat the fruit first with flour (this makes sure the batter adheres well) and then with the batter. Lift out with a fork, hold over the bowl and allow surplus batter to drop back into the bowl. Heat the oil until it is hot enough to turn a stale bread cube golden brown in 30 seconds (190°C./375°F. on a deep-fat thermometer). Drop the rings into the hot oil and fry steadily for 4–5 minutes until golden brown. Drain on absorbent paper, coat in sugar and serve hot.

If frying in shallow fat, turn the fritters after 2–3 minutes and brown the other side.

Peaches in wine

Metric/Imperial	American
4 large, ripe, unblemished peaches	4 large, ripe, unblemished peaches
caster sugar	superfine sugar
lemon juice	lemon juice
red wine or chilled sweet white wine	red wine or chilled sweet white wine

Serves 4

Peel peaches carefully and slice into four goblets. Sprinkle the peaches with plenty of sugar and a little lemon juice. Just before serving, pour enough wine into the goblets to just reach the top of the fruit. Serve immediately. Try using a rosé wine, champagne or sauterne.

Apple crumb pudding

Metric/Imperial	American
50 g./2 oz. butter	¼ cup butter
75 g./3 oz. brown sugar	½ cup brown sugar
1 tablespoon golden syrup	1¼ tablespoons maple syrup
1 teaspoon mixed spice	1 teaspoon mixed spice
225 g./8 oz. fresh breadcrumbs	4 cups fresh breadcrumbs
grated rind and juice of 1 lemon	grated rind and juice of 1 lemon
3 large cooking apples	3 large cooking apples
50 g./2 oz. sugar	¼ cup sugar
75 g./3 oz. raisins	½ cup raisins

Serves 4–6
Oven setting: 160°C./325°F./Gas Mark 3
Cream the butter and brown sugar together. Beat in the syrup. Add the mixed spice, breadcrumbs and lemon rind. Put half this mixture into a greased ovenproof dish. Peel, core and slice apples, mix with sugar, lemon juice and raisins. Put over the crumb mixture, then top with the rest of the crumbs and a foil covering or a lid. Bake for about 30 minutes. Remove the covering or lid and bake for a further 5–10 minutes to crisp the crumbs.

Brandy soufflé

Metric/Imperial	American
about 12 sponge finger biscuits	about 12 sponge finger cookies
6 tablespoons brandy or Curaçao	7½ tablespoons brandy or Curaçao
100 g./4 oz. glacé cherries or mixed candied fruits, chopped	⅔ cup chopped candied cherries or mixed candied fruits
25 g./1 oz. butter	2 tablespoons butter
25 g./1 oz. flour	¼ cup flour
150 ml./¼ pint milk	⅔ cup milk
150 ml./¼ pint single cream	⅔ cup light cream
50 g./2 oz. caster sugar	¼ cup superfine sugar
3 egg yolks	3 egg yolks
4 egg whites	4 egg whites

Serves 4–6
Oven setting: 180°C./350°F./Gas Mark 4
Arrange the sponge fingers in the bottom of a soufflé dish and add half the brandy or Curaçao and the cherries or fruit. Heat the butter in a large pan and stir in the flour. Cook gently, stirring, for 2 minutes. Gradually add the milk and cream. Bring slowly to the boil, stirring constantly, and simmer for 3 minutes, or until thickened. Add the sugar, the remaining brandy or Curaçao and the egg yolks. Beat the egg whites until very stiff and fold into the egg yolk mixture with a metal spoon. Pile the mixture over the sponge fingers. Bake in the centre of the preheated oven for 40 minutes. Serve at once.

CAKES and BAKING

White bread

Metric/Imperial
1.4 kg./3 lb. strong plain flour
25 g./1 oz. salt
25 g./1 oz. lard
25 g./1 oz. fresh yeast
800 ml./scant 1½ pints tepid
 water

American
12 cups all-purpose flour
2 tablespoons salt
2 tablespoons lard
1 cake compressed yeast
3½ cups tepid water

Makes four ½ kg./1 lb. (2 cup) loaves
Oven setting: 200°C./400°F./Gas Mark 6
Sift the flour and salt into a large mixing bowl. Rub in the lard with the fingertips, as for pastry. Dissolve the yeast in the measured water, then tip all the liquid into the flour. Mix well with a wooden spoon or fork until a dough forms, then turn out on to a well floured surface. Knead the dough for 15 minutes, adding extra flour if the dough is too sticky to handle.

To knead, use the heel of your hand to push the dough down firmly, then draw it towards you, fold over and press down again, turning the dough occasionally. Alternatively, knead using an electric mixer.

Put the dough in an oiled plastic bag in the mixing bowl and leave in a warm place (28°C./80°F.) until it doubles in size. Turn the dough out on to a floured surface and knead again lightly. Oil four ½ kg./1 lb. loaf tins (2 cup oblong loaf pans), divide the dough into four, and shape to fit in the tins (pans). Cover the tins (pans) with oiled polythene and leave again, preferably in a slightly warmer place, until dough rises to tops of the tins (pans).

Remove the plastic from the tins (pans). Place 2 tins (pans) on the bottom shelf of the preheated oven and the other 2 tins (pans) on the top shelf. Bake for 20 minutes, then reverse the positions of the tins (pans). Bake for a further 20 minutes or until evenly browned.

Test by turning one of the loaves out of its tin (pan) and tapping the bottom; if it sounds hollow, the loaf is cooked. Turn out on a wire rack to cool.

Wheatmeal bread

Metric/Imperial
15 g./½ oz. dried yeast
1 tablespoon sugar
450 ml./¾ pint tepid water
350 g./12 oz. strong plain
 flour, sifted
350 g./12 oz. wholewheat flour
2–3 teaspoons salt
1 tablespoon salad oil
cracked wheat

American
½ oz. dried yeast
1¼ tablespoons sugar
2 cups tepid water
3 cups all-purpose flour, sifted
3 cups wholewheat flour
2–3 teaspoons salt
1¼ tablespoons salad oil
cracked wheat

Makes 2 loaves
Oven setting: 230°C./450°F./Gas Mark 8
Cream the yeast with 1 teaspoon sugar, and add the water. Leave in a warm place for about 15 minutes, or until the mixture becomes frothy. Put all the remaining ingredients, except the cracked wheat, in a bowl and add the yeast mixture. Mix well, then turn the dough out on to a floured surface. Knead for about 10 minutes, or until smooth and no longer sticky.

Put the dough in an oiled polythene (plastic) bag and leave to rise until doubled in bulk. (About 1 hour at room temperature and overnight in the refrigerator.) Knead the dough back to its original bulk. Divide the dough in half.

Shape one-half into a ball and place it in a well-greased clay 12.5 cm./5 inch flower pot or cake tin. (Do not use a plastic flower pot.) Shape the second piece of dough into a loaf and put on a baking sheet or in a ½ kg./1 lb. loaf tin (2 cup oblong loaf pan).

Cover with an oiled polythene (plastic) bag and leave to rise in a warm place until doubled in bulk or until the dough has risen to the top of the tin. Remove the bag. Brush the tops of the loaves with a little salted water and sprinkle with the cracked wheat.

Bake in the preheated oven for 30–40 minutes, or until the loaves are evenly browned and sound hollow when tapped on the bottom. Leave to cool on a wire rack.

Scones I

Metric/Imperial
225 g./8 oz. plain flour
½ teaspoon salt
½ teaspoon bicarbonate of soda
1 teaspoon cream of tartar
25–40 g./1–1½ oz. butter or
  margarine
25 g./1 oz. sugar
150 ml./¼ pint milk

American
2 cups all-purpose flour
½ teaspoon salt
½ teaspoon baking soda
1 teaspoon cream of tartar
2–3 tablespoons butter or
  margarine
2 tablespoons sugar
⅔ cup milk

Makes 12
Oven setting: 220°C./425°F./Gas Mark 7
Sift the flour, salt, soda and cream of tartar into a bowl.
Rub in the butter or margarine. Add the sugar. Add the
milk to the flour mixture, mixing quickly to a soft dough.
Pat or roll out the dough on a lightly floured surface to
about 1 cm./½ inch thick. Either cut into 12 squares or
5 cm./2 inch rounds. Place the scones on a greased baking
sheet and bake towards the top of the preheated oven for
10 minutes, or until risen and golden brown. Serve warm,
with butter or cream and jam.

Helpful hints
For fruit scones, add 50 g./2 oz. (⅓ cup) mixed dried fruit
to either of these recipes before adding the liquid.

Scones II

Metric/Imperial
225 g./8 oz. plain flour
1 teaspoon bicarbonate of soda
1 teaspoon cream of tartar
25 g./1 oz. butter
150 ml./¼ pint buttermilk

American
2 cups all-purpose flour
1 teaspoon baking soda
1 teaspoon cream of tartar
2 tablespoons butter
⅔ cup buttermilk

Makes 12
Oven setting: 220°C./425°F./Gas Mark 7
Sift the flour, soda and cream of tartar into a bowl. Rub in
the butter. Add the buttermilk to the flour mixture, mixing
quickly to a soft dough. Turn the dough on to a lightly
floured surface and knead until smooth. Roll out to about
2 cm./¾ inch thick. Cut into twelve 5 cm./2 inch rounds.
Leave for 15 minutes before baking.

   Place the scones on a greased baking sheet and bake in
the preheated oven for 10 minutes, or until risen and
golden brown. Serve warm, with butter or cream and jam.

CAKES and BAKING

Family fruit cake

Metric/Imperial
225 g./8 oz. self-raising flour
pinch of salt
100 g./4 oz. lard, cooking fat or
  margarine, or mixed fats
90 g./3½ oz. caster sugar
150 g./5 oz. mixed dried fruit
1 teaspoon finely grated orange
  rind
1 egg, beaten
approx. 6–7 tablespoons cold
  milk, to mix

American
2 cups self-rising flour
pinch of salt
½ cup lard, shortening or
  margarine, or mixed fats
just under ½ cup superfine
  sugar
1 cup mixed dried fruit
1 teaspoon finely grated orange
  rind
1 egg, beaten
approx. 7½–9 tablespoons cold
  milk, to mix

Makes one ½ kg./1 lb. loaf or 15 cm./6 inch cake
Oven setting: 180°C./350°F./Gas Mark 4
Brush a ½ kg./1 lb. loaf tin (2 cup oblong loaf pan) or
15 cm./6 inch round cake tin with melted fat. Line the base
and sides with greased greaseproof (waxed) paper.

Sift the flour and salt into a bowl. Rub in the fat. Add the
sugar, fruit and orange rind. Toss the ingredients lightly
together. Add the egg and milk and mix to a semi-stiff
batter, stirring briskly without beating. Transfer to the
prepared tin.

Bake just above the centre of the preheated oven for
1–1¼ hours, or until well risen and golden or until a
skewer inserted into the centre of the cake comes out
clean. Leave to cool in the tin for 20 minutes, then turn out
and cool completely on a wire rack. Remove the paper
before serving.

Sally Lunn

Metric/Imperial
50 g./2 oz. butter
150 ml./¼ pint plus 4
  tablespoons milk
1 teaspoon caster sugar
2 eggs, beaten
15 g./½ oz. fresh yeast or 2
  teaspoons dried yeast
450 g./1 lb. strong white
  flour
1 teaspoon salt
sugar glaze, made by boiling 1
  tablespoon water with 1
  tablespoon sugar for 2
  minutes

American
¼ cup butter
⅔ cup plus 5 tablespoons milk
1 teaspoon superfine sugar
2 eggs, beaten
½ cake compressed yeast or 2
  teaspoons dried yeast
4 cups all-purpose flour
1 teaspoon salt
sugar glaze, made by boiling
  1¼ tablespoons water with
  1¼ tablespoons sugar for 2
  minutes

Makes 2
Oven setting: 230°C./450°F./Gas Mark 8
Melt the butter slowly in a pan, remove from the heat and
add the milk and sugar. Add the warm milk mixture and
the eggs to the yeast. Blend well. Sift together the flour
and salt, add the liquid, mix well and knead lightly. Divide
the dough between two well greased 13 cm./5 inch round
cake tins and leave to rise in a warm place for about ¾–1
hour, or until the dough fills the tins. Bake just above the
centre of the oven for 15–20 minutes. Turn the loaves out
to cool on a wire rack. Make up the sugar glaze and glaze
the loaves while they are hot.

Afternoon tea ring

Metric/Imperial	American
225 g./8 oz. self-raising flour	2 cups self-rising flour
1 teaspoon baking powder	1 teaspoon baking powder
pinch of salt	pinch of salt
50 g./2 oz. butter or margarine	4 tablespoons butter or
50 g./2 oz. caster sugar	margarine
65 g./2½ oz. mixed dried fruit	¼ cup superfine sugar
1 egg	½ cup mixed dried fruit
cold milk	1 egg
	cold milk

Serves 8

Oven setting: 220°C./425°F./Gas Mark 7

Sift the flour, baking powder and salt into a bowl. Rub in the fat. Add the sugar and fruit and toss the ingredients lightly together.

Beat the egg lightly then make up to 150 ml./¼ pint (⅔ cup) with cold milk. Add to the flour mixture, mixing quickly to a soft dough. Turn the dough on to a floured surface and knead lightly until smooth. Divide the dough into 8 equal-sized pieces and shape each one into a round. Stand in an overlapping ring on a greased baking sheet and brush with a little beaten egg. Bake just above the centre of the preheated oven for 20–25 minutes, or until golden brown. Leave to cool on a wire rack.

Helpful hints

Mix and bake quickly. As soon as the liquid is added the raising agent begins to work; if the tea ring does not go in the oven quickly the gases will escape and the ring will be flat and heavy.

Caramel cakes

Metric/Imperial	American
Shortbread	Shortbread
150 g./5 oz. butter	10 tablespoons butter
100 g./4 oz. caster sugar	½ cup superfine sugar
275 g./10 oz. plain flour	2½ cups all-purpose flour
100 g./4 oz. plain chocolate, broken into pieces, for topping	4 squares semi-sweet chocolate, broken into pieces, for topping
Filling	Filling
100 g./4 oz. butter	½ cup butter
100 g./4 oz. caster sugar	½ cup superfine sugar
2 tablespoons golden syrup	2½ tablespoons light corn syrup
1 large can condensed milk (equivalent to approx. 1 l./1¾ pints skimmed milk)	1 large can condensed milk (equivalent to approx. 4½ cups skimmed milk)

Makes about 30 cakes

Oven setting: 180°C./350°F./Gas Mark 4

Cream the butter and sugar together in a bowl. Work in the flour. Press into a greased 30 ×23 cm./12 × 9 inch Swiss roll tin (jelly roll pan) and bake in the preheated oven for 15–20 minutes, or until the shortbread is golden. leave to cool in the tin (pan).

To prepare the filling, put all the ingredients in a pan and heat gently until the sugar has dissolved, stirring occasionally. Increase the heat and boil the mixture for 5 minutes, stirring constantly. Remove from the heat, leave to cool for 1 minute, then pour on to the cooled shortbread base. Leave to set.

Melt the chocolate in a small heatproof bowl set over a pan of hot water. Spread over the set filling. Mark into serving portions, and leave to cool completely in the tin (pan), then remove carefully.

CAKES and BAKING

Date crunchies

Metric/Imperial	American
100 g./4 oz. wholewheat flour	1 cup wholewheat flour
175 g./6 oz. rolled oats	1½ cups rolled oats
225 g./8 oz. butter or margarine	1 cup butter or margarine
	1⅓ cups pitted chopped dates
225 g./8 oz. dates, stoned and chopped	2½ tablespoons water
2 tablespoons water	1¼ tablespoons lemon juice
1 tablespoon lemon juice	1¼ tablespoons clear honey
1 tablespoon clear honey	pinch of ground cinnamon
pinch of ground cinnamon	

Makes 12–14
Oven setting: 180°C./350°F./Gas Mark 4
Put the flour and oats into a bowl. Rub in the butter or margarine. Turn out the dough on to a floured surface and knead until smooth. Halve the mixture and press one-half over the bottom of a greased 18 cm./7 inch square cake tin (pan).

Simmer the chopped dates with the water until soft. Cool and stir in the lemon juice, honey and cinnamon. Spread the date mixture over the oat dough and cover with the remaining oat dough. Smooth flat with a palette knife. Bake in the centre of the preheated oven for 25 minutes. Cut into fingers while still warm. Leave to cool completely in the tin (pan), then remove carefully. Store away from cakes and biscuits (cookies).

Helpful hints
When chopping dates, use a floured board and a floured knife to prevent sticking.

Victoria sandwich

Metric/Imperial	American
100 g./4 oz. butter	½ cup butter
100 g./4 oz. caster sugar	½ cup superfine sugar
2 large eggs, beaten	2 large eggs, beaten
100 g./4 oz. self-raising flour, sifted with pinch of salt	1 cup self-rising flour, sifted with pinch of salt
jam	jam
whipped cream	whipped cream

Makes one 18 cm./7 inch cake
Oven setting: 180°C./350°F./Gas Mark 4
Grease two 18 cm./7 inch sandwich tins (layer pans) and line the bases with greased greaseproof (waxed) paper. Cream the butter and sugar together until fluffy and beat in the eggs, one at a time, adding a little flour with each egg. Gently fold in the remaining flour.

Divide the mixture equally between the prepared tins (pans) and bake in the preheated oven for 25–30 minutes, or until well risen and the cakes spring back when lightly pressed. Leave the cakes to cool in the tins for 2 minutes, then turn out to cool completely on a wire rack. Remove the paper and when cold, sandwich together with jam and cream.

Helpful hints
The secret of making a good Victoria sandwich lies in the creaming and beating; if sufficient air is not incorporated into the mixture the cake will not be light and spongy.

Cheese chocolate triangle

Metric/Imperial	American
100 g./4 oz. sugar	½ cup sugar
100 g./4 oz. butter	½ cup butter
½ kg./1 lb. curd cheese	2 cups curd cheese
grated rind of ¼ lemon (optional)	grated rind of ¼ lemon (optional)
1 egg	1 egg
few drops vanilla essence	few drops vanilla extract
36 fine sweet biscuits	36 fine sweet cookies
milk	milk
Chocolate coating	Chocolate coating
3 tablespoons cocoa powder	4 tablespoons unsweetened cocoa
100 g./4 oz. sugar	½ cup sugar
2 tablespoons water	2½ tablespoons water
1 teaspoon instant coffee	1 teaspoon instant coffee
75 g./3 oz. margarine	⅜ cup margarine

Serves 4–6

Cream together the sugar and butter. Add the cheese, grated lemon rind, egg and vanilla essence (extract) and beat well until smooth. Dip the biscuits (cookies) in milk and arrange four rows of three biscuits on a sheet of foil. Spread a layer of the cheese mixture on top. Repeat twice more. Cover with the rest of the cheese mixture, and pile up in centre. Put your hands underneath the foil and bring the outer row of biscuits to meet in the centre, forming a triangle. Leave in the refrigerator while making the coating.

Put the cocoa, sugar, water and coffee in pan and boil until thick. Remove and add the margarine, cut in pieces. Beat well. When cool pour over the top of the cake and leave to set overnight in the refrigerator.

Bournvita loaf

Metric/Imperial	American
300 ml./½ pint cold milk	1¼ cups cold milk
275 g./10 oz. mixed chopped dates, figs, sultanas and currants	2 cups mixed chopped dates, figs, seedless raisins and currants
1 teaspoon bicarbonate of soda	1 teaspoon baking soda
25 g./1 oz. butter or margarine, melted	2 tablespoons butter or margarine, melted
100 g./4 oz. caster sugar	½ cup superfine sugar
50 g./2 oz. Bournvita	½ cup malted chocolate powder
1 egg, beaten	1 egg, beaten
275 g./10 oz. self-raising flour, sifted	2½ cups self-rising flour, sifted

Makes one 1 kg./2 lb. loaf

Oven setting: 180°C./350°F./Gas Mark 4

Brush a 1 kg./2 lb. loaf tin (4 cup oblong loaf pan) with melted fat and line the base and sides with greased greaseproof (waxed) paper. Bring the milk slowly to the boil, stirring. Put the fruit, soda, butter or margarine, sugar and Bournvita (malted chocolate powder) into a bowl. Pour on the boiling milk and mix well. Add the egg, then gradually fold in the flour.

Put into the prepared tin (pan) and bake in the centre of the preheated oven for about 1 hour, or until well risen and golden, and a skewer inserted into the centre comes out clean. Leave the cake to cool in the tin (pan) for 5 minutes, then turn out to cool completely on a wire rack.

CAKES and BAKING

Sponge finger gâteau

Metric/Imperial
about 30 sponge finger biscuits
600 ml./1 pint double cream
sugar
1 kg./2 lb. fresh fruit, prepared

American
about 30 sponge finger cookies
2½ cups heavy cream
sugar
2 lb. fresh fruit, prepared

Serves 6
Put one-third of the sponge fingers on a serving dish.
Whip the cream, add sugar to taste. Spread some of the
cream over the fingers, top with some of the fruit. Add
more fingers, more cream and fruit, then a final layer of
fingers, cream and fruit. Allow to stand for 1–2 hours
before serving.

Helpful hints
For added flavour, dip the sponge fingers in a little sweet
white wine, for a few seconds only, before using.

Golden cake

Metric/Imperial
1 small packet instant mashed
  potato (for 2–3 servings)
1½ teaspoons baking powder
75 g./3 oz. margarine
1 tablespoon golden syrup
75 g./3 oz. caster sugar
finely grated rind of 1 orange
2½ tablespoons orange juice
2 eggs
piece of candied peel (to
  decorate)

American
1 small packet instant mashed
  potato (for 2–3 servings)
1½ teaspoons baking powder
6 tablespoons margarine
1¼ tablespoons light corn
  syrup
6 tablespoons superfine sugar
finely grated rind of 1 orange
3 tablespoons orange juice
2 eggs
piece of candied peel (to
  decorate)

Makes one 15 cm./6 inch cake
Oven setting: 180°C./350°F./Gas Mark 4
Line a 15 cm./6 inch cake tin with greased greaseproof
(waxed) paper. Mix the potato powder and baking powder
in a large bowl. Put the margarine, syrup, sugar, grated
orange rind and orange juice into a pan. Heat gently until
the sugar has dissolved, stirring occasionally. Pour on to
the potato mixture and beat well. Separate the eggs and
add the yolks to the potato mixture. Beat the whites until
stiff, then gently fold into the potato mixture with a metal
spoon.

Put into the prepared tin and bake in the centre of the
preheated oven for about 45 minutes, or until well risen
and golden, and firm to the touch. Halfway through the
cooking time, place the candied peel on top of the cake and
cover with paper to avoid over-browning, or reduce the
heat slightly.

Leave the cake to cool in the tin for 5 minutes, then turn
out and cool completely on a wire rack.

Animal cake

Metric/Imperial
225 g./8 oz. butter
350 g./12 oz. icing sugar, sifted
2 tablespoons cocoa powder
boiling water
1 teaspoon vanilla essence
about 24 ginger biscuits or Jaffa cakes
1 chocolate finger biscuit for tail
2 chocolate buttons for eyes
½ glacé cherry for nose

American
1 cup butter
3 cups confectioners' sugar, sifted
2½ tablespoons unsweetened cocoa powder
boiling water
1 teaspoon vanilla extract
about 24 ginger snap cookies
1 chocolate finger cookie for tail
2 chocolate drops for eyes
½ candied cherry for nose

Serves 10–12
Cream the butter and sugar together until fluffy. Reserve about ½ teaspoon.

Mix the cocoa to a smooth paste with water and leave until cold. Beat into the buttercream with the vanilla essence (extract).

Sandwich the biscuits (cookies) together with the buttercream and stand on a board horizontally. Cover all but one end completely with remaining buttercream and ridge with a fork (as shown in photograph). Put the chocolate finger biscuit (cookie) at the covered end for the tail, then decorate the uncovered 'face' with 2 chocolate button (drop) eyes and a cherry nose, holding them in position with reserved buttercream. Put 2 small blobs of white buttercream in the centres of chocolate buttons to represent the eyeballs.

Mocha hazelnut gâteau

Metric/Imperial
175 g./6 oz. butter
175 g./6 oz. caster sugar
3 large eggs
150 g./5 oz. self-raising flour
15 g./½ oz. cocoa powder
40 g./1½ oz. finely chopped hazelnuts
1 tablespoon coffee essence

Filling
350 g./12 oz. butter
600 g./1¼ lb. sieved icing sugar
1½ tablespoons coffee essence
4 tablespoons chopped hazelnuts (filberts)

Decoration
whole hazelnuts (filberts)

American
¾ cup butter
¾ cup superfine sugar
3 large eggs
1¼ cups self-rising flour
1 tablespoon unsweetened cocoa
almost ¼ cup finely chopped hazelnuts
1¼ tablespoons strong black coffee

Filling
1½ cups butter
3¾ cups sieved confectioner's sugar
2 tablespoons strong black coffee
5 tablespoons chopped hazelnuts (filberts)

Decoration
whole hazelnuts (filberts)

Makes 8–10 slices
Oven setting: 180–190°C./350–375°F./Gas Mark 4–5
Cream the butter and sugar, and gradually add the eggs. Fold in flour and cocoa. Add hazelnuts (filberts) and coffee. Divide mixture between two 20 cm./8 inch greased and floured sandwich tins (layer cake pans) and bake for 20–25 minutes above the centre of the oven, until firm to the touch. Turn out carefully and allow to cool.

Make the filling by creaming the butter with the sugar and coffee. Use about a quarter of the mixture to sandwich the cakes together and another quarter to coat the sides. Roll the cake in the chopped nuts, then cover the top of the cake with some of the remaining filling. Pipe rosettes on top with the last of the filling. Decorate with whole hazelnuts (filberts).

CAKES and BAKING

Brioches

French chocolate squares

Metric/Imperial	American
3 tablespoons water	4 tablespoons water
15 g./½ oz. dried yeast	1 tablespoon dried yeast
1 tablespoon plus ½ teaspoon caster sugar	1¼ tablespoons plus ½ teaspoon superfine sugar
225 g./8 oz. flour	2 cups flour
½ teaspoon salt	½ teaspoon salt
2 eggs, beaten	2 eggs, beaten
50 g./2 oz. butter, melted and cooled	¼ cup butter, melted and cooled

Glaze	Glaze
1 egg, beaten	1 egg, beaten
1 tablespoon cold water	1¼ tablespoons cold water
pinch of sugar	pinch of sugar

Makes 12

Oven setting: 230°C./450°F./Gas Mark 8

Grease twelve 8 cm./3 inch brioche tins or deep fluted patty (muffin) tins. Heat the water until lukewarm and pour into a small bowl. Whisk in the yeast and ½ teaspoon of the caster (superfine) sugar. Leave in a warm place for 10 minutes, or until frothy.

Sift flour and salt into a warm bowl. Mix in the remaining sugar. Stir in the yeast mixture, eggs and butter. Beat by hand until the mixture leaves the sides of the bowl. Knead on a lightly floured board for 5 minutes. Place the dough in a slightly oiled plastic bag and leave to rise in a warm place until it has doubled in size — about 1½ hours.

Knead the dough well on a lightly floured board for about 5 minutes. Divide the dough into four equal pieces, then each piece into three. Use about three quarters of each piece to form a ball. Place the balls of dough in the tins and firmly press a hole in the centre of each. Place the remaining small piece of dough in the hole. Place the tins on a baking sheet and cover with a large oiled plastic bag. Leave in a warm place to rise until light and puffy, about 1 hour. Mix the ingredients for the glaze and brush it lightly on the buns. Bake for about 10 minutes. Serve warm with chocolate sauce, if liked.

Metric/Imperial	American
225 g./8 oz. plain chocolate	8 squares semi-sweet chocolate
½ kg./1 lb. sweet plain biscuits, crushed	4 cups crushed sugar cookies
75 g./3 oz. caster sugar	6 tablespoons superfine sugar
100 g./4 oz. chopped walnuts	1 cup chopped walnuts
50 g./2 oz. butter	4 tablespoons butter
1 tablespoon rum, brandy or coffee essence	1¼ tablespoons rum, brandy or coffee extract
1 × 190 g./6½ oz. can evaporated milk	1 × 6½ oz. can evaporated milk
2 eggs, beaten	2 eggs, beaten

Chocolate icing	Chocolate icing
50 g./2 oz. plain chocolate	2 squares semi-sweet chocolate
25 g./1 oz. butter	2 tablespoons butter
2 tablespoons water	2½ tablespoons water
175 g./6 oz. icing sugar, sifted	1½ cups confectioners' sugar, sifted

Makes about 36 squares

Grease a 20 cm./8 inch shallow square cake tin (pan). Line with greased foil, allowing it to extend about 2.5 cm./1 inch above the top edge of the tin (pan).

Break up the chocolate, put into a heatproof bowl set over a pan of hot water and leave until melted. Put the crushed biscuits (cookies) into a bowl. Add the sugar and walnuts. Melt the butter then stir in the alcohol or essence (extract) and evaporated milk. Gradually blend into the melted chocolate with the beaten eggs. Pour on to the biscuit (cookie) crumb mixture and stir thoroughly to combine. Put into the prepared tin (pan) and refrigerate overnight, until firm and set.

Put the chocolate, butter and water in a heatproof bowl set over a pan of hot water until the chocolate melts. Remove from the heat, stir in the sifted icing (confectioners') sugar and beat until cool and thick.

Before serving, ease the cake out of the tin (pan), peel away the foil and cover the top with chocolate icing. When the icing has set, cut the cake into squares.

Weinerbrød

Metric/Imperial	American
20 g./¾ oz. dried yeast	¾ oz. dried yeast
50 g./2 oz. sugar	¼ cup sugar
300 ml./½ pint tepid milk	1¼ cups tepid milk
½ kg./1 lb. plain flour	4 cups all-purpose flour
175–225 g./6–8 oz. butter or margarine	¾–1 cup butter or margarine
1 egg	1 egg
fillings, see method	fillings, see method
225 g./8 oz. icing sugar	2 cups confectioners' sugar
glacé cherries and chopped nuts (to decorate)	candied cherries and chopped nuts (to decorate)

Makes about 12–14

Oven setting: 220–230°C./425–450°F./Gas Mark 7–8

Cream the yeast with 1 teaspoon sugar, add the milk and a sprinkling of flour. Leave in a warm place for about 15 minutes, or until the mixture becomes frothy.

Put the remaining flour into a bowl and rub in 50 g./2 oz. (4 tablespoons) fat. Add the remaining sugar. Divide the remaining fat into two portions and leave to soften. Add the yeast mixture and egg to the flour and mix well. Knead for about 8 minutes, or until smooth.

Return to the bowl, cover with a cloth, leave in a warm place for about 1 hour to rise until doubled in bulk. Knead again and roll out to an oblong shape, about 1 cm./½ inch thick. Spread with one portion of the softened fat, fold in three, turn at right angles, then roll out once more. Spread with remaining fat, fold in three, turn at right angles, roll again, fold and turn.

Roll out the dough to about ½ cm./¼ inch thick and cut into 10 cm./4 inch squares. Put a little filling, i.e. jam, honey, lemon curd or thick apple purée in the centre of each square. Fold the corners into the centre.

Arrange the pastries on warmed baking sheets and leave in a warm place to rise for 20 minutes. Bake in the preheated oven for 12 minutes. Cool on a wire rack.

Beat the icing (confectioners') sugar with just enough warm water to make a spreading consistency. Spread icing over each pastry and decorate with cherries and nuts.

Birthday cake

Metric/Imperial	American
225 g./8 oz. butter	1 cup butter
225 g./8 oz. caster sugar	1 cup superfine sugar
finely grated rind of 2 lemons	finely grated rind of 2 lemons
4 large eggs, beaten	4 large eggs, beaten
225 g./8 oz. self-raising flour	2 cups self-rising flour
2 tablespoons milk	2½ tablespoons milk
Filling	Filling
100 g./4 oz. butter	½ cup butter
225 g./8 oz. icing sugar	2 cups confectioner's sugar
juice of ½ lemon	juice of ½ lemon
Almond paste	Almond paste
100 g./4 oz. ground almonds	1 cup ground almonds
50 g./2 oz. icing sugar	½ cup confectioner's sugar
50 g./2 oz. caster sugar	¼ cup superfine sugar
1 egg white	1 egg white
3 tablespoons apricot jam	4 tablespoons apricot jam
1 tablespoon water	1¼ tablespoons water
Icing	Icing
350 g./12 oz. icing sugar	3 cups confectioner's sugar
4 tablespoons lemon juice	5 tablespoons lemon juice
15 g./½ oz. butter	1 tablespoon butter
few drops pink food colouring	few drops pink food colouring

Makes one 25 cm./10 inch cake

Oven setting: 180°C./350°F./Gas Mark 4

Line a 25 cm./10 inch deep cake tin (spring form pan). Beat butter, sugar and lemon rind together. Beat in eggs. Fold in flour with enough milk to make dropping consistency. Turn into tin. Bake for 50 minutes. Cool. Beat together filling ingredients. Split cake in half and sandwich together with filling. Blend together paste ingredients and knead to a smooth paste. Heat jam and water together. Sieve. Use glaze to brush top and sides of cake. Roll out almond paste to a 25 cm./10 inch circle. Place almond paste on top and press down firmly. Heat together sugar, lemon juice and butter over very low heat. Reserve a little icing. Add pink colouring to icing left in pan. Thin with a little water. Pour over pink icing. Allow to dry overnight. Put remaining white icing in a piping bag and decorate.

CAKES and BAKING

Rich shortbread

Metric/Imperial
225 g./8 oz. butter
100 g./4 oz. caster sugar
275 g./10 oz. plain flour
50 g./2 oz. fine semolina
extra caster sugar

American
1 cup butter
½ cup superfine sugar
2½ cups all-purpose flour
½ cup fine semolina flour
extra superfine sugar

Makes 16 fingers
Oven setting: 170°C./325°F./Gas Mark 3
Lightly grease and flour a 30 × 23 cm./12 × 9 inch square
tin (pan). Cream the butter and sugar together until fluffy.
Add the flour and semolina (semolina flour) to the
creamed mixture, a little at a time, gradually drawing the
mixture together with the fingertips. Turn out the dough
on to a floured surface and knead lightly until smooth.
Press the mixture into the prepared tin (pan). Prick all over
with a fork and sprinkle with the extra sugar.

Chill in the refrigerator for 15 minutes, then bake in the
preheated oven for about 30 minutes, or until pale brown.
Leave to cool in the tin (pan) for 5 minutes, then while soft
cut into fingers. Turn out to cool completely on a wire rack.

Dundee cake

Metric/Imperial
150 g./5 oz. margarine or
  butter
150 g./5 oz. sugar
2 large eggs
225 g./8 oz. self-raising flour,
  or plain flour with 2
  teaspoons baking powder
350 g./12 oz. mixed dried fruit
50 g./2 oz. glacé cherries
50 g./2 oz. chopped candied
  peel
little milk
25–50 g./1–2 oz. blanched
  almonds

American
10 tablespoons butter or
  margarine
⅔ cup sugar
2 large eggs
2 cups self-rising flour, or
  all-purpose flour with 2
  teaspoons baking powder
2 cups mixed dried fruit
⅓ cup candied cherries
⅓ cup chopped candied peel
little milk
¼–½ cup blanched almonds

Makes one 18–20 cm./7–8 inch cake
Oven setting: 160°C./325°F./Gas Mark 3
Line an 18–20 cm./7–8 inch cake tin with greased
greaseproof (waxed) paper, or grease and flour the tin.
Cream the butter or margarine and sugar together until
fluffy, and gradually beat in the eggs. Fold in the sifted
flour, fruit, cherries and peel, and enough milk to give the
batter a soft, dropping consistency.

Put into the prepared cake tin and cover with the
almonds. Brush these with a little egg white (there should
be enough left in the egg shells used to make the cake).
Bake in the centre of the preheated oven for about 1¾
hours, reduce the heat slightly after ¾–1 hour if the cake is
browning too quickly. This cake tends to rise in a pleasant
round instead of being flat. Remove the paper before
serving.

Helpful hints
To freeze, wrap carefully in heavy duty foil and a
polythene (plastic) bag. Thaw at room temperature for 3–4
hours.

Almond triangles

Metric/Imperial
225 g./8 oz. self-raising flour
1 teaspoon ground cinnamon
½ teaspoon each mixed spice
    and ground ginger
150 g./5 oz. butter
75 g./3 oz. dark soft brown
    sugar
50 g./2 oz. blanched slivered
    almonds, toasted
2 egg yolks
milk
apricot jam
1 egg white

American
2 cups self-rising flour
1 teaspoon ground cinnamon
½ teaspoon each ground
    allspice and ground ginger
10 tablespoons butter
½ cup dark brown sugar
½ cup blanched slivered
    almonds, toasted
2 egg yolks
milk
apricot jam
1 egg white

Makes about 16

Oven setting: 190°C./375°F./Gas Mark 5
Sift the flour and spices into a bowl. Rub in the butter. Add
the sugar and almonds, then mix to a stiff but pliable
dough with the egg yolks and milk as necessary.

Turn out the dough on to a floured surface and knead
lightly until smooth. Divide in half and roll out each half to
a 20 cm./8 inch square. Put one square on to a lightly
greased baking sheet, spread lightly with apricot jam and
cover with the other square. Beat the egg white to a froth
then brush over the top.

Bake just above the centre of the preheated oven for
about 30–40 minutes, or until golden brown. Leave to cool
on the sheet until almost cold then cut into triangles.

Coffee walnut layer cake

Metric/Imperial
175 g./6 oz. butter
175 g./6 oz. caster sugar
3 large eggs
1 egg yolk
1 tablespoon coffee essence
175 g./6 oz. self-raising flour
75 g./3 oz. finely chopped
    walnuts

Filling
100 g./4 oz. butter
225 g./8 oz. icing sugar, sifted
1 tablespoon milk

Icing
225 g./8 oz. sugar
4 tablespoons water
pinch of cream of tartar
1 egg white, stiffly beaten
walnut halves

American
¾ cup butter
¾ cup superfine sugar
3 large eggs
1 egg yolk
1¼ tablespoons strong black
    coffee
1½ cups self-rising flour
¾ cup finely chopped walnuts

Filling
½ cup butter
almost 2 cups sifted
    confectioners' sugar
1¼ tablespoons milk

Icing
1 cup sugar
5 tablespoons water
pinch of cream of tartar
1 egg white, stiffly beaten
walnut halves

Makes 6–8 slices

Oven setting: 180–190°C./350–375°F./Gas Mark 4–5
Cream the butter and sugar. Gradually beat in the eggs,
egg yolk and coffee. Fold in the flour and the chopped
walnuts. Grease and flour two 20 cm./8 inch sandwich tins
(layer cake pans). Divide the mixture between the tins
(pans) and smooth flat on top. Bake just above the centre
of the oven for about 25 minutes or until firm to the touch.
Turn out carefully and allow to cool.

Cream butter and sugar together, then add milk. Split
each cake to give four layers, spread with the filling and
put the cake together again. Put sugar and water into a
saucepan, and stir until sugar has dissolved. Boil steadily,
without stirring, until the mixture forms a 'soft ball' when
tested in cold water. Add cream of tartar and beat hard
until cloudy, then pour steadily on to the egg white.
Continue beating until the icing (frosting) thickens, then
spread over the top and sides of the cake. Decorate with
walnut halves.

CAKES and BAKING

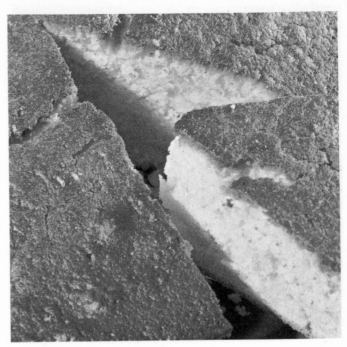

Cream horns

Metric/Imperial
melted butter
400 g./14 oz. puff pastry
  dough
beaten egg
sugar
strawberry jam
300 ml./½ pint double cream
1 teaspoon vanilla essence
3 teaspoons icing sugar, sifted
2 tablespoons milk

American
melted butter
3½ cups puff pastry dough
beaten egg
sugar
strawberry jam
1¼ cups heavy cream
1 teaspoon vanilla extract
3 teaspoons confectioner's
  sugar, sifted
2½ tablespoons milk

Makes 12
Oven setting: 230°C./450°F./Gas Mark 8
Grease 12 cream horn tins (forms) with melted butter.
Rinse a large baking tray (sheet) with water and leave it
damp. Roll out the pastry thinly and cut into 12 long strips,
about 2.5 cm./1 inch wide. Brush one side of each strip
with cold water. Wind each strip, with dampened side
inside, round the tins (forms), starting from the pointed
end and overlapping the strip slightly so that there are no
gaps. Transfer to the tray (sheet), brush with egg and
sprinkle with sugar. Leave in a cool place for 30 minutes.

Bake the cream horns just above the centre of the oven
for 20–25 minutes or until golden brown and puffy.
Remove from the oven and gently lift on to a wire rack.

When almost cold, carefully remove the tins (forms)
from the pastry cases. Put a little jam into the pointed end
of each pastry horn then fill with the cream, whipped until
thick with the essence (extract), sifted sugar and milk.
Decorate each by pressing a fresh strawberry into the top.

Polish cheesecake

Metric/Imperial
approx. 6 tablespoons crushed
  digestive biscuits
700 g./1½ lb. curd cheese
finely grated rind and juice of 1
  lemon
175 g./6 oz. caster sugar
1 teaspoon vanilla essence
2 tablespoons cornflour
3 eggs, separated
150 ml./¼ pint double cream

American
approx. 7½ tablespoons
  crushed graham crackers
3 cups cottage cheese
finely grated rind and juice of 1
  lemon
¾ cup superfine sugar
1 teaspoon vanilla extract
2½ tablespoons cornstarch
3 eggs, separated
⅔ cup heavy cream

Makes one 20 cm./8 inch cake
Oven setting: 160°C./325°F./Gas Mark 3
Grease a 20 cm./8 inch spring form tin (pan) and sprinkle
heavily with crushed biscuits (crackers). Beat the cheese
until smooth with the lemon rind and juice, sugar, vanilla
essence (extract), cornflour (cornstarch) and egg yolks.
Beat the egg whites until stiff. Beat the cream until thick.
Fold the whites and cream alternately into the cheese
mixture with a large metal spoon. When smooth, transfer
to the prepared tin (pan) and bake in the centre of the
preheated oven for 45 minutes.

Turn off the heat, open the oven door and leave the cake
for a further 30 minutes. Remove from the oven and
remove the cake from the tin (pan) when completely cold.
For a browner top cook near the top of the oven for about
35–40 minutes, but watch the cake carefully as it might
brown too much in this position.

Almond cake

Metric/Imperial
175 g./6 oz. margarine or
  butter
175 g./6 oz. caster sugar
3 large eggs
225 g./8 oz. plain flour
1½ teaspoons baking powder
50 g./2 oz. ground almonds
450 g./1 lb. mixed dried fruit
50 g./2 oz. glacé cherries
50 g./2 oz. chopped candied
  peel
little milk
25–50 g./1–2 oz. blanched
  flaked almonds (to decorate)

American
¾ cup margarine or butter
¾ cup superfine sugar
3 large eggs
2 cups all-purpose flour
1½ teaspoons baking powder
½ cup ground almonds
2⅔ cups mixed dried fruit
⅓ cup candied cherries
⅓ cup chopped candied peel
little milk
¼–½ cup blanched flaked
  almonds (to decorate)

Makes one 18–20 cm./7–8 inch cake
Oven setting: 160°C./325°F./Gas Mark 3
Line an 18–20 cm./7–8 inch cake tin with greased
greaseproof (waxed) paper, or grease and flour the tin.
Cream the margarine or butter and sugar together until
fluffy and gradually beat in the eggs. Fold in the sifted
flour and baking powder, then the ground almonds, dried
fruit, cherries, peel and enough milk to give the batter a
soft, dropping consistency.

Put into the prepared tin and bake in the centre of the
preheated oven for 2–2¼ hours, reducing the oven
temperature to 150°C./300°F./Gas Mark 2 after about 1–1½
hours. Leave the cake to cool slightly in the tin, then turn
out carefully on to a wire rack. Brush with a little egg white
(there should be enough left in the egg shells used to make
the cake), cover with a thick layer of blanched and flaked
almonds and brown for a few minutes under the grill
(broiler). Remove the paper before serving.

Schnecken

Metric/Imperial
15 g./½ oz. fresh yeast
1 teaspoon sugar
4 tablespoons warm water
225 g./8 oz. strong flour
½ teaspoon salt
25 g./1 oz. butter
25 g./1 oz. sugar
1 egg

Filling
25 g./1 oz. melted butter
50 g./2 oz. sultanas
25 g./1 oz. chopped mixed nuts
1 teaspoon ground cinnamon
25 g./1 oz. brown sugar

To coat tin and glaze
butter
brown sugar
2 tablespoons water
1 tablespoon sugar dissolved in
  a little boiling water
extra sugar

American
½ cake compressed yeast
1 teaspoon sugar
5 tablespoons warm water
2 cups all-purpose flour
½ teaspoon salt
2 tablespoons butter
2 tablespoons sugar
1 egg

Filling
2 tablespoons melted butter
⅓ cup seedless raisins
¼ cup chopped mixed nuts
1 teaspoon ground cinnamon
1¼ tablespoons brown sugar

To coat tin and glaze
butter
brown sugar
2½ tablespoons water
1¼ tablespoons sugar dissolved
  in a little boiling water
extra sugar

Makes 12
Oven setting: 220°C./425°F./Gas Mark 7
Mix yeast with the teaspoon sugar and 1 tablespoon (1¼
tablespoons) of warm water. Leave in warm place until
bubbly. Mix together flour and salt, and rub in the butter;
add sugar. Pour yeast mixture into centre of the flour
mixture. Add the egg and enough of the remaining warm
water to make a stiff dough. Knead well.

Roll out into a square. Brush with some melted butter,
and sprinkle with the rest of the filling ingredients. Wet
edges and roll up tightly. Brush with the rest of the butter.
Cut into 2.5 cm./1 inch slices. Grease a deep tin lavishly
with butter, sprinkle thickly with brown sugar, and
sprinkle with water. Place slices in tin. Put into greased
plastic bag. Leave in a warm place to double in size.

Bake in the oven for about 20–30 minutes. Leave to cool.
Brush with the glaze and sprinkle with sugar.

CAKES and BAKING

Mushroom cake

Metric/Imperial	American
75 g./3 oz. plain chocolate	3 squares semi-sweet chocolate
2 tablespoons milk	2½ tablespoons milk
150 g./5 oz. self-raising flour	1¼ cups self-rising flour
pinch of salt	pinch of salt
100 g./4 oz. butter	½ cup butter
100 g./4 oz. caster sugar	½ cup superfine sugar
2 eggs	2 eggs
Almond paste	Almond paste
100 g./4 oz. ground almonds	1 cup ground almonds
50 g./2 oz. icing sugar	½ cup confectioner's sugar
2 tablespoons caster sugar	2½ tablespoons superfine sugar
lemon juice	lemon juice
1 egg yolk	1 egg yolk
1 tablespoon warmed apricot jam, sieved	1¼ tablespoons warmed apricot jam, strained
Topping	Topping
50 g./2 oz. butter	¼ cup butter
100 g./4 oz. icing sugar	1 cup confectioner's sugar
25 g./1 oz. plain chocolate, dissolved in 2 teaspoons hot milk	1 square semi-sweet chocolate, dissolved in 2 teaspoons hot milk

Makes one 20 cm./8 inch cake
Oven setting: 190°C./375°F./Gas Mark 5
Grease a 20 cm./8 inch deep sandwich tin (layer cake pan) and line base. Put chocolate and milk in a pan. Melt over low heat. Cool. Sift flour and salt together. Cream butter and sugar, then beat in whole eggs, adding a little flour with each. Add chocolate/milk mixture and a further spoon of flour. Beat well. Fold in remaining flour. Put in tin and bake for 35 minutes. Turn on to rack, remove paper and cool completely. Mix almonds and both sugars. Bind with lemon juice and egg yolk. Knead and roll out into a large circle. Brush with jam and place cake in centre. Press paste against side of cake. Trim. Roll trimmings to form 'stalk'. Cream butter and sugar. Beat in chocolate. Beat well and cool. Spread on top of cake. Mark to resemble a mushroom. Put 'stalk' in centre.

Doughnuts

Metric/Imperial	American
225 g./8 oz. self-raising flour, or plain flour and 2 teaspoons baking powder	2 cups self-rising flour, or all-purpose flour and 2 teaspoons baking powder
good pinch of salt	good pinch of salt
25 g./1 oz. melted butter or oil	2 tablespoons melted butter or oil
1 egg	1 egg
25–50 g./1–2 oz. sugar	⅛–¼ cup sugar
approx. 6–7 tablespoons milk and water	good ½ cup milk and water
jam	jam
oil or fat for deep-frying	oil or fat for deep-frying
sugar	sugar

Makes about 8
Sift the dry ingredients together. Add the butter or oil, the egg and sugar and mix well. Gradually add enough milk to make a soft dough. (If slightly sticky, cover and stand for about 10 minutes.) To make round doughnuts, roll the mixture into balls. Make depressions with the tip of your finger and fill with jam, then re-roll the balls to cover the jam. To make ring doughnuts, roll out the dough on a lightly floured surface and cut into rings.

Heat the oil or fat until it is hot enough to turn a stale bread cube golden in 30 seconds (190°C./375°F. on a deep-fat thermometer). Slide the doughnuts into the hot oil or fat, putting in as many as you can but allowing space between each to turn them over. Cook quickly until they rise to the surface and begin to colour underneath, turn carefully and continue to cook until golden brown all over. Drain over the pan for a few seconds, then on absorbent paper. Roll in sugar, or drop into a bag of sugar and shake vigorously until coated.

Cider crumble cake

Metric/Imperial
500 g./1 lb. 2 oz. self-raising
flour
4½ teaspoons baking powder
100 g./4 oz. moist brown sugar
65 g./2½ oz. dates, stoned and
chopped
3 tablespoons black treacle
300 ml./½ pint cider
2 eggs

Topping
40 g./1½ oz. caster sugar
40 g./1½ oz. flour
40 g./1½ oz. butter
40 g./1½ oz. chopped walnuts
½ teaspoon ground cinnamon
3 tablespoons apricot jam

American
4½ cups self-rising flour
4½ teaspoons baking powder
⅔ cup moist brown sugar
½ cup pitted chopped dates
4 tablespoons molasses
1¼ cups hard cider
2 eggs

Topping
3 tablespoons superfine sugar
6 tablespoons flour
3 tablespoons butter
⅓ cup chopped walnuts
½ teaspoon ground cinnamon
4 tablespoons apricot jam

Makes one 23 cm./9 inch cake
Oven setting: 160°C./325°F./Gas Mark 3
Line a 23 cm./9 inch square cake tin with greased
greaseproof (waxed) paper. Sift the flour and baking
powder into a bowl. Add the sugar and chopped (pitted)
dates. Put the treacle (molasses) and cider into a pan and
heat gently until the treacle (molasses) has melted, stirring
occasionally. Pour on to flour mixture. Add eggs and mix.

Put into the prepared tin and bake in the centre of the
preheated oven for 30 minutes. Meanwhile, prepare the
topping. Mix the sugar and flour together, rub in the
butter and stir in the chopped walnuts and cinnamon.
Remove the cake from the oven, spread with the jam and
press the crumble over the top. Return to the oven for a
further 20 minutes, or until a skewer inserted into the
centre of the cake comes out clean. Leave the cake to cool
in the tin for 10–15 minutes, then turn out and cool
completely on a wire rack. The cake is better left for 2 days
before removing the paper, slicing and serving.

Date and walnut loaf

Metric/Imperial
225 g./8 oz. dates, stoned and
chopped
1 teaspoon bicarbonate of soda
pinch of salt
300 ml./½ pint hot water
275 g./10 oz. self-raising flour
100 g./4 oz. butter or
margarine
50 g./2 oz. chopped walnuts
100 g./4 oz. dark soft brown
sugar
1 egg, beaten

American
1⅓ cups chopped pitted dates
1 teaspoon baking soda
pinch of salt
1¼ cups hot water
2½ cups self-rising flour
½ cup butter or margarine
½ cup chopped walnuts
⅔ cup dark brown sugar
1 egg, beaten

Makes one 1 kg./2 lb. loaf
Oven setting: 180°C./350°F./Gas Mark 4
Grease a 1 kg./2 lb. loaf tin (4 cup oblong loaf pan) with
melted fat. Put the dates, soda and salt into a bowl and
pour over the hot water. Set aside until cool.

Meanwhile, sift the flour into a bowl. Rub in the butter
or margarine, then stir in the walnuts and sugar until well
mixed.

Mix the dry ingredients into the cooled date mixture and
beat in the egg. Put into the prepared tin (pan) and bake in
the preheated oven for 1–1¼ hours, or until a skewer
inserted into the centre of the loaf comes out clean. Leave
to cool completely on a wire rack.

CAKES and BAKING

Bran teabread

Cheese straws

Bran teabread

Metric/Imperial	American
1 tablespoon dried yeast	1¼ tablespoons dried yeast
1 teaspoon sugar	1 teaspoon sugar
150 ml./¼ pint tepid water	⅔ cup tepid water
75 g./3 oz. bran cereal	about 1 cup bran cereal
150 ml./¼ pint milk	⅔ cup milk
½ kg./1 lb. plain flour	4 cups all-purpose flour
1 teaspoon salt	1 teaspoon salt
25 g./1 oz. sugar	2 tablespoons sugar
grated rind of ½ orange	grated rind of ½ orange
1 egg, beaten	1 egg, beaten
100 g./4 oz. icing sugar, sifted	1 cup confectioners' sugar, sifted
chopped glacé cherries, pineapple and angelica (to decorate)	chopped candied cherries, pineapple and angelica (to decorate)

Serves 6–8
Oven setting: 220°C./425°F./Gas Mark 7
Cream the yeast with 1 teaspoon sugar, and add the water. Leave in a warm place for about 15 minutes, or until the mixture becomes frothy. Put the all-bran and milk into a bowl and leave for 10 minutes. Sift the flour and salt into the same bowl. Add the sugar, orange rind, egg and yeast mixture. Mix well, then turn the dough out on to a lightly floured surface. Knead for about 10–15 minutes, or until smooth and no longer sticky. Put the dough in an oiled polythene (plastic) bag and leave in a warm place to rise until doubled in bulk.

Knead the dough lightly again for 1–2 minutes. Divide into three and roll into ropes about 38 cm./15 inches long. Make into a plait (braid) then join the two ends together to make a ring. Stand on a greased baking sheet, cover with an oiled polythene (plastic) bag and leave in a warm place to rise until doubled in bulk. Remove the bag.

Bake towards the top of the preheated oven for about 15–20 minutes or until browned. Cool on a wire rack.

Meanwhile, beat the icing (confectioners') sugar with just enough warm water to make a spreading consistency. Trickle the icing over the tea-bread. Sprinkle with the glacé (candied) fruits when the icing has almost set.

Cheese straws

Metric/Imperial	American
225 g./8 oz. flour, preferably plain	2 cups flour, preferably all-purpose
good pinch of salt	good pinch of salt
pinch of pepper	pinch of pepper
pinch of cayenne	pinch of cayenne
pinch of dry mustard	pinch of dry mustard
100 g./4 oz. butter, margarine or cooking fat	½ cup butter, margarine or shortening
75 g./3 oz. grated Parmesan cheese	¾ cup grated Parmesan cheese
2 egg yolks	2 egg yolks
water to mix	water to mix

Makes about 60 straws and 8–10 rings
Oven setting: 220–230°C./425–450°F./Gas Mark 7–8
Sift the dry ingredients together. Rub in the butter, margarine or fat (shortening). Add the cheese, then the egg yolks and sufficient water to make a soft dough.

Roll out the dough on a lightly floured surface to 1 cm./½ inch thick. Cut into narrow fingers, and arrange on well greased baking sheets. Save a little dough to make rings. Brush the straws and rings with egg white and bake towards the top of the preheated oven for 8–10 minutes. Leave to cool on the baking sheet, then lift off carefully and store in an airtight tin. Put some of the straws through the rings to serve.

Helpful hints
To economize, use finely grated, stale Cheddar cheese instead of Parmesan.

Mince pies

Metric/Imperial
225 g./8 oz. plain flour
pinch of salt
50 g./2 oz. margarine
50 g./2 oz. white cooking fat
3 tablespoons water
½ kg./1 lb. mincemeat
beaten egg
icing sugar

American
2 cups all-purpose flour
pinch of salt
¼ cup margarine
¼ cup shortening
4 tablespoons water
2 cups mincemeat
beaten egg
confectioners' sugar

Makes 12
Oven setting: 200°C./400°F./Gas Mark 6
Lightly grease 12 deep bun tins (muffin cups). Sift the flour and salt into a bowl. Add the fat and cut into the dry ingredients with a pastry cutter or round-topped knife (spatula), then rub in lightly with fingertips. Mix to a stiff dough with water and knead lightly until smooth. Roll out evenly. Cut out 12 rounds and line tins. Fill with mincemeat and moisten pastry edges with water. Cut out slightly smaller rounds and remove centres. Cover mincemeat, pinching pastry edges together to seal. Brush the tops with beaten egg then bake for about 20 minutes just above the centre of the oven. Remove from the tins (cups) when cooled slightly, and sift icing (confectioners') sugar over the tops.

Easter flake cake

Metric/Imperial
225 g./8 oz. plain flour
2 teaspoons baking powder
¼ teaspoon salt
175 g./6 oz. butter or
    margarine, softened
175 g./6 oz. caster sugar
finely grated rind of 1 small
    lemon (optional)
1 teaspoon vanilla essence
3 eggs
2 tablespoons cold milk

American
2 cups all-purpose flour
2 teaspoons baking powder
¼ teaspoon salt
¾ cup butter or margarine,
    softened
¾ cup superfine sugar
finely grated rind of 1 small
    lemon (optional)
1 teaspoon vanilla extract
3 eggs
2½ tablespoons cold milk

Vanilla buttercream
225 g./8 oz. butter
350 g./12 oz. icing sugar,
    sifted
1 teaspoon vanilla essence
6 large milk chocolate flake
    bars, crushed
fondant Easter eggs

Vanilla buttercream
1 cup butter
3 cups confectioners' sugar,
    sifted
1 teaspoon vanilla extract
6 large chocolate flake bars,
    crushed
fondant Easter eggs

Makes one 20 cm./8 inch cake
Oven setting: 160°C./325°F./Gas Mark 3
Make the basic cake as for Chocolate layer loaf, using a 20 cm./8 inch round cake tin (pan). When completely cold, cut into three horizontally.
  To make the buttercream, cream the butter until soft then gradually beat in the icing (confectioners') sugar and vanilla essence (extract). Sandwich the cake together with some of the buttercream, then spread the remainder thickly over the top and sides. Coat completely with crushed chocolate flake bars. Put a few fondant Easter eggs in the centre and stand a couple of fluffy chicks nearby.

CAKES and BAKING

Swedish tea ring

Metric/Imperial
350 g./12 oz. proven white
  bread dough
25 g./1 oz. butter, melted
50 g./2 oz. soft brown sugar
pinch of ground cinnamon
25–50 g./1–2 oz. blanched
  almonds, finely chopped
50–75 g./2–3 oz. icing sugar,
  sifted
glacé cherries and blanched
  whole almonds (to decorate)

American
3 cups proven white bread
  dough
2 tablespoons butter, melted
⅓ cup light brown sugar
pinch of ground cinnamon
¼–½ cup finely chopped
  blanched almonds
½–¾ cup confectioners' sugar,
  sifted
candied cherries and blanched
  whole almonds (to decorate)

Serves 6
Oven setting: 200–220°C./400–425°F./Gas Mark 6–7
Roll out the proven dough to a 30 × 23 cm./12 × 9 inch
rectangle. Brush with melted butter and sprinkle with the
brown sugar, cinnamon and almonds. Roll up Swiss (jelly)
roll style, form into a round and seal the ends.

Transfer to a warmed greased baking sheet. Make cuts
with scissors about 2.5 cm./1 inch apart. Leave in a warm
place for 30 minutes, until the ring has risen. Bake in the
preheated oven for 15–20 minutes, or until lightly
browned. Leave to cool completely on a wire rack.

Meanwhile, beat the icing (confectioners') sugar with
just enough warm water to make a spreading consistency.
Spread the icing over the top of the ring and decorate with
halved glacé (candied) cherries and blanched almonds.

Flapjacks

Metric/Imperial
100 g./4 oz. butter or
  margarine
25 g./1 oz. soft brown sugar
4 tablespoons golden syrup
225 g./8 oz. rolled oats

American
½ cup butter or margarine
2 tablespoons light brown sugar
5 tablespoons light corn syrup
2 cups rolled oats

Makes 18–24
Oven setting: 180°C./350°F./Gas Mark 4
Put the butter or margarine, sugar and syrup in a large
pan. Heat gently until melted, add the oats and mix well.
Spread the mixture smoothly over a greased 20 ×30 cm./8
× 12 inch tin (pan) and bake in the centre of the preheated
oven for 15–20 minutes, or until golden brown and firm to
the touch. Mark into squares or fingers while warm. Leave
to cool completely in the tin (pan) then remove carefully.

Helpful hints
Keep flapjacks in an airtight container, separate from other
cakes or biscuits (cookies).

Vanilla slices

Metric/Imperial	American
225 g./8 oz. puff pastry dough	2 cups puff pastry dough
Filling	*Filling*
300 ml./½ pint double cream	1¼ cups heavy cream
sugar to taste	sugar to taste
few drops vanilla essence	few drops vanilla extract
fruit jam	fruit jam
sifted icing sugar	sifted confectioners' sugar

Makes 6

Oven setting: 240°C./475°F./Gas Mark 9

Roll the pastry out until wafer thin. Cut into 18 fingers. Put on to baking trays (sheets) and leave in a cool place for about 30 minutes. This makes sure they keep a good shape. Bake just above the centre of the oven for approximately 10 minutes until well risen and golden, then switch the oven off for about 5 minutes. Remove from oven, allow to cool then trim the edges with a very sharp knife. Whip the cream, add a little sugar and vanilla. Spread one third of the slices with the cream, top with another slice, then with the jam and a final pastry slice. Dust with sugar.

Helpful hints

Three layers of pastry give a tall and very impressive slice, but two layers of pastry are often used, in which case spread the bottom layer of pastry with jam (jelly) and then with cream, and top with the second layer of pastry. Coat the top of the slices with glacé icing.

Rich dark chocolate cake

Metric/Imperial	American
160 g./5½ oz. caster sugar	¾ cup superfine sugar
3 tablespoons water	4 tablespoons water
40 g./1½ oz. cocoa powder	6 tablespoons unsweetened cocoa powder
75 ml./3 fl. oz. milk	6 tablespoons milk
100 g./4 oz. butter	½ cup butter
2 eggs, separated	2 eggs, separated
100 g./4 oz. self-raising flour	1 cup self-rising flour
1 teaspoon baking powder	1 teaspoon baking powder
65 ml./2½ fl. oz. double cream	⅓ cup heavy cream
65 ml./2½ fl. oz. single cream	⅓ cup light cream

Makes one 20 cm./8 inch cake

Oven setting: 180°C./350°F./Gas Mark 4

Line a deep 20 cm./8 inch sandwich tin (layer pan) with greased greaseproof (waxed) paper. Put 40 g./1½ oz. (3 tablespoons) of the sugar in a pan with the water and cocoa and mix to a paste. Heat gently until the mixture is thick and shiny. Stir in the milk and leave to cool.

Cream the butter and remaining sugar together until fluffy. Beat in the egg yolks and the cocoa mixture. Sift the flour and baking powder together and fold into the mixture. Beat the egg whites until stiff, then fold into the mixture with a metal spoon.

Put into the prepared tin and bake in the preheated oven for about 40 minutes, or until the cake is well risen and golden, and springs back when lightly pressed. Remove the paper and leave the cake to cool on a wire rack. Beat the double (heavy) and single (light) cream together until thick. Split the cake into two layers and use the cream to sandwich them together.

CAKES and BAKING

Scotch pancakes

Metric/Imperial
100 g./4 oz. plain flour
½ teaspoon bicarbonate of soda
1 teaspoon cream of tartar
1 tablespoon sugar
2 teaspoons cooking oil
1 egg, beaten
approx. 150 ml./¼ pint milk

American
1 cup all-purpose flour
½ teaspoon baking soda
1 teaspoon cream of tartar
1¼ tablespoons sugar
2 teaspoons cooking oil
1 egg, beaten
approx. ⅔ cup milk

Makes 16

Sift the flour, soda and cream of tartar into a bowl. Add the sugar and oil, then gradually beat in the egg and milk to form a thick batter.

Heat the girdle (griddle) until hot. Wrap a small piece of suet in a piece of absorbent paper and grease the girdle (griddle) with it. Drop batter on to the hot girdle (griddle), a tablespoonful at a time, leaving room for the batter to run. Cook until golden brown on the underside and bubbles rise on the surface. Turn over and cook the other side.

Keep the pancakes hot in a warm tea-towel while you cook the remaining batter in the same way.

Helpful hints

If a girdle (griddle) is not available, a heavy-based frying pan (skillet) can be used, or the pancakes can be cooked directly on the solid hot plate of an electric stove.

Coconut squares

Metric/Imperial
175 g./6 oz. self-raising flour
pinch of salt
175 g./6 oz. mixed butter and
 margarine
175 g./6 oz. caster sugar
1 teaspoon vanilla essence
3 eggs
plum or apricot jam
desiccated coconut

American
1½ cups self-rising flour
pinch of salt
¾ cup mixed butter and
 margarine
¾ cup superfine sugar
1 teaspoon vanilla extract
3 eggs
plum or apricot jam
shredded coconut

Makes about 12

Oven setting: 180°C./350°F./Gas Mark 4

Grease a Swiss roll tin (jelly roll pan) about 28 × 20 × 4 cm./11 × 8 × 1½ inch and line with greased greaseproof (waxed) paper. Sift the flour and salt into a bowl. Cream the fat, sugar and vanilla essence (extract) together until fluffy. Beat in the eggs, one at a time, adding a tablespoon of dry ingredients with each one. Fold in the remaining flour.

Put into the prepared tin (pan) and bake in the centre of the preheated oven for about 20–25 minutes, or until golden. Leave the cake to cool in the tin (pan) for 5 minutes, then turn out to cool completely on a wire rack. When cold, cut the cake into squares. Brush all over with warmed jam and coat in the coconut.

Catherine wheel birthday cake

Metric/Imperial	American
225 g./8 oz. plain flour	2 cups all-purpose flour
2 teaspoons baking powder	2 teaspoons baking powder
¼ teaspoon salt	¼ teaspoon salt
175 g./6 oz. butter or margarine, softened	¾ cup butter or margarine, softened
175 g./6 oz. caster sugar	¾ cup superfine sugar
finely grated rind of 1 small lemon (optional)	finely grated rind of 1 small lemon (optional)
1 teaspoon vanilla essence	1 teaspoon vanilla extract
3 eggs	3 eggs
2 tablespoons cold milk	2½ tablespoons cold milk

Buttercream	Buttercream
350 g./12 oz. butter	1½ cups butter
½ kg./1 lb. icing sugar, sifted	4 cups confectioners' sugar, sifted
1 teaspoon vanilla essence	1 teaspoon vanilla extract
1 tablespoon cocoa powder	1¼ tablespoons unsweetened cocoa powder

Makes one 20 cm./8 inch cake
Oven setting: 160°C./325°F./Gas Mark 3
Make the basic cake as for Chocolate layer loaf, using a 20 cm./8 inch round cake tin (pan). When cold, cut into three horizontally.

To make the buttercream, cream the butter until soft then gradually beat in the icing (confectioners') sugar and vanilla essence (extract). Divide into two portions. Mix the cocoa to a smooth paste with boiling water, leave until cold then gradually beat into one portion of buttercream. Sandwich slices of cake together using plain buttercream for one layer and chocolate buttercream for the other.

Put star nozzles into two forcing bags (pastry bags) fill each with a different coloured buttercream. Pipe rosettes round the top and sides of the cake, alternating the buttercreams. Chill slightly.

Just before serving, insert candles and holders at an angle to represent a Catherine wheel.

Golden ginger loaf

Metric/Imperial	American
275 g./10 oz. plain flour	2½ cups all-purpose flour
1 teaspoon bicarbonate of soda	1 teaspoon baking soda
½ teaspoon ground ginger	½ teaspoon ground ginger
175 g./6 oz. clear honey	¾ cup clear honey
100 g./4 oz. fat	½ cup fat
175 g./6 oz. sugar	¾ cup sugar
2 tablespoons syrup from jar of preserved ginger	2½ tablespoons syrup from jar of preserved ginger
1½ tablespoons milk	2 tablespoons milk
2 eggs	2 eggs

To decorate	To decorate
1 tablespoon clear honey	1¼ tablespoons clear honey
few leaves of angelica	few leaves of angelica
2–3 tablespoons preserved ginger (cut in neat pieces)	2½–4 tablespoons preserved ginger (cut in neat pieces)

Makes one 1–1½ kg./2–3 lb. loaf
Oven setting: 150–160°C./300–325°F./Gas Mark 2–3
Line a 1–1½ kg./2–3 lb. loaf tin (4–6 cup oblong loaf pan) with greased greaseproof (waxed) paper. Sift the dry ingredients into a bowl. Put the honey, fat and sugar in a pan. Heat gently until the fat melts, pour over the flour and beat well. Warm the syrup and milk in the pan, add to the flour mixture with the eggs and beat until smooth.

Pour into the prepared tin (pan) and bake in the centre of the preheated oven for 1–1¼ hours, or until just firm to the touch; do not overcook. Leave to cool in the tin (pan) for about 15 minutes. Remove the paper, then brush the top with honey and press the pieces of angelica and preserved ginger into position.

CAKES and BAKING

Viennese orange shortbreads

Metric/Imperial	American
100 g./4 oz. flour	1 cup flour
100 g./4 oz. cornflour	1 cup cornstarch
175 g./6 oz. butter	¾ cup butter
100 g./4 oz. icing sugar, sifted	1 cup confectioners' sugar, sifted
finely grated rind of 1 large orange	finely grated rind of 1 large orange
extra icing sugar (to decorate)	extra confectioners' sugar (to decorate)
Filling	**Filling**
finely grated rind of 1 large orange	finely grated rind of 1 large orange
75 g./3 oz. butter	6 tablespoons butter
175 g./6 oz. icing sugar, sifted	1½ cups confectioners' sugar, sifted

Makes 7–8

Oven setting: 180°C./350°F./Gas Mark 4

Sift the flour and cornflour (cornstarch) into a bowl. Cream the butter, icing (confectioners') sugar and orange rind until fluffy. Gradually beat in the sifted flour and cornflour (cornstarch).

Put the mixture into a forcing bag (pastry bag) fitted with a 1 cm./½ inch rose nozzle and pipe out 14–16 neat roses on an ungreased baking sheet. Bake in the centre of the preheated oven for 15–20 minutes. The shortbreads should crisp without becoming too brown. Leave to cool on the baking sheet.

To make the filling, cream the orange rind, butter and icing (confectioners') sugar together. Sandwich the shortbreads with the filling and sprinkle the tops with a little extra icing (confectioners') sugar.

Coffee gâteau

Metric/Imperial	American
3 large eggs	3 large eggs
75 g./3 oz. caster sugar	⅜ cup superfine sugar
75 g./3 oz. self-raising flour	¾ cup self-rising flour
50 g./2 oz. flaked, toasted almonds	½ cup flaked, toasted almonds
chocolate balls	chocolate balls
Icing	**Icing**
350 g./12 oz. sifted icing sugar	2⅔ cups sifted confectioners' sugar
2 tablespoons coffee essence	2½ tablespoons strong black coffee
2 tablespoons rum or brandy	2½ tablespoons rum or brandy
175 g./6 oz. butter	¾ cup butter
25 g./1 oz. crystallized ginger	¼ cup crystallized ginger

Makes 8–10 slices

Oven setting: 190°C./375°F./Gas Mark 5

Grease two 20 cm./8 inch diameter sandwich tins (layer cake pans), then line the bases with circles of greased, greaseproof (waxed) paper.

Whisk the eggs and sugar in a bowl placed over a pan of hot water until the mixture is pale and mousse-like. Remove the bowl from the heat and fold in the flour. Divide the mixture between the prepared tins and bake for 20–25 minutes, or until the centre of each sponge springs back when lightly pressed. Turn out and cool on a wire rack.

Blend together the sugar, coffee and rum or brandy. Cream the butter until soft, add the sugar mixture a little at a time, beating well after each addition.

Put just under half of the icing in a bowl. Chop the ginger and add to this mixture. Use to sandwich the sponges together. Put one heaped spoon of icing aside in a small bowl. Spread the remainder around the sides and over the top of the cake. Press half of the almonds against sides of cake with a palette knife. Decorate the top with remaining almonds and chocolate balls. Pipe the reserved icing in rosettes.

Chocolate layer loaf

Metric/Imperial	American
225 g./8 oz. plain flour	2 cups all-purpose flour
2 teaspoons baking powder	2 teaspoons baking powder
¼ teaspoon salt	¼ teaspoon salt
175 g./6 oz. butter or margarine, softened	¾ cup butter or margarine, softened
175 g./6 oz. caster sugar	¾ cup superfine sugar
finely grated rind of 1 small lemon (optional)	finely grated rind of 1 small lemon (optional)
1 teaspoon vanilla essence	1 teaspoon vanilla extract
3 eggs	3 eggs
2 tablespoons cold milk	2½ tablespoons cold milk
Chocolate icing	Chocolate icing
50 g./2 oz. margarine	4 tablespoons margarine
6 tablespoons water	7½ tablespoons water
4 tablespoons cocoa powder	5 tablespoons unsweetened cocoa powder
½ kg./1 lb. icing sugar, sifted	4 cups confectioners' sugar, sifted

Makes one 1 kg./2 lb. loaf
Oven setting: 160°C./325°F./Gas Mark 3
Grease a 1 kg./2 lb. loaf tin (4 cup oblong loaf pan) and line with greased greaseproof (waxed) paper. Sift the flour, baking powder and salt together. Cream the butter or margarine, sugar, lemon rind (if used) and vanilla essence (extract) together until fluffy. Beat in the eggs, one at a time, adding a tablespoon of sifted dry ingredients with each one. Using a metal spoon, fold in the remaining dry ingredients alternately with the milk.

Put into the prepared tin (pan) and bake in the centre of the preheated oven for 1½–1¾ hours, or until well risen and golden and a skewer inserted into the centre of the cake comes out clean. Leave the cake to cool in the tin (pan) for 10 minutes, then turn out to cool completely on a wire rack. Remove the paper.

Meanwhile, put the margarine in a bowl with the water and gradually beat in the cocoa powder. Beat in the icing (confectioners') sugar until smooth and well combined. When cold, slice the cake twice lengthwise then sandwich and coat the top and sides with chocolate icing.

Almond tarts

Metric/Imperial	American
100 g./4 oz. shortcrust pastry, made with 100 g./4 oz. plain flour, etc.	1 cup shortcrust pastry, made with 1 cup all-purpose flour, etc.
2 tablespoons jam	2½ tablespoons jam
flaked almonds	flaked almonds
apricot jam, warmed	apricot jam, warmed
6 glacé cherries, halved	6 candied cherries, halved
Almond cake mixture	Almond cake mixture
75 g./3 oz. self-raising flour	¾ cup self-rising flour
50 g./2 oz. butter or margarine	4 tablespoons butter or margarine
50 g./2 oz. caster sugar	¼ cup superfine sugar
1 egg	1 egg
25 g./1 oz. ground almonds	2 tablespoons ground almonds
almond essence	almond extract
milk to mix	milk to mix

Makes about 12
Oven setting: 200°C./400°F./Gas Mark 6
Roll out the pastry on a floured surface and cut into about twelve 7.5 cm./3 inch rounds with a fluted cutter. Use to line greased shallow bun tins (tart pans). Put ½ teaspoon jam in each.

Sift the flour into a bowl. Cream the butter or margarine and sugar together until fluffy, then beat in the egg, ground almonds and essence (extract). Fold in the flour alternately with a few teaspoons of milk to make a stiffish batter.

Spoon the almond cake mixture over the jam, to three-quarters fill each tart, and scatter the tops heavily with flaked almonds. Bake the tarts just above the centre of the preheated oven for 25–30 minutes, or until well risen and golden. Turn out to cool completely on a wire rack.

When cool, brush the tops with melted apricot jam and top with half a cherry.

Index

Index

Index

Acknowledgements

The photographs in this book are from the Octopus Library and the following organisations and manufacturers:
American Rice Council
Argentine Beef Bureau
Australian Recipe Service
Birds Eye Foods Limited
British Egg Information Service
Cadbury Schweppes Food Advisory Service
Bournville, Birmingham
California Prune Advisory Bureau
Cookware by Aubecq
The Dutch Dairy Bureau
Eden Vale Limited
Electricity Council
Flour Advisory Bureau
Fruit Producer's Council
Gale's Honey
Hassy Perfection Celery
Herring Industry Board
Kellog Company of Great Britain Limited
Knorr Foods
Lawrys Foods Inc.
Lea & Perrins Worcestershire Sauce
Mazola Corn Oil
National Dairy Council
National Magazine Company
New Idea
New Zealand Lamb Information Bureau
Pasta Foods Limited
R.H.M. Foods Limited
Swiss Cheese Union
Tabasco Sauce
Taunton Cider Company
John West Foods Limited
White Fish Authority

Front Jacket: Paul Kemp
Back Jacket: John Lee
Endpapers & Flaps: John Searle Austin
Half-title, Title, Contents: Roger Tuff